Recovering the Black Female Body

Recovering the Black Female Body

Self-Representations by African American Women

edited by
MICHAEL BENNETT
VANESSA D. DICKERSON

RUTGERS UNIVERSITY PRESS
New Brunswick, New Jersey, and London

Library of Congress Cataloging-in-Publication Data

Recovering the Black female body : self-representations by African American
women / edited by Michael Bennett and Vanessa D. Dickerson.
    p. cm.
    Includes bibliographical references and index.
    ISBN 0–8135–2838–0 (cloth : alk. paper) — ISBN 0–8135–2839–9
(pbk. : alk. paper)
    1. Afro-American women. 2. Body, Human, in literature. 3. American
literature—20th century—History and criticism. 4. American literature—
Afro-American authors—History and criticism. I. Bennett, Michael, 1962–
II. Dickerson, Vanessa D., 1955–

E185.86 .R37 2000
305.48'896073—dc21

                                   00–027657

British Cataloging-in-Publication data for this book is available from the
British Library

Excerpts of poems by Lucille Clifton first appeared in *two-headed woman*,
published by the University of Massachusetts Press, and now appear in *good
woman: poems and a memoir 1969–1980,* published by BOA Editions, Ltd.
Copyright © 1980 by the University of Massachusetts Press. Reprinted by
permission of Curtis Brown, Ltd.

Excerpts from Suzan-Lori Parks's *The Death of the Last Black Man in the
Whole Entire World* are reprinted by permission of the author.

Manufactured in the United States of America

Contents

Acknowledgments

The editors would like to dedicate this book to those African American women who have been especially significant for us and our own understanding of the importance of body politics and of black female self-representations.

Michael would like to acknowledge Hilary Weaver, his oldest friend, whose exploration of her own Native American, African, and European heritage showed how complex are questions of racial identity and representation, which didn't prevent Michael's grandmother from showing how uncomplicated can be our answers to these questions when she admonished, "I don't want you going out with that black girl"; the students in the first African American literature class he ever taught, which was composed almost entirely of black women—one of whom accused him of being racist and sexist when he failed her for plagiarism and the rest of whom made it easy to dismiss this charge while acknowledging that all of us are complicit in a racist and sexist society that requires our commitment to personal vigilance and social action; Gail Shirley and Mary Rose, who worked hard to make the Carter G. Woodson Institute for Afro-American and African Studies such a welcoming and smoothly run place in which to explore issues such as those raised in this book; Debbie McDowell, who commented early on in their relationship that it was a political decision for a white male student to work for a black female professor and who has been a constant source of insight for all of us who think and write about black feminist literature and criticism; Gale Stevens Haynes, the provost at the institution that hired a fresh Ph.D. who "looked black on paper" and who has guided that institution, Long Island University (Brooklyn), to become the kind of place that welcomes students often marginalized at other schools; the single largest demographic bloc of these students, African American and Caribbean women, who have made teaching at Long Island University such a rewarding experience; and, of course, Vanessa Dickerson, who provided the impetus for this volume and who it is always a pleasure to encounter in the most far-flung locales, from Toronto to Thailand. And Michael would especially like to dedicate this volume to his family by "domestic partnership": grandmother-in-law Bessie Lewis, mother-in-law Barbara Battle, sisters-in-law Irann Brown and Javii Pittman, and nieces Danielle, Jennifer, Joanne, Kimberly, Morgan, Shelley, and Sheree.

Vanessa wants to give thanks and credit to the mother who bore her and to the grandmothers (Adner and Mary Lou) and aunts (L'sis, Ba'sis, Bea, Irene, and AV) who helped her to love and respect her own black body; to "Aunt" Sarah, who kept her, body and soul, in the church; to Mama Saunders, who taught her to look always for silver linings; to Ms. Harvey, Ms. Williams, Mrs. Ford, and Mrs. Hairston, those proud and regal black elementary teachers in a segregated system who schooled her in the unlimited powers of the mind and the proper carriage of the black female body; to those sisters in the Wintergreen Collective, those writers, poets, critics, and theorists with whom she has shared not only academic dreams and intellectual conversation but also mango for the body and chicken soup for the soul; to her friends, mother and daughter, Ellen and Yacqui Peete, who cheered her both off and on the tennis court; to her best friend Veloisa Marsh, so magnificently queenly; and to her sister Erline (Girl, when we were growing up together, I never dreamed how many ways you would see this body through). Vanessa especially wishes to acknowledge her daughter, Yanna, whose body gave her the best reason of all for pursuing the idea of this volume. Vanessa wishes to dedicate this book to all the black women—those named and those whose names she cannot recall—who know that in this world sometimes you have to put your hands on your hips and let your backbone slip. "girl,girl,girlgirlgirl."

CARLA L. PETERSON

Foreword:
Eccentric Bodies

In Western reality, there is a clear split between the spiritual and the material. . . . To a Dagara man or woman, the material is just the spiritual taking on form.
—Malidoma Patrice Somé, *Of Water and the Spirit*

I had never seen any paintings of colored people before, and they seemed to me beautiful.
—Harriet Jacobs, *Incidents in the Life of a Slave Girl*

When invoking the term "body," we tend to think at first of its materiality—its composition as flesh and bone, its outline and contours, its outgrowth of nail and hair. But the body, as we well know, is never simply matter, for it is never divorced from perception and interpretation. As matter, the body is there to be seen and felt, and in the process it is subject to examination and speculation. Perception and interpretation come from different sources. Each of us has a sense of the body we inhabit; but others also look at our bodies and interpret them from their own particular standpoint—coincident with, different from, or supplemental to our own. Initiated from the outside, such perceptions are inevitably partial; nevertheless, we often incorporate them into our own sense of our bodies. In addition, as we observe bodies (ours or others'), we need to acknowledge that we are never just looking at individual bodies; by comparison, we connect these to other bodies, placing them within groups—most especially those of gender, family, race, and nation—and endowing them with a group identity. These differing perspectives on the body—ours, others', ours of others', in relation to groups—may overlap, but, just as significantly, they may also diverge and conflict with one another.

The body then is inextricably linked to ideation and subjectivity. In addition, as my first epigraph suggests, among traditional African peoples no clear separation is made between body and spirit; rather, the body is conceived as the material form of the spirit. This conjoining of the material and the spiritual is especially evident in African cosmology's refusal to distinguish clearly between the realms of life and death, which are demarcated only by a boundary of water. In the afterlife, the body survives to demand gratification of such physical needs as hunger and thirst; conversely, the material world of the living is often visited by the spirits of the dead. This African concept of the unity of body and spirit was ruptured, but not destroyed, by the experience of the Middle Passage. The culture, rituals, folkways, and writings developed by enslaved Africans and their descendants bear witness to African Americans' on-going struggle to reconnect body and spirit and endow this newly formed entity with beauty.

With the institutionalization of black servitude and slavery in the United States, the dominant culture endeavored to split the African body and spirit from one another. At the extreme, slaveholding ideology came to deny the very existence of an African soul in order to legitimate the enslavement of beings who, if soulless, could not be considered human. Other thinkers like Thomas Jefferson acknowledged the existence of black interiority but insisted on its essentially debased and disordered nature. In his *Notes on the State of Virginia*, Jefferson asserted that, unlike Native Americans, Africans are incapable of genuine cultural creativity; writers like "Phyllis Whately" [Phillis Wheatley] are at best mere imitators; possessing no Chief Logan whose eloquence rivals that of white orators, African Americans are unable to plead their own cause. Even the later doctrine of romantic racialism propounded by nineteenth-century white abolitionists circumscribed the capacities of African interiority. Celebrated for a naive spirituality that in this instance marks them as superior to the aggressive and entrepreneurial Anglo-Saxon, Africans are nonetheless perceived as immutably fixed in a state of childhood, unself-conscious, inarticulate, and hence incapable of mature self-representation.

As dominant ideologies devalued the African soul, spirit, and inner being, they came to emphasize the body construed as a sign of racial difference that justified the perpetuation of slavery in the South and discrimination and segregation in the North. Within both economic systems of slavery and free labor, the black body was made to perform as a laboring body, as a working machine dissociated from the mind that invents or operates the machine. For black women, the consequences were multiple. In slavery in particular, the black woman not only carried out the physical labor demanded by plantation economy, she also performed the sex work that satisfied the slaveholder's lust as well as the reproductive labor of breeding that ensured the replenishment of his slave stock. In the eyes of the dominant culture what resulted was a simultaneous masculinization and feminization of the black female body, which was consequently perceived as grotesque. Moreover, the legal positioning of the female slave underscores how individual bodies become inseparable from group identity: just as racial distinctiveness marks the slave woman, binds her to the slave system, and converts her into a commodity that can be bought and sold, so the laws of slavery tie her children to her condition regardless of the identity of the father; under these conditions, the integrity of the slave family is under constant assault and its members denied the protections provided by citizenship and membership in the national body politic.

Despite the elaborateness of these racial ideologies, however, the dominant culture exhibited considerable anxiety about the possibility of actually fixing the black body. Indeed, nowhere is the body's subjectivity more evident than in the instability of representations of the black body—an instability that gave rise to irresolvable tensions and contradictions. For example, to the dominant culture the black body was often both invisible and hypervisible. Such was the experience of Sojourner Truth during her stay in the Pierson household in New York in the 1830s; as a domestic, she was a non-presence, but after Pierson's poisoning, she was the first to be suspected of the crime. Or, as noted earlier, the black female body could be perceived as simultaneously feminine and masculine. Hence, Truth's body was considered female by virtue of its reproductive and nurturing capacities, but it was also interpreted as masculine given her physical labor as a field hand in rural slavery and her later unseemly exposure as a public speaker. Yet the most remarkable emblem of the black body's instability perhaps resided in the figure of the mulatta—so fair that she could readily pass for white—who dominated much of nineteenth- and early-twentieth-century American and African American fiction. In this instance, perception of the visible signs of the body—color, hair texture, facial features—is never sufficient; the matter that tells—blood—is now inside, invisible even to the most observant eye.

My following comments on African American women's attempts to represent themselves against these dominant ideologies expand upon the arguments of my book, *"Doers of the Word": African American Women Speakers and Writers in the North (1830–1880)*. Here I have chosen to term the black female body "eccentric," insisting on its double meaning: the first evokes a circle not concentric with another, an axis not centrally placed (according to the dominant system), whereas the second extends the notion of off-centeredness to suggest freedom of movement stemming from the lack of central control and hence new possibilities of difference conceived as empowering oddness. Relocated in a new world, African-descended visual and verbal artists faced the question of how to define and represent, in the words of my second epigraph, the eccentric bodies of "colored people" as "beautiful." Here the issue of articulation becomes especially crucial once we remember Elaine Scarry's contention that under conditions of pain the powerless become voiceless "bodies in pain" dominated by the bodiless voices of those in power. But African American writers insisted on overcoming voicelessness in their efforts to reconcile body and spirit and represent the beauty of the African American self.

In coming to voice, many nineteenth-century black writers turned first to strategies of bodily representation derived from sentimental culture; yet from the outset these could not further the project of reconciling body and soul. Indeed, one sentimental strategy was that of decorporealizing the eccentric black body, rendering it invisible and privileging the soul or mind instead. Throughout his lengthy writing career, for example, Alexander Crummell argued for African Americans' potential for civilization—and hence inclusion in the national body politic—by divorcing black body from mind and focusing on the mind's capacity to attain a level of culture commensurate to that of white Americans. Even as late as 1903, Crummell's disciple W.E.B. Du Bois insisted on titling his collection of essays *The Souls of Black Folk*, even as the text itself attends to the folk's laboring bodies. This strategy was most common, I suggest, in representations of the black male body where it often functioned to attenuate the threat of black male violence.

A second technique of decorporealization was to emphasize the black subject's rhetorical abilities—seen as yet another marker of civilization and potential for citizenship—and to represent his or her language as disembodied. This is the strategy pursued, for example, by Frederick Douglass's narrator in "The Heroic Slave": if the narrator's introductory description of Madison Washington initially emphasizes the slave's physical manliness, it quickly shifts to a focus on his language, and the account of the rebellion in part 4 deliberately de-emphasizes the violence of Washington's actions during the revolt to focus instead on his oratory of liberation that echoes that of the American Revolution. Somewhat differently, in her speaking engagements and poetry recitations Frances Harper often found her audiences fascinated by her body, wondering whether she was a man or a woman, of a natural colored complexion or painted. Harper sought to negotiate these tensions both by drawing attention to her voice—the musicality of its sound, the chasteness of its language—and by stilling her eccentric body, repressing gesture and movement. Yet ultimately neither Douglass's readers nor Harper's audience could forget that language emanates from the body and that the black body is inescapably present.

If the eccentric black body cannot be decorporealized, perhaps it can be normalized. This strategy of normalization was pursued by many nineteenth-century black writers, including women novelists such as Frances Harper and Pauline Hopkins and activists like Josephine St. Pierre Ruffin and Fannie Barrier Williams who were at the forefront of the Black Women's Club Movement. Rather than attempt to render the body invisible or to present the black subject as a disembodied voice, these women acknowledged the corporeality of the black female body but, following the conventions of the dominant literary culture, sentimentalized it, locating it within an idealized middle-class domestic household, imbuing it with moral value, and making it an object worthy of the reader's compassion. Still perceived and interpreted from an outside perspective, the black female body was frequently depicted as racially white (the mulatta figure in fiction) or at least as culturally white (embodying the values of whiteness); as such, it remained regulated and disciplined by the dominant culture.

Such concessions to dominant ideologies do not necessarily signify an assimilationist stance, however. In post-Reconstruction sentimental novels, both the tragic and the triumphant mulatta heroine may be said to enact plots of resistance. The narratives punish the former for her attempts at racial passing, while they portray the latter as resisting abjection and searching instead for ways to assert individual agency. In Harper's 1892 novel, *Iola Leroy*, for example, Iola refuses to pass but determinedly acts on her desire to find her lost mother and reconnect with her black family. Similarly concerned with issues of black agency, club women and other activists of the period radically affirmed African Americans' potential to reach a level of cultural and intellectual achievement that would enable them to enter the national body politic as full citizens.

In striking contrast to these novelists and club women reformers, however, other nineteenth-century black women rejected the sentimental strategies of decorporealization and normalization in order to flaunt the eccentric black female body before their audiences and readers and celebrate its beauty. If the body's very eccentricity functions here as a kind of counterdiscourse, it also represents a determination to define the black female body on its own historical terms and suggests a more successful attempt at reconciling body and spirit. In her speeches, for example, Sojourner Truth insisted on drawing attention to her body; in the process she pointed to the ways in which the bodily labor she performed under slavery—the field work usually reserved to men, the reproductive work of bearing children for the profit of the slaveholder, and the work of nurture that had transformed her breasts from emblems of female sexuality into tools of labor that suckle her master's children—has defined her very sense of self as a black woman worker. Even more compelling are the religious experiences of women evangelists like Jarena Lee and Julia Pell, which boldly affirm the material reality of the black female body. In accordance with their deeply held conviction in incarnation, the Word is made flesh, and the wild, ecstatic movements of their bodies become the visible signs of their mystical communion with God, of the union of their bodies and spirit with the Godhead.

The beginnings of New Negro modernity at the end of the nineteenth century and the start of the twentieth inaugurate a moment in which the representation of the black female body becomes even more complex. If the normalized body of the mulatta is ever present, this period also bears witness to the production of new kinds of fiction in which the black female body becomes a site of deeply felt pleasure; inner strivings and desires find fulfillment in the body. A first tentative step is taken by Emma Dunham Kelley-Hawkins in her fictions of the 1890s, *Megda* and *Four Girls at Cottage City*. In these two novels, Kelley-Hawkins imagines a raceless world in which racial difference and hence racial discrimination do not exist; as a result, her heroines are freed from the yoke of racial oppression and the duties of racial uplift and able to explore the pleasures offered by the modern world. Neither text offers an explicit representation of female sexual desire and its satisfaction, but the girls do openly experience the pleasures of high culture, fashionable dress, household ornamentation, and fine foods. Significantly, they are never consumed by this conspicuous consumption of material goods since, as regenerated Christians, they are equally attentive to the life of the spirit; in these texts, the protagonists are able to bring body and soul into harmony with one another.

Equally significantly, however, in both of Kelley-Hawkins's novels the characters remain racially unmarked and the heroines consistently depicted as fair; we know them as African American only by virtue of the texts' social references. I would suggest that the originality and boldness of Kelley-Hawkins's project necessitated her adherence to the sentimental processes of normalization whereby the black female body is admitted to be eccentric and hence unrepresentable and fairness is acknowledged as the standard of beauty. Several decades later women writers of the Harlem Renaissance would attempt the portrayal of racially marked female characters who freely enjoy the pleasures of the body; they did so with vastly differing results. In Nella Larsen's *Quicksand*, Helga Crane struggles toward full sensual self-expression only to find her eccentric black body transformed into a commodity and ultimately consumed by a society that profoundly misunderstands her. If Zora Neale Hurston continues this tradition of the black female bildungsroman in *Their Eyes Were Watching God*, this novel is notable for the seriousness of its representation of the black folk. The formation that its heroine, Janie Crawford, receives is the growing awareness that her body—represented by Hurston as an eccentric black body with its big breasts, firm buttocks, and long rope of hair—is an important site of self-knowledge, including sexual self-knowledge, that unites body and soul to produce beauty.

What can we say then about the representation of the black female body as we begin the twenty-first century? Perhaps simply that history repeats itself given that this body remains a highly contested site of meaning both within and without the black community and that African American women still struggle with its representation, vacillating between the poles of sentimental normalization and the flaunting of eccentricity. Indeed, the dominant culture continues to exhibit a morbid fascination with the black body—both male and female; and much of this fascination finds wider dissemination than ever through the media of film and television. From a representational point of view, these visual forms encourage a separation of black body from soul, foregrounding the former and rendering the latter practically nonexistent. Thus, television was able to portray Rodney King as a wild jungle animal, O. J. Simpson as an out-of-control killer, and Clarence Thomas (with his own cooperation) as a high-tech lynched black body. In this visual arena, black women have fared no better: Anita Hill was seen as a reincarnation of the nineteenth-century Sapphire figure and Thomas's sister as but another version of today's welfare queen.

What is particularly troubling is the way in which these images of blacks disseminated by the popular media have saturated so many sectors of American society and come even to influence public policy. The backlash against affirmative action and the devolution of welfare reform were made possible in the 1980s and 1990s once popular opinion came (wrongly) to believe that African Americans were the chief beneficiaries of these federal policies. Its prejudices were then reinforced by the stereotypes of the black body discussed earlier: African Americans need affirmative action because, as pure bodies, they are incapable of intellectual thought and cannot compete fairly as workers in the marketplace; black women need welfare because, as irresponsible hypersexual beings incapable of regulating their passions, they resist paid work and insist on producing babies outside of the boundaries of marriage. According to these views, eccentric black bodies are not, and cannot be, successfully incorporated into the national body politic.

Faced with this continued onslaught of negative images, black women have not stood by passively but have responded in a multiplicity of voices that stem from a variety of disciplines and discourses not available to them in the nineteenth century. Strategies of normalization are, of course, still in evidence; witness, for example, Oprah Winfrey's much publicized weight reduction program and appearance on the cover of *Vogue* magazine in a tight-fitting gown that showed off her newly trim waistline. But other strategies have insisted on our need to acknowledge and honor the eccentric black female body. Legal cases have been brought to defend black women's right to wear braided hairstyles in the workplace; critical race theorists have questioned the constitutionality of the criminal prosecution of drug-addicted mothers for exposing their babies to drugs while pregnant, a prosecution that disproportionately affects poor black women. Finally, still other efforts have recognized the continuing separation of black body from soul, the consequent inability to perceive the eccentric black body as beautiful, and the urgent need to heal this split. In a recent hit, "Unpretty," the black hip-hop female group TLC sings about how the black woman has been made to feel "unpretty" and about how this devaluation of black female beauty has led to a divorce between an outside that "looks cool" and an inside that is "blue." I would like to think that artists such as Toni Morrison are charting new directions for us as we begin the twenty-first century with the creation of female characters like those portrayed in *Beloved*. Here Morrison rewrites the history of African American women, painstakingly reporting the violence done to their bodies but affirming the ineffable beauty of these bodies and the possibility of exploring and representing their inner lives.

Recovering the Black Female Body

MICHAEL BENNETT
VANESSA D. DICKERSON

Introduction

On 29 May 1998 a black weekly newspaper, the *Indianapolis Recorder*, reported an incident in which two black women and two white women in a predominantly white section of town called Speedway exited their cars to engage in a very physical fight during which "both parties inflicted visible bodily damage." The black women were arrested and charged with two counts of battery after the five police officers who broke up the fight detected "bruises and bite marks on the white women" but found no evidence of injury to the bodies of the black women (Britt A6). The Speedway incident raises some compelling questions. How does the status of the black female's body differ from that of the white female's? How are bodies historically perceived in America? How are bodies read? If the body is a text, who gets to give the official interpretation about or reading of that text? Whose gaze falls upon the body definitively? What is the relation of the discursive body to the material body?

A closer look at the Speedway incident further underscores the urgency of these questions. The reporter for the *Recorder* continued, "But, upon examination, the Holowkas [the white females who lived in Speedway] clearly were not the only ones to bear wounds. Even after more than a week, Mays [one of the black women who was visiting Speedway] still bears a swell on her right eye, and bite marks on her right hand. Strong [the other black female] has a knot on the back of her head, the result of the blow sustained by the unidentified white male [who joined the fray and withdrew before the arrival of the police], and a scratch on her neck which also is still visible after one week." Still, as the reporter sums it up, "It was the white women's scars that warranted the arrests" (Britt A6). This incident coming on the cusp of the millennium is just one indicator of how the body of the black female remains situated: seldom perceived as the body of the "damsel in distress," in Western culture it is not the rescuable body. The five police officers' responsiveness to the bodies of the white women and disregard for the bodies of the black women reenacts the cultural and historical mandate to value, if not worship and protect, the pale, presumably fragile white female body that is constructed as the more attractive text, easier and more gratifying to read. The officers (all of whom were white and male) saw the darker skin of Mays and Strong; they could not or would not detect the wounds of these black women because the discursive body society has created for the black woman—savage, strong, and ugly—was much more powerful than the material bodies that actually presented themselves. Here is an instance in which, to borrow the words of Robyn Wiegman, "the seeming veracity of flesh can fail to register itself" because the officers, agents of the State, were very much invested in "the binary structure of vision" that shapes "pursuits of knowledge and truth" (21, 4). Five officers chose not to hear the voices of the black women ("Basically, the police officers told us [Mays and Strong] to just be quiet") and not to read their dark bodies. It would seem a discursive text was imposed upon a material body left officially unprized and unguarded. "It was humiliating," commented one of the black women, "and I want them [her white attackers] to experience the same thing we had to. I never felt I needed to be afraid (of police). I now feel I have to guard myself against people who are paid to guard(ed) me [*sic*]" (A6).

These feelings of humiliation and guardedness are wed to suspicion in another incident, this time nationally publicized, involving the black female body.[1] The 14 December 1998 issue of *Newsweek* found a newsworthy story in the fact that some black parents protested when a young white female teacher assigned black writer Carolivia Herron's storybook about a black girl with African-textured hair to her class of black and latino students in a Brooklyn public school. Like the Speedway encounter, the hair imbroglio generates its own barrage of questions. What does it mean that *Newsweek* includes this report under the "National Affairs" section? To what extent does the magazine recognize the black female body as a national affair, or to what extent does it recognize the threatened white female as a national concern? What is to be made of *Newsweek*'s coverage of the hair affair in such terms as "culture wars," "cross-fire," "battle," and "political correctness"? Even more to the point are questions about how some African Americans have come to believe that the topic of black hair texture can be offensive and whether black parents would have been as upset if a black female, a black male, or a white male had presented the story about nappy hair to the Brooklyn class.

These last queries lead up to the larger, more pressing concerns that pervade and drive this volume, the issue of recovery. Although the white teacher, Miss Sherman (as the *Newsweek* reporter at one point is careful to identify her), "fac[es] threats and taunts," she is not the only one to do so. The parents, as did preceding generations of blacks, also believed that they and their children are threatened and taunted constantly by magazines, billboards, movies, media, the gaze of others, even loved ones—all disdainful of or despising African skin and the texture of African hair. The parents may very well have felt themselves and their children especially threatened and taunted by the very fact that the white, blond, straight-haired Miss Sherman was presenting material about the very hair that her own race had so constructed as to grant her seemingly automatic worth and appeal even as it denied black women's claim to value, desirability, or beauty. The black parents' strong reaction to Sherman's reading of *Nappy Hair* manifested the psychic wounds of despised bodies in need of a cure, of affirmation, of recovery.

The Speedway and nappy-hair incidents, just two of many similar stories that do not get reported or recorded, come at a time when African American women are more sensitive than ever to their bodies and how their bodies are perceived. This sensitivity is in part driven by recently acquired access to and participation in media and market forces. JoAnne Cornwell provides an example of this development when she notes that "over the past decade, the last five years especially, we have seen an explosion of self-help books geared toward African American women" because "this country has only recently discovered us as an untapped economic market" and because "our most sensitive and creative people are gaining more access to the printed and visual media" (15). Of course, African American women's sensitivity to their bodies also comes at a time when there is a heightened awareness of the body in the Western world. While Jane Arthurs and Jean Grimshaw acknowledge that "interest in the body has been a constant theme and subtext to a great deal of nineteenth- and twentieth-century theory and discourse" from Darwin to Charcot to Freud and, especially, to Foucault, they also note a "recent dramatic increase in writing about the body" fueled by sexually explicit images in the media, the contemporary "intersection

of the discourses of health, fitness and beauty," "current crises and un-
certainties in gender relations," and "a veritable explosion of academic
interest in the body"(1–6).

———————

The relationship between literature and the body has been a central concern of feminist literary theory since feminism rose to academic prominence in the 1970s and 1980s. French feminists have explored the role
of "writing the body" in *écriture feminine*. Elaine Scarry's *The Body in
Pain*, Susan Rubin Suleiman's *The Female Body in Western Culture*, and
works on reproduction and mothering by such writers as Nancy
Chodorow and Emily Martin have been equally important for Anglo-
American feminists. However, where the black female body is concerned,
many academic studies have been, to borrow Toni Morrison's phrase,
"playing in the dark," as few of these studies have given great shrift to
the bodies of African American women. Most of the early feminist works
on women's bodies focused almost exclusively on white females, or at
least on bodies of unspecified race that were often presumed to be white.
It took the work of African American feminists and other women of color
to demonstrate that all bodies are not treated equally or represented in
quite the same way. Foundational works by Barbara Christian and Patricia
Hill Collins focused less on black female bodies per se than on general
cultural stereotypes of African American women (the mammy, matriarch,
Jezebel, for example). Sander L. Gilman and Karen Sanchez-Eppler have
concentrated on cultural representations of the black female body, but
they were primarily concerned with the dominant images against which
African American women struggled. Only a very few scholars have analyzed African American women's self-representations of their bodies. This
collection of essays is designed to make a contribution to this underdeveloped topic of cultural analysis by working to recover the ways in
which African American women have represented their own selves.

   This volume, then, concerns the recovery of the black female body
in at least two senses: first, recovering the first person (often elided
by cultural studies of the ways in which black women have been represented by the dominant culture) through exploring the continuities
and discontinuities in nineteenth- and twentieth-century century self-
representations by African American women—that is, emphasizing questions of subjectivity and agency as opposed to a relentless focus on the
process of objectification; second, analyzing the strategies employed by
black women to recover their bodies (techniques used to shield, protect,
and nurture) rather than simply enumerating the mechanisms by which
the oppressive gaze of the dominant culture often attempts to strip black
female bodies of any cover. To that end, this collection focuses on forms

of self-representation and cultural production less mediated than the popular culture images, from Aunt Jemima to Anita Hill, often examined as evidence of how black women have been viewed by others. Our concern is how African American women, from slavery to the present, have represented their physical selves in opposition to the distorted vision of the dominant culture.

This collection attempts to carefully intervene in the recently emergent areas of the literary and theoretical study of the black body without reinscribing the dominant discourse's negative construction of African American women or turning the black female body into a spectacle toward some other end. Margaret Homans has pointed out that the writings of women of color frequently have been appropriated by white feminist poststructuralists for the purpose of reconstituting arguments about essentialism. This volume aims, rather, to amplify the counterhegemonic discourse of African American women writers who attempt to recover their bodies—to take back their selves and reappropriate and reconstitute a body that has often been hypereroticized or exoticized and made a site of impropriety and crime.

We would hope that the significance of this volume is not just that it contributes to an underexamined scholarly field but that it amplifies the vibrant energy of African American women's attempts to wrest control of the physical and symbolic construction of their bodies away from the distortions of others. This task is especially important given that the barely subconscious images of black women's bodies promulgated by conservative analysts—for example, the unreasoning fear and loathing toward the supposed fecundity and irresponsibility of black teenage mothers, particularly welfare recipients—threaten to forever warp American social policy. Literally the scapegoats—the sacrificial bodies—of so much of the horrendous conservative assault on the body politic, black women are, like their foremothers, resisting the straitjackets forced on them by others and recovering their own bodies in more seemly garments.

We are pleased that our efforts to analyze this significant discursive formation are framed by two of the very few scholars who have written incisively on the issue of bodily self-representations by African American women: Carla L. Peterson and Deborah E. McDowell. Carla L. Peterson, whose book *"Doers of the Word": African-American Women Speakers and Writers in the North (1830–1880)* is one of the most complete studies of the embodiment of African American women's counterhegemonic discourse in the nineteenth century, provides an extended foreword to frame the issues at stake in recovering the black female body. Deborah E. McDowell, whose foundational essay "Towards a Black Feminist Criticism" was republished and updated, along with other influential work, in *"The Changing Same": Black Women's Literature, Criticism, and Theory*, offers an afterword that completes the frame. The body of this collection is divided into three sections: Covering/Uncovering, Discovering, and Recovering.

The first section, Covering/Uncovering, looks at the ways in which nineteenth- and early-twentieth-century African American women responded to the various material and discursive practices that scripted and enforced "proper" female behavior within the rubric of what has come to be designated as the Cult of True Womanhood: the dominant ideology during this period that constructed "womanhood" as a quality composed of "piety, purity, submissiveness and domesticity" (Welter 21). From its inception, the cult was essentially a whites-only club, but this fact did not necessarily decrease its influence on black women, whether they fruitlessly sought entrance to its precincts, battled against its proscriptions, or protested against its efforts to dismiss their bodies as irretrievably other. Even as the cult waned in the early twentieth century, it still exerted a strong force on African American women either as a model of the demurely covered body or as a challenge to efforts to explore the sexuality of (to uncover) the black female body.

In "Frances Ellen Watkins Sings the Body Electric," Michael Bennett discusses the antebellum poetry and speaking career of Watkins in relation to the poetic productions of Walt Whitman during the same period. Though the pairing of Watkins and Whitman may seem odd, Bennett argues that they shared a common discourse based on their consuming interest in dramatizing the relationship between private and public bodies—a relationship highlighted and troubled by the conflicts, especially over slavery, that led up to the Civil War. Bennett also attends to the very significant differences between the two poets. Devalued by later critics, Watkins's traditional ballad style was highly popular on the antebellum stage, where her poetry was performed before tens of thousands of enthralled spectators. At the same time, Whitman's unconventional free verse, later canonized as a vital part of the "American Renaissance," was confined to the printed page where it was read by few of his contemporaries. Bennett attempts to recover the specific ways in which each poet's body of work was consumed by those who immediately encountered their differently raced and gendered bodies in the antebellum period, before the disembodying force of modern aesthetics canonized the "Great Gray Poet" while assigning the "Bronze Muse" of abolition to obscurity. Bennett notes that in order for Watkins to "sing the body electric" she had to first write and speak the black female body into dialogue with the encompassing social bodies of family, race, and nation—the very bodies from which Whitman hoped to escape in order to sing his "Song of Myself." In other words, Watkins sought freedom from the constraints placed on her body by aligning it with larger entities, while Whitman craved the freedom to explore his own body outside of any intervening forces. Bennett argues that this difference between Watkins's "freedom *from*" and Whitman's "freedom *to*" represents different conceptions of body politics that are still active in contemporary debates between and within feminist and queer theory.

In the next essay, "'The Deeds Done in My Body': Black Feminist Theory, Performance, and the Truth about Adah Isaacs Menken," Daphne A. Brooks explores the politics of the body and performance in relation to the nineteenth-century "racially ambiguous" actress Adah Isaacs Menken. Brooks attempts to read against popular biographical constructions of Menken that privilege a passive construction of her corporeality on the stage over more complex considerations of her performative agency and the shifting limitations of spectatorial politics. Ultimately, Brooks mounts a reinterpretation of Menken's deployment of the body in her most popular theater production, the E. T. Smith stage adaptation of Lord Byron's *Mazeppa* (1861). Feminist readings of this notorious performance—which required several levels of masquerade and culminated in the actress's ride across the stage, scantily clad and bound to a black stallion—have tended to characterize Menken's stage work as "a problem of the body." Yet Brooks fundamentally and critically reconsiders such readings by examining Menken's use of the body as a discursive and performative instrument of subjectivity. Reading for the "opacities" in Menken's representation of the corporeal, evidenced by her manipulation of dominant racial and gender constructions in "double drag" roles, clears a space for considering the critical possibilities of a specifically black feminist performance methodology. In the process, Brooks foregrounds the figure of Sojourner Truth, Menken's contemporary, as a critical model who exemplifies black feminist performative strategies by virtue of the "deeds done" in her own body.

In "The Flower of Black Female Sexuality in Pauline Hopkins's *Winona*," Dorri Rabung Beam notes that a primary goal of black women writers of the nineteenth and early twentieth centuries was to assert their personhood in the face of racist constructions of black women as lascivious. Many argue that such a project entailed, as Lauren Berlant puts it, "the evacuation of erotic or sexual or even sensational life itself as a possible ground of personal dignity for African-American women" (564). This essay contends, however, that such an argument depends on an overemphasis on the domestic novel and on a limited definition of eroticism. Using Hopkins's magazine novel *Winona*, written for *The Colored American*

Magazine in 1902, Beam argues that Hopkins's generic choices, romance and western, lend themselves more readily to an exploration of the "sensational life" than to racial uplift, with its consequent avoidance of sexuality and the body. Hopkins's desire to portray the romantic feelings of her heroine, despite the unrepresentability of those feelings in a racist society, led her to explore the possibilities of "flower language." Specifically, she insinuates a black female sexual self into flower imagery—not as a simple euphemism for the female body or one of its parts but as a metaphor for a more holistic sexuality conjoining bodily, emotional, and imaginative pleasure. By appropriating flower language to interweave representations of body and soul, Hopkins critiques racist distinctions between the ethereal white female body and the fleshly sexualized black female body. Beam uses Gilles Deleuze's notion of "the fold" to illuminate the way Hopkins pleats together generic layers, crevices a black female body within the text, and enfolds pleasure within flower imagery. Hopkins at once uncovers a personal space of control and self-knowledge long denied to black women while covering it with the veil of flower language—even burying it in the landscape of the novel.

The final essay in this section, Meredith Goldsmith's "Shopping to Pass, Passing to Shop: Bodily Self-Fashioning in the Fiction of Nella Larsen," explores the nexus of consumerism and racial passing in two novellas by Harlem Renaissance novelist Nella Larsen, *Quicksand* (1928) and *Passing* (1929), which foreground consumption as a form of bodily self-fashioning. Representatives of the rising black middle class in the 1920s, Larsen's heroines are preoccupied with the interrelation between shopping and passing: some manipulate commodity aesthetics to alter the way their bodies are perceived by both white and black cultures, while others manipulate their light skin privilege to enjoy segregated leisure. At times willfully exoticizing themselves in imitation of black female popular culture figures of the 1920s, at times producing a nonthreatening, domesticated version of African American femininity, Larsen's women attempt to control their racial, class, and gendered status through consumer performance. For Larsen's characters, boundaries between body and commodity blur in the act of consumption, and object culture often serves as a social extension of the body. However, this close association between body and commodity carries its own set of risks: even as Larsen's characters celebrate bodily difference through commodity culture, they are drawn into an uneasy similarity with commodities themselves. The pessimistic closures of both narratives question the effectiveness of the self-conscious celebration of difference and exoticism in which both texts engage.

The next section, Discovering, marks a historical break with the limitations imposed by the Cult of True Womanhood. "Discovering" refers both to efforts by mid- to late-twentieth-century African American women writers to discover the terrain of the black female body outside the opposition between covering and uncovering and to attempts by critics to likewise avoid this binary in critical explorations of the textuality of the body and the embodiedness of texts. In this section, we see that writers and critics have both been attempting over the last few decades to discover the parameters of the black female body when not seen through the bifocal lenses that have tried to limit the view of such bodies to the categories of propriety or perversion.

In "Relocating the Black Woman Subject: The Landscape of the Body in the Poems of Lucille Clifton," Ajuan Maria Mance argues that African American poet Lucille Clifton draws upon the images, themes, and language of myth to create portraits of the black female body that expose the failure of dominant conceptions of adult female subjectivity to account for the possibility of a subject who is both woman and nonwhite. Clifton offers her myths explaining the black woman's subjectivity as an alternative to the marginalizing sociopolitical constructs that erase that figure from view. When she assigns to the black female body qualities like timelessness and magic that exceed the boundaries of traditional womanhood, she replaces the marginalizing system of binary relations (man/woman, black/white, margin/center, public/private) that perpetuates the confinement of womanhood to exclusionary spaces like the middle-class suburban home with a paradigm of meaning based upon simultaneity. According to this model, the African American female subject comes into view, not by virtue of her relationship to the sociopolitical order that exists outside of black womanhood, but through those institutions and identity categories that coexist within black womanhood.

Yvette Louis's "Body Language: The Black Female Body and the Word in *The Death of the Last Black Man in the Whole Entire World*" maintains that a significant part of the project of African American letters has reflected an attempt to re-member and restore the black body through language. Suzan-Lori Parks's 1990 play, *The Death of the Last Black Man in the Whole Entire World*, is a recent expression in a long tradition that posits language as the alchemy by which the African American subject position is constructed out of the devastation of slavery. While embedding the drama deeply within the African American experiences of slavery, violence, and racial oppression, Parks makes use of deconstructed language and dramatic form to contest dominant discourses that have pathologized the black body and presents a counternarrative of the black body as the source of restorative abundance. As the character Black Man repeatedly experiences episodes of violence that rupture his sense of self, Black Woman, a representative, even archetypal female, uses her substantial powers to revive him and sustain the community. While the play and its title apparently foreground the black male body, in fact it is the female body, manifested in speech acts, that transforms the narrative of "flesh" into a subject positionality that proves integral to constructing an integrated self. By re-membering the African American textual body, Parks and her female character transform language into the vehicle through which the black subject not merely survives but thrives.

In "Detecting Bodies: BarbaraNeely's Domestic Sleuth and the Trope of The (In)visible Woman," Doris Witt focuses on a series of detective novels by the African American writer BarbaraNeely. *Blanche on the Lam* (1992), *Blanche among the Talented Tenth* (1994), and *Blanche Cleans Up* (1998) all feature the character Blanche White, a dark-skinned, heavyset, natural-haired, gap-toothed, forty-something African American woman who has chosen to work as a domestic servant rather than become a nurse. Blanche is confident, outspoken, and highly critical of the exploitation of domestic servants. But whereas earlier literary portrayals of African American women servants—such as Alice Childress's character Mildred from *Like One of the Family* (1956)—had focused on workplace dynamics and racial politics, Neely presents Blanche as constantly interpreting the meaning of skin tone, hairstyle, body shape, fashion choices, speech patterns, eating habits, reproductive decisions, and other bodily clues. Witt argues that the detective work Blanche undertakes is very centrally a decoding of contemporary body politics in the United States, as inflected by sexuality, gender, ethnicity, race, class, and disability. In the current cultural climate, when constructivist discourses of the body compete for public acceptance with resurgent biological essentialism and when efforts to redress ongoing collective discrimination against women and minorities are being countered by conservative claims of "reverse discrimination," Neely's portrayal of both Blanche's body and Blanche's efforts to decipher others' bodies demonstrates why the pursuit of social justice has tended to necessitate a contradictory politicization of the body on the part of African American women.

The last essay in this section, Vanessa D. Dickerson's "Summoning SomeBody: The Flesh Made Word in the Fiction of Toni Morrison," begins by noting that the black female body is not a privileged body; it has traditionally not been represented as respected or loved. Historically relegated to the auction block instead of the pedestal, the black female body has been constructed as profane rather than sacred, other rather than ideal. How does the African American woman handle her physical disenfranchisement? How does she negotiate the politics of the body? How does she reappropriate her reviled and colonized being? These questions are arguably at the heart of all of Toni Morrison's fiction. In the novels Dickerson examines, Morrison depicts black female protagonists who come to terms with society's disdain for their bodies through a mental and spiritual improvisation involving a shift of the flesh/body into ambiguity. Making the flesh word, these females enter a liminal space where they can summon the other to themselves, their flesh/bodies becoming the site of love, compassion, and understanding.

———

The third section, Recovering, looks at contemporary efforts by black women to shape, transform, and represent their bodies in various ways, from dieting (or not dieting) and filmmaking to bodybuilding and hairstyling. This section responds both to the recent explosion of multiple forms of self-representation that break through the discursive construction of the body in literary texts and to the materialist criticism responding to these phenomena. The essays in this section clearly participate in developments within contemporary cultural studies that move beyond textuality and into material practices in which bodies are, of necessity, given more weight than they have been afforded in traditional literary criticism.

In a departure from the critical analysis of the texts and bodies of others, Margaret Bass explores her own experience of negotiating contemporary body politics. "On Being a Fat Black Girl in a Fat-Hating Culture" explores the irony that Bass was able to grow up in the Jim Crow South confident in her racial self because of the nurturing of her black self-image by friends and family while at the same time she was taunted and tormented for a much less obvious "handicap": being fat in a culture that rejects that body type. This personal essay traces her attempt to confront the resulting negative self-image from childhood to the present. In the process of this autobiographical exploration, Bass makes important connections between body politics, racism, classism, and, above all, size-ism.

Mark Winokur's "Body and Soul: Identifying (with) the Black Lesbian Body in Cheryl Dunye's *Watermelon Woman*" examines Dunye's film through the lens that she herself suggests, as a response to the absence of a history for which she would like to be the heir: black lesbian filmmaking. Dunye has given us a primary text whose fantasy archaeology preempts any critique and history of itself. As she says of her own work: "The *Watermelon Woman* came from the real lack of any information about the lesbian and film history of African-American women. . . . Since it wasn't happening, I invented it" (Stockwell 69). Dunye is doing in *Watermelon Woman* what queer and race critics both demand as a primary goal of contemporary cultural production: on the one hand, recouping a marginalized history—in this case the history of the black lesbian body—and, on the other hand, postulating that such recouping is ultimately problematic if not impossible. Dunye accomplishes both tasks by inventing a history whose artifice she acknowledges but which she in any case explores. The artifice allows for the analysis of the culture and history of black Hollywood and Philadelphia, while simultaneously critiquing a mainstream culture that excluded blacks and queers and attempted to erase any record of them that might exist.

Jacqueline E. Brady's "Pumping Iron with Resistance: Carla Dunlap's Victorious Body" examines the triply marginalized body (self-made, African American, female) of a former Ms. Olympia, Carla Dunlap, as it is mediated through the documentary movie *Pumping Iron II*. Several feminist readers have commented on the documentary's exciting depiction of transgressive bodies as it recaps the story of four finalists in Caesars Palace World Cup Championship for women bodybuilders, focusing on two opposite types of white female bodies: Rachel McLish as a feminine "natural body" and Bev Francis as a masculine "techno-body." To date, however, no one has considered the surprising ways in which Dunlap, who is the only black contestant and the eventual contest winner, manages to resist some of the heavily hegemonic strictures inherent in the technologies and practices of bodybuilding and filmmaking. Brady contends that bodybuilding, for Dunlap, partly functions as a resistant activity because Dunlap uses it as a collective space where she communes with other women, exploring and critiquing gender constructs of the feminine body.

Finally, Noliwe Rooks's "Wearing Your Race Wrong: Hair, Drama, and a Politics of Representation for African American Women at Play on a Battlefield," is about the self-representation of African American women who choose to adorn their bodies in certain ways. Rooks maintains that the adornment of African American bodies is inextricably linked with the perception of wearing and performing an acceptable racial identity. The central question explored is how one might juxtapose the political and social realities of what certain bodies mean in public life with the more playful desire to see bodily adornment as an expression of individual style. In order to understand the contours of public dramas and interactions involving African American women and hair, the essay looks at three "acts" in what is clearly a larger drama involving race, hair, fashion, and identity played out in the cultural space of

American newspapers during 1996 and 1997. By juxtaposing the discursive with the visual (thanks to interspersed photographs by Bill Gaskins), Rooks also seeks to understand the political and social realities of what style means in relation to raced and gendered bodies in public life and culture.

Black women have been and are now engaged in the process of rethinking and reassessing their own bodies, which are historically and culturally fraught with a significance that goes to the heart of national, if not Western, identity. The black female body carries so much more than its own material weight, as Zora Neale Hurston understood when she had her character Nancy declare in *Their Eyes Were Watching God*, "De nigger woman is de mule uh de world so fur as Ah can see"(14). In slavery, the black female body served as one of the prime technologies of reproduction and commodification. It, more than any other body, politically belies the American declaration of democracy, equality, and freedom. Yet as Robyn Wiegman points out, when "contemporary cultural rhetoric" identifies "blacks and women" as the excluded groups, "lost in the systematic reduction is the black woman whose historical and theoretical presence has quite rightly been pursued in recent years as a way of rethinking the inherently compounded nature of social identity" (7).[2]

Basic to identity, self-image, and being in the physical world is the body, a source of conflict for black women whose ownership of its beauty, pleasure, and potential has been complicated where it has not been denied. Decried as unnatural, ugly, bestial, and unfeminine, the black female's person was excluded, as Hazel Carby has so deftly demonstrated, from the nineteenth-century Cult of True Womanhood. Later, still romanticized as the strong body of a superwoman, the black female body was yet again dehumanized as a machine built for endurance and little else. In short, historically and socially, the black female body tends to be defined and viewed as the antithesis of the good, the true, and the beautiful. Demonized, debased, raped, dismissed—no other body in the United States has been so materially and discursively hobbled.

The essays that follow explore the ways in which black women have confronted this assault by reclaiming and representing their own bodies. Focusing on the ways in which the black female body has been covered, uncovered, discovered, and recovered, this volume considers both how black women have deployed and redeployed language and signs to revise and repossess the discursive body and how the material body has been recovered through performance and other transformative and transgressive acts.

NOTES

1. This same incident is discussed in Rooks's essay in this volume.
2. In *Ain't I a Woman*, hooks notes the disappearance of the black female person when she writes, "We are rarely recognized as a group separate and distinct from black men, or as a present part of the larger group called 'women' in this culture. . . . When black people are talked about the focus tends to be on black *men*; and when women are talked about the focus tends to be on *white* women" (7). This phenomenon is also specified in the title of Hull, Scott, and Smith's *All the Women Are White, All the Blacks Are Men, but Some of Us Are Brave.*

WORKS CITED

Arthurs, Jane, and Jean Grimshaw, eds. *Women's Bodies: Discipline and Transgression.* London: Cassell, 1999.

Berlant, Lauren. "The Queen of America Goes to Washington City: Harriet Jacobs, Frances Harper, and Anita Hill." *American Literature* 65 (1993): 549–74.

Britt, Barato. "Victims in Speedway Incident Claim Malice, Racism." *Indianapolis Recorder* 29 May 1998: A1+.

Carby, Hazel. *Reconstructing Womanhood: The Emergence of the Afro-American Woman Novelist.* New York: Oxford UP, 1987.

Chodorow, Nancy. *The Reproduction of Mothering.* Berkeley: U of California P, 1978.

Christian, Barbara. *Black Women Novelists: The Development of a Tradition 1892–1976.* Westport: Greenwood, 1980.

Clemetson, Lynette (with Evan Halper). "Caught in the Cross-Fire." *Newsweek* 1 Dec. 1998: 38–39.

Collins, Patricia Hill. *Black Feminist Thought: Knowledge, Consciousness, and the Politics of Empowerment.* New York: Routledge, 1990.

Cornwell, JoAnne. *That Hair Thing: And the Sisterlocks Approach.* San Diego: Sisterlocks, 1997.

Gilman, Sander L. "Black Bodies, White Bodies: Toward an Iconography of Female Sexuality in Late Nineteenth-Century Art, Medicine, and Literature." *"Race," Writing, and Difference.* Ed. Henry Louis Gates Jr. Chicago: U of Chicago P, 1986. 223–61.

Homans, Margaret. "'Women of Color' Writers and Feminist Theory." *New Literary History* 25 (1994): 73–94.

hooks, bell. *Ain't I a Woman: Black Women and Feminism.* Boston: South End, 1981.

Hull, Gloria, Patricia Bell Scott, and Barbara Smith, eds. *All the Women Are White, All the Blacks Are Men, but Some of Us Are Brave.* Old Westbury: Feminist, 1982.

Hurston, Zora Neale. *Their Eyes Were Watching God.* 1937. New York: Harper, 1990.

McDowell, Deborah E. *"The Changing Same": Black Women's Literature, Criticism, and Theory.* Bloomington: Indiana UP, 1995.

Martin, Emily. *The Woman in the Body: A Cultural Analysis of Reproduction.* Boston: Beacon, 1987.

Peterson, Carla L. *"Doers of the Word": African-American Women Speakers and Writers in the North (1830–1880).* New York: Oxford UP, 1995.

Sanchez-Eppler, Karen. *Touching Liberty: Abolition, Feminism, and the Politics of the Body.* Berkeley: U of California P, 1993.

Scarry, Elaine. *The Body in Pain: The Making and Unmaking of the World.* New York: Oxford UP, 1985.

Stockwell, Anne. "Film Preview." *The Advocate* 716 (17 September 1996): 69–70.

Suleiman, Susan Rubin, ed. *The Female Body in Western Culture: Contemporary Perspectives.* Cambridge: Harvard UP, 1986.

Tompkins, Jane. *Sensational Designs: The Cultural Work of American Fiction 1790–1860.* New York: Oxford UP, 1985.

Welter, Barbara. "The Cult of True Womanhood, 1820–1860." *American Quarterly* 18 (Summer 1966): 151–74.

Wiegman, Robyn. *American Anatomies: Theorizing Race and Gender.* Durham: Duke UP, 1995.

PART

I

Covering/
Uncovering

MICHAEL BENNETT

Frances Ellen Watkins Sings the Body Electric

It may seem odd to use a phrase from Walt Whitman to describe the poetry of Frances Ellen Watkins. In most respects, they were two very different poets: one a European American man who wrote highly unconventional free verse that would later make him the most famous poet of the "American Renaissance" and the other an African American woman who has been remembered, if at all, as the author of postbellum dialect poetry and the late-nineteenth-century novel *Iola Leroy*, published long after the first success she achieved as a balladeer in the years before she married Fenton Harper (and added his name to hers) in 1860. Yet it was during this early period, in the decade leading up to the Civil War, that Watkins and Whitman shared a common discursive terrain based on their consuming interest in the intersection between the private bodies of America's inhabitants and the public democratic body of which they were a part—a relationship highlighted and troubled by the struggle over slavery. Both poets drew on and developed the abolitionists' discourse of what I have called "bodily democracy"—the extension of formal democracy to the realm of body politics and control over one's own sexuality.[1]

On the basis of this shared discourse, not only are there interesting grounds for comparison of the two poets, but the usual valuation of their importance might, in fact, be reversed. I would argue that the accolades typically accorded to Whitman—the poet of the body, the great democratic poet—are more aptly applied to Watkins. It was Watkins, not

Whitman, whose poetic performances put her work and her self on display throughout the antebellum northern United States, making her one of the most popular American poets before the Civil War. More than ten thousand copies of Watkins's *Poems on Miscellaneous Subjects* (1854) were published in roughly the same period during which fewer than a hundred copies of *Leaves of Grass* (1855) were sold (Boyd 77; Mathiessen x). These figures make one question how the title "the poet of democracy" has been applied to a man who was seldom read and little admired during his own time while a woman whose poetry was publicly performed to large and enthusiastic crowds—and then read, memorized, and esteemed by tens of thousands—has been not only denied the same recognition but practically forgotten. It was, after all, Whitman himself who claimed, in the concluding line of the 1855 preface to *Leaves of Grass*, that "the proof of a poet is that his country absorbs him as affectionately as he has absorbed it" (2727). By this measure, the "Good Gray Poet" was considerably less significant to antebellum American culture—a less vital part of the democratic body—than was the "Bronze Muse" (Boyd 52) of the abolitionist movement.

This judgment does not speak to the relative "merit" of each poet's work, but the fact that it is so difficult for contemporary readers to imagine a valuation giving more prominence to Watkins than to Whitman does speak to the decontextualizing effects of modern aesthetics and to the loss of memory that occurs when public performances are reduced to written accounts. To modern ears, the claim that Watkins was a more significant poet than Whitman sounds sacrilegious, but to most of their antebellum contemporaries it was a matter of course: Watkins was a popular poet who appeared frequently on the public stage, while Whitman was a journalist whose poetic productions were unknown beyond a small circle. We have lost the immediacy that Watkins's audience felt when she bodied forth her poetry on the stage, just as it is all too easy to lose the cultural memory and historical immediacy embodied in any performance. As Joseph Roach points out, the relationship between memory and history is central to the study of performance, for without efforts to recover the body in performance, "memories torture themselves into forgetting by disguising their collaborative interdependence across imaginary borders of race, nation, and origin" (xi). In the effort to recover the interdependence of the poets discussed in this essay and to examine the ways in which they trouble the imaginary borders alluded to by Roach, it makes perfect sense to compare Watkins and Whitman and to remember when and how the former was valued more highly than the latter.

This judgment has, of course, been reversed in subsequent years—a fact that speaks to the process by which memories fade and to the different sociocultural positions that "gray" male and "bronze" female bodies ultimately assume in the United States. The consequent valuation of Watkins and Whitman and their body of work has much to do with the racial and gender hierarchies that put their selves in different relationship with surrounding social bodies. Even though both sang the body electric—the democratic chant of individual bodies merging to form one nation—this song was inflected differently by the two poets and heard differently by their audiences. The first section of this essay considers how Watkins, even to be considered part of the body electric and to lay claim to the promise of American freedom, had to first write the black female body into relation with the encompassing social bodies of family, race, and nation. The next section explores how Whitman hoped to disencumber his self from these same encompassing bodies in order to enjoy what his mentor Emerson called an "original relation to the universe" (21). In other words, Watkins sought freedom from the constraints placed on her body by aligning it with larger forces, while Whitman craved the freedom to explore his own body outside of any intervening forces. This difference between Watkins's "freedom *from*" and Whitman's "freedom *to*" is explored in the last section of this essay, which speaks to how these different conceptions of body politics are still active in contemporary debates between and within feminist and queer theory.

> Heard you that shriek? It rose
>   So wildly on the air,
> It seemed as if a burden'd heart
>   Was breaking in despair
> ("The Slave Mother" 58–59)[2]

The first stanza of what is probably Watkins's most famous antebellum poem begins with a sound far different than Whitman's famous song celebrating himself. Instead, Watkins begins with a "shriek" that echoes the trials and tribulations suffered by the black female bodies simultaneously valued and devalued by antebellum American culture. In bringing to the public's attention the bodies that made such sounds, Watkins had to contend with the dominant culture's efforts to portray the African body as subhuman and the black female body as lascivious (Foster, *Witnessing* 131–32). Carla L. Peterson has written about the ways in which Watkins responded to these images by attempting, in her public appearances, to "decorporealize the body . . . and present the self as a disembodied voice" (22). I am interested, however, in the ways in which Watkins foregrounded the discourse of the democratic body even as she sought to shield her person from assault. Watkins attempted to transfigure the black woman's body from the locus of enslavement to a site of

resistance. Her strategy was to challenge the peculiar institution's definition of the slave's body as wholly public—existing solely as the property of another—while insisting that the private self exists within a social
network of family, race, and nation. The existence of what Lauren Berlant
has called "the slave's two bodies—sensual and public on the one hand;
vulnerable, invisible, forgettable on the other" (263)—necessitated a dual
strategy in Watkins's poetry and performances: shielding the public body
(hers and the slave's) while making public the invisible body.

Thus Watkins's discourse of the body was very different from the
more conventional rhetorical efforts of women like Maria Stewart who
sought to cover the black female body in the cloak of "true womanhood."
Even as Watkins participated in efforts to shield the black female body
from undue public scrutiny, her poetry provided a detailed examination
of the "body in pain" (Scarry), whether from slavery, poverty, or as the
victim of gendered violence. Her participation in the feminist-abolitionist
discourse of the body not only emphasized control of the individual self
but also highlighted the peculiar institution's destruction of familial ties.
The abolitionists' repeated emphasis on slavery's ability to capriciously
separate family members provided Watkins with a somewhat different
take on the sentimental convention of tragically parted loved ones.

In poems such as "The Slave Mother," Watkins employs what Jane
Tompkins has famously called the "sentimental power" of antebellum
women's writing within a specifically racialized context by exploring
slavery's violation of the mother-child relationship. The loss of a child—
a convention in sentimental novels by white female authors—is refigured as the core predicament of enslaved black women in the abolitionists'
repeated references to families and homes torn asunder by slavery. Maggie
Sale and Claudia Tate have noted that, in response to this threat, the
"assertion of a fundamental bond between mother and child" (Sale 159)
took on a different meaning for African American women who were stereotyped as lacking that mother-child connection—a myth perpetuated
to justify the forced separation of slave parents and children. In "The
Slave Mother," Watkins emphasizes the horrible grief of a mother whose
son is being sold away from her; the mother's despair is written upon
her body:

> Saw you those hands so sadly clasped—
>   The bowed and feeble head—
> The shuddering of that fragile form—
>   That look of grief and dread?
> Saw you the sad, imploring eye? (59)

The questioning format provides a fairly conventional appeal to a presumably female audience to identify with the suffering of a mother, but at the same time it presents an unconventional insistence on recognizing the public display of private griefs inflicted upon black women.

In another poem also entitled "The Slave Mother" (this one subtitled "A Tale of the Ohio"), Watkins further challenges her audience with an image that does not fit the sentimental conventions: a mother's attempt to kill her children. Based upon a tragic incident in the life of Margaret Garner—which also served as the source for the central plot in Toni Morrison's novel *Beloved*—Watkins depicts a mother who is willing to sacrifice her children's lives rather than see them returned to slavery, attempting to kill them before she is captured by bounty hunters and returned to the South. In a revealing pronoun slippage from first to third person, Watkins writes, "I will do a deed for freedom / She shall find each child a grave" (85).[3] The absolute fact of the children's mortality is used to deny their definition as property. Given that children's status as free or slave was determined by their mother's condition, the act of birth was in itself an act of enslavement that this mother refuses to perpetuate. The ultimate assertion of the sanctity of the familial bond is the willingness to forego life itself if that bond will not be recognized. The strangled version of freedom rendered by this act committed under appalling circumstances provides evidence of Peterson's claim that Watkins "reconfigured sentimental values in her poetry by insisting on the extent to which public interests at all times infiltrate the private sphere of African-American familial life" (156).

This erosion of the public/private distinction was increasingly evident in the antebellum discourse of the racialized body. In response, Watkins challenged the dominant discourse that depicted dark skin as a mark of inferiority. She questioned the basis of this racist judgment in her poetic tribute to Harriet Beecher Stowe's character Eliza Harris: "How say that the lawless may torture and chase / A woman whose crime is the hue of her face?" (61). In "To the Cleveland Union Savers," Watkins identifies herself as "One of the Fugitive's Own Race"—which is seen as a badge of honor—and transfers the mark of sin from a racial signification to the moral blight of slavery's evil:

> There is blood upon your city,—
> Dark and dismal is the stain;
> And your hands would fail to clea[n]se it,
> Though you should Lake Erie drain. (94)

The body is stained by acts, not by innate conditions, and the "hue" of Watkins race is a source of pride, not shame. In the poem "Ethiopia," all of Africa is personified as a wrongly injured female body casting "the tyrants yoke from off her neck / His fetters from her soul" (62) as she rises to her true glory. Rather than serving as a category that separates superior and inferior peoples in the United States, race becomes a transhistoric and transatlantic category connecting American slaves to the glories of Mother Africa.

Closer to home, Watkins recognizes that the only lasting protection of the enslaved person's body comes not from the ties of family and race but from being integrated into the nation's body. In her speeches, Watkins pictures slavery as a "monstrous Juggernaut of organized villainy" that "fattens and feasts on human blood" (52, 45). This monstrous body could only be challenged by an equally powerful democratic body in which all are "bound together in a great bundle of humanity" (217). In the battle for the soul of the nation, the "icy hands of slavery" chill the "country's heart" (86), but Watkins exhorts the nation to lay aside its divisions and "Be Active" together to "staunch the wounds that bleed" where "oppression's feet of iron / Grind a brother to the ground" (76–77). Only the body electric can band together with enough charge to dispel the juggernaut of slavery. Bodily imagery is used to envisage African Americans' claim to the protections of citizenship in a postemancipation United States.

In addition to transmuting the slave from the condition of property into the network of family, race, and nation, Watkins also wrote private griefs into public discourse through the form of her poetry. As Peterson notes, the ballad form favored by Watkins "grew out of oral folk culture as the product of an anonymous author who voices the concerns of the community" (128). Maryemma Graham argues that Watkins's transposition of the genre into a vehicle of social protest embodying the dramatic details of black experience "transformed the common ballad into a distinctly Afro-American discourse" (lii). Whether or not this is the case, it is certainly true, as Peterson maintains, that Watkins took advantage of the "simplicity and regularity" of the ballad and hymn forms to make the rhetoric of the feminist-abolitionists "appeal to people's understanding" (130).

The very form of Watkins's poetry, unlike that of Whitman's supposed democratic poetics, was designed to reach a mass audience and move them to action. Watkins's early statement of her aesthetic principles in the poem "Be Active" claims that art should be designed to appeal to a "high and holy mission":

> Set to work the moral forces,
> > That are yours of church and state;
> Teach them how to war and battle
> > 'Gainst oppression, wrong, and hate. (76–77)

To prompt this desired action, Watkins uses the body of the poem to get her reader to visualize the effect of oppression: "*gazing* on his mighty wrong" to truly "*see* that sad despairing mother" and that "pale and trembling maiden." The result of this new vision is figured as violent action: to "Hurl the bloated tyrant" and "Crush these gory, reeking altars." What has been referred to as the "highly bodily form" (Peterson 126) of sentimentality because of the genre's emphasis on tears, moans, and pain is transfigured from a form of private grief to one of public action.

This transformation is underscored by the performative aspect of Watkins's poetry. Based upon various contemporary reviews of Watkins's speaking engagements, Elizabeth Ammons concludes that Watkins was "an extraordinary artist in the oral tradition" (62). Ammons goes on to note that much of the political charge of Watkins's work came from the way in which she "wove her poems into the countless public speeches she delivered" (64). Watkins's ballads highlighted the connections and disconnections between the black female body and the democratic body through both the form of the poems and the structure of their presentation upon the abolitionist stage. Literary criticism too often fails to flesh out our understanding of the relationship a public poet like Watkins created with her audience, to develop a theory of embodied performance. Despite recent efforts to correct this oversight, a performative perspective has been absent from most explorations of nineteenth-century African American women engaged in the process of self-representation.[4]

Such a perspective is necessary if we are to explore how the antebellum judgment that Watkins, not Whitman, was the great poet of the democratic body became so dramatically reversed as their physical bodies passed away and their body of works passed through the decontextualizing machinery of modern aesthetics. The shift in attention from Watkins to Whitman was not, of course, simply the result of the disinterested process of time sorting out the wheat from the chaff; there are fundamental gendered and racial differences between the discursive locale of each poet. These differences, embodied in the form and content of their poetry, help explain why the physical presence of Watkins on the abolitionist stage, performing her rhyming ballads on the effects of slavery, captured the attention of antebellum audiences while the less topical and never-performed poetry of Whitman failed to appeal to his contemporaries though his substantial body of unconventional poetry was canonized by academics taught to devalue conventional, popular cultural productions that draw much of their power from a performative context.

I celebrate myself,
   And what I assume you shall assume,

> For every atom belonging to me as good belongs to you.
>   ("Song of Myself" 2727)[5]

Though Watkins works from an understanding of the vexed relationship between the private and public body of the slave, necessitating her
efforts to write the black female body into encompassing social bodies
while shielding it from harm, the very first lines of "Song of Myself"
make it clear that Whitman assumes a comfortable relation between his
own body and that of his compatriots and country. Seeming to deny the
distinction between public and private, "Song of Myself" famously begins with the implicit understanding that by celebrating himself Whitman
is celebrating the body electric. He casually states that "what I assume
you shall assume" because the self is a physical entity composed of a
material that "belonging to me as good belongs to you." The equality of
Whitman's body with others is "assume[d]," meaning that it need not
be proved; his body is seamlessly blended with his fellow humans, their
institutions, and even with the whole of nature since all material is composed of the same atoms. In later versions of "Song of Myself," Whitman
makes the privilege of his position clear. The body's preeminence is
foregrounded as "creeds and schools" are held "in abeyance" (*Complete*
25). Whitman's body exists in such easy relation with humanity and nature that it can simply cast off the constraints of social ideologies and
institutions. This is a body existing in very different relation to its society than the body of Frances Ellen Watkins. Far from writing himself
into the networks of family, race, and nation, these are the very institutions from which Whitman attempts to extricate himself in order to enjoy full bodily freedom.

In Watkins's poetry, sexuality exists only implicitly in the procre-
ation needed to establish the sanctity of the mother-child bond, while
in Whitman's the sexual body is not tied to the family but to explicit
celebrations of desire and homoeroticism. Even when Whitman writes
of procreative sex, the focus is not on the resulting family bonds but on
the urge to procreate—on desire rather than the results of desire: "Urge
and urge and urge, / Always the procreant urge of the world" (2728).
And then there are the celebrations of homosexual, or at least homoerotic, unions that are only metaphorically procreative:

> . . . comes a loving bedfellow and sleeps at my side all night,
>   and close on the peep of the day,
> And leaves for me baskets covered with white towels bulging the
>   house with their plenty. (2729)

This is but one of several passages in "Song" that reveal the untroubled eroticism of privileged male bodies at play.[6] Probably the most famous of these passages is the scene in which the nude, well-lit bodies of male bathers, embodied in the painting *The Swimming Hole* by Whitman's friend Thomas Eakins, are contrasted with the shaded, costumed body of the proper woman watching them. While watching the bathers, this woman "hides handsome and richly drest aft the blinds of the window" (2734); yet, despite her exterior conformity to the codes of bodily propriety, the woman imaginatively joins the twenty-eight bathers: "Where are you off to lady? for I see you, / You splash in the water there, yet stay stock still in your room" (2735). Whitman reminds his readers of the relative freedom of white male bodies, which cavort unclothed in the great outdoors, in contrast to the female body, which remains hidden in the dark under layers of fabric and standing stock still—finding freedom only in male-centered imaginings. Bodily freedom for Whitman exists in opposition to the notions of female propriety into which Watkins hopes to insert black women—that is, Watkins seeks the protection of the very conventions that Whitman flouts.

The same is true of how each poet approaches the relationship between individual bodies and the social network of race. Again, Watkins devotes herself to constructing a positive image of her race to argue for the equality of black and white bodies, while Whitman seeks to deconstruct the very notion of race. In the famous sixth stanza, answering a child's question "What is the grass?" (2730), Whitman links together even those bodies most radically separated by slavery: "Kanuck, Tuckahoe, Congressman, Cuff" (2731). Whitman argues that the grass, "Growing among black folks as among white" (2731), erases the distinction between racial categories, using slang to equate a French Canadian living outside the reaches of slavery and the Fugitive Slave Law, a white Virginian, a member of the U.S. House of Representatives (ipso facto, a privileged white male), and an African American. These disparate bodies are equated syntagmatically and even conjoined through alliteration on the "k" sound of each designation—essences mingle fluidly into one another in a sort of linguistic miscegenation. Whitman's efforts to erase the body's racial markers through linguistic miscegenation are matched by his interest in the "biological" equivalent: "I saw the marriage of the trapper in the open air in the farwest, /.... the bride was a red girl" (2734). Even Whitman's observation of birds with various colors of plumage is internalized in such a way that it could be read as an allegory of America's own mixed races: "I believe in those wing'd purposes, / And acknowledge red yellow and white playing within me" (2736). Rather than writing his body into an encompassing racial network, like Watkins, Whitman writes various races into his own body, and the country for which he stands, indivisible.

Whitman also engages in the problematic attempt to elide the distinctions between different components of the national body. His radical leveling instinct makes each body equal without regard to its place in the national hierarchy of citizenship. Several lists of America's inhabitants, compiled from his experience as a journalist on a city beat, comprise a catalog of the high and low in American society in hopes of erasing the distinctions that separate them. The "half-breed" and "the quadroon girl . . . sold at the stand" become just another part of the corporeal scenery, along with the "deacons," "lunatic," and "cleanhaired Yankee girl" (2737–38). Again using alliteration to erase the distinction between social categories, Whitman juxtaposes the "opium eater" and "prostitute" with the "President" (2738), folding all these bodies into the body of the poet: "And these one and all tend inward to me, and I tend outward to them, / And such as it is to be of these more or less I am" (2739) (later versions added: "And of these one and all I weave the song of myself" (*Complete* 36). Ultimately, this laudable democratic impulse is compromised by the ease with which Whitman is allowed an imaginative bodily space that escapes the markers of age, gender, race, and class:

> I am of old and young, of the foolish as much as the wise,
> Regardless of others, ever regardful of others,
> Maternal as well as paternal, a child as well as a man,
> . . . Of every hue and trade and rank, of every caste and
>   religion (2739–40)

There are clearly deep philosophical and ideological problems with the assumption that one man's body can stand in for the whole nation. In fact, when Whitman tries to mandate a sense of unity and agreement between and within his and the nation's body, his own unpopularity and the Civil War would seem to disprove this faith. He claims that his thoughts are really the thoughts of "all men in all ages and lands" and that "[i]f they are not yours as much as mine they are nothing, or next to / nothing" (2740). Returning to the criteria by which Whitman asks us to judge his success as a poet—that poet's absorption by American society—Whitman was clearly a failure in his own time.

Whitman's unpopularity in antebellum America resulted both from the radical themes of his poetry and from the unconventional form of *Leaves of Grass*. Just as Watkins and Whitman sought bodily freedom through opposing paths—one embracing larger social bodies and one fleeing them—so they embodied this search in dramatically different forms. While Watkins's ballads projected private griefs into the public forum without conflating these two realms, Whitman's free verse collapsed the public and private distinction, breaking down the relationship between the individual poet's voice and larger social and aesthetic structures. In the antebellum United States, Watkins's familiar ballad form enabled her to link the private to the public both within her poems, which balanced her individual voice with the culturally sanctioned structures of rhyme and rhythm, and in her presentation of these poems to large audiences. At the same time, Whitman's free verse obliterated both this internal relation between individual voice and social structure and the external relation to a public audience. Despite Whitman's intention to sing the body electric, "Song of Myself" did not prove to be a popular ballad sung for large audiences but rather a very personal tune that Whitman hummed almost on his own.

None of this denies that Whitman's free verse provided a perfectly appropriate form for his efforts to break down distinctions between different components of the national body—a form that could embody the drama of democratic identity. Through cataloging, alliteration, and the interplay between single end-stopped lines and the larger poetic structure, Whitman sought to balance and reconcile the major conflicts in the body politic, yoking the many together into one (separate person and en masse, liberty and union, South and North, farm and city, labor and capital, black and white, female and male, religion and science)— e pluribus unum. But, as we have seen, Whitman's use of these techniques and his paratactic style—creating, as they do, a leveling effect in which nothing is subordinated—had some unintended consequences. Even though Whitman claims that his style ensures that there will not be "a single person slighted or left away," he proceeds through a kind of guilt by association to yoke together those marked as other because of their skin color with those marked as other because of some variety of socially defined moral failing: "The keptwoman and sponger and thief, are hereby invited . . . the / heavy-lipped slave is invited . . . the venerealee is invited, / There shall be no difference between them and the rest" (2741). The slave is equated with those who have engaged in some act of social or moral crime. Certain hierarchies are kept in place even as the form attempts to break them down. Indeed, Whitman's free verse still makes room for the opposite of freedom—the logic of slavery.

I do not wish to disagree with the current consensus of Whitman scholars that "there is an intimate connection between Whitman's poetic language and political philosophy" embodied in his "democratic poetics" (Dimock 71, 73). Indeed, I have argued that the form and content

of "Song of Myself" work together to break down antidemocratic hierarchies within the social body by folding them all into the private self
of the poet. But the contrast between Whitman and Watkins shows the
problem with uncritically celebrating the fact that, by "presenting himself as a model democrat who speaks as and for rather than apart from
the people," Whitman is "a breaker of bounds: he is female and male,
farmer and factory worker, prostitute and slave, citizen of America and
citizen of the world" (Erkkila 7). The liberatory force of this maneuver
is compromised when Whitman "speaks as and for" bodies that, though
not free to simply erase boundaries or become citizens, are perfectly capable of speaking for themselves. The dividing point between Watkins's
and Whitman's self-representations is the line between performance and
performativity, the line between inhabiting a character's body and being interpellated by the conventions of embodiment (Diamond 5).[7]
Watkins's appearances on the abolitionist stage enabled her both to perform a range of poetic characterizations and to show that a black woman
could inhabit a position as a free subject. Whitman's attempt to cross
the same line between the performance of various characters/selves and
the performativity of markers like race and gender founders on his inability to assume a subject position that speaks for the range of bodies
he would represent. Whitman assumes too much when he assumes that
the various tones of the body electric can be harmonized into one, however capacious, song of a white male self.

This contrast between the poetics of Watkins and Whitman has tremendous significance for understanding both antebellum and contemporary
body politics. Once loose of the constraints of family, race, and nation,
Whitman used his free verse to celebrate himself as a microcosm that
stands in for larger social entities, a feat made possible by the easy relationship between individual white male bodies and the encompassing
social body of the United States. Whitman exercises the freedom to explore his own body for private enjoyment and as a symbol of social adhesiveness, erasing the distinction between public and private.[8] Watkins,
however, used her ballads to write herself into the very social bodies
(family, race, nation) that Whitman rejected, a task required by the uneasy relationship between black female bodies and the body electric.
Watkins searches for bodily freedom from the forces that seek to ensnare
her—and her brothers and sisters in bondage—by insisting on the distinction between public protections for the body and private rights to
the body (to counter slavery's erasure of this distinction). Watkins and
Whitman each sought bodily freedom but in ways that were ultimately

not only opposed but even antithetical in terms of how that freedom was represented and conceptualized.

In pursuit of bodily freedom, Whitman assigns himself the task of being the one true representative of others who are very capable of representing themselves. Because the poet stands in for all those figures who are blended into the song of himself, Whitman erases the subjectivities of those who comprise the body electric. Whitman claims to speak for the voiceless, though they do in fact have voices that are likely to be drowned out by his own:

> Through me many long dumb voices,
> Voices of the interminable generations of slaves,
> Voices of the prostitutes and of deformed persons,
> Voices of the diseased and despairing, and of thieves and dwarfs,
> Voices of cycles of preparation and accretion, . . .
> Through me forbidden voices
> Voices of sexes and lusts . . . voices veiled and I remove the veil,
> Voices indecent by me clarified and transfigured. (2746)

The assumption that slaves and others are "dumb" or that, if they can speak, their voices are "indecent" and must be "clarified and transfigured" by the poet reveals a fundamental flaw with Whitman's body politics in the arena of representation. Rather than allowing slaves and assorted others to speak for themselves, Whitman becomes them:

> The mother condemned for a witch and burnt with dry wood, and
>   her children gazing on;
> The hounded slave that flags in the race and leans by the fence,
>   blowing and covered with sweat, . . .
> All these I feel or am. (2758)

Beyond empathy, he describes a sort of transubstantiation. In the 1855 "Preface," Whitman sets himself the task of embodying America and the American "race" because "a bard is to be commensurate with a people," to respond to the country's spirit by "incarnat[ing] its geography and natural life" (2714). This lofty goal creates a crisis in representation as Whitman calls upon the poet not just to depict the body electric but to become it—a usurpation of bodies inhabited by the likes of Watkins and those she represents.

The issue of representation, however, also presents difficulties for Watkins's body politics. Born free, Watkins was not in the same position as the slave mothers she so often depicts. One could argue that Watkins engages in a form of ventriloquism similar to that of Whitman when she frequently adopts the persona of a slave. On closer inspection, however, Watkins is usually careful to distinguish between her own condition and that of the enslaved. In most of her antebellum poetry and all of her speeches, she maintains a distinction between the first and third person. Only in her poem "The Slave Mother: A Tale of the Ohio" does Watkins shift from one point of view to the other in ways that destabilize bodily boundaries, but this is still a far cry from the explosion of representations in Whitman's "Song of Myself."[9]

More to the point, Watkins's famous representations of slave mothers involve a form of self-representation. The calculus of racial politics in the antebellum United States figured Watkins's black female body as a sign of enslavement, meaning that Watkins's body quite literally stood in for the subjects of her poetic representations in ways that are just not true for Whitman. Watkins recognized that slavery and prejudice caused a collapse of public and private realms both within the family of the slave mother and for all those whose bodies were likewise coded as racially other. In fact, Watkins came to her work in the antislavery movement through the recognition that the political climate of the 1850s made all African Americans subject to enslavement. William Still reports that Watkins became active in the abolitionist movement after she heard about a "free" black man who was captured in Maryland, Watkins's native state, and sold as a slave based on an 1853 law that remanded into slavery any person of color who entered the state (757–58). This Maryland law, combined with the impact of the Fugitive Slave Law (which was easily twisted to enslave African Americans who were not, in fact, runaway slaves), made it clear to Watkins that her body was on the line. She depicted the possibility of her own capture in an 1857 speech to the New York City Anti-Slavery Society: "A man comes with his affidavits from the South and hurries me before a commissioner; upon that evidence *ex parte* and alone he hitches me to the car of slavery and trails my womanhood in the dust" (102). While Whitman is busy breaking down the public/private distinction in order to make his body represent the body electric by an act of will, Watkins recognizes and works to counter the act of law that does break down the private/public distinction that she hopes to resurrect.

The other problem evident in the contrast between the body politics of Watkins and Whitman has to do with their different conceptions of bodily freedom. On the one hand, Watkins is interested in what I have called the "freedom *from*" model usually associated with feminist theory: freedom from the social and cultural constraints placed upon the body. Whitman, on the other hand, pursues the "freedom *to*" model that has circulated within queer theory: a freedom to pursue the liberation of the body. As Rosemarie Tong points out, the central tenet of "traditional liberal feminism" is that "female subordination is rooted in a set of customary and legal constraints that blocks women's entrance and/or success in the so-called public world" (2); the body politics of traditional feminism is focused on gaining freedom *from* these constraints. In contrast, queer theory, at least in its early manifestations, was conceptualized along the lines of what Annamarie Jagose calls a "liberationist" model of homosexuality (92), with a body politics focused on the freedom *to* explore the boundaries of queer subjectivity. Of course, we are now used to thinking of these two versions of freedom as circulating together. The freedom *to* explore the body can only be enjoyed when the body has won at least qualified freedom *from* the narratives and structures that try to ensnare it. As I hope to show in this concluding section, however, these two kinds of freedom in the "classic" form I have outlined here were not reconcilable as played out on the terrain of the opposed body politics of Watkins and Whitman, though the different discursive strains of each poet's work did eventually come together in ways envisioned by Watkins *avant le lettre*.

When Whitman's conception of freedom is viewed through the lens of Watkins's body politics, its limitations become clear. The freedom celebrated by Whitman—the white male body enjoying its desires without limits—is precisely the kind of bodily freedom that curtailed the liberty of black women in the antebellum United States. Whitman's depiction of his body—"Walt Whitman, an American, one of the roughs, a kosmos, / Disorderly fleshy and sensual . . . eating drinking and breeding," (2746)—relied on the very qualities of white male bodies ("disorderly," "fleshy," "sensual") that led to what Watkins, in a letter to John Brown's wife, Mary, designated as "a plundered cradle and a scourged and bleeding woman" (49). One can only imagine how the following passage from Whitman would sound to Watkins, who was invested in preserving the sanctity of marriage to prevent the violation of the female slave's body: "I turn the bridegroom out of bed and stay with the bride myself, / And tighten her all night to thighs and lips" (2757). This was, the abolitionists' insisted, the course of action of all too many slave masters with regard to their slaves.

The rapacious quality of Whitman's bodily freedom, devouring all into himself, is in a certain respect precisely the logic of slavery—the emptying out of one body so that it may be fully possessed by another. And this omnivorous desire does not stop with other humans; Whitman expresses his need to display his body and come into full contact with the whole of nature: "I will go to the bank by the wood and become undisguised and naked, / I am mad for it to be in contact with me" (2727).

How different this is from Watkins's efforts to shield her body and protect it from the world. How different as well is the animalistic imagery that Whitman uses in celebrating the absolute freedom of his body: "I think I could turn and live with animals . . . they are so placid and self-contained, / I stand and look at them sometimes half the day long" (2752). When Whitman enumerates the places where he is "afoot with [his] vision" (2753), he includes the place "Where the bull advances to do his masculine work, where the stud / to the mare, where the cock is treading the hen." (2755). Whitman equates the desires of the human body and the rutting of animals at precisely the same time that Watkins is working hard to dissociate the black female body from animalistic associations.

To counter the equation between slaves and animals, a central trope challenged by many slave narrators, Watkins highlights the very human quality of suffering endured by slave mothers.[10] The final stanza of "The Slave Mother" makes it clear that one of the chief purposes of displaying the tremendous grief that can be read from the body of a female slave separated from her child is to prove that she is not an animal but a mother, just like many of Watkins's white female readers: "No marvel then, these bitter shrieks / Disturb the listening air: / She is a mother . . ." (59) The colon introduces the point of the poem like an equal sign in an equation. [11] A similar contrast between the bodily imaginary of slavery (which reduces humans to animals) and that of the abolitionists (which insisted on a distinction between the two) is evident in Watkins's "Eliza Harris." At the beginning of the first stanza, Eliza is described as "like a fawn from the arrow, startled and wild," but by the end she is described in fully human terms "for she is a mother" (60–61). Watkins is all too aware of the danger, especially in antebellum America, of erasing the distinction not just between public and private bodies but between humans and animals as well.

Ultimately, the differences between the body politics of Watkins and Whitman flow from the fact that the white male body can easily be represented in American culture as a zone of self-pleasure and control, while black women have had to resist efforts to keep their bodies within the confines of pleasure for others, labor, and even property. Whitman's discourse of the body came from a more privileged site than did Watkins's, and their corporeal selves existed in a very different relation to the larger sociopolitical bodies in which they resided. Lacking the means to overthrow this inequitable access to bodily representation, Watkins's innovation is to take over these confining roles and turn them into spaces of power. The black female body becomes the site of meaningful political action through a process of claiming autonomy that simultaneously enables the self to engage in fair exchange with encompassing bodies—familial, racial, and national. In this way, Watkins sidestepped many of the constraints of the Cult of True Womanhood and, though lacking the degree of freedom accorded to Whitman, created a radical poetry of the body. Watkins composed in a different key than Whitman and utilized her own forms, but her ballads and hymns sing the body electric in hopes that we shall assume what she assumed—that deeper than the words that divide slave and free there is a struggle to embody liberty, "written in living characters upon the soul" (100).

This image portrays freedom as a combination of bodily struggle and discursive resistance —a conception that I want to argue was truly ahead of its time. Though Michel Foucault is usually credited as the thinker who helped us to escape the binary between "freedom *from*" and "freedom *to*" by teaching us to conceptualize all freedom as subject to a micropolitics of resistance, Watkins anticipates this insight. Whitman's conception of bodily freedom is based on a fantasy of complete liberation from societal norms, which could only be believed by someone privileged enough to entertain the notion that it was possible to truly escape such norms. Watkins, whose body was not granted such privileges, is much more attuned to the realities of how power functions in a modern state, requiring a constant effort to win limited freedoms rather than the assumption of total emancipation—a concept that had a much more specific meaning for her. In Foucauldian terms, Watkins's bodily politics is based on an understanding that freedom can only be won through acts of resistance within the domain of power, whereas Whitman fantasizes about liberation from all forms of power and control.[12]

In short, Frances Ellen Watkins and other early black feminists launched a tradition of looking at body politics as a matter of strategic resistance, an insight that has only recently been thoroughly developed within feminist and queer theory. Confronting a white feminist movement that saw freedom *from* patriarchal society as a form of liberation, black feminists and other women of color have pointed to "power relations *between women*—of different races, classes, and cultures"—as equally in need of contestation (Ruiz and DuBois xii). Black feminist thought has always been forced to recognize that bodily freedom is bounded by rigorous exclusions. It is a freedom that must be continually won through acts of resistance. According to the Foucauldian narrative, this same realization came to queer theory when nonnormative sexualities were written into medico-juridical discourses that constructed the modern homosexual. But we must remember that "Song of Myself" was written before this discourse became operative in the United States—it fails to anticipate later developments in queer theory because it came into existence before such concepts had any currency.[13] The exclusion of Whitman's body from the discourse of the homosexual, let alone the queer, marks a decisive historical break with later developments, while Watkins anticipated later developments in black feminist theory because of a sadly consistent treatment of black female bodies in the United States.

In fact, this black feminist tradition of constructing a body politics of resistance provides a challenge not only to Whitman but also to later queer theorists influenced by Foucault, who, like Whitman, tends to imagine bodies without race or gender. To the extent that Watkins and those black feminists who followed her insisted on the specificity of bodies in resistance, they provide a corrective for those who try to trace a queer body politics from Whitman to Foucault and beyond. Watkins's work reveals that she was aware that freedom for the black female body required more than the elimination of slavery. Emancipation technically meant the liberation of slaves, but freedom for those of African descent has proved to be much more complicated in the United States. The Thirteenth Amendment may have freed the slaves, but it did not bring freedom to those whose bodies continued to be coded as racially and gendered others, as evidenced by the ongoing acts of bodily resistance on view in the essays that follow.

Frances Ellen Watkins and Walt Whitman performed the discourse of bodily democracy, working to transform the performativity of raced and gendered bodies in the United States. To the extent that the performative options for such bodies were transformed after the Civil War, Watkins and Whitman, along with the radical abolitionists, succeeded in putting this discourse into material practice. To the extent that their performances remain unfinished and obscured by time, especially in the case of the practically forgotten antebellum stage appearances of Watkins, I offer this genealogy of their performances, attending "not only to 'the body,' as Foucault suggests, but also to bodies—to the reciprocal reflections they make on one another's surfaces as they foreground their capacities for interaction" (Roach 25). Roach argues that this process "recovers the 'counter-memories' or the disparities between history as it is discursively transmitted and memory as it is publicly enacted by the bodies that bear its consequences" (26). Recovering the bodies of Watkins and Whitman in their "reciprocal reflections" reawakens their poetic enactments on behalf of bodies that bore the consequences of life in a slave state.

The task of recovering the bodies of Watkins and Whitman at the same time recovers the possibilities manifest in their historical situation in that, as Judith Butler claims, "the body is a historical situation . . . a manner of doing, dramatizing, and reproducing a historical situation"

("Performative" 272). This insight from performance studies is, Marvin Carlson notes, indebted to Kenneth Burke's formulation of language and thought as "'situated modes of action'" such that "'every text is a strategy for encompassing a situation'" (17). According to Burke's pragmatic method, a poem's structure is described most accurately by thinking of its function (a poem is, after all, designed to do something), and one should observe the design of the poem as an embodiment of this function. Burke claims that "implicit in poetic organization there is the assertion of an identity" (39). The problem, as we have seen, with viewing Whitman's poetry in this way is that the identity he constructs is outside the realm of possibility for those who are not in the privileged position of the white male body. At the same time, one could argue that the strength of his poetry is that it hopes to make his own empowered identity available to all. From this perspective Watkins's and Whitman's poetry clearly falls into the category that Burke calls "incantatory"—poetry that provides an exhortation to make ourselves over in the image of the poem's imagery (117). The difference between Watkins and Whitman is that in making this incantation and exhortation, in singing the body electric, Whitman sang of himself while Watkins transposed the song into a key that unlocked the potential for future singers not just to remake themselves in her image but to take their own turn on the stage of history and thus transform it.

NOTES

1. My analysis of the abolitionist discourse of bodily freedom is expanded and expounded upon in the larger work of which the current essay is a part, *Democratic Discourses: Antebellum American Literature and the Abolition Movement*.
2. Unless otherwise indicated, all quotations from Watkins's poetry and prose are taken from *A Brighter Coming Day*, edited by Frances Smith Foster.
3. This is one of the rare moments when Watkins slides from representations of slave bodies into self-representations of her own black female body, as will be discussed later.
4. The effort to develop a theory of embodied performance has recently become a popular project, generating a series of works on this topic published by Routledge in the last few years. See, for example, Butler (*Excitable*), Carlson, Diamond, Parker and Sedgwick, Phelan, and Schneider. Attempts to apply this perspective to African American women living before the twentieth century have, however, been few and far between. See Peterson and Daphne Brooks's essay in this volume.
5. For ease of reference, I refer to the first poem in *Leaves of Grass* as "Song of Myself" though, except where noted, I am using the 1855 edition in which that poem bore no title. The title most commonly associated with the poem did not appear until 1881, after the 1856 version called "Poem of Walt Whitman, An American," but it is the title that has been retroactively inscribed on the 1855 version by most readers. Also for ease of reference, I sometimes refer to the fifty-two stanzas of the poem, even though these, too,

were added later. I focus on the 1855 version because it is most historically proximate with the antebellum poems of Watkins and the abolitionist discourses to which I refer. I also focus on the 1855 text because, as the editors of the *Heath Anthology* point out, "in later editions of the poems, Whitman toned down some of the more radical stylistic, linguistic, and thematic features of the original edition" (2727). The occasional references to the 1881 version of "Song of Myself," taken from *Complete Poetry and Selected Prose*, are indicated by parenthetical references to *Complete*; citations from "Song of Myself" not preceded by *Complete* are taken from the 1855 version reprinted in the Heath Anthology.

6. Several other passages of homosexual/homoerotic love could be cited here. Among the most explicit is the end of what later became the twenty-first stanza: "Thruster holding me tight and that I hold tight! / We hurt each other as the bridegroom and the bride hurt each / other" (2744). By the time the poem was rewritten into stanza form, however, this and several other of the more explicit passages were removed or softened. As I will argue more fully in the concluding section of this essay, Whitman's self-editing would seem to have to do with his efforts to distance himself from the emerging discourse of the homosexual, or "Uranian" as it was termed at the time. For more on the mid-nineteenth-century development of the discourse of homosexuality, including the derivation of the term "Uranian," see Bronski 21–22.

7. In distinguishing between performance and performativity, I have paraphrased a somewhat narrowed version of what Diamond suggests in her introduction to *Performance and Cultural Politics*. It should be noted, however, that Diamond, like almost every commentator on performance studies, cautions that these terms are contested categories. For further ruminations on the various and variable meanings of performance and performativity, see the authors listed in Note 4.

8. For commentary on the homosexual/homosocial inflection of the word "adhesiveness" in Whitman's poetry and thought, see Bronski 16–21.

9. An interesting contrast could also be made between Watkins's poems about slave mothers and John Greenleaf Whittier's "The Farewell," which is narrated entirely in the persona of "a Virginia Slave Mother" (1816). This poem, written by a white male much more firmly connected to the abolitionist movement than was Whitman, might further complicate the ethics of representation raised by the contrast between Watkins and Whitman.

10. See, for example, the numerous equations made between slaves and animals in the first chapter of Frederick Douglass's and Harriet Jacobs's narratives.

11. This equation—which might be represented as "the separation of slave mother and child + the slave's overwhelming grief = the slave mother must be human because she displays the same emotions as other (white) mothers"—is on display in several of Watkins's poems, including "The Slave Auction," "The Slave Mother: A Tale of the Ohio," and, more obliquely, in "Rizpah, the Daughter of Ai."

12. For more on Foucault's understanding of the difference between resistance and liberation, see Halperin 16–18.

13. AIDS has quite certainly changed the early gay liberationist perspective I have summarized as "freedom to" by revealing the necessary component of "freedom *from*" in queer theory. AIDS activism has entailed a struggle to free the body from the deadly snares of government prejudice and medical bureaucracy, and the development of "safer sex" guidelines certainly reveals a consciousness of the limitations of a "freedom *to*" perspective.

WORKS CITED

Ammons, Elizabeth. "Legacy Profile: Frances Ellen Watkins Harper (1825–1911)." *Legacy* 2.2 (1985): 61–66.

Bennett, Michael. *Democratic Discourses: Antebellum American Literature and the Abolition Movement.* New Brunswick: Rutgers UP, forthcoming.

Berlant, Lauren. "The Queen of America Goes to Washington City: Harriet Jacobs, Frances Harper, Anita Hill." *Subjects and Citizens: Nation, Race, and Gender from Oroonoko to Anita Hill.* Ed. Michael Moon and Cathy N. Davidson. Durham: Duke UP, 1995. 455–80.

Boyd, Melba Joyce. *Discarded Legacy: Politics and Poetics in the Life of Frances E. W. Harper (1825–1911).* Detroit: Wayne State UP, 1994.

Bronski, Michael. *Culture Clash: The Making of Gay Sensibility.* Boston: South End, 1984.

Burke, Kenneth. *The Philosophy of Literary Form.* Berkeley: U of California P, 1973.

Butler, Judith. *Excitable Speech: A Politics of the Performative.* New York: Routledge, 1997.

———. "Performative Acts and Gender Constitution: An Essay in Phenomenology and Feminist Theory." *Performing Feminisms: Feminist Critical Theory and Theatre.* Ed. Sue-Ellen Case. Baltimore: Johns Hopkins UP, 1990. 270–82.

Carlson, Marvin. *Performance: A Critical Introduction.* New York: Routledge, 1996.

Diamond, Elin, ed. *Performance and Cultural Politics.* New York: Routledge, 1996.

Dimock, Wai Chee. "Whitman, Syntax, and Political Theory." *Breaking Bounds: Whitman and American Cultural Studies.* Ed. Betsy Erkkila and Jay Grossman. New York: Oxford UP, 1996. 62–79.

Douglass, Frederick. *Narrative of the Life of Frederick Douglass, An African Slave. Written by Himself.* 1845. Rpt. in *The Classic Slave Narratives.* Ed. Henry Louis Gates Jr. New York: NAL Penguin, 1987. 243–331.

Emerson, Ralph Waldo. "Nature." *Selections from Ralph Waldo Emerson: An Organic Anthology.* Ed. Stephen E. Whicher. Boston: Houghton, 1960. 21–56.

Erkkila, Betsy. "Introduction: Breaking Bounds." *Breaking Bounds: Whitman and American Cultural Studies.* Ed. Betsy Erkkila and Jay Grossman. New York: Oxford UP, 1996. 3–20.

Foster, Frances Smith. Ed. with Introduction. *A Brighter Day Coming: A Frances Ellen Watkins Harper Reader.* New York: Feminist, 1990.

———. *Witnessing Slavery: The Development of Ante-bellum Slave Narratives.* Westport: Greenwood, 1979.

Graham, Maryemma. Introduction. *Complete Poems of Frances E. W. Harper.* Ed. Graham. New York: Oxford UP, 1988. xxxii–lvii.

Halperin, David M. *Saint Foucault: Towards a Gay Hagiography.* New York: Oxford UP, 1995.

[Jacobs, Harriet.] Brent, Linda. *Incidents in the Life of a Slave Girl.* Ed. L. Maria Child. 1861. Rpt. in *The Classic Slave Narratives.* Ed. Henry Louis Gates Jr. New York: NAL Penguin, 1987. 333–515.

Jagose, Annamarie. *Queer Theory: An Introduction.* New York: New York UP, 1996.

Lauter, Paul, et al., eds. *The Heath Anthology of American Literature.* 1st ed. vol 1. Lexington: Heath, 1990.

Matthiessen, F. O. *American Renaissance: Art and Expression in the Age of Emerson and Whitman.* London: Oxford UP, 1941.

Parker, Andrew, and Eve Kosofsky Sedgwick, eds. *Performativity and Performance.* New York: Routledge, 1995.

Peterson, Carla L. *"Doers of the Word": African-American Women Speakers and Writers in the North (1830–1880).* New York: Oxford UP, 1995.

Phelan, Peggy. *Unmarked: The Politics of Performance*. New York: Routledge, 1993.

Roach, Joseph. *Cities of the Dead: Circum-Atlantic Performance*. New York: Columbia UP, 1996.

Ruiz, Vicki L., and Ellen Carol DuBois. Introduction to the Second Edition. *Unequal Sisters: A Multi-Cultural Reader in U.S. Women's History*. Ed. Ruiz and DuBois. 2nd ed. New York: Routledge, 1994.

Sale, Maggie. "Critiques from Within: Antebellum Projects of Resistance." *Subjects and Citizens: Nation, Race, and Gender from Oroonoko to Anita Hill*. Ed. Michael Moon and Cathy N. Davidson. Durham: Duke UP, 1995. 145–68.

Scarry, Elaine. *The Body in Pain: The Making and Unmaking of the World*. New York: Oxford UP, 1985.

Schneider, Rebecca. *The Explicit Body in Performance*. New York: Routledge, 1997.

Still, William. *The Underground Railroad*. 1879. New York: Arno, 1968.

Tate, Claudia. *Domestic Allegories of Political Desire: The Black Heroine's Text at the Turn of the Century*. New York: Oxford UP, 1992.

Tompkins, Jane. *Sensational Designs: The Cultural Work of American Fiction 1790–1860*. New York: Oxford UP, 1985.

Tong, Rosemarie. *Feminist Thought: A Comprehensive Introduction*. Boulder: Westview, 1989.

Whitman, Walt. "Song of Myself." Lauter et. al. 2727–78.

Whittier, John Greenleaf. "The Farewell." Lauter et. al. 1816–18.

DAPHNE A. BROOKS

"The Deeds Done in My Body"

Black Feminist Theory, Performance, and the Truth about Adah Isaacs Menken

Less than three months after she was laid to rest in the summer of 1868, actress Adah Isaacs Menken's elusive personal history cemented itself in the public imaginary. In an effort to untangle the New Orleans–born entertainer's notoriously circuitous identity politics, journalist G. Lippard Barclay scrambled to publish a pamphlet on Menken; in his modest volume, he claimed with great moral conviction that his editor had sternly directed him to "write of her nothing but the truth" (43). Yet Barclay's efforts went largely ignored by a generation of scholars and media critics who approached documenting and researching the enigmatic actress's adventurous life and work with varying degrees of accuracy and integrity. Barclay's "truthful" agenda failed to quell the controversy and allure that blanketed Menken's short career, and it did little to discourage future generations of fallacious narratives about the actress. Tellingly, in the decades following her death and in the wake of events in which her remains were literally exhumed, transferred, and reburied, Menken's legendary body (of work) lingers as a hotly contested site of analysis, a corporeal conundrum that repeatedly surfaces as an object of textual appropriation in popular and scholarly projects (James 14–16).[1]

Menken dominated the spectacle-driven transatlantic theater circuit for much of the 1860s, until her untimely death from stage injuries and an infection. She initially gained global notoriety for performing the eponymous lead in the 1861 production of *Mazeppa*. Strapped to a black

Figure 1. Adah Isaacs Menken, portrait by Sarony, circa 1866. *The Harvard Theatre Collection, The Houghton Library.*

stallion and cutting a treacherous path across the stage in "flesh-colored" tights and a tunic before full-house audiences in the United States and Europe, Menken's at once voluptuous and yet ambiguously costumed figure launched a groundswell of pop cultural fascination. The spectacle of her "disrobing" in the cross-dressed role of a heroic rebel warrior evolved into the central attraction during this nightly extravaganza. Yet with so much attention paid to that which she "laid bare" on the stage, the facts of her personal life have largely remained a source of occlusion and contention. This controversy has, in part, led to theater historians' immortalization of Menken less for her roles as a thespian and

THE TRUTH ABOUT ADAH ISAACS MENKEN   43

more as an object of public curiosity who claimed at least half a dozen
pseudonyms throughout her lifetime, named five different individuals
to be her father, identified just as many husbands in sixteen years, and
boasted a colorful array of alleged celebrity paramours and confidants
ranging from Alexandre Dumas *père* to Algernon Charles Swinburne and
Mark Twain. Perhaps the most provocative controversy in twentieth-
century scholarship on the actress, however, revolves around genealogical
politics—the increasing corroboration of Menken's African ancestry, her
putative Creole cultural background, and her own attempts to publicly
obfuscate family lineage.

An inventive participant in the elision and effacement of her own
personal history, Menken spent a good deal of her career circulating narratives by print and word of mouth that complicated the public perception of her identity, in turn inspiring a generation's worth of feeble
attempts to crack the code of her "authentic" racial past. This biographical
obsession with "uncovering the secret" of Menken's cultural and racial
genealogy has paradoxically obscured her subjectivity in the work of
many scholars who collapse a reading of the "truth" of her identity into
the scene of corporeal unveiling in her professional work. At least seven
full-length biographies, as well as numerous journal articles and several works of fiction, foreground Menken's racially ambiguous body and
situate her figure as an open corporeal text inviting circumscription by
the sleuthlike biographer. Menken, in these projects, comes across not
so much as a theatrical pioneer of the mid-nineteenth-century extravaganza genre but more as a hapless criminal beckoning apprehension; an
unruly figure, she is drawn to the theater, these texts suggest, by her essentially libidinous role as "the naked lady." Look no further, these biographies assert, than at the body before you on the stage to find the
"true" Adah Isaacs Menken.[2]

This suggestion, however, seems to grossly oversimplify the life and
career of an entertainer who was, between 1861 and 1863, the highest
paid actress in England and America. Indeed, what is missing from this
remarkably extensive yet egregiously facile biographical and scholarly
discourse on Menken is a critical and methodological approach that allows for a more complex reading of her performative agency. An actress
who intervened in the representation of her own body politics both on
and off of the stage, Menken remains a rich and unrecuperated site of
contradictions and intersections in performance culture. Her work has
rarely been considered in the context of critical feminist cultural analysis, and few scholars have attempted to map a connection between her
manipulation of racial and gender categories and the nature of her work
as a legendary "shape actress."[3] What would it mean, for instance, to

explore the ways in which the labyrinths of Menken's identity performances complicate the terms of her "exposure" as a female entertainer?
How, if at all, might we discuss her work in the racially marked contexts that she simultaneously invoked and confounded? Only by critically recontextualizing biographical as well as theatrical "scenes" in
multiple Menken narratives do we come closer to a consideration of the
interplay between her continuum of identity constructions and her
equally volatile body politics.

I intend to read against popular and long-standing representations
of Menken that fix and reduce her stage materiality. I attempt instead to
resituate the actress in a black feminist theoretical context that allows
us to read her as radically using her body as a performative instrument
of subjectivity rather than existing merely as an object of spectral rav-
ishment and domination. What concerns me here is the possibility of
locating an "imaginary body" that ultimately functions as representational resistance and that equally problematizes the ways in which we
conceive of racial, gender, and corporeal spectacle in nineteenth-century culture.[4] Reading across the gaze of the white male spectator, I am
most interested in mining what we might call a politics of opacity that
black feminist theory enables. Thus the first section considers the methodological quagmire that Menken's life and work poses. I question
whether it is possible to articulate an interpretative strategy of reading
that negotiates black feminist theory and performance, as well as the
politics of the body. The remainder of the essay responds to this initial
query by examining the nexus between corporeal subjectivity and cultural agency as it specifically comes to bear upon Menken. Here I argue
that the opaque operates as a method of contestation and invention for
the public, performative, and racially ambiguous nineteenth-century female figure. From this standpoint I aim to reposition Menken as an actress and a cultural figure deeply rooted in transatlantic theater culture.
A phantasmagoric body of (un)truthfulness that exemplifies the power
of performance as a site of (re)covering, Menken's spectacular figure disrupts the conventional relationship between audience and performer in
nineteenth-century theater culture. This project picks up where Barclay
and other Menken "detectographers" have left off in that it aims to interrogate this arcane cultural icon from the standpoint of a different kind
of "truth" and takes the unlikely figure of Sojourner Truth, Menken's
black feminist contemporary, as a critical and methodological point of
departure. For it is Truth's repeated and legendary characterization of
her own black, female, and very public body that forces an overt consideration of the corporeal as a site of spectacularly resistant opacity.

The Truth about Menken

*I feel that if I have to answer for the deeds done in
my body just as much as a man, I have a right to
have just as much as a man.*
—Sojourner Truth (Gage, "Address")

*For this opacity . . . must be considered in relation to
the dominative imposition of transparency and the
degrading hypervisibility of the enslaved, and
therefore, by the same token, such concealment
should be considered a form of resistance.*
—Saidiya Hartman, *Scenes of Subjection*

When the landmark abolitionist and feminist activist
Sojourner Truth claimed equality by virtue of the "deeds done" in her
body, she articulated a means of rescuing that very body from nineteenth-
century proscriptions of racial and gender abjection by locating agency
precisely within her flesh. This sort of corporeal challenge draws unlikely yet nevertheless resonant comparisons of Sojourner Truth to her
contemporary, Adah Isaacs Menken. Both Truth, born to slave parents
of "unmixed" African ancestry in 1797, and Menken, born in 1839 a free
Southern woman of putative African and European lineage, face the threat
of functioning as circumscribed corporeal spectacles in some of their
more prominent biographical narratives. Truth, for instance, has been
canonized as an illiterate "Amazon" lecturer whose "witnessing" of slavery before all-white audiences depended upon a deployment of the "violated" slave woman's body, reconfigured as a site of "physical endurance"
(Mullen 5). Similarly, studies of Menken often construct her as a mute
yet perilously salacious stage diva who dominated theater circles with
her notorious striptease.[5] However, recent efforts of contemporary feminist theorists to reappropriate Truth's body from these sorts of fetishistic agendas perhaps clear a space for considering the subversive power
of "bodily deeds." Such efforts inform my own reading and recontex-
tualization of Menken as both a biographical and a performative subject. Thus, I will initially turn to the criticism of Truth as a methodological
point of departure in exploring Menken.

White abolitionist Frances Gage's influential memoir of Sojourner
Truth historically canonized her as an "authentic" body of racial and
gender knowledge who faithfully fulfilled the desires of the white spectral
eye/I. This "tall, gaunt black" female figure who marches through Gage's
"Reminiscences" from 1851 is both imposingly present in the body and
suspiciously absent in her ability to enforce a narrative control over that
body. Rather, according to Gage, the "deep tones" of her oratory, which

rivet white Northern spectators, serve to convert and deliver her audience from the moral bankruptcy of complicity with slavery. Having taken her audience of "streaming eyes, and hearts beating with gratitude" into "her strong arms" and having "carried [them] safely over the slough of difficulty" (1960), Gage's Truth relinquishes interiority in favor of preserving the full emotional conversion of her white audience.[6] This sort of problem wherein the black abolitionist is reduced to the serviceable corporeal perhaps has much to do with the fact that her discursive body is so limited. As with the crisis in Menken studies in which the actress left behind only the slightest "fragments" of autobiography, Truth's lifelong illiteracy and a scarcity of self-authored documents leave a void in critical work on her life and activism.[7]

As historian Nell Painter speculates, Truth's "biographical problem becomes a larger question of how to deal with people who are in History but who have not left the kinds of sources to which historians and biographers ordinarily turn" ("Sojourner Truth"13). Like Menken biographies, which simultaneously document and reinvent the legend of the "free-loving" actress, the myths and false reports regarding Truth (for instance, as being prematurely deceased) are clearly "all the more valuable as a reflection of Truth's mid-nineteenth-century persona" (9).[8] I would argue further that the representation of the socially "deviant" woman's constructed persona in both these cases reinforces the ways in which racially marked female bodies occupy a vexed and contested terrain in scholarly (and not so scholarly) discourse. In turn, the conspicuous voids in discursive material on Truth and Menken have contributed to this intense privileging of their bodies as "authentic" texts of identity. The question becomes, then, what kinds of critical methodologies might be used to interrogate the subjectivity of historical figures such as Truth and Menken, figures who have been largely denied the right to claim discursive property as well as the patriarchal fantasy of "writing themselves into being"? Does the scene of performance offer itself as an avenue for these women of the flesh to instead act themselves into being, to act themselves into history?[9]

These questions continue to circulate in current critical debates that perpetuate the reduction of Truth into "authentic," corporeal knowledge, a source of labor for some other agenda. As black feminist critic Deborah McDowell cogently observes, Sojourner Truth is too often employed as a sign to "rematerialize" poststructuralist, epistemological theory, particularly in the work of contemporary white feminist scholars where she is frequently "summoned from the seemingly safe and comfortable distance of a historical past" and transformed into a material and iconographic bridge to "experiential" politics (253). Her points here extend

Valerie Smith's influential work on this topic, as do Margaret Homans's recent critical responses. Smith finds that "it is striking that at precisely the moment when Anglo American feminists and male Afro-Americanists begin to reconsider the material ground of their enterprise, they demonstrate their return to earth, as it were, by invoking the specific experiences of black women and the writings of black women" (45).[10] In response to Smith's observations, Homans, a white feminist critic, painstakingly conscious of racial and gender positionality politics, attempts to question what happens when black women make use of their own materiality within narratives in which they are the subjects; she attempts to make a distinction between an African American woman working *through* her body for her own discourse and Anglo-American feminists working black figures into their discursive projects. In her reading of texts by contemporary black women writers, Homans contends that when these writers "image their own bodies, they set up a constructive dialogue between poststructuralist and humanist views of identity rather than either reducing the black woman's body to sheer ground or matter or, to the contrary, using that body to validate disembodiment" ("Women" 87).

What is most interesting about Homans's analysis for my purposes of recontextualizing and reinterrogating the work of Menken is the significance of performance in this move toward manipulating the borders of the material and the epistemological in black feminist (self-) representation. In a Patricia Williams narrative passage on which Homans focuses, "staging" the self and employing one's body as a performative instrument are of central importance. Williams constructs a moment of seeing herself in a dream: "the me-that-is-on-stage is laughing loudly and long. She is extremely vivacious, the center of attention. . . . She is not beautiful in any traditional sense . . . like a claymation model of myself. . . . I hear myself speaking: *Voices lost in the chasm speak from the slow eloquent fact of the chasm. They speak and speak, like flowing water*" (201). Williams here conjures multiple visions of herself onstage, while yet another self sits in the audience looking on at this "claymation model" who is "laughing loudly and long." Watching this constructed self perform and speak "like flowing water," the projected "voices" of this Other Williams surf into the "fact of the chasm," a void, a space, an aphotic opening. In this passage, where Williams assumes the role of both performer and spectator, Homans observes that "there are two Williamses but they collaborate to make possible the pleasure of voyeurism," and thus Williams celebrates what Homans reads as "embodiment and identity" with "the denaturalizing of identity" ("Women" 89). Performance is the vehicle that enables this process; the "scene," as it were, allows Williams to negotiate an epistemological trajectory from her spectacular "claymation" self onstage to her voyeur figure looking on.

We might, then, think of the "chasm" in the "dream" as a sphere where multiple voices are born, where multiple possibilities exist for the black female cultural producer. Her figure, in this context, is both spectacularly visible and imaginatively elusive in its ability to "denaturalize," bifurcate, and multiply. This "eloquent fact" of the chasm operates as the critical point of departure in black feminist performance and its authorial repossession of body politics. A dark point of possibility, the chasm functions as a figurative site for the opaque reconfiguration of the black and female body on display. This trope of darkness represents a kind of shrouding that allows for corporeal unveiling to yoke with the (re)covering of flesh. Indeed, I suggest that we think of this location as a metaphorical site where black feminist performance flourishes, as a space where opacity works to contest the "dominative imposition of transparency" (Hartman 36). Yet unlike the colonial invention of exotic "darkness" that has historically been made to envelop bodies and geographical territories in the shadows of global and hegemonic domination, this form of black performative opacity, as Hartman suggests convincingly of black song, has the potential to "enabl[e] something in excess of the orchestrated amusements of the enslaved" (36). In the cases of Truth and Menken, opacity has the potential to further liberate "free" yet socially, politically, and culturally circumscribed bodies.[11]

Thus I wish to read for the spectacular opacities rooted in this form of corporeal representation in order to discover the Truth about Menken. It seems increasingly imperative to consider this kind of narrative possibility in relation to black feminist theory as an alternative means to interrogating the work of women whose complex bodies have been trivialized in most critical discourses. If, as performance theorist Jeanie Forte has argued, there are "reasons why . . . it is crucial for Anglo American feminism, and particularly feminist performance theory, to focus on the body at this historical juncture" (249), then the same can be said within African American feminist contexts. Reading these particular negotiations of black feminist performance provides a means to recuperating a narrative strategy that, for nineteenth-century socially, politically, and culturally marginalized women in particular, circumvents the dichotomy between being visible and abject and being "pure" and disembodied. To locate the veiled corners of these female cultural producers' work perhaps allows us to locate the ways in which they strategized "bod[ies] in representation" (249).

This kind of a methodological approach is particularly significant in reexamining the discursive representations of Truth and Menken. De-

spite the obvious objectification of both women in past and present biographical discourses, a re-consideration of their bodies in performance
might allow us to locate the ways in which the opaque potentially produces revisionist and transformative subjectivities. It is, however, critical to point out that in using Truth's performative representations as a
springboard into exploring Menken's, I in no way intend to elide the
vast complexities of their formidable differences. Rather, my effort to
consider Menken in relation to Truth is driven by a critical desire to
complicate the discourses surrounding the actress that, up to this point,
have avoided exploring the convergence of race and gender as ideological constructs in her life and career.[12] With this in mind, I wish to return in brief to the legendary scene of Sojourner Truth's body on display
so as to examine the ways in which she restrategized the public spectacle of her body through performance politics, transforming her corporeality into a contested terrain of social and cultural consumption. This
potent moment in abolitionist history ultimately offers a critical model
that might finally be applied to reexamining Menken's staged body.

The scene in which Sojourner Truth is forced to disrobe before an
all-white audience in rural Indiana is canonized in American historical
discourse. Yet the cultural familiarity with this moment depends on the
imagery of an anonymous account of Dr. T. W. Strain's interrogation of
Truth. A white man suspicious of Truth's sex, Strain demands that

> Sojourner submit her breast to the inspection of some of the la-
> dies present, that the doubt might be removed by their testimony.
> There were a large number of ladies present, who appeared to
> be ashamed and indignant at such a proposition.
>
> Confusion and uproar ensued, which was soon suppressed
> by Sojourner, who immediately rising, asked them why they sus-
> pected her to be a man. The Democracy answered, "Your voice
> is not the voice of a woman, it is the voice of a man, and we
> believe you are a man." . . . Sojourner told them that her breasts
> had suckled many a white babe, to the exclusion of her own
> offspring and she quietly asked them, as she disrobed her bo-
> som, if they, too, wished to suck! She told them that she would
> show her breast to the whole congregation; that it was not her
> shame that she uncovered her breast before them, but their
> shame. (Sterling 151–53)

In this passage, wherein Truth remains potentially buried in the discourse
of a nameless spectator, her use of the corporeal as a narrative strategy
amounts to a performative twist: her breasts relay a textual meaning articulating the history of a slave past and work in contestation of discursive

circumscription here by her allusion to what she calls "the deeds done in [her] body" (Gage, "Address" 1962). These "deeds" simultaneously mark her violation as a slave woman and potentially (re)cover her flesh as unreadable to a "shamed" congregation forced to acknowledge their spectatorial and social complicity in her abjection. For the Northern audience to read Truth's figure as she deploys it here is to affirm the repressed atrocities of slavery that her body harbors and to face their own implicit role in that scene. Harryette Mullen observes pointedly that Truth's "shameless gesture denies social propriety, its oppressive power to define, limit, or regulate her behavior" (3). Truth's demand to have her audience "see" her body according to her own narrative framing also establishes a way to read for the opacity, or for what Elin Diamond might call the "non-truth," of the scene.[13]

Indeed, with this unveiling of Truth before her white audience there appears to be more than one black female figure meeting the gaze of Dr. Strain here. The moment of initial supposed transparency that enables Truth's male spectators to seemingly view the dominant script of the mammy figure whose breasts are made available for "suckl[ing]" immediately transforms into a point of visual excess and occlusion, a suggestion of the extraneous corporeal (sub)texts that the spectator cannot, in fact, see at all. In this scene where Truth rejects the spectator's gaze by reminding her audience of her own absent offspring whom she is denied the right to nurse, she splinters the security of the viewer's intimacy with her body. The hidden narrative of black "motherhood" rather than "mammyhood" operates as a looming disruption that Truth invokes, a specter of contradistinction to the (un)veiled black body of deception who speaks not like a woman. This voice alone calls attention to Diamond's extended refiguration of feminist mimesis-mimicry as a destabilizing "alienation-effect," a point "in which the production of objects, shadows, and voices is excessive to the truth/illusion structure of mimesis, spilling into mimicry, multiple 'fake off-spring'" (371). A kind of "excessive" representation that overturns the subjectivity of the viewer, Truth's appearance here simultaneously assumes the role of the exploited slave by stripping and rejects that role by offering to her "shamed" spectators a body that is a text of multiple social and historical inscriptions that double and cover over each other. From the darkness of the void that she herself creates, multiple Truths are put into play.

It would seem that a moment encapsulating Menken's disrobing could have little in common with the complex distillation of power at work in the moment of Truth's exposure. Separated from Truth by her class status and by a public construction of whiteness that protected the actress from the hardships of American racism (and that shielded her from slavery altogether), Menken approached corporeal representation from a standpoint of relative privilege. Yet in the context of nineteenth-century gender politics, she negotiated a deployment of her body as a canvas of narrative authority that, similar to Truth's efforts, went against the grain of self-abnegation. Wrapping her body in the mosaic of mythography that she shrewdly perpetuates, Menken stages a critical striptease that brings to fore the strategic elements of her performative acts. A well-circulated anecdote exemplifies this point; it concerns how Menken, upon meeting the French journalist Adrian Marx during her stint in Paris, "revealed" herself in several ways to him during an interview that followed one of her sold-out performances. Biographer Allen Lesser describes the scene:

> Menken nonchalantly stripped to her form-fitting tights and then put on her costume for the next act in full sight of her visitor . . . he was certain that she had stood completely nude before him. "She changed costume," he recalled, "and let me see, without modesty and without embarrassment, the marvelous beauty of her body." . . . In answer to a question about her childhood and youth, about which everyone was curious, she launched into a fantastic narrative compounded of every adventure story she had ever read. Indians had captured her in her youth, she said, bending down so that he could feel "the depth of the scar left on her head" by a tomahawk flung at her when she escaped. She had also fought for the south disguised as a soldier, she added, pulling her skirt up above her thigh to show him "the trace of the balls she had received in war." (170)

The passage is extraordinary in the way that it initially showcases the spectacle of Menken's "completely nude" body standing "nonchalantly" before Marx's helplessly ogling gaze. He marvels over Menken's unchecked boldness and apparent candor at allowing him to sneak a peak, "without modesty and without embarrassment," at her naked frame. Marx, in this presumed moment of intimacy and bonding, presses onward with his interview, querying the actress in regard to her childhood. The disingenuous responses that Menken offers, a largely discounted captivity narrative as well as a cross-dressing war tale, are corroborated through the marks and scars inscribed as text onto her body. Here the initial scene of disrobing transforms into a moment of (re)covering as well. At this very moment in the anecdote we are made to bear witness to the way in which Menken uses her body, not as evidence of some "incontrovertible truth" but as an instrument of ontological deception, part of the performance of Menken's passing before a rapt and naive spectator.[14]

To be sure, the narrative manifests Amy Robinson's definition of passing, which considers "the apparatus of the pass" as a "spectatorial transaction" rather than one that is merely ontological. Robinson lobbies for a method to explore passing as the product of skillful reading on the spectator's part as opposed to the visual markers of the passer. She contends that "to read the apparatus of passing in the stead of an inviolate prepassing identity is to value telling over knowing because the availability of codes of deception does not predict access to the authenticity of the subject of deception" (723). The skill to read as well as the skill to perform the pass is ultimately what disrupts arbitrary definitions of identity, for this notion of "the pass" itself as a process, as an apparatus, "catalogues discontinuity and disjunction." Robinson's theory of passing is predicated upon performance, what she sees as a "triangular theater" composed of the passer, the hegemonic dupe, and the "literate member" of the passer's "in-group" community out of which the subject has transmigrated. The pass, she argues further, can only be successful when it is witnessed by the literate "in-group" member (723–28).

Building on Robinson's work, I wish to contend that, as readers of Menken's as well as Truth's biographical and performative narratives, we might, for a change, assume the role of the "in-group" member who knows the "lie" rather than the "truth" about these women and who, along with her contemporaries, as well as various biographers, participates in a "triangular theatre" that recontextualizes the performing female subject's pass(ages) from one body to the next. This type of analysis seems crucial particularly with respect to re-reading Menken, a racially vexing figure whose ambiguous identity generated legendary historical anecdotes such as one in which she was said to have proclaimed to her lover Dumas père that she too was "a quadroon" (Mankowitz 174). If we assume that Menken operates in her biographical canon as what Jennifer Brody would call a "mulattaroon" figure, an "unreal, impossible ideal whose corrupted and corrupting constitution inevitably causes conflicts in narratives that attempt to promote purity" (16), then the exigencies for this sort of critical methodology are all the more apparent.[15] Interrogating the negotiation and the site of the pass in the context of this mulattaroon actress's many varied performances forces us to read through and across not one, but potentially two hegemonic dupes—that is, those in the narratives of nineteenth-century public, racialized women and the biographers who manufacture their narratives. Hence, I demonstrate how Menken extends the efforts of Truth's reappropriation of the corporeal. I will reveal how, through her highly stylized, "seminude" performances, the actress stages a veiled redeployment of her own controversial materiality. In this sense, then, her work also represents a formidable and resourceful critical paradigm for contemporary black feminist theory and practice. Menken enacts a means to resistance through the performance of her own bodily deeds.

Shape and Substance: Drag/racing the Body of Adah Isaacs Menken

Perhaps she did not belong so much to the theater as to the circus.
>   —John S. Kendall, "The World's Delight"

To be inauthentic is sometimes the best way to be real.
>   —Paul Gilroy, "' . . . To Be Real'"

While competing in their research and racing to assert their pivotal roles as detectives in their studies of Adah Isaacs Menken, numerous biographers are uncharacteristically in agreement on one subject: Menken's weakness as an actress and the way in which the spectacle of her body functioned as a primary vehicle in her quest for professional success. Noel Gerson, Wolf Mankowitz, and Bernard Falk all take pains to retell the legend of Menken's introduction to her career as a world-renowned "shape actress" whose "pink fleshlings" overrode any salvageable acting skills. Each of these authors foregrounds a retelling of the tale in which Shakespearean actor James Murdoch, after performing in a haphazard production of *Macbeth* with the actress, is said to have offered the parting advice that Menken "search out for herself some 'sensational spectacle' in which 'your fine figure and pretty face will show.'"[16] Murdoch's suggestion, offered time and again by subsequent researchers, presents itself as the ultimate "proof" of Menken's status as merely a passive "shape" exhibition as opposed to a stage performer of substance.

This opinion was largely canonized by the influential drama critic William Winter, who declared in his review of Menken's 1866 *Mazeppa* performance that she "has not the faintest idea of what acting is. She moves about the stage with no motive, and therefore, in a kind of accidental manner. . . . in short [she] invites critical attention, not to her emotional capabilities, her intellectual gifts, or her culture as an artist, but solely to her physical proportions" (Lesser 175). Winter maintained that Menken lacked vision, analytical clarity, and command over her craft in the role that made her a celebrity. Fame came to her, he argued, as a result of alluring "physical proportions." On the West Coast as well,

Figure 2. Menken as Mazeppa. *The Harvard Theatre Collection, The Houghton Library.*

the actress was simultaneously a box-office success and the subject of journalistic skepticism. Her most famous dual critic and hard-won fan, Mark Twain, was ever reluctant to review a "shape actress" who apparently "didn't have any histrionic ability or deserve any more consideration than a good circus rider!" Winter and Twain each envisioned the spectacle of a powerless (female) body, divested of reason and voice and existing exclusively and basely in relation to materiality (Lyman 270, 276).

These kinds of critiques would persist throughout the actress's career, resurfacing most often during her repeated revival performances of *Mazeppa*. In this her most famous role, Menken was, more often than not, conceived of by both critics and biographers in reductive terms as a mere body, stripped, as it were, of representational complexity. The production itself seemed only to promote this perception. First adapted for the stage in 1830 by English playwright Henry Milner, the drama retells Byron's tale of royal Tartar heir Mazeppa who, upon falling in love with the Polish Castellan's daughter, Olinska, attempts to invade the Polish encampment in order to rescue his betrothed, only to have his plan fail. Captured, stripped, and tortured by the Poles, Mazeppa is forced to ride a wild black stallion across the rugged Tartar landscape. He is subsequently rescued by and reunited with his long-lost father, the elderly Abder Khan, who successfully plots with Mazeppa to seek vengeance upon the ruling Poles in a climactic battle scene tableau. As Lesser points out, from its origination as a stage production the "high point of the spectacle" in *Mazeppa* was "the scene in which the hero is 'stripped' onstage, lashed to the back of the wild horse and carried along a narrow runway up to the top of the theater" (77). However, until American theater entrepreneur E. T. Smith was said to have approached Menken, no woman had ever played the part, and no performer of either sex had actually ridden during the famous horse sequence, opting instead for a dummy to substitute. Smith in 1861 claims to have initially envisioned the concept of placing Menken's physical "beauty" properly in distress in the old equestrian drama as an extremely lucrative box-office venture.

For this reason, critics and scholars have frequently written off Menken's *Mazeppa* production as an insubstantial spectacle that carried an otherwise skill-less actress to worldwide fame in the 1860s. A transatlantic body of spectacularly real deception, Menken was widely perceived by the press, and particularly the British press, as manifesting the bawdy sensationalism of early-nineteenth-century theater.[17] *Mazeppa*'s connection to the popular and evolving extravaganza genre only contributed to this perception; visually, the production was perhaps closely linked to playwright Dion Boucicault's innovative contributions to the field of "realist" spectacle, with its sprawling scenery and elaborate stunts.[18] Menken's and Smith's *Mazeppa* clearly aspired to Boucicault's paradoxical method of representing "realism" through a distinct reliance on the spectacle of artifice. In *Mazeppa* this effort was enacted through and across the site of Menken's spectacularly "real" and curvaceous female body. Falk speculates that "before him the spectator saw a lovely female form traced in winning line by flesh-coloured tights. . . . It was not unintentional that the path Menken scaled was zigzag, and required fifteen minutes . . . to traverse, long enough to permit the eye a satisfying feast of a seductive form" (53). Mankowitz adds that the production included "a formidable array of theatrical illusions. But the two most sensational illusions of all were the voluptuous figure of Adah Isaacs Menken as Ivan Mazeppa, a sexual transformation requiring an extremely willing suspension of disbelief; and more sensational still, the nakedness of the star" (18–19). Here he characterizes this spectacle as rooted both completely and self-consciously in an artificial insistence on representing the conspicuously "female" figure of Menken in drag as the Tartar warrior and also passing that spectacle of her "nakedness" off as "authentic" despite the fact that the actress wore stockings to maintain the "illusion" of nudity. Spectacle, in any case, resided in the (in)authenticity of Menken's disrobed figure on the stage.

This morally bankrupt entertainment, what London theater critic H. B. Farnie lamented as being one of the "many corruptions from America" (Mankowitz 130–31), was thus repeatedly read as a predictable manifestation of popular codes on both sides of the Atlantic, which dually conflated the actress with the sexual availability of the prostitute and the figure of the black woman.[19] Moral anxiety concerning Menken's performances as *Mazeppa* could, for instance, be traced to the production's clear and frequent engagement with Victorian pornographic coding and imagery. In reviewing Menken's success in the role, theater critics have maintained that the "basis of Menken's popular appeal in *Mazeppa* was undoubtedly sensationalism and not a very subtle kind of pornography" (WPA 57). Her costume's combination of "loose folds of white linen" and "flesh-coloured tights" that traced her "lovely female form" boldly referenced contemporaneous pornographic markers, which, as Tracy Davis describes, "flagrantly violated the dress codes of the street and drawing room" in Victorian culture, "flaunting the ankles, calves, knees, thighs, crotch and upper torso" ("Actresses" 106).

Although the rare review rallied to Menken's defense, such as the *London Era*'s claim that her "upper limbs" were "no more delicately exposed than those of ballet and burlesque ladies" (Mankowitz 135), Davis points out in her work on Victorian theatrical nudity that it was

MENKEN.

Figure 3. Menken as a "stripped" Mazeppa. *The Harvard Theatre Collection, The Houghton Library.*

precisely the sorts of vestiary devices found in ballet and extravaganza productions that incorporated costuming traditions promoting a way of "seeing nudity" ("Spectacle" 323). Davis argues that while "Victorian designers did not divest actresses of their clothes, they invested considerable ingenuity in creating costumes that simulated nudity—or at least signified it, keeping the referential body to the fore" (326). The purpose of pink tights and white, tightly bound, gauzelike wrappings, then, was to simulate nudity through props and devices in order to lead spectators to believe that they were, in fact, witnessing a nude—and importantly, a nude "white"—female body like that displayed in pornographic postcards and publications.[20] Thus, to cultural as well as moral pundits of the period, Menken's *Mazeppa* costume placed her firmly in a tradition of the sexual commodification of the "white" female body in theater and popular Victorian subculture.

Even to the critic with a discerning eye, nothing was presumed to have been left uncovered in this display of sheer whiteness. As Lesser contends, for the "excited masculine imagination," her "'classic Dress' concealed none of the exotic delights to which they had looked forward" (134).[21] Even Menken fan and supporter Mark Twain actively pointed out that Menken had "but one garment on—a thin tight white linen one" and she "dressed like the Greek Slave." But unlike Hiram Powers's morally revered figure of classic sculpture, Twain assures, Menken's postures are "not so modest " (78). Indeed, the very putative sexual availability combined with the racial complexities of this white-looking body perhaps aligns Menken's *Mazeppa* more deeply and more problematically with the sensational imagery of John Bell's 1868 statue *The Octoroon* than with Powers's *Greek Slave*. In a critical analysis of the Bell Royal Academy sculpture that brings forth the visual and thematic similarities to Powers's work, Joseph Roach observes that the "octoroon repines unresistingly in the almost ornamental chains of her bondage," recalling the positioning of *The Greek Slave*. Roach concludes, however, that Bell's work panders to a public fascination with white-looking female bodies that, when stripped and chained, are excessively eroticized rather than morally transcendent (220)—a quality that Joy Kasson associates with Powers's work. Although Twain's association of Menken with *The Greek Slave* offers the potential to represent what Kasson reads as the sculpture's "suppressed possibility of resistance" through a spiritual transcendence of the body, most Menken critics suggest that the actress's career-making production of *Mazeppa* sustained a troubling and reductive insistence on the reification of the actress's body, not unlike the thematics of Bell's *Octoroon*.[22]

The racial ambiguity inherent in Bell's statue and Menken's Creole-

to-Spanish-to-Jewish identity politics (dueling significations that Menken
as well as many scholars have evoked for generations) complicates the
politics of female exposure. Both sculptures shed light on the multiple
and intersecting racial and gender codes that specifically affect white
actresses and public black women in the nineteenth century. These two
groups, as Sander Gilman has observed, are specifically aligned from a
spectatorial standpoint in that both European and European American
"public" women (such as actresses and prostitutes) and women of African descent were, more often than not, visually commodified through
their bodies (256). The point here is not to suggest that the political and
socioeconomic position of white women who supported themselves
through the theater is at all equivalent to that of free black women who,
beginning with Maria Stewart in the 1830s, risked ridicule and sometimes bodily harm in order to publicly speak in support of abolitionism, prohibition, and suffrage, among other causes. Rather, the fact that
both groups were perceived as revealing and inhabiting bodies that were
vulnerable and open to varying degrees of public possession provides a
significant and challenging context when reconsidering Menken's performances of *Mazeppa*. For just as the white actress was expected to display "what is cloaked (anatomically and experientially), supposedly
revealing truths about womanhood . . . promulgating a mystery as deep
and as artificial as the colonial photographer's penetration in the Ori-
ental harem" (Davis, "Actresses" 121), so, too, was the black woman's
body, according to Peterson, "always envisioned as public and exposed"
(20).

Yet like the Bell sculpture with its opaque rendering of an unveiled
body, Menken's *Mazeppa* hero/heroine rides a formidable continuum of
double drag that ultimately complicates notions of racial and gender-
marked corporeal exposure; her work insists on a complex form of
counterintuitive viewership that paradoxically sensationalizes the way
that the female figure is obscured. In other words, just as the Bell statue
and an entire subculture of antebellum slave auctions promoted public
fascination with the eroticized subjugation of "white-looking" black
bodies, so, too, did Menken's *Mazeppa* entice and seduce audiences
through a demand to gaze upon the spectacle of a body that is not
what it appears to be—a body dressed as a man that one is expected to
know is inherently female and a body that conveys "whiteness" but simultaneously professes the constructedness of race itself. Despite this
layered imagery, the majority of Menken critics and scholars have overlooked the complexities of what she (un)veiled on stage. Her "problem,"
according to numerous biographers and critics, was that the gaze of the
male spectator and a production of heavily encoded nude imagery

encouraged "the onlooker to trace the lines of the posed figure," an act that Falk argues was "bad for masculine morals and treachery to the feminine species" (14). The real "treachery," according to feminist theater historian Faye Dudden is that in spite of Menken's recognition of her body as a financial "asset" in an ever-expanding transatlantic theater market, she faced what Dudden sees as an "attenuation of the self" as a result of the production's insistence on her status as mere physical commodity.[23]

Dudden contends that Menken's theatrical experience and what she reads as popular exploitation are indicative of much larger gender problems in nineteenth-century American culture. To Dudden, Menken's theatrical career represents "the problem of the body" for nineteenth-century American actresses. She explains that "the actress has been equated with the whore so persistently that no amount of clean living and rectitude among actual performers has ever served to cancel the equation. Acting is linked to sexuality because it is an embodied art—in contrast to the relatively disembodied business of writing. . . . To act you must be present in the body, available to be seen." Like Davis, Dudden ultimately reads the "crisis" of the actress and of all nineteenth-century public (white) women as being a "problem" that forces one to be "present in the body" and "taken as a sexual object against one's will." Clearly, however, Dudden's critical observations are couched in an oversimplified dichotomization that conceptualizes "acting" as an "*embodied* art," fundamentally at odds with other aesthetic spheres (2–3).[24] From a black feminist standpoint as well, women on the margins of culture by virtue of their race and class have always been seen/scene. From this perspective, the significance of performance resides in its ability to exacerbate that moment, to disrupt and obfuscate spectatorial desire precisely through a creative use of "embodied art."

In contrast to this position, Dudden's analysis problematically privileges the authority of the male spectator over the agency of the female performer. What is sorely missing from her study is a more critical consideration of what it meant for an actress to willfully engage in a theatrical relationship with audiences that foregrounds the body. Instead, she asserts that from the 1830s forward the "way that theatre evolved exacerbated the body problem by making male visual pleasure and the sexualized image a routine element of commerce and hence of public life" (4). Although she points to very real systems of social and political power in the nineteenth century that were predicated upon gender as well as racial stratification, Dudden's argument acquiesces to an uncomplicated reification of the female body in this equation. In other words, Dudden juxtaposes the hegemonic power of the male gaze with an unproblematized notion of women's bodies as authentically constructed. Indeed, she contends that this "body problem" is, no doubt, analogous to a "hall of mirrors" that "rob[s] women of any authentic sense of self" (4). In the process, what Dudden fails to consider is how Menken's visual representation is founded upon the ambiguity of the body as a site of knowledge not only in her biographical discourse but in her very performances as Mazeppa. She overlooks the larger possibility of the female performer's role in acting *through* the body as a site of resistance to the male gaze. Dudden might have considered the inauthenticity of the female body as represented in theater as a theoretical approach that opens up a space for reinterrogating the nineteenth-century actress's agency. This critical perspective offers a method to explore Menken's potential engagement in narrating her body imaginatively, resiliently, and opaquely in her *Mazeppa* performances.

As the Tartar heir, Menken assumed a drag, or "breeches," role that required her to strip to a costume that simulated her (female) nudity. This role was built on an endless series of falsities: Menken, an actress of African descent passing for "white,"—in drag as the Tartar hero who disguises himself in order to rescue Olinska but who is forced to reveal a decidedly, perhaps even exaggerated, "naked" female form in the end. Misha Berson observes that Menken's version of *Mazeppa* "tested the waters for a new kind of stage androgyny: a woman revealing her female sexuality through a male role" (57). Indeed, Berson's observation reinforces the notion in nineteenth-century transatlantic theater culture that gender cross-dressing for actresses only served to "highligh[t] rather than disguis[e] sexual difference" (Davis "Actresses" 106). Davis, in fact, warns that in the "Victorian theater, adult female performers were never sexless. . . . Femininity was intractable and the point was to reveal it" (107). Feminist critics have steadfastly contended that, for nineteenth-century women performers, the acting profession is never fundamentally concerned with masquerade but rather with upholding a paradoxical striptease wherein the female body is made bare through the spectacle of covering it. In retrospect, Menken biographer John S. Kendall could claim with confidence that Menken "had the kind of figure which never looked so alluringly feminine as when clad in male attire" (855).

But what of the transracial body who drags herself across the stage, as it were, through multiple layers of masquerade? Could a racially transgressive actress wearing pink tights suggest the metaphoric nature of race as a construct? Could this "flesh" that is made "nude" through costume/covering make use of the fakery of "whiteness" as yet another shield of obstruction at the very moment in which the female body undoes its gendered drag? Does the very notion of the mulattaroon's appropriation of Victorian pornography's fetishization of "white" female corporeality perhaps "unmask the performative nature of whiteness" and "expos[e] the construction" of racial purities (Brody 9)? Despite the complex questions that her acts clearly elicit, Menken's work is most often perceived as a reactionary product of nineteenth-century theater culture. Davis, for instance, argues that the artifice of drag only enticed the male spectator to uncover the sexual disguise onstage, that "sexuality had its own narrative logic that distinguished . . . Mazeppa from Godiva, and Menken from Maddocks" (*Actresses* 114). Marjorie Garber critiques this perspective by examining the ways that the subversiveness of cross-dressing and the ambiguity of identity politics that accompany it have often been avoided by critics who choose "to look *through* rather than *at* the cross-dresser, to turn away from a close encounter with the transvestite, and to want instead to subsume that figure within one of the two traditional genders" (9). Garber suggests that the spectator who witnesses the cross-dresser or the drag performance attempts to control the potential transgressive power of such an act by imposing an organizational gaze onto the figure, disregarding the notion of liminality altogether.[25]

Yet the content of Menken's performances potentially complicates and resists this sort of tyrannical categorization. Menken's theatricality can also be read as a series of cultural exchanges that drew attention to artifice as constitutive of the actress's public persona and her body politic. In *Mazeppa*, Menken calls attention to her materiality through resourceful performative acts that subvert the Victorian sexual reification of her body.[26] The intersections of gender and racial drag function as key elements that contribute to these disruptive performance strategies. Like the deployment of "pink gauze" as a representation of "whiteness," the actress's legendary Tartar warrior costume disrupts the feminist critique of women in (male) drag that was believed to have ultimately underscored and exposed the actress's (female) sexuality. The apparent transparency and disposability of the male costuming instead levels a critique at the patriarchal fantasies the costume figuratively and literally embodies. As Garber points out, the tradition of male cross-dressing performance has "turned on the artifactuality of women's bodies" rather than questioning the presumed authenticity of the male body as the norm. Garber adds that "to deny female fetishism is to establish a female desire for the phallus on the male body as *natural*" (125). From this standpoint, both racial and gender cross-dressing, here manifested in the racially transgressive female's invocation of both the phallus and the coverage of whiteness, present a crucial critique of identity construction in nineteenth-century culture; the artifice of both "manhood" and "white" femininity are put into play and stripped of their arbitrary power. Menken's palimpsested and contradictory racial as well as gender identities thus reflect Judith Butler's influential claim regarding the inauthenticity of the body itself. Butler argues for a clearer understanding of the way in which "the body is a historical situation . . . and is a manner of doing, dramatizing, and reproducing a historical situation" ("Performative" 272). Put another way, Butler suggests that the body is also a theatrical situation, "stylized" and transformed through gendered appearances.[27]

My point here is not to disregard the very real body of Adah Isaacs Menken, a resilient figure who traveled the transatlantic divide and labored adventurously on the stage during the socially and juridically volatile period of the mid–nineteenth century. Rather, I wish to suggest that Menken's symbolic manipulation of the corporeal in her performances was, in itself, a means to theatricalize her body in socially and culturally disruptive ways that have not always been apparent to audiences and critics alike. She embraced a concept of vaudevillian chaos that ran the gamut of genre and production style, testing and challenging her audiences along the way, and wresting the power of the theatrical exchange from the spectator only to plant it firmly, richly, and darkly in that place between the audience and the performer. In this opaque performative space, the groundbreaking "naked lady" of theater reinvented the terms of racial and gender "exposure."

NOTES

A number of people have been so generous as to read earlier drafts of this work. In particular, I wish to thank Valerie Smith, P. Gabrielle Foreman, Sonnet Retman, and Barbara Christian for their helpful suggestions. Thanks also to Rutgers University Press's anonymous reader for providing insightful comments.

1. Menken was originally buried in Paris's Pere la Chaise Cemetery on 10 August 1868. In April 1869 Menken's friend and confidant Edwin James spearheaded the exhumation and transference of her remains to the Cemetery Montparnasse. Mankowitz 237–44; James 14–16.
2. For a study of the connections between Menken biographies, identity politics, and the literary genre of sensation, see my "Lady Menken's Secret." Recent contemporary studies of the actress tend to trace Menken's genealogical history back to New Orleans, where she is believed to have been born as Philomene Croi Theodore in 1839 to a "free man of color" and his French Creole wife. The public moniker that she kept for a major portion of her life came as a result of her marriage to her first (authenticated) husband, the musician and businessman-turned-theater manager Alexander Isaac Menken. The most recent biography of Menken, written by Wolf Mankowitz, focuses in detail on the actress's family history. See also Lesser, Falk, and Gerson.
3. Female entertainers who worked as "shape actresses" often performed in

extravaganza productions called "leg shows," which specialized in the "show of leg" and other suggestive body parts in order to accentuate the sexualized female form. See Dudden.

4. I borrow the formulation of "imaginary bodies" from Gatens.

5. For more on the problematics of Menken biographical discourse, see my "Lady Menken's Secret." See also Mankowitz's controversial depiction of his relationship with biographer Noel Gerson (Mankowitz 185–89). Mankowitz's savvy work manifests a sophisticated awareness of the complexities of Menken's identity politics; yet he ultimately foregrounds his own subjectivity as a biographer at the expense of the actress's position in the text.

6. For more on Truth's oratory, see Peterson 47–53.

7. Painter argues that the *Narrative*'s longevity as a mainstay and as an exclusive source of Truth is due primarily to a "virtual lack of autobiographical documents" and Truth's own life-long illiteracy ("Sojourner Truth" 13). For a more detailed study of Truth's life and iconography, see Painter *Sojourner Truth*. Menken's "Notes of My Life" first appeared posthumously in the 6 September 1868 edition of the *New York Times*. Lesser is the only biographer who includes the piece in its entirety in an appendix to his biography (253–64).

8. Harriet Beecher Stowe, for instance, weaves a string of inaccuracies in her article on Truth, claiming in an egregious error that Truth was deceased at the time of her writing. For an analysis of Stowe's article, see Yellin 81–87 and Painter, *"Sojourner Truth"* 8–12. See also Washington's note on editions of Sojourner Truth's *Narrative* (125–27). For an example of the machinations of Menken mythography, see Gerson's largely erroneous work, *Queen of the Plaza*.

9. In their introduction to *The Slave's Narrative*, Davis and Gates argue that "the slave narrative represents the attempts of blacks to *write themselves into being*" (xxiii). This historically male-dominated strategy of canon formation sets the stage, so to speak, for the yoking of black ontological politics with the erasure of the (female) corporeal. Homans examines this gendered bifurcation in African American literary and cultural criticism wherein "the body that is troped as female" in the poststructuralist theories of many black male scholars is one "whose absence . . . theory requires" ("Racial" 81).

10. See also duCille's important work "The Occult of True Black Womanhood," which takes to task the problem of black women's persistent role in contemporary academic discourse as "infinitely deconstructable 'othered' matter" (70).

11. In her study of the performance of blackness in antebellum culture, Hartman declares that her "task is neither to unearth the definitive meaning of song or dance nor to read song as an expression of black character as was common among nineteenth-century ethnographers but to give full weight to the opacity of these texts wrought by toil, terror, and sorrow and composed under the whip and in fleeting moments of reprieve" (36). My use of the term "opacity" here differs somewhat from the Irigarian theory that "women represent the sex that cannot be thought, a linguistic absence and opacity" (Butler *Gender* 9). Rather than arguing for representational absence, I am instead suggesting that "opacity" in this context characterizes a kind of performance rooted in a layering and palimpsesting of meanings and representations. From this standpoint, "opacity" is never a mark of absence but is always a present reminder of black feminist agency and the body in performance.

12. At present, outside of the Kendall essay, there are very few critical works that have examined Menken at length in the context of blackness and the

politics of racial ambiguity. See, for instance, Monfried. Her adopted "Jewishness" has, however, been a subject of provocative discussion, particularly in works such as Falk's *The Naked Lady* and in Mankowitz. In his 1957 historical study of San Francisco, Dickson makes passing reference to the likelihood of Menken's father being a "'free' Negro of Louisiana" (70). See also Cofran's short article on Menken's genealogy, which briefly notes that the actress's father was a "free man of color" (52). More recently, Menken has been recuperated into a nineteenth-century black women's canon of poetry. For instance, her posthumous collection of poems entitled *Infelicia* (1868) is included in the *Schomburg Library of Nineteenth-Century Women Writers* series supplement.

13. Here I build on Judith Butler's nearly canonical revelation that "gender proves to be performative" and "always a doing" constituted by "deeds" (Butler *Gender* 25). Yet I wish to draw a distinction between my reading of Truth's role as a performative subject in this scene and Butler's groundbreaking theories of performativity, which call into question the existence of "a doer behind the deed" in gender construction. As Patrick Johnson queries in his cogent work on blackness, sexuality, and performance theory, "the body might be a blunt field of 'matter' inscribed and reinscribed, a site of infinitesimal signifiers, but does not the body signify in specific historical and cultural ways?" Johnson calls for the specific theory and practice of black queer critical methodologies and contends that "the body, too, has to be theorized" to "not only describe the ways in which it is brought into being" but so as to also articulate "what it *does* once it is constituted and the relationship between it and the other bodies around it." Hence, my reading of Truth in this scene is driven by a concern to identify how she employs performance as a means to resituating her body in multiple social and historical situations. Rather than jettisoning Truth as the "doer" of her "deeds," I employ performance as a lens through which to locate the moments when Truth makes her body "matter," as it were, in crucial social and political ways. Diamond, in her work on feminist performance theory, interrogates the viability as well as the efficacy of performance as an intervention in forms of patriarchal mimesis that merely reproduce the abject female form. Invoking Luce Irigaray's critical transmutation of the Platonic cave of illusions into a female womb/ theater structure as a point of departure, Diamond suggests that feminist appropriations of mimesis in performance posit "an irreducible conundrum: the nontruth of truth-reality constructed as a shadow-and-mirror play" (371). For Diamond, this "resistant" mimesis transforms the female body into a site of trickery that draws the male spectator into the reflection of the woman. Modleski has explored the politics of mimetic art as well in the work of African American performer Anna Deavere Smith. Yet I find Modleski's study problematic in the way that it often elides and sometimes romanticizes the role of the black female body on the stage.

14. For the most recent and complete version of Menken's captivity narrative, see Mankowitz 41–44. The tale is assumed to be largely fictional since Menken was said to have claimed to have been raised partly in Texas when the incident occurred, and no documents corroborate such a claim. Terry and Urla contend that "the body has been understood to be given by nature, and thus to be real and objective, capable of overriding even the most abstruse attempts of an individual to disguise his or her true self" (6). Menken's actions here reveal how the body can, in fact, become part of an inauthentic "disguise."

15. Brody demonstrates persuasively how an "American invention and New World product, the mulattaroon was a blood vessel who could be described

as being neither black nor white, yet also both white and black. Throughout most of the nineteenth century, the struggle to definitively define her
unstable constitution . . . was a real concern. Although answers to the problem of her identity and her identifications varied, the mulattaroons usually
served as an interstitial ideal whose complicated constitution both marked
and masked the nineteenth century mesalliance known as miscegenation" (16).

16. Indeed, Mankowitz's opening chapter begins with this anecdote. Murdoch
was said to have had to prompt the actress on her lines throughout the performance (Mankowitz 6; Gerson 115; Falk 49). Lesser, arguably the biographer most attentive to the details of Menken's career as an actress, at one
point reductively asserts that her "contribution" to American theater was
that "she offered the female figure unadorned" (75).

17. In anticipation of her 1864 London debut at Astley's theater, the *London Review* argued that she was "'a notorious woman from America, with no more
real talent for the stage than an ordinary fish-hag might possess,' who had
'found a manager willing to let her stride about with pink legs, bare arms,
and something which looks like three-fourths of a shift'" (Falk 93). Others
have lavished praise on Menken's creative involvement in the production.
Rourke maintains, for instance, that "she indubitably transformed a tawdry
equestrian play into something which meant a reversion to poetry" (44).

18. Gerson, in fact, argues that the famed playwright and producer's influence
was far-reaching in East Coast theater culture by the time Menken debuted
in Albany, New York, as the heroic Tartar. He states that "the hand of
Boucicault was plainly evident. Any play that hoped to succeed in New York
had to include two elements that had made Boucicault popular. Unabashed
melodrama predominated, and somewhere during the performance a touch
of realism on a grand scale was required. Audiences demanded a diet that
would jolt the emotions and leave them round-eyed with wonder" (36). For
more on Boucicault's innovations in Victorian theatre, see Booth.

19. For more on the equation of the theatre with sexual depravity, see Johnson
3–36. Ryan argues that between 1825 and 1850 in New York, "women engaged in sexual commerce found themselves in exotic and motley company"
including actresses, jugglers, and even puppet show performers (1–8). See
also Gilman.

20. The sheer, stark whiteness invoked in this kind of coding points to the odd
contradiction of nineteenth-century popular culture wherein nudity was most
often conceived of and idealized as white; yet clearly it was black female
flesh that was most vulnerable to sudden and aggressive exploitation and
violation.

21. Menken wrote a widely published rebuttal to theatre critic Farnie in which
she defended her performances of *Mazeppa* on the moral grounds that it
invoked classical Greek sculpture (Mankowitz 131).

22. Twain's allusion here to the 1840s' statue *The Greek Slave* is a provocative
one given the ostensible similarities between Powers's work, which foregrounds the spectacle of the naked female body in chains, and Menken's
role in *Mazeppa*. In the original stage adaptation of *Mazeppa*, the Castellan
of Laurinski orders his servants to "tear the garb" off of the captive Mazeppa,
to "lash the traitor" and bind him in cords. See *Mazeppa* 4. Like the *Mazeppa*
production, Powers's statue of a European woman taken into slavery by the
Turks is meant to reference a tale of abduction and bondage through the spectacle and display of female nudity and submission. Kasson argues, however,
that Powers's heroine successfully "redirected the viewer's gaze from the female subject's body to her face, stressing her emotions: anxiety, fortitude,

and resignation" (178). For an insightful reading of the racial politics of *The Greek Slave*, see Brody 67–71.

23. In a broad and oversimplified argument regarding Menken's career, Dudden maintains that the actress's theatrical work hit a precipitous decline as her body aged. Dudden argues in an almost punitive tone that, by the time of her death, "Menken had proved that displaying her body might be lucrative for a woman, but she also demonstrated that, given the realities of aging, the resulting career might be pathetically brief" (164). Although Menken is often said to have been less than thrilled with one of her final roles in Paris as a mute heroine in *Les Pirates de Savanne*, most biographical accounts report that she was nonetheless a box-office success through her final performances in the summer of 1868. See Mankowitz 231–38.

24. Dudden's characterization of writing as a "disembodied" art form overlooks a vast array of critical feminist works, particularly by French scholars, that interrogate the site of writing as inextricably linked to the (female) body. See, for instance, Moi. Dudden ultimately fails to consider the ways in which acting might itself serve as an art form offering a means to the "embodied subjectivity" that Grosz envisions in her important work on corporeal representation and feminist politics.

25. Indeed, as Butler points out in her work on the politics of passing, the surveillance of liminal bodies functions as both an act of fetishizing the other and reinforcing the hegemonic position of the spectator, for "the spectre of racial ambiguity . . . must be conquered" in the end (*Bodies* 172).

26. This method of foregrounding the body as a site of resistance is not unlike that employed by black women abolitionists such as Truth, who, Peterson argues, strategically "call[s] attention to the materiality of the black female body in both its productive and reproductive functions in order to subvert the dominant culture's construction of it" (22). Peterson contends that African American women lecturers had to function as "actresses" who constantly negotiated their self-representation in a bid to resist dominant racial and gender stereotypes.

27. See also Butler's *Gender Trouble*. In both a provocative and a problematic twist, Menken would later in her career become one of only a handful of women performing minstrelsy. Clearly, in one sense, her decision to don burned cork suggests an ultimate rejection and ridicule of blackness. Yet perhaps one might read her minstrel characters—like her cross-dressing as Mazeppa—as transgressing white patriarchal circumscription from within its very borders rather than simplistically succumbing to it. One could perhaps contend that she, in fact, positioned what Eric Lott might call her mythologized "wench" persona in a "breeches" role, smoking cigars and cracking profane jokes while also invoking the show of her female physique as a way of potentially undoing the total subjugation of racially and gender abject bodies in minstrelsy.

WORKS CITED

Barclay, G. Lippard. *The Life and Career of Adah Isaacs Menken, the Celebrated Actress*. Philadelphia, 1868.

Berson, Misha. "The San Francisco Stage: From Gold Rush to Goldenspike, 1849–1869." *San Francisco Performing Arts Library and Museum Journal* 2 (1989): 75–79.

Booth, Michael R. *Victorian Spectacular Theatre: 1850–1910*. Boston: Routledge, 1981.

Brody, Jennifer DeVere. *Impossible Purities: Blackness, Femininity, and Victorian Culture*. Durham: Duke UP, 1998.

Brooks, Daphne A. "Lady Menken's Secret: Adah Isaacs Menken and the Race for Sensation." *Legacy: A Journal of American Women Writers* 15:1 (1998): 68–77.

Butler, Judith. *Bodies That Matter: On the Discursive Limits of "Sex."* New York: Routledge, 1993.

———. *Gender Trouble: Feminism and the Subversion of Identity.* New York: Routledge, 1990.

———. "Performative Acts and Gender Constitution: An Essay in Phenomenology and Feminist Theory." *Performing Feminisms: Feminist Critical Theory and Theatre.* Ed. Sue-Ellen Case. Baltimore: Johns Hopkins UP, 1990. 270–82.

Cofran, John. "The Identity of Adah Isaacs Menken: A Theatrical Mystery Solved." *Theatre Survey* 31 (May 1990): 47–54.

Davis, Charles T., and Henry Louis Gates Jr. "Introduction: The Language of Slavery." *The Slave's Narrative.* Ed. Davis and Gates. New York: Oxford UP, 1985.

Davis, Tracy. *Actresses as Working Women: Their Social Identity in Victorian Culture.* New York: Routledge, 1991.

———. "The Actress in Victorian Pornography." *Victorian Scandals: Representations of Gender and Class.* Athens: Ohio UP, 1992. 99–133.

———. "The Spectacle of Absent Costume: Nudity on the Victorian Stage." *New Theatre Quarterly* 5 (1989): 321–33.

Diamond, Elin. "Mimesis, Mimicry, and the 'True-Real.'" *Acting Out: Feminist Performances.* Ed. Lynda Hart and Peggy Phelan. Ann Arbor: U of Michigan P, 1993. 363–82.

Dickson, Samuel. *Tales of San Francisco.* Stanford: Stanford UP, 1957.

DuCille, Ann. "The Occult of True Blackwomanhood: Critical Demeanor and Black Feminist Studies." *The Second Signs Reader: Feminist Scholarship, 1983–1996.* Ed. Ruth-Ellen B. Joeres and Barbara Laslett. Chicago: U of Chicago P, 1996.

Dudden, Faye E. *Women in the American Theatre: Actresses and Audiences, 1790–1870.* New Haven: Yale UP, 1994.

Falk, Bernard. *The Naked Lady.* London: Hutchinson, 1934.

Forte, Jeanie. "Focus on the Body: Pain, Praxis, and Pleasure in Feminist Performance." *Critical Theory and Performance.* Ed. Janelle G. Reinelt and Joseph R. Roach. Ann Arbor: U of Michigan P, 1992. 248–62.

Gage, Frances. "Address to the First Annual Meeting of the American Equal Rights Association." Lauter et al.1962–63.

———. "Reminiscences by Frances D. Gage of Sojourner Truth, for May 28–29, 1851." Lauter et al. 1959–61.

Garber, Marjorie. *Vested Interests: Cross Dressing and Cultural Anxiety.* New York: Harperperennial, 1992.

Gatens, Moira. *Imaginary Bodies: Ethics, Power and Corporeality.* New York: Routledge, 1996.

Gerson, Noel. *Queen of the Plaza: A Biography of Adah Isaacs Menken.* By Paul Lewis (pseud). New York: Funk, 1964.

Gilman, Sander. L. "Black Bodies, White Bodies: Toward an Iconography of Female Sexuality in Late Nineteenth-Century Art, Medicine, and Literature." *"Race," Writing, and Difference.* Ed. Henry Louis Gates Jr. Chicago: University of Chicago Press, 1985. 223–61.

Gilroy, Paul. "'. . . To Be Real': The Dissident Forms of Black Expressive Culture." *Let's Get It On: The Politics of Black Performance.* Ed. Catherine Ugwu. Seattle: Bay, 1995. 12–33.

Grosz, Elizabeth. *Volatile Bodies: Toward a Corporeal Feminism.* Bloomington: Indiana UP, 1994.

Hartman, Saidiya. *Scenes of Subjection: Terror, Slavery, and Self-Making in Nineteenth-Century America.* New York: Oxford UP, 1997.

Homans, Margaret. "'Racial Composition': Metaphor and the Body in the Writing of Race." *Female Subjects in Black and White: Race, Psychoanalysis, Feminism.* Ed. Elizabeth Abel, Barbara Christian, and Helene Moglen. Berkeley: U of California P, 1997. 77–101.

———. "'Women of Color' Writers and Feminist Theory." *New Literary History* 25 (1994): 73–94.

James, Edwin. *Biography of Adah Isaacs Menken, with Selections from Infelicia.* New York: [1881?].

Johnson, Claudia. *American Actress: Perspectives on the Nineteenth Century.* Chicago: Nelson-Hall, 1984.

Johnson, E. Patrick. "'Quarrying' Queerness, Queering Blackness: Reading Marlon Riggs' *Black Is, Black Ain't.*" University of California, San Diego. La Jolla, 24 Feb. 2000.

Kasson, Joy. "Narratives of the Female Body: The Greek Slave." *The Culture of Sentiment.* Ed. Shirley Samuels. New York: Oxford UP, 1992. 172–90.

Kendall, John S. "'The World's Delight': The Story of Adah Isaacs Menken." *Louisiana Historical Quarterly* (1938): 846–68.

Lauter, Paul, et al., eds. *The Heath Anthology of American Literature.* 2nd. ed. Vol. 1. Lexington: Heath, 1994.

Lesser, Allen. *Enchanting Rebel [The Secret of Adah Isaacs Menken].* New York: Beechhurst, 1947.

Lott, Eric. *Love and Theft: Blackface, Minstrelsy, and the American Working Class.* New York: Oxford UP, 1993.

Lyman, George D. *The Saga of the Comstock Lode: Boom Days in Virginia City.* New York: Scribner's, 1934.

McDowell, Deborah. "Recycling: Race, Gender, and the Practice of Theory." *Studies in Historical Change.* Ed. Ralph Cohen. Charlottesville: U of Virginia P, 1992. 246–63.

Mankowitz, Wolf. *Mazeppa: The Lives, Loves and Legends of Adah Isaacs Menken: A Biographical Quest.* New York, Stein, 1982.

Mazeppa; or, the Wild Horse of Tartary. A Romantic Drama in Two Acts. New York: [183?]. Special Collections Library, University of California, Los Angeles.

Menken, Adah Isaacs. *Infelicia. Collected Black Women's Poetry.* Ed. Joan R. Sherman. Vol. 1. New York: Oxford UP, 1988. 1–124.

———. "Notes of My Life." *New York Times* 6 Sept. 1868.

Modleski, Tania. "Doing Justice to the Subjects: Mimetic Art in a Multicultural Society: The Work of Anna Deavere Smith." *Female Subjects in Black and White.* Ed. Elizabeth Abel, Barbara Christian, and Helene Moglen. Berkeley: U of California P, 1997. 57–76.

Moi, Toril. *Sexual/Textual Politics: Feminist Literary Theory.* New York: Routledge, 1985.

Monfried, Walter. "The Negro Beauty Who Bewitched Two Continents." *Negro Digest* 14 (1965): 86–90.

Mullen, Harryette. "'Indelicate Subjects': African-American Women's Subjugated Subjectivity." *Sub/versions: Feminist Studies.* Santa Cruz: University of California, 1991. 1–7.

Painter, Nell. "Sojourner Truth in Life and Memory: Writing the Biography of an American Exotic." *Gender and History* 2.1 (1990): 3–16.

———. *Sojourner Truth: A Life, a Symbol.* New York: Norton, 1996.

Peterson, Carla. *"Doers of the Word": African-American Women Speakers and Writers in the North, (1830–1880).* New York: Oxford UP, 1995.

Roach, Joseph. *Cities of the Dead: Circum-Atlantic Performance*. New York: Columbia UP, 1996.

Robinson, Amy. "It Takes One to Know One: Passing and Communities of Common Interest." *Critical Inquiry* 20 (Summer 1994): 715–36.

Rourke, Constance. *Troupers of the Gold Coast; or the Rise of Lotta Crabtree*. New York: Harcourt, 1928.

Ryan, Mary. *Women in Public: Between Banners and Ballots, 1825–1880*. Baltimore: Johns Hopkins UP, 1990.

Smith, Valerie. "Black Feminist Theory and the Representation of the 'Other.'" *Changing Our Own Words: Essays on Criticism, Theory, and Writing by Black Women*. Ed. Cheryl A. Wall. New Brunswick: Rutgers UP, 1990. 38–57.

Sterling, Dorothy, ed. *We Are Your Sisters: Black Women in the Nineteenth Century*. New York: Norton, 1984.

Terry, Jennifer, and Jacqueline Urla. "Introduction: Mapping Embodied Deviance." *Deviant Bodies: Critical Perspectives on Difference in Science and Popular Culture*. Ed. Terry and Urla. Bloomington: Indiana UP, 1995. 1–18.

Twain, Mark. "The Menken—Written Especially for Gentlemen." *Mark Twain of the Enterprise: Newspaper Articles and Other Documents, 1862–64*. Ed. Henry Nash Smith with the assistance of Frederick Anderson. Berkeley: University of California, 1957. 78–80.

WPA. *San Francisco Theatre Research, Vol. 4, First Series, Abstract from WPA Project 8386 O.P. 465–03–286*. San Francisco: 1939. San Francisco Performing Arts Library, San Francisco.

Washington, Margaret, ed. *Narrative of Sojourner Truth by Olive Gilbert*. New York: Vintage, 1993.

Williams, Patricia. *The Alchemy of Race and Rights: Diary of a Law Professor*. Cambridge: Harvard UP, 1991.

Winter, William. *New York Tribune*: 1 May 1866.

Yellin, Jean Fagan. *Women and Sisters: The Antislavery Feminists in American Culture*. New Haven: Yale UP, 1989.

DORRI RABUNG BEAM

The Flower of Black Female Sexuality in Pauline Hopkins's *Winona*

It is well known by now that a primary goal of black women writers of the nineteenth and early twentieth centuries was to assert their personhood in the face of racist constructions of black women as animalistic and lascivious. Many argue that the cost of such a project entailed, as Lauren Berlant puts it, "the evacuation of erotic or sexual or even sensational life itself as a possible ground of personal dignity for African American women" (564). To complicate this notion, I turn to Pauline Hopkins's magazine novel *Winona: A Tale of Negro Life in the South and Southwest*, written in serial installments for *The Colored American Magazine* in 1902. Hopkins's generic choices—interweaving romance and western—lend themselves more readily to an exploration of the "sensational life" than to racial uplift, with its connotation of transcending the sexual and bodily.

The project of racial uplift was a many-faceted tactic employed by elite black intellectuals and leaders of the late nineteenth and early twentieth centuries to simultaneously combat racism and claim full, integrated citizenship in the United States, a momentous task given that the opportunities of Reconstruction had rapidly receded in inverse proportion to the rise of virulent white supremacism. Confronting a concept of race steeped in oppressive stereotypes, scientific racism, and white cultural supremacy, black proponents of uplift proposed accessing full citizenship by subscribing to dominant bourgeois class and gender codes, optimistic that racial difference could be subsumed in a society based on class stratification. For these African Americans, "the appropriation of gentility meant approximating racial equality" (Tate 59), so the uplift program trafficked in counterstereotypes of refined, educated African Americans in traditional gender roles.

Domestic novels and genteel poetry were the primary forms that uplift discourse took in black women's writing. These genres provided the ideal venue for the positive representation of the black family's bourgeois values and the feminine virtue of the black heroine, particularly her sexual purity and even passionlessness. Thus, though marriage is often the manifest goal in these African American domestic novels, courtship is eclipsed or displaced, as in Emma Dunham Kelly-Hawkins's *Megda* or Amelia E. Johnson's *Clarence and Corrine*, or converted into a politicized coupling of companionate race workers devoted as much to their duty as to each other. The honeymoon of Frances Harper's Iola Leroy is, as Claudia Tate puts it, "an occasion for public service" (170) not private pleasure. At the same time, as Tate points out, the "codes that sanction the heroine's unquestioned social station . . . restrict topics for fictional treatment, restrict the manner of their presentation, and define the work's audience. . . . These codes demanded, in particular, that they delete . . . not only allusions to sexual passions but anger as well" (63).

Hopkins herself felt the pressure of these codes, but the absence of a domestic trajectory in her story signals a willingness to explore other venues for representing black female experience. My aim is not to undercut the politics of the domestic novel but to release *Winona* from those generic expectations. Simply put, *Winona* is interested in exploring autonomous female sexual desire; it does not, as a domestic novel would, concern itself with a story of female development and preparation for a gender-schematized position within the racial family terminating in a testimony to racial achievement or national citizenship. It shows little proclivity for domestic realism in its vast range of adventure; there is hardly a house in sight. *Winona* imagines not a social role for its heroine but a private self. Instead of sublimating it to political, economic, or social advancement, Hopkins seems interested in representing eroticism for its own sake—itself a political move for an early-twentieth-century black woman writer. Still, Hopkins was affected by the same strictures as her contemporaries. It is precisely because gender, race, and genre were tightly bounded categories that allowed little room to explore passion, anger, romance, and sex in a black woman's text that the representational strategies Hopkins employs are remarkable, embodying the pleasures and passions that her black heroine's body is not supposed to own.

A primary strategy in Hopkins's novel is to alternately trouble, shift, and incapacitate the signifying power of bodies despite the apparent immutability of skin and sex markers. Hopkins's political goal was to expose the artificiality of binary categorizations of race and gender, while simultaneously carving out an interior space for the black subject. As she put the matter in her preface to *Contending Forces*, her objective was to "*faithfully portray the inmost thoughts and feelings of the Negro with all the fire and romance which lie dormant in our history*" (14). As if to ensure that Winona's "inmost thoughts and feelings" remain under her control, rather than fueling racist myths, Hopkins envelops her story within other covering stories. Pleasure is often secreted in the nooks and crannies of the text; to read into these folds is to discover not evacuated ground void of sensation or sexuality but a space manifold with possibility.

To illustrate the supple layering of Hopkins's text, I use Gilles Deleuze's notion of "the fold," which conceptualizes space using a metaphorics of matter as layers of earth, folds of fabric, and creases of bodies. The texture, style, or expression of any matter is defined not by its heterogeneous parts, but by the way the matter is folded. The fold provides a way to think of Hopkins's text as pliable, as unfolding to reveal new enfoldings (literally, im*plic*ations, "-plic" being derived from the Latin root for fold or pleat) and refolding (complicating), just as Hopkins both explicates and complicates anew the raced and gendered script she has been assigned. This conceptualization also allows us to see how Hopkins goes about the hard work of constructing an embodied identity that shows black women to be both victims of rape by white men and agents of an autonomous and pleasurable sexuality, a sexuality embodied not least in the folds of the body of her text. Hopkins goes about this task not with schizophrenic attention to alternating modes of protest and pleasure but with conjoined attention to systemic victimization and individual agency, for both are entwined in the fabric of embodied black female experience. In the final analysis, the intricacies of Hopkins's text complicate Deleuze's theory by incorporating dimensions of race and gender in theories of the fold.[1]

The narrative of *Winona* follows two trajectories: a romance plot involving Winona and a white Englishman, Warren Maxwell, and a westernlike plot that centers on Winona's adopted black brother, Judah. Critics, taking the covering story at face value, invariably emphasize the western, leading them to lament the absence of female agency.[2] Tate has observed that "rescue missions largely displace the courtship story, with the exception of intermittent romantic flashes between Maxwell and Winona" (201), and, indeed, Winona often functions as an object to be rescued and abducted by different bands of men. However, a reading of *Winona* as formulaic (rather than pliant) proves unsatisfactory, as complexity opens up at unanticipated intervals—wrinkles in the midst of the western. The novel is just as importantly, if not as overtly, a "tale of romantic happenings," as Hopkins herself states in the very first paragraph, and the titular character is central to this romance (287). Not to be dismissed, the "romantic flashes" in the novel are textual folds where Hopkins's suddenly sensual language employs a vocabulary of dreams, flowers, and spirits—delaying the action of the plot and lingering over seemingly superfluous nonevents (even more attenuated by the serialization of the novel). These textual folds create a sense of Winona's interiority. Hopkins's need to maintain tight control over the eroticism of her text is echoed in the strangely inscrutable and often silent Winona. Thus *Winona* illustrates Hazel Carby's contention that "the representation of the struggle for sexual autonomy was to remain a crucial organizing device of the narrative structures of black women writers" (39); however, this struggle is not always waged at the level of plot or character but in compressed pockets of textual encoding.

While this essay primarily follows the romance strand of *Winona*, once the hidden folds of the text are explored, we find that the two strands are implicated, one in the other. My reading also registers the western's dual movements in both protecting and exposing the body of *Winona*'s text. The western envelops the erotic story of Winona even as it unfolds her sexual vulnerability in a racist society through western thematics of captivity and escape, here displaced onto the slaveholding South. Moreover, the western and romance, like geological seams or veins of rock, each contain a concentrated deposit of circumscribed pleasures—anger and righteous violence are Judah's portion, while eroticism is Winona's. These strands are clearly gendered, but, because they are creviced in the same textual matter, the desires explored in each inform the other: Winona is able to turn violence back against those who turned it against her, while action, as sheer unrestricted movement, is eroticized. Winona's very presence in the western signals a disruption of both a feminized romance plot and a masculinized action plot. All of this collapsing of generic bodies into each other is symptomatic of the way in which Hopkins will bend categories, cross boundaries, and shift contents of physical bodies throughout.

The key to unfolding the encoded pockets of *Winona* is the language of flowers. It was not uncommon for women of Hopkins's era to assign flowers to their feelings. In fact, this was the business of flower dictionaries, increasingly popular throughout the nineteenth century.[3] According to these dictionaries, each flower, operating as a unit of meaning, expressed a particular sentiment and was usually paired with a verse that articulated that feeling. As Alice Dunbar-Nelson's story "Violets" (1895) demonstrates, flower language was intended to facilitate communication between lovers. In Dunbar-Nelson's story, each flower in a bouquet exchanged by lovers "whisper[s] a love-word" (918), and her heroine interprets each flower in a letter accompanying the bouquet (she is concerned that her lover "may not be able to read their meaning," revealing flower language to be a fairly feminized code). Thus flower language provided, as Beverly Seaton has observed, "the vocabulary needed to conduct a love affair" (122).

But flower dictionaries hinted at more extensive semiotic possibilities for what was often called the "mystical" language of flowers. Even Sarah J. Hale's prosaic but popular dictionary claimed some interest in the mystical dimension of flower language; she hoped to "stimulate the young to the observance of the hidden meanings which may lie concealed in the flower volumes of nature" (iv). Such language invites a heuristic project with rather remarkable possibilities for nineteenth-century female decoders. Women were asked to cultivate flowerlike qualities—essentially to be a flower as illustrations from Cleaveland's translation of *The Flowers Personified* indicate (fig. 1). In fact, women were urged to study botany because, as one late-century handbook for girls put it, "in learning to know Nature, you are learning to know yourselves" (Seaton 22). Among other "hidden meanings" concealed in flowers was the floral reproductive system, a recent botanical discovery explained in detailed scientific language in many flower dictionaries.

Flower dictionaries often left blank pages for readers' commentary and annotation, thus inviting each reader to become an editor of flower language and launch independent interpretations. This is precisely what Sarah Mapps Douglass, a black Philadelphian and educator, did when faced with the blank space of an album page in her pupil Mary Anne Dickerson's album. There she painted a full-page watercolor of a sprig of fuchsia (fig. 2) and paired it with her reading of the flower:

> "All the species of fuchsia droop their heads toward the ground in such a manner that their inner beauties can only be discerned when they are somewhat above the eye of the spectator. In a meaner flower this might not attract attention, but most of the fuchsias are eminently beautiful, both in form and color; and this modest bending of the head is the more remarked from the singular and peculiar beauty of the parts involved in the calyxe which they would thus seem anxious to conceal." Beautifully and significantly typifying modesty.

Figure 1. Charles Granville. "Dahlia." *The Flowers Personified: Being a Translation of Grandville's "Les Fleurs Animees."* Trans. N. Cleaveland. New York: R. Martin, 1849. *Library Company of Philadelphia.*

Douglass's interpretation is most interesting for its departure from the standard vocabularies of flower dictionaries. An intrinsic color vocabulary, often made explicit through a color glossary in an appendix (or even called attention to in the very title, for example, Burke's *The Coloured Language of Flowers*), dictated that white, not red, flowers typified purity and modesty.[4] That Douglass chooses to epitomize the "exotic" and colored fuchsia as "modest" seems to be a calculated refutation of those color vocabularies applied both to flowers and to female sexuality—the lurking signified of flower language. Certainly such lurking meaning was

Figure 2. Sarah Mapps Douglass. "Fuchsia." Album entry. July 1846. Mary Anne Dickerson Album. *Library Company of Philadelphia.*

not lost on Douglass, the first well-known black sex educator, however "anxious to conceal" the fuchsia's "inner beauties" she might be.

While Christopher Looby and Paula Bennett have recently and con-vincingly reclaimed the language of flowers as a widely available erotic discourse in the nineteenth century, I want to stress that flower language also laid special emphasis on the "soul" of the flower. In flower dictio-naries, very few flowers are used to describe physical characteristics; it was a language interested primarily in "inward states" (Seaton 126), especially of women. Elaine Scarry, in speaking to the universality of flower imagery in our imaginative expressions (whether painting, philosophy, or poetry), argues that flowers provide "an arc between the material and the immaterial" (102). Their material substance, combined with what Aristotle called their "rarity" (their quick, almost ephemeral existence, and their growth, or ascension, toward the heavens) and with what Scarry characterizes as their very willingness to become the stuff of our imaginations, contributes to the idea that flowers are "always already in a state of passage from the material to the dematerialized" (104). This arc between the material and immaterial was formulated in nineteenth-century flower language in a gender-specific way as the arc between the flower's corporeality (miming not only faces, or the curve of the eye as in Scarry's formulation, but also the female body) and the flower's soul. Flower language therefore lent dimension to representations of a female self in a way that allowed women to hold together body and soul by enfolding both sexuality and spirituality within the petals of the flower.

Long a field of alternative signification—Scarry refers to a flower as "the work table on which the less easily imagined becomes imaginable" (95)—flower language offered Hopkins and her contemporaries a space to explore an embodied identity that was not caught in a mimetic relationship to white femininity. The array of floral figurations available— the spectrum of shapes, colors, and sizes—made flower language a particularly pliable semiotic of femininity. It provided a way to depathologize black female desire through a metaphorics steeped in both gentility and benign natural imagery. Black women writers almost always decentered flower language conventions to some degree. Charlotte Forten castigated the showy white camellia in her flower fable "The Flower Fairies' Reception" (Peterson 223). Dunbar-Nelson is careful to distinguish the "wild, shy kind" of violet, her signature flower, from those in the florists' shops (915). Both writers thereby signal that they would embrace genteel femininity on their own terms.[5] Thus flower symbolism, bound to its sexual and racial hidden meanings, was put into play by black women writers. Its pliability facilitated an active reading protocol versed not in the transparencies of language nor in the static conventionalities of symbols but in the constant unfolding of metaphoric possibilities, the layering and enfolding of meaning, and the malleability of a code open to endless editing—or arrangements, as it were.

This alternative language yielded a whole system of hidden meanings that attempted to push further than the surface semiotics of floral appearance, of color and form (skin and genitals), to express the ever elusive, seemingly ineffable and unspeakable soul of the flower. Theoretically then, flower language suggested the possibility (by no means always realized) of expressing a female self outside of the bounds of dominant race and gender constructions. Flower language allowed Hopkins to approach the issue with which black women writers would continue to grapple in the coming century—in Deborah McDowell's words, "how to express female sexual desire . . . without becoming an icon of racist projection" (97).

Hopkins's *Winona* offers one of the most striking and elaborate uses of flower language among her contemporaries. Hers is a complex appropriation sensitive to the pitfalls and privileges involved in such a model of femininity and aware that flower language had various ways of reinscribing race. Hopkins begins *Winona* by rendering Winona's sexual coming-of-age in flower language, a scene to which I will return shortly. Some background on Winona will prove helpful: the child of a racially mixed marriage, Winona is raised by her white father when her mulatto mother dies soon after Winona's birth. Her mother was a slave who escaped to upstate New York on the Underground Railroad. There she met Winona's father, who had eschewed white culture to live with an Indian tribe, inhabiting an island on the border of the United States and Canada. White Eagle, as the tribe calls Winona's father, and Winona's mother were legally married in Canada under English law. Winona is raised with Judah, an older adopted brother who is black, the son of a runaway slave woman who escaped with Winona's mother but died in the process. Also included in the immediate family is Nokomis, an Indian woman who acts as housekeeper. Winona's happily mixed family is part of a larger "mixed community of Anglo-Saxons, Indians, and Negroes" (287) that lives in the Buffalo, New York, area. At the precise moment when she is made more vulnerable by her budding sexuality, Winona is abducted and sold into slavery via the newly created Fugitive Slave Law (the story is set in the 1850s). After two years, Winona is rescued from slavery and taken west where she and her rescuers join forces with John Brown's version of Free Soil politics in Kansas.

Winona contains the most optimistic exposition of integration in Hopkins's work, returning as it does to a high point of interracial political coalition (John Brown's radical brand of abolitionism) while simultaneously integrating the private sphere through an honorable interracial romance between Winona and a white English hero, Warren Maxwell. Winona's rejection of her black adopted brother Judah as a contender for her hand in marriage marks Hopkins's break from "the sibling model of ideal love," the dominant model in black women's fiction at the turn of the century (Tate 176). By abandoning what had become a generic requirement, Hopkins departs from the marriage-as-duty-to-the-race thematics of black women's domestic fiction in order to explore marriage and courtship as passionate rather than ideal love. As Siobhan Somerville has pointed out, "Hopkins's insistence on claiming African American desire, which included the possibility of interracial desire, was part of her larger attempt to refuse the racialized boundaries that Jim Crow and antimiscegenation legislation increasingly imposed and naturalized during the 1890s and 1900s" (140). Furthermore, the narrative of heterosexual desire turns out to be a pretense—yet another cover— for an autoerotic exploration of her heroine's own sexuality. Thus Hopkins retreats from the public politics of racial uplift in order to explore the private politics of an autonomous black female sexuality.

Hopkins appropriates flower language to describe her own black heroine and to critique racist distinctions between a delicate white female body and a fleshly sexualized black female body. Probably no flower was more racially coded than the magnolia. The heavily scented flower was central to white women's erotic encodings for its ethereality; the fragrance was a sort of sensuous rendering of a white female erotic self that avoided the snares of embodiment, that remained elusive and unseen, that could not be plucked or harvested. Of course, its whiteness was the visual analogue of the delicate sensuality the scent evoked. One flower myth claimed that magnolias, though naturally of a "dazzling hue," "drooped and grew *sallow*" when plucked "like princesses captive in the prison of the barbarous foe" (Fuller 300; my emphasis). In a familiar calculus, as the flower shifts from an inviolable and high-souled presence to a material object that has been plucked and bruised, its loss of whiteness is the chief signifier of its degraded state.

Hopkins sets about materializing this discourse of white female sexuality in spite of itself. Her initial description of Magnolia Farm, the plantation to which the recently captured Winona is brought, appears to be straight out of the "moonlight and magnolias" school of popular plantation fiction:

> The air was redolent with the scent of flowers nor needed
> the eye to seek far for them, for the whole front of the dwell-
> ing ... [was] rendered picturesque by rich masses of roses and
> honeysuckle that covered them.... Mingled with the scent of
> the roses was the fragrance of the majestic magnolia whose buds
> and blossoms nodded at one from every nook and unexpected
> quarter. (315–16)

But this is not a picturesque scene for Winona, whose master, Colonel Titus, is biding his time until she is old enough for her sexual wares to be sold at a handsome price; Magnolia Farm is the home of Colonel Titus,

and we are told that "all was grist that came to his mill" (316). The ubiq-
uity of the magnolia and its fragrance takes on an insidious quality, for
Winona's story bears witness to the hideous underbelly of the "moonlight and magnolias" school.

As if to make this very point, Hopkins stages the following scene at
Magnolia Farm. Maxwell and Judah are

> sitting in the darkness, the sweet scent of the magnolia envel-
> oping them in its fragrance, the faint sound of insect life min-
> gling with the murmur of rustling leaves. Warren Maxwell
> listened to whispered words that harrowed up his very soul. To
> emphasize his story, Judah stripped up his shirt and seizing the
> young white man's hand pressed it gently over the scars and
> seams stamped upon his back [by Colonel Titus's whip]. (334)

Hopkins thus burdens the ephemeral evocation of white female sexuality with the materiality it so eschews. In this case, she saddles it with a
materiality so grotesque, so horrific, that when Maxwell's nose fills with
the fragrance of magnolias while his hands trace the welts on Judah's
back it becomes impossible not to forever associate the two sensations.
Hopkins inverts the magnolia's meaning so that instead of standing in
direct opposition to the bruised, commodified, utterly material and spir-
itless brown or black flower, it is now bound in a symbiotic relationship with the sexual and physical abuse of black bodies. These
associations are folded into the very perfume of white female sexuality.

Hopkins further challenges the racist constructions of flower language by choosing the Indian-pipe as the flower that figures her heroine's
sexuality. The Indian-pipe is a fungal wildflower that cannot be domesticated, nor is it to be found in flower dictionaries, signaling Hopkins's
departure from traditional, and white, femininity. In Winona's first encounter with the Indian-pipes on the remote island of her childhood,
"[a] distant gleam among the grasses caught the girl's quick eye. She ran
swiftly over the open and threaded her sinuous way among the bushes
to drop upon her knees in silent ecstacy [sic]. In an instant Judah was
beside her. They pushed the leaves aside together, revealing the faint
pink stems of the delicate, gauzy Indian-pipes" (291). Occurring as it
does in the first chapter of the novel, the figure of the Indian-pipe, including the (rather elaborate) mise-en-scène and dialogue Hopkins contrives to accompany it, serves as a key to the rest of the novel. The
concluding chapter returns to the scene to assure the reader that the
Indian-pipes still "lay concealed among the bushes as of old" (434), another signal that Hopkins intends her flower language to fulfill a semiotic
function with significance for the full comprehension of the whole of

her narrative. Creviced in the landscape, the Indian-pipe is a tight tex-tual bud whose plicated meaning unfurls throughout the narrative, al-lowing Hopkins, via her own arrangement of flower language, to explore the many layers of an embodied black female self.

Winona's "sinuous way" and "silent ecstacy," when read in the con-text of flower language, alert us to the possibility that this discovery of the concealed Indian-pipes entails an erotic awakening for Winona. When Winona parts the leaves to reveal the small, waxy, nodding flowers of the Indian-pipe (fig. 3), Hopkins employs a system of clitoral imagery— of small but precious objects (buds, seeds, jewels)—that Paula Bennett has shown to be used by (white) women writers throughout the nine-teenth and twentieth centuries. "In the waxlike jewel, the flower bud," Bennett argues, women writers "found the images [they] needed to rep-resent woman to herself—not as a space to be entered but as a presence to be uncovered and adored" (244).[6] The identification of the Indian-pipes with an eroticized Winona is immediately confirmed when Judah feels "a strange sense of pleasure stir his young heart as he involuntarily glanced from the flowers to the childish face before him . . . the olive complexion with a hint of pink like that which suffused the fragile flowers before them . . . gave his physical senses pleasure to contemplate. From afar came ever the regular booming of Niagara's stupendous flood" (291–92). Obviously, Judah, too, is awakened to Winona's sexuality.

But why, if Hopkins has already concealed the flower of her black heroine's sexuality on a remote island and under the cover of highly eu-phemistic language, must she also bleach the color of her flower? It would not be in keeping with Hopkins's explicit goal of ridding culture of any such superficial racial identity to transvalue binaries by choosing an op-positional vocabulary of colored or exotic flowers. Winona's variously colored body—her "brown hand" (289), "brown fingers" (309), "olive complexion" (292), "soft, dark face" (356), "white throat" (359)—is in-tended to show that it is "in vain to find the dividing line supposed to be a natural barrier between the whites and the dark-skinned race" (287). The remarkable thing about Hopkins's choice of Indian-pipes is that they have no chlorophyll, a widely known attribute of this indigenous flower. Thus Hopkins chooses a "colorless" or, if chlorophyll may be thought of as the floral equivalent of melanin, a racially unmarked flower. The translucence of the flower's membranes enforces Hopkins's ideal of a society that sees past skin color.

The scene between Winona and Judah continues to both advance and complicate Hopkins's intervention in the raced and gendered erotics of flower discourse. "But they turn black as soon as you touch them,"

Figure 3. Mabel Loomis Todd. Watercolor painting of Indian-pipes. Gift to Emily Dickinson, Fall 1882. *Emily Dickinson Collection, Archives and Special Collections, Amherst College Library. Amherst.*

Judah says, ostensibly returning his thoughts to the Indian-pipes after his arousing contemplation of Winona. Winona responds, "Yes, I know; but we will leave them here where they may go away like spirits; Old Nokomis told me." To which Judah scoffs, "Old Nokomis! She's only a silly old Indian squaw. You mustn't mind her stories," adding that "in school you learn not to believe all the silly stories that we are told by the Indians" (292). If the meditation on the Indian-pipes is a meditation on Winona's own budding sexuality, the import is that while she might thrive in the color-blind pan-ethnic community, coded as "natural" in the novel, her removal from that community will be the death of her spirit and, consequently, of her own pleasure in her sexuality, precisely because she will be viewed and treated as "black" in a racist society. That is, the color of her skin will code her as a plucked flower: impure and a husk, only a body with no spiritual interiority.

To extend the implications of Hopkins's revised floral color vocabulary, it must be pointed out that the color black often functions in the novel as a sign of what is done to African American bodies as a result of a racist social order—a social order that violently imposes meaning on what Hopkins would otherwise have us see as the artificial category of race. In moments that reflect as much on the violence concurrent with Hopkins's writing as on the antebellum race struggles her story narrates, Hopkins evokes "the ghostly ruins of charred houses [that] lifted their scarred skeletons against the sky in a mute appeal for vengeance" (360) as a metonym for the charred ruins of lynched and burned bodies, burned homes, and raped women that littered her own post-Reconstruction landscape—the actual horrific blackening of African American bodies. She bends the formula that equates a black flower with impurity to show that the black flower has instead been violated.

Co-opting the gruesomely visual and public sign of white racist violence toward black men—the lynched and burned body—to protest the often unseen and unmentionable crime of rape, Hopkins questions "the worth of a white man's love for a woman of mixed blood; how it swept its scorching heat over a white young life, leaving it nothing but charred embers and burnt-out ashes" (357–58). Though ostensibly referring to the quick cooling of a white man's lust, the ambiguous syntax of the sentence—the uncertainty over just who is burning or being burned—seems to imply that "scorching heat" can apply to the violence committed by white lust, charring and violating the African American woman, like a blighted Indian-pipe. One reading of the Indian-pipe, then, is as a sign of white racist violence. In this reading, blackness refers not to skin color but to an identity violently enforced and persecuted—branded and burned. Where blackness invokes burned bodies, the Indian-pipe that turns black when violated is a powerful and visceral symbol of the black woman's abused body, scorched by white violence. Male-dominant attitudes espoused by both white and black men have consistently refused to view rape as a hate crime, choosing instead to view it as an act of passion in which the female victim is somehow complicit, particularly when she is black. If, as Hazel Carby has asserted, "the institutionalized rape of black women has never been as powerful a symbol of black oppression as the spectacle of lynching" (39), then Hopkins, through flower language, rends the veil from the body that suffers this obscured history, granting material resonance to its pain.

True to the erotic discourse of flowers, Hopkins is as concerned with the spiritual dimension as she is with the physicality of her flower, choosing as she does a flower that is at once highly delicate and ephemeral (melting away like a spirit), even as it remains physically suggestive of female genitalia. Judah's focus on only the physical attributes, his alternating rhapsody on and repulsion from the color of the flower depending on what side of the color line it appears, and his dismissal of its spiritual attributes (again due to the colored origin of the story) mark him as already marred by contact with a racist society. Later, he presumes that Winona "ought naturally" to marry him, not Maxwell, because they are both black—"of the same condition in life in the eyes of the world" (378, 377). While Judah's love for her is tender and honorable, he does not consider whether her spirit is as closely affinitized to him as her color. Flower language does indeed prove to be "the vocabulary needed to conduct a love affair" (Seaton 122), for when Judah rejects the discourse's insistence on the flower's (Winona's) soul, he finds he has no suit. It is Maxwell who follows the "arc between the material and the immaterial" that the Indian-pipes evoke: he sees "the soft, dark face [of Winona] so full of character, so vivid with the light of the passionate soul within" (356). By rejecting Judah, who attempts to impose a color line on her desire, Winona asserts an autonomous sexual desire that refuses to be objectified in a struggle between men over ownership of her body. Moreover, Judah's rhetoric is overlaid with the patriarchal slant of many race leaders who expended much effort to ensure that black women married within the race (when, in fact, significantly more black men than women married interracially). By effecting this type of racial conservation, male leaders hoped both to assuage concerns (not least their own) about black women's purity and to maintain the integrity, or purity, of the race (Gaines 120–27). Sexuality, for black women, thus became a matter of reproducing the race. Exposing this masculinist project through Judah's relation to Winona, Hopkins then dispenses with it to clear the way for Winona's sexual autonomy. By bucking racial conservation, she destabilizes racial identity—not for the last time in the novel.

In his preoccupation with the way the dominant society defines race through biology, Judah misses another, more liberating, idea of race dear to Hopkins's political project in all her fiction: a culturalist notion of race.[7] Winona's alliance with Nokomis in the Indian-pipe scene is reminiscent of other bonds, in other novels, between Hopkins's mulatto heroines and racialized maternal figures. As an (albeit shadowy) mother figure for Winona and as the source of flower lore, Nokomis recalls Madame Frances, the black fortune-teller and aunt of the heroine in *Contending Forces*, and foreshadows Aunt Hannah, the black slave, voodoo practitioner, and grandmother of the central female character in *Of One Blood*. These women have telling links to the heroines; as in a novel of passing, these related and racialized bodies "tell on" the biological race of the heroine and are a source of information about racial history and cultural knowledge. Winona is not passing, a strategy Hopkins resolutely condemned, but she is distanced from a black slave past by the removal of her mother from the narrative. Though the death of Winona's slave mother seemingly sets Winona free to pursue assimilation into white society, the presence of Nokomis undermines that very project by pulling Winona back into a racialized dynamic (one characterized as oppositional to white culture) that threatens her vaunted colorlessness.

A storyteller and the purveyor of the mystical language of flowers, Nokomis also has a knowledge potentially useful to Winona. Her story of the Indian-pipes allows Winona to access an alternative reading of them and of her body. More than material husks, Indian-pipes in Nokomis's version have spirits, a being beyond their color, and Hopkins holds out this possibility to Winona. This is not something Judah's school, in its attention to the color rather than essence of knowledge, has taught him; consequently, his single-minded attention to race and oppression leads him to near despair. His embittered view of how race relations operate is a significant layer of Hopkins's protest but not the sum total of her message. Winona, on the other hand, though she certainly feels her oppression, has spiritual resources on which to rely. Her ability to imagine a self outside of bodily categories resonates with the ideal of the novel, that, in one of its variations, is stated as "there is no respect of persons with God" (374).

Yet that imagined self is still coded as racialized, as Hopkins returns flower language to its non-white origins. By ascribing flower language to a nonwhite source, Hopkins may have thought of herself not as appropriating a white discourse but as *re*appropriating a nonwhite, even

African, discourse. Many flower dictionaries made much of their ancient and non-European origins—for example:

> The indestructible monuments of the mighty Assyrian and Egyptian races bear upon their venerable surfaces a code of floral telegraphy that Time has been powerless to efface, but whose hieroglyphical meaning is veiled, or, at the best, but dimly guessed at in our day. India, whose civilization had attained its full vigour whilst that of Greece was in its cradle, has ever been poetically ingenious in finding her magnificent Flora significations applicable to human interest. (Ingram 1)

Indeed, despite the flurry of amalgamating activity in Hopkins's idealized locale, flower language and its accompanying mystical insight into nature linger and haunt the text as a racialized knowledge, in this case Native American. At the same time, Native American and, though unspoken, African histories and identities intersect in *Winona*. The "island [that] has no name" (294), on which Winona and her tribe live is suggestive of America before its discovery, but it also evokes Africa when Winona and Judah are snatched from it. The colonization of the two continents are fused in the "violent invasion of this world [of the island] by two white men whose first language is gunfire, not words" (Ammons 214). As a veiled Africa, the island functions (as Africa often did in black texts of this time) as an "uncolonized territory of the spirit" (Sundquist 559). Uncolonized and nameless, the island is a prelapsarian body before race is named, before the notion of race violently issued from contact with other peoples.

Though colorless, then, the Indian-pipe invokes a historical black experience of slavery and violence as well as a nonwhite cultural identity (a mystical colored spirituality and interiority). Both senses are specifically gendered, for the Indian-pipe speaks to a history of institutionalized rape of black women and to a culturally based mystical knowledge that includes a knowledge not only of spirits but of the female body. The stories of Nokomis—her flower language, in which Winona has invested her faith but which Judah has discredited—enfold three aspects of a potential black female self in the hidden meaning of the Indian-pipe: that self's history of oppression, a potentially radical alterity accessed through nonwhite cultural resources (a possible Africanity), and sexuality. Considered taboo by many middle-class blacks in the service of racial uplift and integration and manipulated by the dominant white society in the service of primitivist stereotypes, these discredited stories must be both recovered and protected from racist interpretation and circulation.

By picking Winona off of her island and sending her over the border and into slave territory (thus plunging the black reader into the past), Hopkins refuses either an idealized version of colorlessness where the material consequences of racism are effaced or, alternatively, the return to an idealized cultural identity that predates race (the golden age the island invokes). Perched between slavery in the United States and freedom in Canada, between legal rape under United States law and legal marriage under English law, between a horrible past of oppression and a hope for an ideal future without racism, Winona's symbolic predicament recalls the position of the post-Reconstruction black who must adjudicate between optimism about full and equitable citizenship and despair over ever-increasing racism. Evasion of history is not an option Hopkins offers to Winona or her readers. Winona will have to recover the liminal space she needs to explore her sexuality despite the racist society in which she lives.

Though Winona experiences the extreme sexualization of slavery in which she is regarded only as a body to be trafficked by white men, this portion of her life is foreshortened in the story. Instead, it is Maxwell, in yet another seemingly impossible fold of Hopkins's text, who must undergo the violent racialization portrayed by the blackened Indian-pipes. A white man and English to boot, Maxwell knows little (and believes less) about the cruelty and inhumanity of slavery. Most of the portion of the novel that occurs in Kansas with John Brown, the western plot, is devoted to Maxwell's education in the realities of racism. Rather than relying on mere sympathy to solidify the coupling of Winona and Maxwell, Hopkins makes Maxwell realize that "experience is a stern teacher" (395) and schools him in a politicized version of the Golden Rule: "Remember those in bonds as bound with them" (374).

Maxwell's horrific bodily indoctrination into the ways of slavery includes being the object of mob violence, being placed on display "much as is a wild beast caged in a menagerie" (382), and experiencing a "trial" that is a "farcical mockery of justice" (382). Not least, Maxwell is in danger of being burned at the stake in a scene that refuses to avert the reader's gaze from a single detail; in fact, Hopkins rewinds the scene between monthly installments so that the pile under Maxwell is lit twice (368, 370). Hopkins not only lifts the veil of Maxwell's ignorance about black history, she marches him across the color line—twice, in case he does not get it the first time. Maxwell is "saved" only to be further tortured with imprisonment and the promise of execution, but not before his skin has been scarred by the fire. Like Winona, Maxwell is raced by a racist society, literally blackened like the Indian-pipes. Race unfolds as a fiction with material consequences, a mobile category whose organizing principle is domination, not biology. The "exchange of situation" (386) between the dominated and the oppressors that the Bible promises and Hopkins delivers serves to reverse the imperialist experience of the western at the same time that it makes Maxwell, because of that very reversal, a fit match for Winona. Hopkins reveals the costs of western fantasies of lawlessness and freedom while appropriating the revenge mode of the western to subject her romance hero to a stern lesson. Cast from a privileged position and made into the object of imperial domination, Maxwell learns what it is like to occupy a body that is, at least momentarily, no more privileged than Winona's.

If having Maxwell live out one trajectory of racial embodiment enfolded in the Indian-pipes seems not only to blacken him but also to feminize him through an association with flower language, that is because Hopkins does not miss the opportunity to reveal rape as another act of terrorism endured by black women. A hole in the floor of Maxwell's prison cell "afforded diversion for the invalid who could observe the full operation of the slave system" (384) by watching the treatment blacks received in the cell below. Indeed, one day he sees "a Negro undergoing the shameful outrage, so denounced in the Scriptures," which causes him to fall "fainting with terror and nausea upon the floor" (385). The implications are doubled: Maxwell vicariously experiences the rape that Winona has narrowly escaped as the sight and sounds of the rape penetrate his eyes, ears, and cell through the small hole, while his voyeurism implicates him in the white man's act.

If Hopkins invades and bends the generic form of the western in order to invest it with a radically different spirit, this move is replicated by Winona on a more personal scale. When Maxwell is first captured by the mob, Judah's overseer (Bill Thompson) tries to bargain with Maxwell for information on the whereabouts of Winona and Judah. At the moment when he is considering his reply, Winona mystically appears to Maxwell even though she is physically far away: "Winona stared at him across the shadows of the dim old woods. 'Be true,' she whispered to the secret ear of his soul. With rapture he read aright the hopeless passion in her eyes when he left her. He knew now that he loved her" (363). Winona, as the agent (staring, whispering) in this encounter, is represented as exercising her power of suggestion according to mesmerist beliefs, in which Hopkins was well versed and which she often deployed in her fiction.[8] Like mesmerists who demonstrated their power of control over trancees on the itinerant lecture circuit, Winona takes up a position of control over Maxwell's mind and body. She in fact invades his body through "the secret ear of his soul" and by obtruding herself upon his vision. Once in possession of Maxwell, she infuses him with new spirit: "With sudden boldness he answered his tormentor. 'You have no right to claim either Winona or Judah as your slave. They are as free as you or I. I will never aid and abet your barbarous system, understanding it as I do now'" (363). Maxwell's epiphany has long been coming, but the suggestion of Winona gives him new zest in his convictions. A black woman in possession of a white man's body, particularly when she makes that body commit political acts on her behalf, is surely a powerful image unavailable in the dominant discourse.

Winona uses mystical knowledge to exercise control over her own body as well. After escaping slavery and joining John Brown's camp in the frontier territory of Kansas, Winona's return to a natural, geographically liminal, and racially integrated setting like that of her childhood island helps her to recapture the sense of self promised by the Indian-pipes, to fuse body and soul: "Some impulse of the wild things among whom she had lived drove her to a hole in under the bluff. It was necessary to descend to find it. Presently she was in a tunnel which led to a cavern" (375–76). Significantly, Hopkins has once more placed the female body onto the landscape, as indicated by the "hole in under the bluff" and the "tunnel which led to a cavern" and with her previous description of this landscape as "naked woods" with "the cup-like shape of the hills," and "ribs of rock" (358). Again Hopkins ascribes Winona's primal knowledge of the female-body-in-the-landscape onto Winona's Indianness (just as Nokomis was the source of flower lore) and furthers the idea that a nonwhite mystical knowledge allows Winona to access an erotic identity that is both sexual and spiritual. This identity is an alternative to the utterly bodily identity Winona was assigned in slavery; instead, it returns her to the holistic model of femininity offered through flower language and Hopkins's particular arrangement of its metaphorics in the Indian-pipe. While in Hopkins's *Of One Blood* the "undiscovered country within ourselves" (448) is materialized in a hidden ancient African city, the undiscovered country in *Winona* is the hidden female body, thus giving a gendered inflection to notions of a hidden self usually associated with a Du Boisian, and male, mode of identity formation. Precisely because the female body is hidden (just as it is geographically underground, so Winona must rely on "underground," or occult, knowledge to locate it), Hopkins realizes her "desire for a pure black womanhood, an uncolonized black female body" so elusive in her other works (Carby 144).

Though I agree with Ann duCille when she emphasizes that late-nineteenth-century black women writers (Francis Harper specifically) did not displace sexuality but rather placed it into a safer realm (45), Hopkins does not place Winona's "nook" in the woods for Maxwell's benefit in order to facilitate his coupling with Winona; the "nook" is strictly for Winona to explore. The autoerotic valences of such an exploration cannot be overlooked. Upon entering this female space, Winona "made herself a divan of dried moss and flung herself down at full length to think" (376). Via the feminine landscape, Winona has entered her own body as sole proprietor. Posed for her own pleasure, not someone else's, Winona can now engage in what can only be called an autoerotic fantasy:

> Time's divisions were lost on those days when the girl felt that she neglected no duty by hiding herself in her nook. She had come upon the eternal now as she lay in a sweet stupor until forced to arouse herself. She stared across the space that divided Maxwell from her with all the strength of her inner consciousness. That light which falls on the spot where one's loved one stands, leaving the rest of the landscape in twilight, now rested about him. With rapture she saw again the hopeless passion in Warren's eyes. Her hands and feet were cold, her muscles knotted, her face white with the force of the cry that she projected through space: "Come back to me!" (376)

A climactic moment in many ways, this scene proves *Winona* to be an exception among other late-nineteenth and early-twentieth-century black women's fiction, of which Tate has said: "There is love in these novels; however, it is not passionate ardor but rather compassionate duty, spiritualized affection, and sentimental attachment" (167). Clearly Winona experiences—both physically and emotionally—that most censored feeling, passionate ardor. Ensconced in the earth, rooted to her moss divan, Winona is once again like the Indian-pipes. As in that scene, Hopkins releases the compressed intensity of a textual fold, a creviced bud, a hidden nook, and, it hardly needs saying, Winona's embodied pleasure.

At the same time, and also like the Indian-pipes, she is free to "go away like a spirit." In a quite literal way, there is spiritualized affection, for this scene narrates an out-of-body reunion with Maxwell. It is important to remember that such spiritualized affection was not necessarily antithetical to eroticized feeling. As Hopkins's deployment of flower language's "arc" between spirituality and corporeality demonstrates, it was a necessary strategy for binding emotional with sensual feeling. By emphasizing her soul's response, Hopkins mitigates against racist readings of black sexuality as entirely physical, even animalistic, and places her heroine's desire on another plane altogether. By stressing spiritual affinity, she exposes the artificial distinction upon which antimiscegenation laws were based. Winona literally channels her desire across "the space that divided her from Maxwell," across the color line. Here one minute, spirited off the next, this quality of ephemerality renders her not available as a commodity. Even attempts to "fix" or determine her color will be confused, just as Judah wavered over the color of the Indian-pipes. Released from a racially determined sexuality, Winona is free to enjoy erotic moments of "sweet stupor," "arous[al]," and "rapture."

If ecstasy—like that which Winona experienced when she first discovered the Indian-pipes and gazed upon them with "silent ecstacy"—by definition means "a being put out of its place," then when the Indian-pipes go away like spirits, they are directly analogous to Winona's own pleasure. Politically speaking, Winona is a being out of her proper place. She neither occupies the white-assigned position of sexual Jezebel nor the defensive posture (assumed by both white and black women) of passionless maiden. Far from passionless, Winona is shown in these mystical romantic flashes to be the agent of her own desire, channeling it at will, and able to "arouse herself." In these moments, she is not "put out" of her place, she puts herself out of it. This freedom of movement, of entering or transcending her (or Maxwell's) body at will, is informed by both anger that protests its constrictions and pleasure that revels in its unboundedness. The eroticized movement of Winona's spirit is an embodiment of African American desire, but it is not a body bound by the specular constraints of skin or gender.

Hopkins effects "an exchange of situation," a crossing of the color line, that is not an act of passing or uncritical assimilation but of usurping and occupying white space (of Maxwell's body, of the Western, of flower language) in order to transform it and empty it of privilege. In doing so even momentarily—by allowing a black soul to "possess" a white body, or blackening the white body, or meeting somewhere else altogether in the ether—the color line becomes difficult to place. This is the model of interracial relations *Winona* offers, a confusion of bodily identities and an affinity of souls, but one that nonetheless impresses upon each body and mind the historical effects of race. The envisioned relationship between the races (which Hopkins does not conflate with current realities) is neither one of passing nor rape precisely because the body's burden of representation has been released by a new emphasis on spirit. That spirit, however, emanates from a spirituality situated outside of white structures and bodies, remaining primarily a futuristic vision and limited to the microcosmic interracial relation between Winona and Maxwell. They cannot remain in Winona's nation because their bodies continue to signify without their consent.[9]

Yet the hidden body of the text remains, and it is strictly for Winona—and perhaps by extension, the black female readers of *The Col-*

ored American Magazine—to explore. In the layering and doubling of
Hopkins's novel, textual body and physical body interweave. A counterpoint of passion and protest, Hopkins's novel dilates and recedes, extends protest, retracts stereotypes, and unfurls alternatives. Its very
movement defies static formulas just as Hopkins's permutations of embodied black female identity slip away from stereotypes and counter stereotypes. If, under the insidious illogical system through which race is
produced in a racist society, the black woman impossibly occupies two
bodies—"sensual and public on the one hand; vulnerable, invisible, forgettable on the other" (Berlant 556)—Hopkins unfolds two other bodies
for Winona. Hopkins represents the vulnerability of the raced body
through the blackened Indian-pipes and reveals the "scorching" violence
by which bodies are raced; she goes public with this body to protest its
violation. Nonetheless, she also claims ownership to a sensual body by
privatizing it, even spiritualizing it, so that only her heroine knows how
to access it. She wants to reveal both pain and pleasure as embodied
experiences of African American women. At the same time, by envel-
oping one body and unfolding another she controls how and by whom
that body is seen. Hopkins at once uncovers a personal space of control
and self-knowledge long denied to black women while covering it with
the veil of flower language—even burying it in the landscape of the novel.
The two gestures work in tandem folds, for this erotic space cannot remain her own if it is exposed. Yet this very act of covering and uncovering the black female body through the language of flowers is also an
act of recovery, of renaming; ultimately, it is an act of self-creation and
a labor of self-love.

NOTES

Research for this essay was supported in part by an Andrew W. Mellon Foundation fellowship at the Library Company of Philadelphia. A shorter version of this essay was presented at the 1997 American Studies Association
Convention in Washington, D.C. I would like to thank John Charles, Kim
Chabot Davis, Susan Fraiman, Lisa Harper, Eric Lott, and Deborah McDowell
for their advice on various versions of this essay.

1. See Deleuze for more on theories of the fold. For excellent discussions, to
   which I am indebted, of how the fold applies to conceptual space, see
   Rajchman and Lynn. For a discussion of the usefulness of Deleuzian theories to feminist theories of the body, see Braidotti and Grosz, though neither author specifically discusses theories of the fold.
2. Following Carby, Ammons and Tate have viewed *Winona* as marred by its
   dime novel formulation. By emphasizing the western plot, these readings,
   especially Carby's and Ammons's, elide the narrative trajectory that I explore.
   Carby discusses only Judah, to the neglect of Winona. Ammons's essay
   is important for calling attention to the complexity of *Winona*, but she
   dwells on the contradictions she believes inhere in Hopkins's adaptation of

the western, including the absence of female subjectivity in that form. Tate, while treating the romance, feels the western displaces the "woman-centered discourse of female development" (208). I argue that *Winona* embarks on a different project from the domestic novels Tate seeks to affirm. I cover rather different ground than these critics, focusing on the romance plot bound up in Hopkins's portrayal of Winona.

3. So popular were flower dictionaries that John Ingram's 1887 dictionary was able to claim that, "in the United States, the language of flowers is said to have more votaries than in any other part of the world; and said with justice, if we may judge by the number and splendor of the works on the subject which have appeared there during the last few years, and the intimate acquaintance which American writers display with floral symbols" (7). Many women writers edited flower dictionaries, including Sarah Hale, Elizabeth Oakes Smith, Frances Osgood, Emma Embury, and Louisa May Alcott. Late-century flower language books include the still-reprinted Kate Greenaway's *Language of Flowers* (1884); Alice Ward Bailey's *Flower Fancies* (1889); Walter Crane's various illustrated flower fables, such as *Flora's Feast* (1889) and *A Flower Wedding* (1905); Lizzie Deas's *Flower Favorites: Their Legends, Symbolism, and Significance* (1898); and various anonymous flower dictionaries like *The Language and Poetry of Flowers* (1885) and *The Language of Flowers: A Complete Alphabet of Floral Emblems* (1875). See Seaton for a full bibliography.

4. Ingram's preface is typical of such a color vocabulary. It claimed: "That the 'white investments' of the childlike Daisy should, as Shakespeare says, 'figure innocence,' is self-evident" (6).

5. See Peterson 222–23 for a reading of Frances Harper's and Forten's use of gardens as an allegory of the nation.

6. Compare Hopkins's Indian-pipe, for instance, to the imagery in this stanza of Amy Lowell's later poem "The Weather-Cock Points South" (1919), quoted by Bennett as an example of clitoral imagery: "I put your leaves aside, / One by one: / The stiff, broad outer leaves; / The smaller ones, / Pleasant to touch, veined with purple; / The glazed inner leaves, / One by one / I parted you from your leaves, / Until you stood up like a white flower / Swaying slightly in the evening wind" (245).

7. For excellent discussions of Hopkins's use of Ethiopianism and Egyptology in her next and last novel, *Of One Blood, or, the Hidden Self*, see Sundquist and Gillman. Hopkins's interest in the African origins of civilization and particularly the mystical components of that civilization is developed most strikingly in *Of One Blood*, and documented in her history, *A Primer of Facts Pertaining to the Early Greatness of the African Race*.

8. See Schrager and Gillman for discussions of Hopkins's creative use of mesmerism and the philosophy of William James.

9. For a different reading of interracial relations in *Winona*, see McCann.

WORKS CITED

Ammons, Elizabeth. "Afterword: *Winona*, Bahktin, and Hopkins in the Twenty-first Century." Gruesser 211–19.

Bennett, Paula. "Critical Clitoridectomy: Female Sexual Imagery and Feminist Psychoanalytic Theory." *Signs* 18 (1993): 235–59.

Berlant, Lauren. "The Queen of America Goes to Washington City: Harriet Jacobs, Frances Harper, Anita Hill." *American Literature* 65 (1993): 549–74.

Bordo, Susan. *Unbearable Weight: Feminism, Western Culture, and the Body*. Berkeley: U of California P, 1993.

Boundas, Constantin V., and Dorothea Olkowski, eds. *Gilles Deleuze and the Theater of Philosophy.* New York: Routledge, 1994.

Braidotti, Rosi. "Toward a New Nomadism: Feminist Deleuzian Tracks; or Metaphysics and Metabolism." *Gilles Deleuze and the Theater of Philosophy.* Boundas and Olkowski 159–83.

Burke, Anna Christian. *The Coloured Language of Flowers.* London: Routledge, 1886.

Carby, Hazel V. *Reconstructing Womanhood: The Emergence of the Afro-American Woman Novelist.* New York: Oxford UP, 1987.

Cleaveland, N., Esq., trans. *The Flowers Personified: Being a Translation of Grandville's "Les Fleurs Animees."* New York, 1849.

Deleuze, Gilles. *The Fold: Leibniz and the Baroque.* Trans. Tom Conley. Minneapolis: U of Minnesota P, 1993.

Douglass, Sarah Mapps. "Fuchsia." Album entry. 14 Nov. 1846. Mary Anne Dickerson Album. Library Company of Philadelphia.

duCille, Ann. *The Coupling Convention: Sex, Text, and Tradition in Black Women's Fiction.* New York: Oxford UP, 1993.

Dunbar-Nelson, Alice. *The Works of Alice Dunbar-Nelson.* Ed. Gloria T. Hull. Vol. 1. New York: Oxford UP, 1988.

Fuller, Margaret. "The Magnolia of Lake Pontchartrain." *The Essential Margaret Fuller.* Ed. Jeffrey Steele. New Brunswick: Rutgers UP, 1995. 44–49.

Gaines, Kevin K. *Uplifting the Race: Black Leadership, Politics, and Culture in the Twentieth Century.* Chapel Hill: U of North Carolina P, 1996.

Giddings, Paula. *When and Where I Enter: The Impact of Black Women on Race and Sex in America.* New York: Morrow, 1984.

Gillman, Susan. "Pauline Hopkins and the Occult: African-American Revisions of Nineteenth-Century Sciences." *American Literary History* 8 (1996): 57–82.

Grosz, Elizabeth. "A Thousand Tiny Sexes: Feminism and Rhizomatics." Boundas and Olkowski 187–210.

Gruesser, John Cullen, ed. *The Unruly Voice: Rediscovering Pauline Elizabeth Hopkins.* Urbana: U of Illinois P, 1996.

Hale, Sarah J. *Flora's Interpreter, and Fortuna Flora.* Rev. ed. Boston, 1853.

Hopkins, Pauline. *Contending Forces: A Romance Illustrative of Negro Life North and South.* Ed. Richard Yarborough. New York: Oxford UP, 1988.

———. *Of One Blood; or, the Hidden Self. The Magazine Novels of Pauline Hopkins.* Ed. Hazel Carby. New York: Oxford UP, 1988.

———. *A Primer of Facts Pertaining to the Early Greatness of the African Race and the Possibility of Restoration by Its Descendants—with Epilogue.* New York: Cambridge, 1905

———. *Winona: A Tale of Negro Life in the South and Southwest. The Magazine Novels of Pauline Hopkins.* Ed. Hazel Carby. New York: Oxford UP, 1988.

Ingram, John. *The Language of Flowers; or, Flora Symbolica.* New York, 1887.

Looby, Christopher. "Flowers of Manhood: Race, Sex, and Floriculture from Thomas Wentworth Higginson to Robert Mapplethorpe." *Criticism* 37 (1995): 109–56.

Lynn, Greg. "Architectural Curvilinearity: The Folded, the Pliant, the Supple." *Architectural Design* 63.2 (1993): 8–15.

McCann, Sean. "'Bonds of Brotherhood': Pauline Hopkins and the Work of Melodrama." *ELH* 64 (1997): 789–822.

McDowell, Deborah E. *"The Changing Same": Black Women's Literature, Criticism, and Theory.* Bloomington: Indiana UP, 1995.

Peterson, Carla. *"Doers of the Word": African American Women Speakers and Writers in the North (1830–1880).* New York: Oxford UP, 1995.

Rajchman, John. "Out of the Fold." *Architectural Design* 63.2 (1993): 60–63.

Scarry, Elaine. "Imagining Flowers: Perceptual Mimesis (Particularly Delphinium)." *Representations* 57 (1997): 90–115.

Schrager, Cynthia D. "Pauline Hopkins and William James: The New Psychology and the Politics of Race." Gruesser, 182–209.

Seaton, Beverly. *The Language of Flowers: A History.* Charlottesville: UP of Virginia, 1995.

Somerville, Siobhan. "Passing through the Closet in Pauline E. Hopkins's *Contending Forces*." *American Literature* 69 (1997): 139–166.

Sundquist, Eric. *To Wake the Nations: Race in the Making of American Literature.* Cambridge: Harvard UP, 1993.

Tate, Claudia. *Domestic Allegories of Political Desire: The Black Heroine's Text at the Turn of the Century.* New York: Oxford UP, 1992.

MEREDITH GOLDSMITH

Shopping to Pass, Passing to Shop

Bodily Self-Fashioning in the Fiction of Nella Larsen

Representatives of the rising black middle class, Nella
Larsen's African American heroines are preoccupied
with the interrelation of consumption and self-transformation. Helga
Crane, of *Quicksand* (1928), shops to pass, using consumption as a tool
to claim a coherent identity within the African American middle class,
while Clare Kendry and Irene Redfield, coheroines of *Passing* (1929),
pass to shop, exploiting their light-skin privilege to take advantage of
segregated leisure. Using the tools offered by a burgeoning consumer
culture to alter how their bodies are perceived, Larsen's protagonists simultaneously manipulate their bodies to gain access to objects of elite
consumption. Fashioning identities through the material apparatus of
clothing, makeup, and decor, Larsen's heroines appear to embrace willfully inauthentic, performative selves.

In this essay I argue that the social performances of Larsen's characters provide an important insight into the split between agency and
social construction that theorists have described as characteristic of
performativity. Judith Butler's efforts to clarify the involuntary nature
of performativity in *Bodies That Matter* neatly encapsulates the dilemma
of Larsen's characters. Responding to criticism of the notion of
performativity articulated in *Gender Trouble*, she writes that

> if I were to argue that genders are performative, that could mean
> that I thought that one woke in the morning, perused the closet
> for some more open space for the gender of choice, donned that

gender of that day, and then restored the garment to its place at night. Such a willful and instrumental subject, one who decides *on* its gender, is clearly not its gender from the start and fails to realize that its existence is already decided *by* gender. Certainly, such a theory would restore the figure of a choosing subject—humanist—at the center of a project whose emphasis on construction seems to be quite opposed to such a notion. (*Bodies* x)

The metaphor of the closet, with its abundance of garments representing a plethora of identities from which the subject can choose freely, is telling. Throughout *Bodies That Matter*, Butler struggles to distinguish performativity from the consumerist theatricality of her example, the agent who "chooses" an identity as if it were a garment. However, the slippage between self-conscious theatricality—in which consumerism emerges as a mode of racial, class, and gender identity construction—and performativity, a system in which the reiteration of "regulatory norms" (2) of such categories calls subjects into being—is precisely the problem that Larsen's novellas explore. As dress and adornment mark a liminal boundary between self and world, consumerism does not merely demonstrate the individual consumer's attempts at identity construction; it also vividly depicts the forces that militate against such self-construction. Larsen's characters use dress, adornments, and object culture to metonymize erotic, racial, class, and gendered desires. Through the reading of costume, decor, color, and light, I examine both the pleasures and the consequences of Larsen's characters' efforts at bodily self-fashioning.

As Larsen's fiction shows, however, the acceptance of consumerist theatricality subjects African American women to a particular set of risks. African American women in the early twentieth century felt particular pressure to avoid the labels of "exotic"" and "primitive." As part of his principle of "sober economy," for example, Booker T. Washington urged an aesthetic of primness upon middle-class black women, imposing dress codes on the teachers and students at the Tuskegee Institute and Fisk University.[1] More generally, the ascendance of the heroine as consumer runs the risk of reproducing women's role in a culture dependent upon what feminist anthropologist Gayle Rubin calls "the traffic in women" (177), which reduces women to objects of exchange and reinforces homosocial bonds between men. Middle-class women offered no possibilities of productive labor may become, in Charlotte Perkins Gilman's phrase, "priestesses of consumption" (118), increasingly dependent on their husbands to supply the capital for their consumer habits. As the heroines of Larsen's fiction appropriate selfhood through performance,

they are drawn into uncomfortable proximity with the figures of the actress and the prostitute, women who are defined by, but manipulate, their
own commodity status and who were frequently racial and ethnic minorities. However, as the rise of consumer culture offered women new
access to the public sphere, late-nineteenth- and early-twentieth-century
narratives of female consumption—among them Stephen Crane's *Maggie*
(1893), Theodore Dreiser's *Sister Carrie* (1900), Anzia Yezierska's *Bread
Givers* (1925), and Jessie Fauset's *Plum Bun* (1929) as well as Larsen's
own—lend particular insight into the yearnings of middle-class women
for political and social autonomy.[2] By forging narrative economies in
which African American women must constantly vacillate between the
role of consumer and that of object of consumption, Larsen's fiction provides a particularly compelling example of how black female identities
may be both enabled and endangered by the possibility of consumerist
masquerade.[3]

The Consuming Desires of Helga Crane

Larsen's childhood experiences of racism, nativism,
and class disenfranchisement fueled the desires of Helga Crane, the heroine of *Quicksand,* to attain a middle-class African American identity
through consumption. Born in the 1890s, Larsen was the daughter of a
white Danish immigrant mother and a black father, believed to have emi-
grated to the United States from the Danish Virgin Islands. Before Larsen
was three, her mother married another white Dane, leaving Larsen as
the only black member of a white household.[4] Whether out of compassion or disdain, Larsen's mother and stepfather sent her to a boarding
school associated with Fisk University and then to the university itself;
her contact with her family appears to have ended in her teenage years.
She had a short career as a teacher at Fisk, where she deeply resented
the codes for dress and behavior that Washington imposed, and then
briefly married Elmer Imes, a scion of the African American elite. After
a bitter divorce, Larsen returned to her career as a nurse, and remained
estranged from her family for the rest of her life. At her death in 1960,
her sister denied her existence. Perhaps because of a personal history
shot through with racial, class, and ethnic conflict, Larsen became deeply
committed to attaining middle-class security—a desire repeatedly voiced,
yet rarely realized, by her heroines.[5]

The conflict between corporeal fantasies of middle-class desire and
bodily realities of race and gender drives Helga Crane's narrative. The
child of a white immigrant mother and black father, Helga is stifled by
the homogenous atmosphere of Naxos, the Tuskegee-inspired black
college where she teaches. While Helga longs passionately for beauty,

attempting to craft a "commodity aesthetic" by arranging herself and her world when she has the opportunity to do so, she is reduced to commodity status through her frequent association with the very objects she desires. As Jean-Christophe Agnew explains, a "commodity aesthetic" implies a collapse of boundaries between the self and the desired object, "celebrat[ing] these moments when the boundaries between the self and the commodity world collapse in the act of the purchase. Such an aesthetic regards acculturation as if it were a form of consumption and consumption, in turn, not as a form of waste or use, but as deliberate and informed accumulation" (135). By focusing on the moment of collapse of boundaries between self and other, Agnew fails to call attention to the consequence of such a fragmentation of the self, especially for nonwhite and female subjects. Once Helga senses the failure of her commodity aesthetic, she marries a preacher and returns to the rural South, believing that marriage, children, and sexuality will fulfill her sense of longing. At the close of the novel, the realities of reproduction trump Helga's dreams of consumer desire: trapped in a claustrophobic cycle of pregnancy and childbirth, Helga is left with nothing but the fantasy of "freedom and cities" (Larsen 135).

Considering Helga's narrative in the context of women's roles as both consumers and objects of consumption illuminates a set of issues in the novel usually given scant critical attention. Several critics have explored at least one facet of Larsen's use of color imagery, for example, but few have focused on Larsen's extensive and complicated poetics of color.[6] In addition, almost no critical attention has been devoted to Larsen's dense and textured descriptions of costume, light, art objects, and decor. Yet the modern department store, perhaps the most important consumer institution of the 1920s, supplies the backdrop for Larsen's lush poetics of color and description. Early-twentieth-century innovations in the production of color, glass, and light revolutionized department store merchandising and thus accelerated the rise of consumer culture. In contrast to the relatively stable color system that prevailed in most of the nineteenth century, by the early twentieth century advances in the dyeing process offered over a thousand shades and hues; neon lighting and mass-produced plate glass theatricalized the experience of shopping. Window trimmers were encouraged not to merely arrange piles of objects, as had been characteristic of Victorian displays, but to create coherent scenes of luxurious living, tableaux that focused more intensely on objects than on the characters who used or wore them. Display designers organized the shopwindows of major department stores by color, exploiting the range of hues in one color, or created vibrant contrasts by using a different color in each window of the store.[7] In *Quicksand,*

Larsen uses the color vocabulary of the 1920s to underscore the especially liminal position of African American women with respect to the burgeoning consumer culture.

Like the window trimmers, Larsen employs color to create a harmonious interplay between the bodies of her characters and the signifiers of bourgeois sophistication that they crave. In addition, however, she enlists color imagery to code her characters within a feminine trajectory of sensuality, marriage, and reproduction. Larsen's characters self-consciously manipulate bodily surfaces to convey interior states: when Helga quits Harlem for Denmark, for example, she chooses "as a symbol" of her decision a "cobwebby black net [dress] touched with orange" in which she resembles "something about to fly" (56). Larsen consistently links the colors green and red to her heroines' sexuality; the name of Helga's husband, the Reverend Pleasant Green, signifies both the erotic thralldom that draws Helga to him and the fecundity that will characterize Helga's married life. Red carries conventional associations of uncontrolled female eroticism: having mistakenly wandered into church wearing "a clinging red dress," Helga is characterized by the women surrounding her as "a scarlet woman," "a pore los' Jezebel" (118), as if Helga's costume were identical with her sexual desires. The last name of Irene Redfield, the heroine of *Passing*, literalizes through its juxtaposition of red and green the heroine's conflict between her own desires and her commitment to the roles of mother and wife. Advancing the heroines' sexual conflicts through color, Larsen offers us a way of seeing that operates in tandem with the consumer aesthetics of the era.

Rather than creating an opposition between beautiful object and body, Larsen fuses the two, applying the new color vocabulary of the era to her characters. She challenges the racist aesthetic coded into the binary of white and black by creating a multihued spectrum of racial coloration, presenting both her light- and dark-skinned black characters in the vocabulary of art and tasteful pleasures. Faces range from "ivory" to "alabaster" to "mahogany"—materials used for decorating wealthy bodies or furnishing homes of the well-to-do. "Tea" and "biscuits," food for the upper middle class, figure Helga Crane's feet and Brian Redfield's fingers. The students at Naxos appear in shades of "ebony, bronze, and gold." At a nightclub in Harlem, Helga marvels "[f]or the hundredth time" at the various "gradations within this oppressed race of hers. A dozen shades slid by. There was sooty black, shiny black, taupe, mahogany, bronze, copper, gold, orange, yellow, peach, ivory, pinky white, pastry white" (59).[8] In the equation of "shade" and "person," Larsen aestheticizes and celebrates the diversity of Harlem; even as she does so, however, she risks reifying its subjects as commodities for audience consumption.

The aesthetic of the shopwindow dominates *Quicksand* from its first scene, in which Helga Crane frames herself with commodities. The interplay of light and shadow focuses the reader's attention on Helga:

> Only a single reading lamp, dimmed by a great black and red shade, made a pool of light in the blue Chinese carpet, on the bright covers of the books which she had taken down from their long shelves, on the white pages of the opened one selected, on the shining brass crowded with many-colored nasturtiums beside her on the low table, and on the oriental silk which covered the stool at her slim feet. . . . This was her rest, this intentional isolation for a short while in the evening, this little time in her own attractive room with her own books. (1)

Contrasts emerge, however, between woman as consumer and arranger of art and woman as art object, as the narrator goes on to admire Helga's "skin like yellow satin," "well-turned limbs," and a "sharply cut face." Helga initially seems a model of bourgeois feminist self-possession: with "her own attractive room" filled with "her own books," she establishes selfhood through the ownership of things. Despite her felicitous taste, however, the decorative rhetoric that surrounds Helga suggests that she, too, is a potential and alluring object of possession. In this tableau, Larsen intimates that Helga's narrative will vacillate between the two poles of woman as consumer and woman as object of consumption.[9]

Larsen contrasts Helga's elegance with the factory-like milieu of Naxos, the black college where she teaches.[10] Larsen characterizes the students of the college as "products" (3); the college, Helga tells us, was "a machine," "a big knife with ruthlessly sharp edges ruthlessly cutting all to a pattern" (4). Helga's passion for elegant clothes in sensual, "queer" colors—"dark purples, royal blues, rich greens, deep reds"—and "soft, luxurious" fabrics (18), Larsen explains, has always been at odds with the aesthetic of sober economy on which Naxos was founded. Helga's dissatisfaction with Naxos, we learn, has been amplified by a white minister who has come to the school to preach a version of Washington's critique of consumption: "he hoped, he sincerely hoped, that they wouldn't become avaricious and grasping, thinking only of adding to their earthly goods . . . it was their duty to be satisfied in the estate to which they had been called, hewers of wood and drawers of water" (3).

Helga is desperate to restore to Naxos's black female students the love of color that she believes to be part of their "inherent racial love of gorgeousness" (18). "One of the loveliest sights Helga had ever seen," Larsen writes, "had been a sooty black girl decked out in a flaming orange dress, which a horrified matron had next day consigned to the dyer. Why, she wondered, didn't someone write *A Plea for Color?*" (18).[11] Despite the primitivist overtones of her sentiments, in her desire for "a plea for color" Helga craves not only a diversity of colors in art and clothing but an appreciation of heterogeneity within the race as well. In her view, the "sooty black girl" can be just as beautiful as the amber-hued Helga, if her beauty is properly framed. Watching one of her few friends at the school, she wonders "just what form of vanity was that had induced an intelligent girl like Margaret Creighton to turn what was probably nice live crinkly hair, perfectly suited to her smooth dark skin and agreeable round features, into a dead, straight, greasy, ugly mass" (14). The contrast between "live" and "dead" is significant; if the hair, a synecdoche of self, can be deadened through an internalization of white standards of beauty, the consequences to the body and psyche seem equally threatening.[12] Helga rejects the assimilation to the white ideals supported by Washington's dress and style regulations, choosing the elite consumables she craves as a means to craft an autonomous aesthetic.

In her attempts to reclaim individual beauty and style, however, Helga has no choice but to enter a pattern of pecuniary emulation like that described by Thorstein Veblen in *The Theory of the Leisure Class*, in which she must imitate the spending patterns of leisure-class women. Helga's efforts to recuperate the material goods she lacks and the spiritual fulfillment she seeks require that she masquerade as a woman of means. First buying her way out of the Jim Crow car of the northbound train, she spends her money too quickly in Chicago on "things which she wanted, but did not need and certainly could not afford," including a book and a "rare old tapestry purse" (35, 32). In making these purchases, Helga compensates for her feeling of rejection by her white uncle and his new wife, who have refused to see her. Using these objects as both frame and mask, she can imaginatively possess the sense of history she lacks and simultaneously emphasize her own sense of beauty and rarity. Forced into competition with her white middle-class relatives who have rejected her, Helga uses material objects to reinforce a tenuous sense of self.

Helga's shopping, however, risks reiterating the status of woman as an object of consumption. For this reason, her consumerism parallels her association with prostitution, a trope recurring throughout the novel. Overqualified for domestic work and undertrained for middle-class employment, "it seemed that in that whole energetic place nobody wanted her services. At least not the kind that she offered. A few men, both white and black, offered her money, but the price of the money was too dear. Helga Crane did not feel inclined to pay for it" (34). Larsen's exploitation of metaphors of price and value embodies Helga's vacillation between consumer and object of consumption. Even as her economic situation draws her dangerously close to prostitution, in which her "services" would become a commodity for sale, Larsen constructs Helga as a consumer, with her sexuality turned into payment for the money men would offer her. Helga's consuming habits provide a means to control the way her body is perceived, thus serving as the only alternative to her intense bodily self-consciousness.

Helga is not the only character who uses costume and decor as extensions of the performativity of the gendered, classed, and racial body. In the depiction of Anne Grey, Helga's mentor among the Harlem elite, Larsen uses commodity aesthetics to show the sense of belonging to an American haute bourgeoisie that Harlem's elite enjoys. Helga moves to Harlem and is befriended by Anne, a wealthy African American war widow who "ape[s]" the "clothes," "manners," and "ways of living" (48) of the white upper classes yet claims contempt for all whites; championing African Americans in abstraction, she responds to black cultural expression with disgust. Ironically, despite her name that suggests a mixture of races and colors, she is particularly appalled by miscegenation and snubs Audrey Denney, a light-skinned African American who lives downtown rather than in Harlem and gives mixed parties (61). Regardless of her sexual and racial repression, however, Anne has achieved the harmonious interplay between her body and physical space that Helga craves, appearing excluded from the nexus of consumer and consumed. Ensconced in Anne's home, Helga is struck not only by the beauty of her things but by their voluminousness:

> Beds with long, tapering posts to which tremendous age lent dignity and interest, bonneted old highboys, tables that might be by Duncan Phyfe, and others whose ladder backs gracefully climbed the delicate wall panels. These historic things mingled harmoniously and comfortably with brass-bound Chinese tea-chests, luxurious deep chairs and davenports, tiny tables of gay color, a lacquered jade-green settee with gleaming black satin cushions, lustrous Eastern rugs, ancient copper, Japanese prints, some fine etchings, a profusion of precious bric-a-brac, and endless shelves filled with books. (44)

Despite the quantity of Anne's possessions, Helga does not characterize her as vulgar because her "mingling" of styles signifies Anne's successful entry into an Anglo-African American middle class. In its interplay of vivid colors and orientalist motifs, the description of Anne's space repeats certain elements of Helga's rooms, but here Larsen adds "historic things" metonymizing the American past, emphasizing the sense of tradition that Helga lacks. Moreover, Anne's membership in the black elite seems to lend her the bodily self-confidence Helga does not possess: in Helga's view, Anne "possessed an impeccably fastidious taste in clothes, knowing what suited her and wearing it with an air of unconscious assurance" (45).

Nonetheless, the claustrophobic quality of the middle-class African American world, signaled by the excessive quality of Anne Grey's decor, proves stifling for Helga. Anne emerges as a symptom of what Helga found so distasteful at Naxos: the mimicry of Anglo-American mores, interests, and aesthetics in an attempt to construct a black bourgeoisie. To extricate herself from this constricting world, Helga quits Harlem for her Danish relatives, believing that to be adored for her otherness will assuage the "lack somewhere" (7) she has always felt. Helga's foray into white European culture forcefully demonstrates, however, that her efforts to differentiate herself from black America must come at a price that eventually proves "too dear" (34).

As Larsen positions Helga as the archconsumer she has longed to become in her years of aesthetic deprivation, she simultaneously marks Helga's white relatives' desires to craft her as an exotic primitive.[13] Helga realizes quickly that in Denmark she is to be "[a] decoration. A curio. A peacock" (73); her Danish relatives promote her, and thus their own social status, by clothing her in exotic styles and fashions reminiscent of blues divas (duCille 94–97) and Josephine Baker, who hovers on the margins of the Copenhagen section of the novel (Wall 103).[14] Larsen alerts the reader to her heroine's problematic status in Europe through the wildly excessive clothes her relatives purchase for her:

> There were batik dresses in which mingled indigo, orange, green, vermilion, and black; dresses of velvet and chiffon in screaming colors, blood-red, sulphur-yellow, sea-green and one black and white thing in striking combination. There was a black Manila shawl strewn with great scarlet and lemon flowers, a leopard-skin coat, a glittering opera-cape. There were turban-like hats of metallic silks, feathers and furs, strange jewelry, enameled or set with odd semi-precious stones, a nauseous Eastern perfume, shoes with dangerously high heels. (74)

One might argue that the "black and white thing in striking combination" is exactly what her Danish relative relatives would like her to be. They encourage her to "capitalize on her difference" (Wall 101), to exaggerate her blend of racial heritages. Larsen repeats the same images she uses earlier to characterize Helga's aesthetic but exaggerates them:

orientalist motifs become "nauseous" and explicitly primitive, reducing Helga to an object of exotic colonial adventures like the leopard whose skins will make her coat. Whereas both Helga and Anne excel at creating a harmonious interplay of color, here colors are "mingled" to intoxicating effect. The "screaming" colors Aunt Katrina and Uncle Poul urge upon her overwhelm the subtlety Helga seeks in her aesthetic arrangements. Through Helga's clothes, Larsen foreshadows that Helga's accession to consumerism is inseparable from the evacuation of selfhood characteristic of the commodity.

While for the first time in her life she possesses both the money and the comforts she has always desired, Helga now has little to fill her time but shopping and arranging herself aesthetically. At first she revels in the sensuous consumptive pleasures she has been denied. In Chicago she had skipped meals to buy accessories; in Denmark "an endless and tempting array" of food satisfies her cravings (77). While not much of a skater, the "attractive skating-things" (78) she can wear mitigate a few tumbles. In striking contrast to her previous experience as a consumer, however, here Helga is allowed to make no decisions: her aunt and uncle select her costumes for the many social events she attends. Helga's sense of her own objectification by the white Danes is underscored by the word that falls "freely, audibly" (73), from their lips—*Den Sorte*, the Danish word for the color black. Larsen shows that Helga's desire for aestheticization has the potential to backfire with a vengeance: having previously argued that blacks should feel pride in the heterogeneity of their colors, here she is reduced to no more than a color.

The closure of the Denmark section of the novel makes clear the extent to which Helga's efforts to control the representations of her body have come at the expense of a growing ambivalence toward the materiality of her own body. During her residency in Denmark, Helga has become increasingly disgusted with her own aura of difference and its sexualization by her Danish companions. At a vaudeville performance, for example, Helga is appalled by a pair of black performers who sing ragtime tunes while "pounding their thighs, slapping their hands together, twisting their legs, waving their abnormally long arms, throwing their bodies about with a loose ease" (83). The sexual language Larsen uses here, stressing the sinuosity and flexibility of black bodies, signals Helga's anxiety about the possible similarity between these bodies and her own. Helga displays a comparable ambivalence when Axel Olsen, an artist who is one of Helga's suitors, paints a portrait of her depicting her as an exotic primitive. Although Larsen never steps outside Helga's point of view to describe the portrait accurately, Helga interprets it as "not herself at all, but some disgusting sensual creature with her features"

(89).[15] By letting Helga's point of view predominate, Larsen shows Helga caught between binaries of racial and gendered modes of representation. Through her assumption that the painting represents her as a "disgusting sensual creature," we see that she cannot imagine any other alternative to the role of (implicitly white, nonsexual) "lady" than that of explicitly sexualized black primitive. Realizing how the gaze of her Danish relatives has intensified her own feelings of objectification, Helga seeks to reclaim a sense of her beauty and rarity by returning to Harlem.

The novel's title, *Quicksand*, however, reminds us that changes in location inevitably fail to heal Helga's anxiety and ambivalence. As the novel moves toward its conclusion, Larsen introduces both the continuity and the tension between erotic and consumer desires, for Helga begins to believe that sexuality will provide the solace she has been seeking. As suggested by the etymological link of the word "consumption" to the word "consummation" (Bowlby 20), consumerism implies an absorption of the purchased object by the self, an erotically charged but temporary suspension of boundaries. Having rejected Axel's marriage proposal and realizing she has lost a chance at love with the erudite Dr. Anderson, principal of Naxos, Helga undergoes a religious conversion and marries a Southern preacher, the Reverend Mr. Pleasant Green. Larsen represents Helga's embrace of religion as a capitulation to the sexual desires she has repressed throughout her past. Wandering into a church, she is horrified, then entranced, by the press of bodies, which recalls the vaudeville dancers in Denmark; her resistance swept away, she yields to the "brutal desire to shout and sling herself about" (113).[16] In the orgasmic release that accompanies her conversion, Helga allows the reverend to accompany her to her hotel; the two are married in the "seductive repentance" (118) of the next morning. Eroticism initially replaces consumerism, as Helga admits to herself that "things . . . hadn't been, weren't enough for her" (116).

In the shift from consumption to consummation, Helga for the first time experiences complete peace of mind. As she claims to herself that she has transcended the world of things, her religious convictions and sexual satisfaction mitigate "the choppy lines of the shining oak furniture" and "the awful horribleness of the religious pictures" (121). Significantly, Larsen figures Helga's newfound comfort as "anaesthetic" (118), suggesting not just the soothing of pain but the muting of her sensitivity to art. Attempting to aestheticize her surroundings by "subduing [their] cleanly scrubbed ugliness . . . with soft inoffensive beauty," Helga abjures her previously sensuous tastes, now regarding them as "fripperies" (121). Offering rural black women a form of aesthetic redemption and renouncing her own desires, Helga at first appears to have resolved the opposition between consumer and consumed that has characterized the entire novel.

In the final section of the novel, Larsen emphasizes the contrast between the material self-fashioning of the black urban female body, represented by Helga, and the bodily realities of black rural women. The lives of the "dark undecorated" (121) women Helga encounters in Alabama are organized by a seemingly endless cycle "of births and christenings, of loves and marriages, of deaths and funerals" (121). Far removed from the tableaux of urban department store shopwindows, to them Helga is simply an "uppity No'the'nah" (119). The presence of Clementine Richards signals the new irrelevance of Helga's aesthetic. As if Axel's painting of Helga had come to life, Clementine is "a strapping black beauty of magnificent Amazon proportions and bold shining eyes of jet-like hardness. A person of awesome appearance. All chains, strings of beads, jingling bracelets, flying ribbons, feathery neck-pieces, and flowery hats" (119). While in their primitivist characteristics the representations of Helga in Denmark and Clementine in the South seem markedly similar, these two efforts at black female self-fashioning differ significantly. Where the "barbaric bracelets" (70) and wildly colored clothes Helga's Danish relatives urge on her increase her sense of immobility, Clementine is all motion, "jingling bracelets" and "flying ribbons" (119). Where Helga's white audience fetishistically views her body as a series of discrete parts—"[s]uperb eyes . . . color . . . neck column . . . yellow . . . hair . . . alive . . . wonderful" (71)—the physically imposing and sexually autonomous (as Larsen's labeling her an "Amazon" suggests) Clementine resists such anatomization. Divorced from an urban world of surfaces, Clementine seems to have absorbed the pleasures of bodily self-fashioning without assuming its risks.

Near the end of the novel, the conflict between urban consumerist fantasy and rural bodily reality escalates even further. Wishing that her body could again become a static art-object, "something on which to hang lovely fabrics" (123), Helga now moves with "lumbering haste" (125), weakened from her repeated pregnancies. Worn out from the birth and death of her fourth child, she fantasizes a return to the middle-class world of "freedom and cities" (135). However, these abstract ideals are represented by the specifics of commodity culture: "clothes and books . . . the sweet mingled smell of Houbigant and cigarettes in softly lighted rooms filled with inconsequential chatter and laughter and sophisticated tuneless music" (135). Helga claims she will "retrieve all these agreeable, desired things" (135) but succumbs to her postpartum weakness instead.

One might suggest that it is the inexorability of consumer desire that Larsen's novel documents so compellingly, for both in the form and con-

tent of the novel Larsen creates an aesthetic lens through which her heroine is only visible as framed by commodities. In the gap between the
novel's last two paragraphs, the narrative voice shifts out of Helga's consciousness to that of a distant narrator. While Helga has dreamed of
clothes and books, of perfume and jazz, the novel's last paragraph strips
Helga of her individuality: "And hardly had she left her bed and become able to walk again without pain, hardly had the children returned
from the homes of the neighbors, when she began to have her fifth child"
(135). With its first word, "And," its grim repetition of the word "hardly,"
and its use of the pronoun "she" rather than Helga's name, the final sentence underscores the cyclical, impersonal nature of Helga's reproductive state. In the earlier portions of the novel, Helga has manipulated
the practices of consumption and adornment as a means of individual-
izing her body and simultaneously of differentiating it from the material realities of working-class female black life depicted in the final section
of the novel. However, the last line of the novel, with its generalizing
nature, transforms Helga's body into part of the mass of rural black women
in labor.[17] With this grim closing gesture, Larsen signals the triumph of
the material realities of race, class, and gender over the performative identity Helga has struggled so poignantly to claim.

Passing *and the Class Politics of Bodily Style*

In contrast to *Quicksand*, in which passing as middle
class emerges as an attempt to appropriate a coherent racial identity, the
racial masquerade of *Passing* permits the appropriation of a class identity. Where in *Quicksand* Larsen demonstrates through the character of
Helga Crane the risks to the self of controlling one's bodily representations through performative self-fashioning, *Passing* enacts these risks
through its style, metonymizing the black female body through representations of the material world: colors, light, objects, and decor. While
Passing does not use consumption as a metaphor of self in the consistent manner of its predecessor, the critique of consumption Larsen provides in *Quicksand* complicates the sexual and racial repression many
readers have located in *Passing*. The "aches," "passions," and "wild desires" (145) of the heroines have not only an erotic inflection, but a
consumerist one as well.[18]

Passing maps the efforts of competing heroines, Irene Redfield and
Clare Kendry, to control representations of the black female body. The
two are former childhood friends, the first a comfortably affluent Harlem
dweller and the second a formerly impoverished orphan who has passed
to marry a wealthy white man, Jack Bellew. Clare occupies a shadowy

racial borderland, masquerading as a white woman in her marriage yet making sorties into Harlem to recover the black world she has lost through passing. Allowing her husband to call her "Nig" (170) and joking about a possible touch of the tar brush, she performs a version of near-white femininity for her husband. Irene herself is involved in the merchandising of blackness through her race work; in close proximity with the white intellectual elite, for whom Harlem may serve as literary or political material, she is eager to promote a domesticated version of black femininity.[19] Each heroine is thus engaged with the relationship between racial passing, upward mobility, and self-commodification; Clare accepts, while Irene denies, the relationship between these terms.

Irene and Clare renew their acquaintance through a chance meeting in the segregated rooftop tearoom of Chicago's Drayton Hotel. Irene has repaired there in a state of near collapse after an unsuccessful shopping trip: six stores have failed to yield the sketchbook she has promised her son. Larsen's setting of the scene suggests the dizzying and threatening possibilities inherent in a consumer world of surfaces, in which "the glass of the shop-windows threw out a blinding radiance" (146). Irene initially appears an unsophisticated consumer, a woman who will shop all day in inferno-like heat to please a child and end the day unsatisfied. Clare appears to have made more felicitous choices: clad in a "fluttering dress of green chiffon whose mingled pattern of narcissuses, jonquils, and hyacinths was a pleasant reminder of cool spring days," she has selected things that were "just right for the weather, thin and cool without being mussy, as summer things were apt to be" (148). Irene is intensely self-conscious of her body and its possible failings: while Clare stares at her, Irene "slid her eyes down. What, she wondered, could be the reason for such persistent attention" (149). An amalgam of social envy and erotic anxiety structures Irene's reactions to Clare; Irene, for instance, judges Clare's frank smile "just a shade too provocative" for the waiter who comes to take her order.[20] With Irene and Clare's chance meeting, Larsen sets in motion a Veblenesque pattern of emulation. As Veblen writes, emulative dyads create a "chronic dissatisfaction" within the "normal average individual" with respect to one's perceived class superiors (31). Irene's self-conscious response to Clare's stare entails just such a sense of inferiority; intensely envious of Clare's success in the white world even as she rejects it, Irene unconsciously emulates Clare's performance of whiteness.

Consumer spaces in which bodies are on display become sites for passing; simultaneously, however, they objectify the subjects who circulate through them. Irene gazes at Clare as if she were the inhabitant of a showwindow, underscoring the motivations behind both women's efforts to pass. Each is passing, Irene for a day and Clare for life, to enjoy the pleasures of the white leisure class. Irene justifies her passing to herself as a magical self-transformation in which she has no agency: "It was, she thought, like being wafted upward on a magic carpet to another world, pleasant, quiet, and strangely remote from the sizzling one that she had left below" (147). On the other hand, Clare is aware that her passing contains much more dangerous possibilities. Having crossed the color line to marry Jack, a man "with untold gold" (159), Clare passes despite, if not because of, the constant risk of exposure. That consumerism becomes a site for both the pleasures and dangers of passing is suggested in Clare's description of being snubbed by her black childhood friends in public places: "once I met Margaret Hammer in Marshall Field's. I'd have spoken, was on the very point of doing it, but she cut me dead . . . I assure you that from the way she looked through me, even I was uncertain whether I was actually there in the flesh or not" (154). Clare's statement makes vividly clear the possibilities for both self-extinction and self-gratification in the act of consumption. "The cut" administered by the phallicly named Margaret Hammer engenders complete self-effacement and an ironic reversal: where Clare has passed to eradicate her sense of invisibility as a working-class black woman, she is now reduced to complete invisibility as a leisure-class white woman.

Jacquelyn McLendon notes that the women spend the afternoon trading signs of "whiteness and middle-class status" (113) to reinforce their developing homosocial bond. Smoking, which literalizes the link between consumption and bodily absorption, constitutes one of these signs. Cigarettes serve as a synecdoche for consumption in early-twentieth-century culture, for, as Oscar Wilde writes in *The Picture of Dorian Gray*, "cigarettes are the perfect type of the perfect pleasure. They are exquisite, and they leave one unsatisfied" (8). Rachel Bowlby observes that cigarettes were "one of the most ubiquitous and widely advertised late nineteenth-century commodities," and "could connote the indolence of the beautiful life of the dandy but also . . . the sexually transgressive associations of the independent 'new woman'" (7, 8). Connoting both the dandy's sense of style and the New Woman's freedom, here cigarettes also mark the clandestine erotics of Irene and Clare's relationship and the class privilege that permits such pleasures: less attractive and less tasteful women, as we learn later in the novel, do not smoke. Cigarettes also lend themselves to Larsen's poetics of color: the smoke in which Irene and Clare wrap themselves blends both light and dark, metaphorizing their passing and veiling their mutual attraction. Blurring the boundary between body and commodity, transforming black and white into ambiguous gray, smoking concretizes the aesthetics of both passing and consumption.

Larsen's means of representing the near-white female body helps to expose the class valences of racial passing. Her depiction of Gertrude Martin, a childhood friend of both women who has also married a white man, makes clear that the kind of passing Clare and Irene practice is coextensive with comforts of the upper middle class. The circumstances of Gertrude's passing are different from Clare's: her white husband knows her origins, as do most of her friends.[21] Gertrude's sartorial style, or lack thereof, places her in a vastly different category than that which Clare and Irene occupy. While Gertrude's racial passing is successful, her class passing is in doubt:

> Gertrude . . . looked as if her husband might be a butcher. . . . She had grown broad, fat almost, and though there were no lines on her large white face, its very smoothness was somehow prematurely ageing. Her black hair was clipt, and by some unfortunate means all the live curliness had gone from it. Her overtrimmed Georgette crepe dress was too short and showed an appalling amount of leg, stout legs in sleazy stockings a vivid rose-beige shade. Her plump hands were newly and not too competently manicured—for the occasion, probably. (167)

Gertrude's bad bob—which Larsen implies has endured chemical straightening procedures—her shoddy manicure, and her ill-fitting dress bespeak failed class emulation. Each aspect of Gertrude's body suggests the failure of her efforts to rise above her class. Moreover, the colors Larsen uses to characterize Gertrude are stark and ugly compared with the subtle shading of Irene and Clare. Successful passing comes to be associated with upper-middle-class blacks like Irene and Clare, for despite Clare's poor upbringing, she was born with "that dim suggestion of polite insolence with which a few women are born and which some acquire with the coming of riches or importance" (161). Not only sartorial style but physical beauty comes to be an element of successful passing.

Perhaps for this reason, images of the sexualized female body dominate Irene's imagination as her frustration with Clare increases. Irene labors to diminish the threat Clare poses to her through repeated references to Clare as either an actress or a prostitute, figures seen as nearly identical in their sexual commodification in early-twentieth-century thought. For example, Irene discourages Clare's coming to the Welfare League Ball, a gathering of the black elite and white sympathizers, with the suggestion that she will be taken for a "lady of easy virtue looking for trade"

(199). However, Irene denies that she maintains the same relationship with white spectators as Clare does. She performs an unthreatening version of black middle-class femininity, transforming Harlem itself into a marketable product for white audiences through her race work. Clare transforms her body into a marketable product for the pleasure of white spectators in order to secure the life she wanted, although at a price; Irene denies the extent to which she, too, participates in marketing African American identity for white consumption.

Irene's attempt to distance herself from Clare simultaneously represents an effort to extricate herself from the cycle of emulation in which both women are engaged. When Clare arrives at the Redfield home to prepare for the party, Irene feels painfully inadequate in comparison with her friend:

> Clare, exquisite, golden, fragrant, flaunting, in a stately gown of shining black taffeta, whose long, full skirt lay in graceful folds about her slim golden feet; her glistening hair drawn smoothly back into a small twist at the nape of her neck; her eyes sparkling like dark jewels. Irene, with her new rose-coloured chiffon frock ending at her knees, and her cropped curls, felt dowdy and commonplace. (203)

Larsen's description sets up an ideal to which Irene implicitly believes she should aspire. The repetition of adjectives has the air of an advertisement, and Clare herself speaks in the flattering language of an ad, causing Irene to remark to herself on her overuse of superlatives (204, 209). While Larsen renders Clare as a static object, description without action, her portrayal of Irene renders her painfully embodied; one can sense her embarrassment even in her exposed knees. Through references to her short pink dress and cropped hair, Larsen transforms Irene into a slightly more sophisticated version of Gertrude Martin, emulating the successful passer in vain. Clare's "exquisite" beauty, which facilitates her pass, undermines Irene's sense of class position, the one thing in which she feels secure.[22]

Throughout *Passing*, Larsen uses objects to metonymize the black female body; as the novel draws to a close, the proliferation of these objects prefigures Clare's demise. Attending the party at which Irene becomes convinced of Brian's infidelity, Clare is clothed in colors that recall her racial liminality, "cinnamon-brown" accented with "amber" and "a little golden bowl of a hat" (220). What at first appears a simple description of a cloche comes back to mind moments later, as Irene, with "rage boil[ing] up in her" (221), either smashes or drops a delicate china teacup. The "white fragments" at her feet prefigure the near-white fragments into which Clare's racially ambiguous body will shortly shatter. Arguably, one might hear an echo of Henry James's *The Golden Bowl* (1904) in this scenario. [23] At this juncture, Irene, like Maggie Verver in James's novel, believes that she has secured an understanding of her husband's infidelity, symbolized in James's novel by the flaw in the gilt bowl, once believed to be golden. Larsen brilliantly tropes on James here, racializing, gendering, and classing his metaphor by replacing the golden bowl with the white china teacup. Where Maggie smashes the golden bowl—and thus the fiction of her husband's fidelity—by finding its hidden flaw, Irene simultaneously smashes Clare's near whiteness, her own bourgeois gentility, and the history of miscegenation that both women share. Irene attempts to justify her act to her white friend Hugh Wentworth:

> "It was the ugliest thing that your ancestors, the charming Confederates ever owned. I've forgotten how many thousands of years ago it was that Brian's great-great-grand-uncle owned it. But it has, or had, a good old hoary history. It was brought North by way of the subway. Oh, all right! Be English if you want to and call it the underground." (223)

In smashing the teacup, Irene symbolically obliterates her own history of slavery (implied in Larsen's reference to the "underground," a trope on the Underground Railroad) and miscegenation (suggested in the slippage between "your ancestors" and "Brian's great-great-grand-uncle"). Yet through her use of the teacup, delicate and infinitely breakable, as a symbol of black middle-class female history, Larsen makes clear the tenuousness of light-skinned black middle-class female subjectivity.

While for Clare and Irene racial passing comes to serve as the opposite face of bourgeois consumption, Larsen does present one character who can enjoy class privilege and remain unaffected by the desire for racial transformation: Felise Freeland. As Irene's merger of passing with conspicuous consumption initiated the two women's first encounter, it also brings on the novel's denouement. Arm in arm with the darker-skinned Felise on a shopping trip in midtown Manhattan, Irene experiences a comfortable homosocial bond, in contrast to her feelings while in physical proximity with Clare. The women collide with Jack Bellew, who instantly discerns the truth. Surveying him "with the cool gaze of appraisal she reserved for mashers" (226), Irene moves on, explaining to her friend, "I don't believe I've ever gone native in my life except for the sake of convenience, restaurants, theatre tickets, things like that. Never socially I mean, except once. You've just passed the only person that I've ever met disguised as a white woman" (227). Here, the trajectories of consumerism and passing, imbricated throughout the novel, work at cross-purposes. Irene admits to passing to enjoy the pleasures of segregated consumerism, despite its risks of public exposure and humiliation. However, her enjoyment of these pleasures is tainted by the same risks that heighten it. Frightened by the certain results of her encounter with Bellew, Irene gives up her shopping trip, while Felise returns to admiring a coat in a shopwindow.

How might we understand Felise, who, in her own words, "queers" (227) Irene's passing by showing her color in relation to Irene's? Her name alone signifies unambiguous security in her black identity; her confidence contrasts with the vexing liminality of the mulatta. While Felise, too dark to pass, is unembarrassed about exposing Irene, she takes unqualified pleasure in consumerism. Felise counsels Irene to recover from a low mood through "buy[ing] yourself an expensive new frock, child. It always helps. Any time this child gets the blues, it means money out of Dave's pocket" (219). Clare's desire for "things" has caused her to deny her racial identity through a marriage that constantly harbors the risk of exposure; Irene's claim that she only passes to enjoy segregated leisure, given what we see of her activities, suggests that she may pass more often than she cares to admit. Only Felise, who, like Clementine Richards in *Quicksand*, is a minor character given almost no narrative attention, appears to have acknowledged the pleasures of consumerism without fantasizing its transformative possibilities. In contrast to Irene's metaphorizing of literal upward motion into upward mobility at the Drayton, no "magic carpet" "wafts" (147) Felise's guests up to the top of her Harlem apartment building. Their color notwithstanding, they all go up by what Brian calls "nigger-power" (236). Significantly, Felise's apartment may only be reached by walking up stairs, through physical labor; she maintains an awareness of the materiality of the body that Irene has lost in her fantasy of racial and class transformation.

The color spectrum Larsen creates in *Passing* narrows dramatically with the novel's final chapter. A snowstorm covers Harlem; seemingly innocent contrasts of black and white in fact foreshadow Clare and Jack's final encounter. Before the Freelands' party, Irene watches as snow fills in the "ugly irregular gaps" on the sidewalk; as Clare and Irene enter the Freelands' apartment building, they keep to the cement path that "splits" the "whiteness" of the garden. The complementarity of black and white, which Larsen has exploited from the very beginning in her depiction of Clare ("ebony" eyes in an "ivory" skin, for example), returns with an ominous difference.

Jack, having discovered Clare's association with the Redfields, storms the Freelands' party and denounces Clare as "a nigger, a damned dirty nigger!" (238). Even in the moment of Clare's public exposure, Larsen represents her as an aesthetic object; despite the fact that the fictions of her life have just been shattered, Clare stands calm and "composed" (238). As Clare jumps, falls, or is pushed through the window, Irene registers the implications of her loss in a way that reifies Clare even further: "Gone! The soft white face, the bright hair, the disturbing scarlet mouth, the dreaming eyes, the caressing smile, the whole torturing loveliness that had been Clare Kendry. That beauty that had torn at Irene's placid life. Gone! The mocking daring, the gallantry of her pose, the ringing bells of her laughter" (239). Irene verbalizes the fragmentation of Clare's body as it smashes against the sidewalk in her reduction of Clare to a series of parts for the whole. Larsen distributes the synecdoches of Clare's difference onto the darker-skinned members of the party, who, like Clare, undergo a bodily transformation: "the golden brown" of Felise Freeland's "handsome face" had "changed to a queer mauve colour" (241). Brian's "lips" are "purple and trembling" (241). The color purple, of which mauve is a shade, has signified Clare's exoticism from the first page of the novel, as Irene opens the letter that announces Clare's return to New York. In her final juxtaposition of color schemes, Larsen transfers the symbolic colors of race- and class-passing onto the characters who cannot pass. For Irene, who can choose whether to pass, "everything" goes "dark" (242). The color Clare has brought to Irene's monochromatic life is finally subsumed in polarities of black and white.

Through color imagery and the rhetoric of object culture, Larsen crafts a style politics that shows the interrelationship of black middle-class female subjectivity, consumerism, and passing. The melding of passing and consumption in which Irene Redfield and Clare Kendry engage serves as an attempt to deny the material realities of race and gender. For both heroines, the novel's conclusion displays the brutal consequences of these efforts. One dies and one lives, but each is finally reduced to her color.

Conclusion

In her life and her fiction, Nella Larsen attested to the struggle of black female middle-class self-representation in the 1920s. Resenting the Washingtonian aesthetic of sober economy for the banal homogeneity it imposed, she nonetheless realized the risks to black female subjectivity posed by the self-conscious celebration of difference. In her catapult to fame, Larsen embraced aestheticism and consumer pleasures, yet she finished her life as a nurse, returning both to the ethos of service and the uniforms she scorned in her years at Fisk and Tuskegee. Larsen's characters negotiate similar poles, simultaneously representing modes of radical self-fashioning and the failure of those efforts.

The concluding moments of both *Quicksand* and *Passing* reiterate the power of dominant cultural representations of black femininity to diminish the personhood of individual black women: while the intense beauty of Larsen's fiction lies in the celebration of aesthetic pleasures— of color, light, costume, and decor—the final words of both her novellas may provide the most compelling lessons. The material realities of the black female body that each heroine attempts to escape through costume, performance, and self-adornment ultimately prove inexorable. *Quicksand* and *Passing* poignantly document the allure of self-aestheticization for black middle-class women in the 1920s; however, the "quicksands" of Larsen's conclusions remind us at what costs the pleasures of bodily self-fashioning were achieved.

NOTES

1. Washington advocated modest consumption, as exemplified in his belief in the "gospel of the toothbrush," and sharply criticized "showy" blacks who used installment plans to buy items they could not afford (113, 174–75).
2. See Felski's analysis of consumption as a means of increasing women's object status. Despite her pessimism on this score, Felski considers the entrance of women into the public sphere through consumption as an opportunity for increased agency and, ultimately, political power.
3. Doane provides a useful account of women's position between consumer and commodity.
4. See Davis and Larson. Both authors, but particularly Davis, construct Larsen's primary trauma as her "abandonment" by her mother, Marie Larsen. However, Hutchinson's reconstruction of Larsen's relationship with her mother has shown how the compression of Larsen's mixed-race heritage into a homogenous narrative of African American history ignores important elements of her personal history ("Nella").
5. Much of the following supports Carby's contention that *Quicksand*'s importance lies in its status as perhaps "the first text by a black woman to be a conscious narrative of a woman embedded within capitalist social relations" (171). For an essay that has many parallels with both Carby's and my own, see Rhodes.
6. Hostetler provides the most extensive analysis; see also McDowell xviii-xix, xxvii-xxix.
7. See Leach 65 and Abelson 41–44. As Abelson explains, many female shoplifters reported feeling "seduced" into theft by the theatricality of the displays. Among the most influential window trimmers was L. Frank Baum, who wrote *The Art of Decorating Dry Goods Windows* (1900) at the same time as *The Wizard of Oz* (1900). For an analysis of Baum's poetics of color, which might be read provocatively against Larsen, see Culver.
8. Michie reads this catalog, and Larsen's representation of light-skinned black women in general, as part of a pattern of "sororophobic contrasts," female attempts to reject alliances with other women. Such contrasts are implicit in the class conflicts I treat in this essay.
9. Interpreting this first scene in light of the journey trope in African American fiction, Hostetler argues that the tableau imprisons Helga in the first of many social spaces that she must escape to live without hypocrisy (37).
10. As several critics have noted, "Naxos" is an anagram for Saxon. In her wordplay, Larsen suggests that black imitation of white culture produces a distorted

mirror image, whereas Helga consumes in an effort to create an autonomous aesthetic. As Banta observes, Larsen calls upon a Taylorist vocabulary of mass production to differentiate Helga from the Naxos pupils (7, 277).

11. Both Hostetler and Dittmar argue that Helga's desire to beautify the women around her allegorizes the position of the frustrated female artist.

12. Hair is a particularly potent symbol of identity in African American narratives. In James Weldon Johnson's *Autobiography of an Ex-Coloured Man*, for example, the narrator marks his decision to pass for white by shaving his mustache.

13. On white audiences' ostensible craving for the exotic primitive in black culture, see Douglas 98–99; Huggins 84–136; and Levering Lewis 224–29. Hutchinson offers an important critique of the trope of exoticism in African Americanist literary criticism (*Harlem*).

14. Wall gives a detailed analysis of the similarities between Helga and Baker (103–11), underscoring that the difference between the two is in Baker's ability to manipulate her image as exotic primitive, while Helga acquiesces to it. Silverman also contextualizes Helga's status as exotic primitive against Baker. On Baker's consumer habits, see Rose 113, 131, 143; on her love of sumptuous clothes, many of which she designed herself, see Baker and Chase 120–21, 275.

15. Given the renewed biographical interest in Larsen's mother, it seems crucial that the only viewer who objects to the dominant critical praise of the portrait is the Danish maid Marie, who bears Larsen's mother's name. Marie is the only Danish character who does not exoticize Helga by viewing her within a pre-existing system of representation. Attention to Marie's brief appearance in the novel might constitute one step in reconsidering the role of the white mother that, as Hutchinson has shown, is frequently occluded from critiques of Larsen's work ("Nella").

16. On Larsen's representation of the conversion scene in relation to nineteenth-century theories of the spontaneous agency of the crowd, see Esteve.

17. As Cutter argues, the stifling end of *Quicksand* leaves us, in Barthesian terms, as consumers of the text, whereas the ambiguity of the conclusion of *Passing* transforms us into textual producers. My thinking departs from Cutter's primarily in that the binary of consumption and production creates a false opposition that early twentieth-century understandings of consumer culture do not fully support.

18. Many critics have commented on the erotic dynamics of Irene and Clare's relationship. McDowell has read the novel as a narrative of repressed lesbian desire. Blackmer offers a fascinating reading of Irene's anxieties around Clare as a form of "lesbian panic," arguing that Larsen critically revises the erotic triangle of Gertrude Stein's *Melanctha*. Blackmore has located male homoerotic impulses in the representation of Brian Redfield, who considers sex "a joke" and yearns to flee Manhattan for Brazil.

19. DuCille offers the best reading of the complementarity of Clare and Irene, arguing that the dialectical relationship between the two women figures the dialectic of the Harlem Renaissance itself: modernism versus late Victorianism, free love versus marriage, passing versus race pride. In duCille's reading, Clare's return to Harlem suggests a yearning for the respectability she has lost in crossing to the white world.

20. As Brody suggests, Irene's response to Clare's behavior may inhere in the fact that the waiter is black (1058).

21. Gertrude appears only once in the novel, at the tea party where Irene discovers Jack Bellew's hatred of blacks. In their mutual dupe of Bellew, Gertrude and Irene function as what Robinson calls "in-group clairvoyants" (716), the third parties necessary for a successful pass.

22. Brody also underscores the element of class competition in *Passing*, suggesting that Clare's rags-to-riches narrative might be read as the "embodiment of Irene's bourgeois fantasies" (1060).

23. As Davis notes, Larsen read James for her librarian's examinations at the New York Public Library. While Lay, McLendon, and Wall have noted parallels between Larsen's work and that of James and Wharton, the possibility of self-conscious revision has yet to be fully examined.

WORKS CITED

Abelson, Elaine. *When Ladies Go A-Thieving: Middle-Class Shoplifters in the Victorian Department Store.* New York: Oxford UP, 1989.

Agnew, Jean-Christophe. "A House of Fiction: Domestic Interiors and the Commodity Aesthetic." *Consuming Visions: Accumulation and Display of Goods in America, 1880–1920.* Ed. Simon Bronner. New York: Norton, 1982. 133–55.

Baker, Jean-Claude and Chris Chase. *Josephine Baker: The Hungry Heart.* New York: Random, 1993.

Banta, Martha. *Taylored Lives: Narrative Productions in the Age of Veblen, Taylor, and Ford.* Chicago: U of Chicago P, 1994.

Blackmer, Corinne. "African Masks and the Arts of Passing in Gertrude Stein's *Melanctha* and Nella Larsen's *Passing.*" *Journal of the History of Sexuality* 4 (1993): 230–63.

Blackmore, David. "The Unusual Restless Feeling: The Homosexual Subtexts of Nella Larsen's *Passing.*" *African American Review* 26.3 (1992): 475–84.

Bowlby, Rachel. *Shopping with Freud.* London and New York: Routledge, 1993.

Brody, Jennifer DeVere. "Clare Kendry's 'True Colors': Race and Class Conflict in Nella Larsen's *Passing.*" *Callaloo* 15.4 (1992): 1053–65.

Butler, Judith. *Bodies That Matter: On the Discursive Limits of "Sex."* New York: Routledge, 1993.

———. *Gender Trouble: Feminism and the Subversion of Identity.* New York: Routledge, 1999.

Carby, Hazel. *Reinventing Womanhood: The Emergence of the Afro-American Woman Novelist.* New York: Oxford UP, 1987.

Culver, Stuart. "What Manikins Want: *The Wonderful Wizard of Oz* and The Art of Decorating Dry Goods Windows." *Representations* 21 (1988): 97–116.

Cutter, Martha. "Sliding Significations: Passing as a Narrative and Textual Strategy in Nella Larsen." *Passing and the Fictions of Identity.* Ed. Elaine K. Ginsberg. Durham: Duke UP, 1996. 75–100.

Davis, Thadious. *Nella Larsen, Novelist of the Harlem Renaissance: A Woman's Life Unveiled.* Baton Rouge: Louisiana State UP, 1994.

Dittmar, Linda. "When Privilege Is No Protection: The Woman Artist in *Quicksand* and *The House of Mirth.*" *Writing the Woman Artist: Essays on Poetics, Politics, and Portraiture.* Philadelphia: U of Pennsylvania P, 1992. 133–54.

Doane, Mary Ann. *The Desire to Desire: The Woman's Film of the 1940s.* Bloomington: Indiana UP, 1987.

Douglas, Ann. *Terrible Honesty: Mongrel Manhattan in the 1920s.* New York: Farrar, 1995.

duCille, Ann. *The Coupling Convention: Sex, Text, and Tradition in Black Women's Fiction.* New York: Oxford UP, 1993.

Esteve, Mary. "Nella Larsen's 'Moving Mosaic': Harlem, Crowds, and Anonymity." *American Literary History* 9.2 (1997): 268–86.

Felski, Rita. *The Gender of Modernity.* Cambridge: Harvard UP, 1995.

Gilman, Charlotte Perkins. *Women and Economics.* 1898. New York: Harper and Row, 1966.

Hostetler, Ann. "The Aesthetics of Race and Gender in Nella Larsen's *Quicksand.*" *PMLA* 105.1 (1990): 35–46.

Huggins, Nathan. *Harlem Renaissance.* New York: Oxford UP, 1971.

Hutchinson, George. *The Harlem Renaissance in Black and White.* Cambridge and London: Harvard UP, 1995.

———. "Nella Larsen and the Veil of Race." *American Literary History* 9.2 (1997): 329–49.

Larsen, Nella. *Quicksand* and *Passing.* Ed. Deborah McDowell. New Brunswick: Rutgers UP, 1986.

Larson, Charles. *Invisible Darkness: Jean Toomer and Nella Larsen.* Iowa City: U of Iowa P, 1993.

Lay, Mary. "Henry James's *The Portrait of a Lady* and Nella Larsen's *Quicksand*: A Study in Parallels." *The Magic Circle of Henry James.* Ed. Amritjit Singh. New York: Envoy, 1989. 73–84.

Leach, William. *Land of Desire: Merchants, Power, and the Rise of a New American Culture.* New York: Pantheon, 1993.

Levering Lewis, David. *When Harlem Was in Vogue.* New York: Oxford UP, 1981.

McDowell, Deborah. Introduction to *Quicksand* and *Passing.* New Brunswick: Rutgers UP, 1986. ix–xxxv.

McLendon, Jacquelyn. *The Politics of Color in the Fiction of Jessie Fauset and Nella Larsen.* Charlottesville: U of Virginia P, 1995.

Michie, Helena. *Sororophobia: Differences Among Women in Literature and Culture.* New York: Oxford UP, 1992.

Rhodes, Chip. "Writing Up the New Negro: The Construction of Consumer Desire in the 1920s." *Journal of American Studies* 28.2 (1994): 191–207.

Robinson, Amy. "It Takes One to Know One: Passing and Communities of Common Interest." *Critical Inquiry* 20.4 (1994): 715–36.

Rose, Phyllis. *Jazz Cleopatra: Josephine Baker In Her Time.* New York: Vintage, 1989.

Rubin, Gayle. "The Traffic in Women: Notes Toward a Political Economy of Sex." *Toward an Anthropology of Women.* New York: Monthly Review, 1975. 157–210.

Silverman, Debra. "Nella Larsen's *Quicksand*: Untangling the Web of Exoticism." *African American Review* 27.4 (1993): 599–614.

Veblen, Thorstein. *The Theory of the Leisure Class.* 1899. New York and London: Penguin, 1978.

Wall, Cheryl. *Women of the Harlem Renaissance.* Bloomington: Indiana UP, 1995.

Washington, Booker T. *Up From Slavery.* 1901. New York: Penguin, 1990.

Wilde, Oscar. *The Picture of Dorian Gray.* 1890. London: Hammondsworth, 1949.

PART
II
Discovering

AJUAN MARIA MANCE

Re-locating the Black Female Subject

The Landscape of the Body in the Poems of Lucille Clifton

Indeed, a fundamental task of black critical think-ers has been the struggle to break with the hege-monic modes of seeing, thinking, and being that block our capacity to see ourselves oppositionally, to imagine, describe, and invent ourselves in ways that are liberatory.

—bell hooks, *Black Looks*

In *Black Women, Writing and Identity,* Carole Boyce Davies describes the capacity of African American women's literature to disrupt and transform prevailing social structures: "Black women's writing re-negotiates the questions of identity; once Black women's experience is accounted for, assumptions about identity, community and theory have to be reconsidered" (3). For nearly 150 years, African American women poets have used their representations of black women's lives as a tool for renegotiating popular assumptions about iden-tity and race that have limited the category of woman to female sub-jects who are white. This narrow conception of womanhood originated during the mid–nineteenth century, when, for all women, failure to con-form to the requirements of what came to be known as "true woman-hood" (that is, domesticity and isolation within the single-family home) was perceived as rebellion against woman's essential nature.[1] African American and poor-white (mostly immigrant) women's labor outside of the home—and the tenement, multifamily, or extended-family dwellings in which these women lived—was widely interpreted as evidence of their fundamental inability to fulfill woman's preordained role within family and society.[2]

The post-Reconstruction period is the first time we see a critical mass of black women poets writing to challenge the gender norms based on this exclusionary vision. During the four decades between the end of Reconstruction and the beginning of World War I, writers like Maggie Pogue Johnson, Josephine Henderson Heard, and the Thompson sisters, Clara and Priscilla, produced poems that assert African American womanhood as a form of adult female subjectivity that popular assumptions about the relationship between gender and race fail to take into account. In this earliest stage of resistance, black women poets use representations of African American home life and intrafamilial relationships to expose the politics of exclusion and containment that perpetuate the white bourgeois feminine ideal. In particular, black women's representations of family love, womanly compassion, and marital fealty, in settings other than the European American household, expose the degree to which that site has been used to preserve womanhood as a racialized identity category.

Since that period—during the Harlem Renaissance, the post–World War II era, the Black Arts movement, and the contemporary period—African American women poets have used a variety of strategies first to dislodge womanhood from its association with the white middle-class home and then to write into possibility a subject who is woman and not white.[3] Most often, African American women poets have appropriated those strategies used by writers involved in related struggles (the idealization of Africa by black male poets of the Harlem Renaissance; the urban existentialism of black novelists in the postwar period; the elevation of African American manhood by male writers of the Black Arts movement), modifying them to respond to those concerns that neither the Eurocentric mainstream of the feminist movement nor the masculinist leadership of the black liberation movement have cared to address.

One strategy easily modified to confront the issues and interests of the subject who is both woman and black involves using poetry as a forum for depicting black female subjects in flagrant disregard of the boundaries that have traditionally limited their visibility. Betsy Erkkila traces the origins of this strategy back to the nineteenth-century poet Emily Dickinson. In *The Wicked Sisters*, Erkkila positions Dickinson as the first in a line of American women poets who resist hegemonic constructions of womanhood by depicting female subjects positioned "at odds with and wickedly in excess of their identity as Woman" (4). Erkkila believes that these poets have developed what amounts to a poetics of "wicked excess," in which they use sarcasm, fantasy, exaggeration, and other techniques to call attention to their willful existence outside of the narrow spaces left open for traditional womanhood. Expanding upon her insight, this essay begins to uncover how African American women poets of the contemporary period create black female subjects whose willful transgression of the physical and discursive boundaries that have limited black women's visibility disrupts those established relationships between subject and setting that have maintained womanhood as a white middle-class identity category. Such poems construct a relationship between race, resistance, and transgression that suggests the possibility of a distinct black women's poetics of "wicked excess."

A crucial step in African American women writers' pursuit of an aesthetic that embraces excess (as a manifestation and marker of outsider status) has been the identification of a symbolic or figurative setting for black womanhood that is liberatory and transformative. Lucille Clifton is one of a growing number of African American women poets for whom the black female body displaces the private suburban home to become the site whose features, traits, and interactions with its physical setting most effectively illustrate the relationship of the African American female subject to the institutions and identity groups that constitute her discursive surroundings.[4] Since the mid-1970s, Clifton has used the language and imagery of myth to create portraits of the black female corpus that, in resisting the narrow definitions of womanhood that have hidden the African American woman from view, undermine the system of sociopolitical hierarchies that perpetuates her invisibility.[5] When she describes the relationships that have marked and defined her existence as a black woman, Clifton attributes to her body and the bodies of those African American women who populate her surroundings (family, friends, ancestors) an array of features and talents, ranging from the mundane to the magical. These features and characteristics reflect her vision of the relationship of the black female subject to the institutions and identity groups that have determined her position and meaning.

Karla Holloway describes the use of myth in literature by black women writers as "a metaphorical revisioning of experiential knowledge" (87). For African American women poets, the deliberate incorporation of language and images associated with myth becomes a way to articulate commonalities in black women's experience without collapsing into essentialism.[6] Jacqueline de Weever describes the impact of this process on the world outside of the mythic text: "If fiction establishes lines to a world other than the real . . . [then] the mythic narrative establishes lines to a world that is not only beyond the real world, but that, at the same time, transforms it" (4). Jane Campbell carries this notion one step farther, as she identifies the specific effect of mythmaking upon race relations in the United States: "mythmaking . . . constitutes a radical act, inviting the audience to subvert the racist mythology that thwarts and defeats Afro-Americans, and to replace it with a new mythology rooted in the black perspective" (x). Building upon the framework of common experience, black women writers use myth to control and redirect the way that the African American woman subject becomes visible. When readers interact with and accept the mythic landscape arranged by the black woman poet, they abandon the mythic landscape organized and presented by white Americans and other privileged constituencies. The African American woman poet offers her myths explaining black woman's subjectivity as an alternative to the marginalizing sociopolitical constructs that aid those identity groups who enjoy "center" status in maintaining their privileged discursive position.

When Clifton assigns to her black female subjects fantastic traits and mythical capabilites that exceed the boundaries of traditional womanhood, their flagrant disregard for the roles that would limit their function and meaning challenges the positionality of those institutions and identity groups whose visibility depends upon the preservation of blackness and womanhood as opposing categories. Her black female bodies replace the marginalizing system of binary relations (man/woman, black/white, margin/center, public/private) that perpetuates the confinement of womanhood to exclusionary spaces like the middle-class suburban home with a paradigm of meaning based upon simultaneity. Within this new paradigm of meaning, the African American female subject comes into view, not by virtue of her relationship to the institutions (womanhood, domesticity, marriage) and identity categories (whiteness, maleness) located outside of black womanhood but through those institutions, identities, and ideas that coexist within the boundaries of that position.[7] Within the paradigm of simultaneity, the coexistence within the African American female subject of blackness and womanhood is indicated through the poet's use of images suggesting duality. The notion, central to Clifton's Afro-mythic cosmology, that history, culture, and memory position black women in the United States and their African ancestors as different manifestations of the same subject position is represented through images evoking the idea of a timelessness that renders the space and time separating these two constituencies virtually inconsequential. African American women's subjectivity becomes simultaneously a fact of the past and a condition of the present. Other seemingly contradictory qualities that converge within African American womanhood—the seen and the unseen, the possible and the impossible—are opposing pairs whose coexistence within black womanhood is indicated, in Clifton's work, through the poet's invocation of the magical.[8]

In many ways Clifton's *two-headed woman*, published in 1980, marks the beginning of her interest in depicting the transgressive black body. Having employed myth in much of her prior work, *two-headed woman* sees Clifton's first widespread application of mythic images and frameworks to the figure of the African American woman.[9] Four poems in this volume ("to merle," "homage to my hips," "homage to my hair," and "i was born with twelve fingers") share this focus. In subsequent volumes, Clifton's interest in this theme either dissipates or combines with other interests (for example, women and illness, women and aging, or women in the Bible), so that very few of her subsequent poems link the specific goal of re-writing African American woman's subjectivity with the figure of the mythic black body.[10] Among the notable exceptions are "daughters" in *The Book of Light* (1993) and "Sisters: For Elaine Philip on Her Birthday" in *An Ordinary Woman* (1974).

In "to merle," Clifton greets her beloved friend, named in the title, with words whose playful excess locate the black woman subject simultaneously in the contradictory moments of present and past:

> say skinny manysided tall on the ball
> brown downtown woman
> last time i saw you was on the corner of
> pyramid and sphinx (1–4)

Clifton's greeting juxtaposes the seemingly opposing traits that coexist within the body of her black woman friend. Beyond the obvious reference to physical size, skinny implies thinness or simplicity—thin as inconsequential or the antithesis of complex. For Merle, however, thinness and complexity coexist without contradiction; she is simultaneously "skinny" and "manysided." Similarly she is both brown (that is, black) and a woman, a pairing unacknowledged within a system of meaning that understands womanhood as inherently white. Even the circumstances under which Clifton offers her greeting suggest the pairing of opposites. Clifton and Merle are friends in the present but are linked by an ancient bond, forged when the pyramids were new; they are American, but their shared subjectivity looks to the physical and symbolic space of Africa as its setting of origin.

Clifton-as-speaker recognizes her long-absent friend not only by her "skinny," "brown" body but by her language: "ten thousand years have interrupted our conversation / but I have kept most of my words / til you came back" (5–7). In this passage, Clifton's relationship to Merle takes on a broader, more historical function, as a symbol of the connections that exist between black women separated by time and space. The notion that the contradictions, characteristics, and language by which Clifton and Merle recognize each other have survived for "ten thousand years" locates the African American woman subject outside of the dominant systems of meaning that do not allow for such temporal excesses. The idea of a friendship whose roots lie at the "corner of / pyramid and sphinx" suggests that the connections between contemporary African American women have a basis far beyond the temporal and spatial boundaries that circumscribe their present condition. Indeed, the connection that Clifton shares with Merle and, by extrapolation, with all women of African descent is rooted in the persistence of her own cultural memory—her stubborn refusal to abandon those long-established systems of meaning ("my words") by which she is able to identify herself and others as women who are black. In fact, when Clifton writes that "I have kept most of my words / til you came back," she is essentially bearing witness to the enduring power of remembrance.

In the end, the long-anticipated reunion between poet and friend symbolizes the reconnection of African history-as-memory with those black women of the present who are its inheritors. Clifton, like many of her contemporaries, uses myth to fill in those circumstances and events in the history of the African American female subject that traditional Western forms of documentation have failed to record. Hence the memory that constitutes the basis of her reestablished link with Merle (as representative of all black women) is imperfect; Clifton reports that she has kept "most" but not all of her words.

That the women in this poem are joined in sisterhood not by marriage or blood but by shared language and locus (instead of the single-family suburban home, which leaves little space for the woman who is not white, the figures in this poem become visible in the space of the black female body) suggests the social and political constructedness of black womanhood and other identity categories that are usually perceived as essential or causal. The poem concludes:

what i'm trying to say is
i recognize your language and
let me call you sister, sister,
i been waiting for you. (8–11)

Clifton's emphasis upon speech ("i recognize your language") and naming ("let me call you sister") suggests that in recognizing and greeting each other as African American women, the black female subjects in the poem successfully speak across, and thus weaken and eradicate, the long-observed boundaries that, in separating blackness from womanhood, have hampered the visibility of women who exist at the point where these identity categories intersect. These acts of seeing highlight, by contrast, the resistance within prevailing social structures to seeing or even acknowledging the possibility of woman subjects who are not white.

Like their counterparts in "to merle," the aging black women friends in Clifton's "Sisters: For Elaine Philip on Her Birthday" recognize each other by their bodies. The appearance of their bodies, however, indicates shared rituals or cultural practices, not shared genes or common bloodlines. Clifton describes the rites with which both women marked their youth. The phrases that she uses to describe these shared activities are culled from black vernacular and suggest the shared language that figured so prominently in the previous discussion. She writes: "me and you / be greasing our legs / touching up our edges" (5–7).

Clifton recalls the rituals with which she and Elaine marked their transition to maturity and motherhood:

> me and you
> got babies
> got thirty-five
> got black
> let our hair go back (15–19)

Their common rituals denote the sisters' shared signification as African American women, an identity group that becomes visible through the vehicle of the body not by virtue of the essential or physical qualities that it exhibits but through the cultural practices that the black woman subject performs on that body and the values and interests that these practices suggest. Clifton's emphasis on ritual is a deliberate departure from notions of African American identity that rely on false and bigoted notions of biological "race." She writes:

> me and you be sisters.
> we be the same.
> me and you
> coming from the same place. (1–4)

As she advocates a vision of African American women's subjectivity that is based in the black female body and the rituals that mark and maintain it, Clifton is careful not to reduce identity or sameness to monoliths. Thus, despite the similar processes by which she and Elaine Philip invent themselves as black—that is, through the exercise of body rituals that link them to the larger community of African American women—Clifton closes the poem with a passage highlighting important differences between the two. Her brief focus on each woman's chosen medium of expression calls attention to the persistence of distinctions even among subjects within a single common identity group:

> me and you
>
> . . . .
>
> be loving ourselves
> be loving ourselves
> be sisters
> only where you sing
> i poet. (14, 20–24)

Without undermining Clifton's larger theme of connections between black women, the notion that some women "sing" and some women "poet" challenges the assumption that subjects within a marginalized group are indistinguishable from one another, an idea that gives rise to stereotyping and other forms of bias.

In "i was born with twelve fingers," Clifton places images of the black female body at the center of an allegory that explains aspects of the encounter between African American women and those sociopolitical forces—from the nineteenth-century Cult of Domesticity to Eurocentrism in the mainstream of today's feminist movement—that have sought to limit or exclude them. Like "Sisters: For Elaine Philip on Her Birthday," this poem emphasizes the body as a reflection of the discursive link that exists between African American women. But while "Sisters" relies on the imagery of the colloquial body, rendered familiar within the community of black women by the cultural practices it manifests (the figures in the poem "touch up [their] edges," "let [their] hair go back," "be greasing [their] legs"), "i was born with twelve fingers" depicts a black woman figure whose physical traits initially seem strange and unfamiliar. More specifically, the latter poem replaces the image of black sisterhood made manifest through African American women's exercise of common cultural practices, offering instead the surprising image of a family of black women, each of whom exhibits the physical anomaly of a sixth finger on each hand: "i was born with twelve fingers / like my mother and my daughter" (1–2).

These six-fingered hands exceed our expectations for the "normal" body in the same way that African American women's dual, interlocking identities exceed mainstream expectations for "normal" (that is, white) womanhood. Like the six-fingered hands of the Clifton family women, the black woman subject confounds the American cultural imagination; her simultaneous embodiment of both blackness and womanhood transforms the spaces left open for the signification of each.

Clifton uses an image of the strange black fingers poking into a pool of fresh milk to dramatize how the dual, interlocking identities exemplified by the African American female subject and her "strange" black body intervene in and disrupt efforts to maintain the idea of woman as a racialized category in which blackness may not coexist:

> each of us
> born wearing strange black gloves
> extra baby fingers hanging over the sides of our cribs and
> dipping into the milk (3–6)

The haunting image of Clifton's small, twelve-fingered hands (her "strange black gloves") reaching over the side of the crib disrupts popular and cherished notions of infant beauty and childhood innocence—the pure simplicity of babyhood and life in the nursery—and lays the foundation for renegotiation of the boundaries that define motherhood and other identities within womanhood. Milk, with its flat color and texture and its links to familiarity, wholesomeness, and comfort, symbolizes both the bland homogeneity of Eurocentric conceptions of womanhood and the secure, predictable dominance that whiteness enjoys when the black female subject is erased from view. Into this peaceful preservation of the racial status quo Clifton inserts the black female body, represented in this passage by the spectacle of her six-fingered hands, whose oddness inspires fear even as it demands a reassessment of those conceptions of the female body that do not allow for such excesses (it is unclear whether her six-fingeredness or her blackness is the greater curiosity).

Clifton remembers the cosmetic, "normalizing" surgery to remove the sixth fingers as a great loss for all of the women in her family. "[O]ur wonders were cut off" because, she explains, "somebody was afraid we would learn to cast spells" (8, 7). Clifton offers this recollection as a metaphor for how identities and institutions at the discursive center rely on assimilation, or the erasure of difference, as a means to lessen the challenge to hegemony issued by those whose difference positions them as marginal. (In "Sisters" a comparative move would be to describe black women being discouraged from practicing the body rituals that enable them to recognize one another.) Such attempts eventually fail, however, because those who wish to separate the Clifton women from their difference grossly underestimate the persistence of historical and cultural memory. The poet explains, "they didn't understand / the powerful memory of ghosts" (9–10). Clifton's allusion to the "memory of ghosts" conjures up notions of the common West African belief that the spirits of the ancestors dwell among the living. Unseen but ever present, the ancestors eat, sleep, and otherwise participate in the daily lives of their communities, where their presence as living manifestations of history is cherished and cultivated.[11] Their advice is often sought on issues of culture, tradition, and genealogy. A somewhat modified version of this belief remains a powerful element in the belief system of many of America's oldest black enclaves.

In "daughters," another semiautobiographical meditation on the question of ancestry, Clifton depicts the potential of the black woman subject to transform her discursive surroundings as a secret passed from one generation to the next. Where "i was born with twelve fingers" is allegorical, however, "daughters" is literal. Its text consists of the poet's meditation on an old photograph of her great-grandmother. She is the "woman who shines at the head / of my grandmother's bed, / brilliant woman" (1–3). Though unnamed in the poem, this woman ancestor is almost certainly based upon the poet's great-grandmother, a Dahomey woman who was kidnapped from Africa and sold into slavery in the United States.[12] This in and of itself would appear to be of great interest to the poet, whose ability to trace her ancestry to a particular place and people on the African continent is a rare and coveted privilege within the African American community. For Clifton, however, the significance of her great-grandmother's position as a conduit of cultural and historical memory clearly surpasses the importance of any blood ties that she and her female ancestors may share. Clifton is interested in the secrets of culture, history, and memory that, when passed down between black women, perpetuate in the daughters of the present the discursive position occupied by the mothers, grandmothers, and great-grandmothers of the past.

To pass these fragments of ritual and ancestry from one generation of women to the next is to transmit a system of meaning, so that each generation of daughters locates the subject position of black women at the same intersection of gender, history, and race that their mothers did before them. Clifton imagines her great-grandmother sharing this secret knowledge with her own daughter, the poet's grandmother: "i like to think / you whispered into her ear / instructions" (3–5). Passed down from great-grandmother to grandmother to mother to daughter, these secrets distinguish the women in this family group as unique and magical figures who wear their difference—their power to transform—on their bodies: "i like to think / you are the oddness in us" (5–6). Clifton understands the transmission of this "oddness" in terms that suggest a link with the ancient West African practice of ceremonial scarification: "you are the arrow / that pierced our plain skin / and made us fancy women" (7–9). During scarification, tribal and familial patterns are etched into the skin (identity and history are literally written on the body) in a painful ritual that elides the process of beautification with the application into the flesh of traditional, ancestral markings. Like the recipients of scarification,

Clifton and her daughters are marked women who inherit their unique ancestral legacy as both painful burden and transforming pleasure. As in the scarification rituals of sub-Saharan Africa, the metaphorical piercing of flesh that turns Clifton and her kin from plain women into fancy uses physical inscriptions in blood and flesh to mark symbolic changes in status and meaning. Touched by the legacy of their ancestor's difference, Clifton's grandmother, mother, and daughters become "my wild witch gran, my magic mama, / and even these gaudy girls" (10–11).

As the poem draws to a close, the poet leaves us with the image of her great-grandmother as a living ancestral presence who wishes no more elaborate honor than simply to be remembered:

> it is enough,
> you must have murmured,
> to remember that i was
> and that you are. (16–19)

Thus Clifton offers this benediction as her promise to perpetuate the memory of the women who have preceded her:

> woman, i am
> lucille, which stands for light,
> daughter of thelma, daughter
> of georgia, daughter of
> dazzling you. (19–23)

Clifton's short praise poems, "homage to my hair" and "homage to my hips," turn away from an emphasis on relationships between African American women to focus on the interaction between the black woman subject and the African American man. The previous poems in this study have used the relationship between black women joined in camaraderie and kinship to explore the substance of Clifton's mythic womanhood. These brief "homage" poems use the cross-gender relationship between African American women and men to revise and explore the meanings assigned to the black female body. In particular, "homage to my hair" and "homage to my hips" celebrate the capacity of the African American woman subject to transform and disrupt categories like masculinity and whiteness, whose visibility depends on the confinement or erasure of black female subjectivity, simply by reinscribing either or both of her constituent identities (blackness and womanhood) with new meaning.

In "homage to my hair," Clifton focuses on changing the meaning of blackness by transforming the language and images linked with nappy hair, a characteristic whose association with black bodies has been used both to single out and ostracize African American women and men. For Clifton's speaker, nappy hair is neither primitive nor comical, neither alien nor exotic. She writes into visibility a head of bushy black hair whose movement and texture simply overwhelm the narrow spaces in which such derogatory characterizations are conceived. It is unruly and excessive, it "jump[s] and dance[s] . . . my God," (1–2) with powers that derive from its propensity to overrun neatly drawn boundaries and challenge expectations. The black male figure in the poem becomes the friendly opposition on whom Clifton's speaker illustrates the reconstructive power of this feature that they share:

> i'm talking about my nappy hair!
> she is a challenge to your hand
> Black man,
> she is as tasty on your tongue as good greens
> Black man,
> she can touch your mind
> with her electric fingers (3–9)

In "homage to my hips," Clifton continues her pursuit of a new and emancipatory vision of the black female corpus, shifting her focus downward to its highly contested midsection. Like "homage to my hair," the woman speaker of "homage to my hips" uses the suggestion of a male addressee as the background against which to convey her new vision of a frequently stereotyped black feature. Clifton reinterprets the outrageousness and excess associated with the African American female body as a source of power and a point of pride. Epitomized in the notorious swing of her "big," "free hips," the black woman's failure to conform to conventional notions of womanliness and femininity is recast as deliberate resistance. Far from hiding her difference, Clifton celebrates her excess, openly proclaiming that her broad hips overwhelm the "little petty places" created to contain her:

> these hips are big hips
> they need space to
> move around in.
> they don't fit into little
> petty places. these hips
> are free hips.
> they don't like to be held back.
> these hips have never been enslaved,
> they go where they want to go
> they do what they want to do (1–10)

Like her nappy hair, Clifton's audacious hips have been known to unsettle the men who engage with their powers:

> these hips are mighty hips.
> these hips are magic hips.
> i have known them
> to put a spell on a man and
> spin him like a top! (11–15)

The poet's decision to leave her readers with this playful image of a man, stunned and reeling at the sheer majesty of her black body, reintroduces the same attitude of friendly opposition that we encountered in "homage to my hair." Clifton invites the unnamed men to whom her poem is addressed to reexamine the symbolic position of the black woman's corpus, not as oppressors but as allies. Indeed, Clifton's emphasis upon reconfiguring the black female corpus—once a symbol of the physical and sexual oppression of all black bodies—as an emblem of freedom suggests that her attempt to rewrite the positionality and meaning of the African American female body may prove equally liberating for black men. Certainly, Clifton's boast that "these hips have never been enslaved" positions the black woman's body as a symbolic link for all blacks to the distant, precolonial past.

When Clifton and other African American women poets collapse the distinctions between history and myth, sorcery and science, conjuring and creativity, they assert—mischievously, unabashedly, self-indulgently, and with pleasure—their newly reclaimed power to define the limits of their own subjectivity.[13] Black women's joy in their newly recovered power of making is evident in their writings that bend and taunt the conventions of the mainstream, not wholly eliminating or exploding traditional identity categories but alleviating them, so that other possibilities may come into view.[14] It is this pleasure in resistance and reconstruction that is intimated in Erkkila's phrase "wicked excess," a term that implies willful mischief. The interaction between Clifton's self-awareness as creator and her playful unrestraint appears in her poems as deliberate, pleasurable, and often wicked self-indulgence in the act of remaking. Excessive display is one of the means by which she and other women poets writing against the hegemony of the mainstream highlight the role of process—of making—in those institutions and identity categories most commonly understood as absolute.

I have come to describe such literary acts of resistance and recreation as "myth-play," a term that connotes the joy and euphoria that accompany African American women poets' recuperation and exercise of the power of making identity. In this context, "myth" establishes identity as fabrication-in-progress; rather than a fixed position, identity is a process. I use "myth," instead of "fiction" or "tale," to acknowledge that identity categories—though they are not material, essential, or otherwise empirical—explain material conditions and power relationships that are quite concrete. Like story myths (Kipling's "How the Camel Got His Hump," the biblical creation myths, and others), the identity categories to which "myth" refers comprise a discourse created in order to explain some "real" aspect of the world in which the myth-makers live. Similarly, in this context the word *play* refers to the exercise of reclaimed power in the process of identity construction. The term *play* is particularly relevant to the poets' exercise of power reclaimed because it connotes indulgence. "Play" implies the self-conscious exercise of agency, not merely in responsible service to the emancipation of the group (though that certainly is a significant part of black women poets' representation of the black female body and landscape) but in celebration of visibility, empowerment, and the return to voice. Thus "myth-play" expresses the black woman poet's engagement in the construction of her identity category in accordance with the needs of African American women (as they write to disrupt sociopolitical relationships that deny them subjectivity) and also in response to their desires and pleasures.

In the early twentieth century, James Weldon Johnson urged young black writers to take on the "serious work" of "wearing away the stereotyped ideas about the Negro" (Birch 34). Today, black women poets encourage each other in the "serious work" of play—playing with gender, race, and other frameworks traditionally used to impose limits upon signification and subjecthood. African American women poets create a new vision of the African American female subject to replace the old and constraining notions that have limited womanhood on the basis of race and class. In so doing, Clifton and her black female contemporaries destroy old myths that refuse to acknowledge their existence and create new myths that, in rejecting discursive formulations that resist black women's subjectivity, write the black female subject into view.

Play is, above all else, the recuperation of the prerogative and power to create and re-create meaning; it is rooted in the writer's reassertion of ownership, so that play becomes a way of reclaiming. Contemporary African American women poets reclaim the black woman's body by re-creating the meaning of its component parts, blackness and womanhood. The transforming influence of African American women poets' playful revisions of black female subjectivity are not, however, limited to these categories. In "Eating the Other," bell hooks describes several strategies through which African Americans and other nonwhite peoples might reinscribe the historical meanings assigned to black and brown bodies.

Hooks explains that members of nondominant identity groups can use their histories of struggle against Euro-dominance to reconstruct themselves so that tragic losses and defeats are recast in ways that encourage celebration:

> The contemporary crises of identity in the west, especially as experienced by white youth, are eased when the "primitive" is recouped via a focus on diversity and pluralism which suggests the Other can provide life-sustaining alternatives. Concurrently, diverse ethnic/racial groups can also embrace this sense of specialness, that histories and experience once seen as worthy of only disdain can be looked upon with awe. (25–26)

In this passage hooks is talking, quite simply, about the power of play. For hooks, play is characterized by a subject's conscious choice to review his or her discursive position, to reinspect an aspect of his or her identity that has negative connotations, and to reinscribe it with positive meaning. For example, play allows African American women poets like Clifton to review the tragic history of black women's enslavement and reinterpret it as evidence of endurance, a characteristic that merits pride and celebration.

In "Selling Hot Pussy," hooks uses a scene from a recent African American film to capture the willfully audacious and revisionary spirit of literary and artistic play when it is employed as a vehicle through which to review (and to re-view—to evolve a new way of seeing) the black body:

> A scene in Spike Lee's film *School Daze* depicts an all black party where everyone is attired in swimsuits dancing—doing the butt. It is one of the most compelling moments in the film. The black "butts" on display are unruly and outrageous. They are not the still bodies of the female slave made to appear as mannequin. They are not a silenced body. Displayed as playful cultural nationalist resistance, they challenge assumptions that the black body, its skin color and shape, is a mark of shame. (63)

Hooks believes that this scene challenges hegemonic constructions of blackness and beauty and resists mainstream conceptions of worth that marginalize black bodies. Clifton's sister-friends and magical mothers perform similarly, as each of these women manifests the transformative excess of the black and female subject who challenges the institutions that would erase her from view. If Lee's "black butts" are "unruly and outrageous," so too are the six-fingered hands of Clifton and her women ancestors. If Lee's *School Daze* answers the specter of the shackled, "still" bodies of African slaves with the spectacle of playful, unfettered black bodies in motion, then Clifton counters that very same memory with an exuberant vision of hair that can "jump up and dance" and hips that "need space to move around in." In "I was born with twelve fingers," "homage to my hips," "homage to my hair," and other body portraits, Clifton invents the African American woman as transgressive, transformative subject. Articulated in the ancestral language of "to merle" and marked and accentuated with the body rituals of "Sisters," the wicked excess of these black bodies in motion flaunts Lucille Clifton's recuperated power to define and invent subjectivities. The poems I have discussed in this essay read the African American body through the lens of myth and magic in order to conduct the reader through an experience of the interaction between subjectivity, gender, and race that is rooted in Clifton's perspective as a black woman. As Holloway and other black feminist critics suggest, such an experience of a mythic landscape ordered according to the interests of a subject who locates herself within a nondominant identity group transforms the world outside of the textual landscape and demands of the subjects who populate that world a new awareness of the sociopolitical and economic origins of privilege, position, and meaning.

NOTES

1. See Welter for a more detailed discussion of how the idea of "true womanhood," the culture of domesticity, and the rise of the American middle class transformed nineteenth-century notions of gender, race, and nation. See Cott for a detailed examination of the essentialist foundations of the "true womanhood" ideal.
2. See Carby for a discussion of the role of nineteenth-century literature in perpetuating this exclusionary ideal.
3. See Hull for a discussion of African American women poets during the Harlem Renaissance; Erkkila for a detailed investigation of African American women poets and resistance in the decades after World War II; and Russell for an overview of African American women writers in the Black Arts movement.
4. Such poets include Audre Lorde, Toi Derricotte, and Ntozake Shange.
5. Although Clifton published her first book in 1969, at the height of the Black Arts movement, it is not until her third book of poetry, An Ordinary Woman, published in 1974, that we begin to see poems that focus upon the African American woman's body as metaphor for the position of the black female subject within the larger society.
6. See Collins for a further exploration of experience as a framework for developing an anti-essentialist vision of African American women's subjectivity.
7. See Collins for a more detailed exploration of the cognitive gap between dominant systems of meaning based on "either/or dichotomous thinking" and black feminist systems of meaning based upon the paradigm of simultaneity.
8. I use the term magical based on my understanding of the meaning and function of "magical realism," which was apparently first coined in the 1920s

by German art critic Franz Roh but is most frequently associated with Latin-American writers of the contemporary period. In particular, I am interested in the propensity of magical realist writers for using images of the unreal (impossible actions, objects, settings, and circumstances) to depict or describe real, material circumstances—most often those of the marginal or the oppressed—that the dominant discourse fails to account for (that is, those whose experiences outside of the descriptive capacity of the dominant language and meaning systems occur as a side effect of their existence in discursive spaces far outside of the sociopolitical and economic mainstream).

9. To explore Clifton's use of mythic images and paradigms for purposes other than the representation of black women, see *Good Times* (1969) and *Good News about the Earth* (1972). Clifton's Kali Trilogy (*An Ordinary Woman*'s "Kali," "The Coming of Kali," and "Calming") also provides an important example of her early exploration of mythic themes and figures. The poems in this trilogy depict a black Hindu goddess whose simultaneous embodiment of multiple and contradictory identities foreshadows Clifton's later application of mythic themes and imagery to the African American woman's body.

10. See "poem to my uterus," "to my last period," "eve's version," "the garden of delight," "adam thinking," "eve thinking," and "the story thus far" in *Quilting* (1991); "amazons," "lumpectomy eve," "consulting the book of changes: radiation," "1994," and "scar" in *The Terrible Stories* (1996); and "sarah's promise" and "naomi watches as ruth sleeps" in *The Book of Light* (1993).

11. See Smith for an exploration of this and other "Africanisms" that have made their way into black American cultural and religious practices.

12. See Clifton's *Generations* for a more detailed account of the poet's known ancestors.

13. See "From the House of Yemanja," "Scar," and "A Woman Speaks," in Lorde's *The Black Unicorn* and "Oh, I'm 10 Months Pregnant" and "We Need a God Who Bleeds Now" in Shange's *A Daughter's Geography.*

14. Yaeger writes, "As women play with old texts, the burden on the tradition is lightened and shifted; it has the potential for being remade" (18). The same can be said of poems that invent mythologies to highlight and explain elements of women's daily lives. Such poems, in elevating the ordinary lives of black women, expand the meaning of holiness and the sacred beyond its common (and limited) association with Euro-patriarchal dominance.

WORKS CITED

Birch, Eva Lennox. *Black American Women's Writing: A Quilt of Many Colors.* New York: Harvester Wheatsheaf, 1994.

Campbell, Jane. *Mythic Black Fiction: The Transformation of History.* Knoxville: U of Tennessee P, 1986.

Carby, Hazel V. *Reconstructing Womanhood: The Emergence of the Afro-American Woman Novelist.* New York: Oxford UP, 1987.

Clifton, Lucille. *An Ordinary Woman.* New York: Random, 1974.

———. *Generations: A Memoir.* New York: Random, 1976.

———. *Good News about the Earth: New Poems.* New York: Random, 1972.

———. *Good Times: Poems.* New York: Random, 1969.

———. *Next: New Poems.* Brockport: BOA, 1991.

———. *Quilting: Poems, 1987–1990.* Brockport: BOA, 1993.

———. *The Book of Light.* Port Townsend: Copper Canyon, 1993.

———. *The Terrible Stories.* Brockport: BOA, 1996.

————. *Two-Headed Woman*. Amherst: U of Massachusetts P, 1980.

Collins, Patricia Hill. *Black Feminist Thought: Knowledge, Consciousness and the Politics of Empowerment*. New York: Routledge, 1991.

Cott, Nancy. *The Bonds of Womanhood: "Woman's Sphere" in New England, 1780–1835*. New Haven: Yale UP, 1977.

Davies, Carole Boyce. *Black Women, Writing, and Identity: Migrations of the Subject*. London: Routledge, 1994.

de Weever, Jaqueline. *Mythmaking and Metaphor in Black Women's Fiction*. New York: St. Martin's, 1992.

Erkkila, Betsy. *The Wicked Sisters: Women Poets, Literary History, and Discord*. New York: Oxford UP, 1992.

Holloway, Karla F. C. *Moorings and Metaphors: Figures of Cultures and Gender in Black Women's Literature*. New Brunswick: Rutgers UP, 1992.

hooks, bell. *Black Looks: Race and Representation*. Boston: South End, 1992.

Hull, Gloria T. *Color, Sex, and Poetry: Three Women Writers of the Harlem Renaissance*. Bloomington: Indiana UP, 1987.

Lorde, Audre. *The Black Unicorn: Poems*. New York: Norton, 1978.

Russell, Sandi. *Render Me My Song: African-American Women Writers from Slavery to the Present*. New York: St. Martin's, 1990.

Shange, Ntozake. *A Daughter's Geography*. New York: St. Martin's, 1983.

Smith, Theophus, H. *Conjuring Culture: Biblical Foundation of Black America*. New York: Oxford UP, 1994.

Wall, Cheryl. *Women of the Harlem Renaissance*. Bloomington: Indiana UP, 1995.

Welter, Barbara. "The Cult of True Womanhood, 1820–1860." *American Quarterly* 18 (Summer 1966): 151–75.

Yaeger, Patricia. *Honey-Mad Women: Emancipatory Strategies in Women's Writ-*

YVETTE LOUIS

Body Language
The Black Female Body and the Word in Suzan-Lori Parks's The Death of the Last Black Man in the Whole Entire World

Suzan-Lori Parks's 1990 play, *The Death of the Last Black Man in the Whole Entire World,* is a recent addition to the tradition within African American letters of positing language as the alchemy by which an African American subject positionality is constructed out of the devastation of slavery. Parks's self-representations of the black female body attempt to re-member and restore the black body through language. While embedding the drama deeply within the African American experiences of slavery, violence, and racial oppression, Parks makes use of deconstructed language and dramatic form to contest dominant discourses that have pathologized the black body and represents a counternarrative of the black body as the source of abundance. Although the black male body is apparently foregrounded in this play, the black female body is constructed as the discursive site of restoration for black subjectivity.

The Death of the Last Black Man in the Whole Entire World was originally produced by BACA Downtown in Brooklyn in 1990 and subsequently at the Yale Repertory Theatre in 1992. Parks, who had won an Obie in 1990, was announced by Yale Rep as one of three American women playwrights featured in their 1992 Winterfest who were "noted for inventing new languages." A favorable review by Kevin Kelly in the *Boston Globe* declared Parks "some rare kind of witchcraft genius," affirming that the play built "an astonishing power" and that "there's no mistaking the majesty, the power and the originality behind" Parks's work.

Kelly nonetheless complained that her work can be "obtuse." Considered "avant-garde" because of its surrealistic form and deconstructed language, the play manipulates African American stereotypes to retell history in order to creatively and imaginatively construct a new black subjectivity. The play is deeply rooted in the African American experience of slavery and racial violence, yet Kelly found that what "Parks is saying is so essential to her—and so many light-years away from what has been considered the 'black experience.'" As Hortense Spillers states, the history of black female subjectivity has been one of "relative silence" and "such silence is the nickname of distortion" (73). Hence, Parks retells the past to engage in what Stuart Hall has called "not the rediscovery but the production of identity" ("Cultural" 224). What may seem obtuse to some readers might be easier to read for those who walk out of a theater into what bell hooks has described as "a void where they are still invisible, their history unknown, their reality denied" (149). Parks's representation of black female subjectivity attempts to "undo *and* reveal" the "distortion" Spillers describes (73). In spite of Parks's "witchcraft genius" at inventing new languages, identities, and subjectivities, public discourse reconfirms the isolation of the African American female subject.

Although the play's title might suggest otherwise, it is precisely the negation and devaluation of black female identities and intellectual production that Parks's work addresses in her theatrical representations of the black female body. The play makes use of stereotypes of the black body, but it neither essentializes blackness nor suspends itself in binary oppositions. Rather, Parks's critique of stereotypes falls within the "practices of representation" Hall has described, namely, "[t]he struggle to come into representation . . . predicated on a critique of the degree of fetishization, objectification and negative figuration which are so much a feature of the representation of the black subject" and that reflect "a concern not simply with the absence or marginality of the black experience but with its simplification and its stereotypical character" ("New" 442). The play's use of irony unveils the historical and ideological origins of such images and discourses, as well as their racist and sexist cultural and social uses.

Parks's play tells the story of the repeated death experiences of the character called simply Black Man. He is hung from a tree that is subsequently hit by lightning, is "fried" in an electric chair, and falls twenty-three stories. The play's context is the history of racial violence and of the discursive and conceptual associations of the black body with the fragmentation that made "flesh" its primary narrative. Spillers describes the transition from "body" to "flesh" that discursively accompanied slavery: "the captive body reduces to a thing . . . mak[ing] a distinction . . . between 'body' and 'flesh.' . . . If we think of the 'flesh' as a primary narrative, then we mean its seared, divided, ripped-apartness, riveted to the ship's hole, fallen, or 'escaped' overboard" (76). The slave body is present in the play, suffering in its material reality the social and cultural practices that arose from the narrative of black "flesh." By foregrounding the body of the character Black Man, trapped in a seemingly endless cycle of dying, Parks dramatizes what Claudia Tate has described as the "plotting of desire" in black male texts, "in which the hero's desire for public respect is repeatedly frustrated" (108). Against the dramatization of repeated assaults on Black Man that repeatedly defer his quest for social equality, the character Black Woman is re-presented as the discursively constructed black female body through whom the perpetually fragmented black male body is re-membered; she provides the integration and shelter instrumental to his survival. Through Black Woman's actions, the movements of her body, and most important, her speech acts, Parks constructs the black female body as a discursive body, making *The Death of the Last Black Man in the Whole Entire World* a black female text in which, as Tate explains, "discourses of desire are satisfied, not deferred" (108). Black Woman carries out her politicized actions within the daily tasks of the domestic sphere, tasks that remind us that "she is an historical subject, bound to the material circumstances of her day" (182). Yet she is not voiceless. Instead, Parks construes a discursivity for Black Woman that amplifies her sphere of influence and constructs a black female subjectivity that becomes the site for reconstructing and recuperating the black body and identity of Black Man. This construction of the black female body as a discursive body has profound implications for the formation of African American female subjectivity.

The deconstructed language in the play mimics the fragmentation of the objectified black body, and Parks's discursive mastery over signs expands the possibilities for black female self-representation. Parks emphasizes representations of the black female body that counteract the degenerative effects of the narrative of violence upon black flesh. By repeating a series of phrases, stories, and monologues with accumulating revisions and altering connotations, signifiers seem to shape-shift from their assumed meanings. The cumulative effect of these disjointed surreal elements makes for a surprisingly moving theatrical experience. Her disruption of logical structure and discontinuity of language seem to free up the emotive potential of the words. The pressures—external and internalized—under which the representative characters find themselves are abstracted and seem to float freely through the language. This strategy makes the pressures easier to read. There are moments of ironic recognition that are surprising because they arise out of such a fragmented linguistic form. By isolating, repeating, and revising signifiers, a dissonance is created that reveals how external representations of black life serve to disempower the subject. Representations of the fragmented black body can be read as conventional signs much in the way the free-floating words in the play can be read as conventional signs. The relationship between the material presence of the enslaved female body as a symbolic object and language as a system of signifying symbols reveals the possibility for the recuperation of the formerly enslaved identity through the speech act. Mastery over and manipulation of the narrative enables Parks to re-assemble the fragmented parts of the black self through the gathering together and reconfiguration of signifiers. Parks appropriates the speech act to transform the narrative of "flesh" to the subject positionality of a more integrated black female self, emphasizing the signifier as a contested space in which resistance and a recuperation of identity can take place.

The Death of the Last Black Man in the Whole Entire World may be read as a response to the pathologizing of the black family, black gender relations, and black bodies. Interpretations such as those put forth in the Moynihan Report have dominated and generated the discourse about African American "problems." Moynihan's report of 1965 claimed that "the Negro community has been forced into a matriarchal structure which, because it is so far out of line with the rest of American society, seriously retards the progress of the group as a whole, and imposes a crushing burden on the Negro." (75). In the aftermath of Moynihan's report, public discourses have often pathologized the African American community as an underclass and the black woman as responsible for its alleged failings. The recent political preoccupation with welfare reform and unwed motherhood, for instance, has "given a 'Black face' to welfare that has made it easier for conservatives to blame African American families than to go to the socioeconomic roots of poverty" (Herring 20). Hazel Carby sees this scapegoating mechanism as a hysterical response to "the movement of black women between rural and urban areas and between southern and northern cities"—a historical development that "generated a series of moral panics" in which the problems that black women encountered were characterized "not as the lack of job possibilities for black women with the conclusion that the employment market should be rigorously controlled, but on the contrary, as a problem located in black women themselves" (740–41). One contemporary "moral panic" that Parks's play may be read as a response to is the so-called crisis of the black male, as presented in a 1994 New York Times Magazine cover story entitled "The Black Man Is in Terrible Trouble. Whose

Problem Is That?" (Herbert) and in a recent *Sports Illustrated* cover story with a picture of a black child over the caption "Where's Daddy?" (Wahl and Wertheim).

Can the media's sudden declaration of a black male crisis and what Doris Witt has described as "the state-sponsored hysteria over 'welfare queens', 'quota queens', and 'condom queens'" (24) be construed as yet another chapter in the cycle of "moral panics" that have historically justified increased control over the black female body? If the public discourse on the male crisis can be read as a backlash against the burgeoning black female voice and black female power, precisely at the historical moment in which the black female subject begins to claim a voice and be recognized, then Parks's play can be read as a response that foregrounds black female subjectivity and represents the black female body as a regenerative symbol.

Parks's play contests the relentless pathologization of the African American male and female by clearly contextualizing the black community's troubles within the system of patriarchy and racial supremacy under which African Americans have lived for hundreds of years. Relations between Black Man and Black Woman empower them and have political implications that can facilitate the community's survival, even while withstanding external and internalized pressures. Parks clearly establishes a loving and nurturing relationship between Black Man and Black Woman, thereby contradicting the negative discourse that blames African American women not only for supposedly troubled black gender relations but also for the low socioeconomic status of the African American male. Parks's interpretation of the role of black female characters is similar to Barbara Christian's position that

> because of their origins and history, African-American women could lay claim to a viable tradition in which they had been strong central persons in their families and communities, not solely because of their relationship to men, but because they themselves had bonded together to ensure survival of their children, their communities, the race. . . . African-Americans as a race could not have survived without the "female values" of communality, sharing and nurturing. (364)

There is the danger, however, that Parks's representation of the black female body may reify what Michele Wallace has termed the myth of the superwoman:

> From the intricate web of mythology that surrounds the black woman, a fundamental image emerges. It is of a woman of

> inordinate strength, with an ability for tolerating an unusual
> amount of misery and heavy, distasteful work. This woman does
> not have the same fears, weaknesses, and insecurities as other
> women, but believes herself to be and is, in fact, stronger emo-
> tionally than most men. (107)

Parks constructs a black female subject that is empowered, albeit necessarily limited by the historical and material constrictions of slavery,
but runs the risk of reifying a stereotype of black womanhood. The result, which is clearly not an exact blueprint for the contemporary black
woman, offers a revisionist point of departure, for Wallace also emphasizes that there is a discordance between the historical reality and the
perpetuated stereotype. According to Wallace, "the record shows that
black men and women emerged from slavery in twos, husbands and
wives. Only as American blacks began to accept the standards for family life, as well as for manhood and womanhood embraced by American whites, did black men and women begin to resent one another"
(23–24). If, as Deborah Gray White claims, "mutual respect characterized relationships between the sexes" (22) in slave gender constructions,
then Parks, as a contemporary black female writer, is retelling such gender
constructions as a point of departure for representing contemporary black
gender relations.

Why this preoccupation in the late twentieth century with representations of the black female slave body? Parks reaches back into history in order to reposition African American identity within what Hall
calls "narratives of the past." If, as Hall claims, "cultural identity . . . is
a matter of 'becoming' as well as of 'being'" and if it is subject to the
continuous 'play' of history, culture, and power" ("Cultural" 225), then
Parks retells history in order to re-present the black female body and
black female subjectivity. Perhaps the best place to begin a reinvention
of the construction of black womanhood, through representations of the
black female body, is in recuperating and reinterpreting the history of
slavery, to offer contemporary audiences the possibility of recognizing
the shared support and bonding that gave the African American community the strength to survive the holocaust that was slavery. These positive qualities are especially relevant at a time when African American
men, women, and children are subjected to the social, economic, and
cultural material realities that impoverish them and when they have to
combat the perpetual dissemination of images of the objectified black
body through increasingly efficient media technologies.

Although Parks entitled the play *The Death of the Last Black Man
in the Whole Entire World*, the content of the story emphasizes the

repeated *survival* of Black Man under the ministrations of the black female body.[1] The contradiction between title and content, between text
and subtext, underlines a criticism of anthropological, scientific, public discourse, and other uses of language that have contributed to the
genocide of groups of people, specifically the peoples of the African
diaspora. Parks's discursive re-presentation is crucial because "how things
are represented and the 'machineries' and regimes of representation in
a culture do play a *constitutive*, and not merely a reflexive, after-the-
event, role" giving "the scenarios of representation—subjectivity, identity,
politics—a formative, not merely an expressive, place in the constitution of social and political life (Hall, "New" 443). Parks focuses on how
the language generated by policymakers and disseminated to the popular consciousness by various media presents the colonized body as cultural artifact. While accentuating how the fetishizing of the black body
permeates discourses that have detrimental economic, social, cultural,
and political consequences, she also reveals how gaining mastery over
signifiers entails the possibility of transforming the black body from a
representation of violence and dehumanization to representing a subject
with a greater degree of agency.

Parks's play dramatizes how public narratives often construct the
rending of the black body as normative. The character named Voice on
thuh TV states: "Upon careful examination thuh small sliver of thuh tree
branch what was found has been found tuh be uh fossilized bone frag-
ment. With this finding authorities claim they are hot on his tail" (89–
90). We see how, as Spillers puts it, "the anatomical specifications of
rupture, of altered human tissue, take on the objective description of labo-
ratory prose" (67). The word "tail," representing how the objectification
of the black body becomes a controlling "tale," is a potent reminder of
how language was manipulated to discursively animalize Africans and
rationalize racial supremacy and domination. The Voice on thuh TV illustrates how language is used to represent the black subject by naming
black body fragments. In a moving scene, Black Man concisely relates
his history to Black Woman, conflating his experiential knowledge of
violence with the animalized ancestry invented by racial supremacists:
"[t]hey . . . [p]ulled me out of thuh trees then treed me then tired of me."
After his painful experience, Black Woman tells him: "You smell." He
exclaims: "On me in my bones. Oh! My shame! On me in my bones.
Maybe I should bathe. Oh! My shame." Words like "tail" and "bones"
evoke the historical death and deterioration that resulted from slavery.
They point out that the black body was constructed as artifact and "consumed" by the economic and ideological systems that created American society. They also linger as painful signifiers of the shame that arises

from the process of objectification. It is Black Woman who offers Black Man solace by proposing that there are possibilities for him beyond his shame. She tells him: "Must be somewhere else tuh go aside from just go gone. Huh" (89).

Black Woman repeatedly instructs Black Man to "gobble up" anything he wants to make his own, proposing to him that the act of writing constitutes incorporation (84). Black Man then internalizes the larger perspective she suggested and passes that knowledge on to another black male character, And Bigger And Bigger And Bigger. Bigger recounts his history: "Sir name Tom-us and Bigger be my christian name. . . . I am grown too big for my own name" (87). His wish is "tuh fit in back in thuh storybook from which I camed" (88). At the end of Richard Wright's *Native Son*, Bigger Thomas is on death row, and in Parks's play, Bigger repeats, "Would somebody take these straps off uh me please? I would like tuh move my hands" (86). Black Man offers Bigger the solution he learned from Black Woman: "My text was writ in water. I would like tuh drink it down" (88). Black Woman proposes that to be able to in-*corp*orate oneself is why the act of writing, with its repetition and revision of language, is so crucial to the survival of Black Man and the African American community. She presents a coherence and reassurance to the fragmented black body of the play. Incorporation serves to rewrite the black female body as the site of transformation and empowerment.

Gender and cultural context are crucial to this play not only because it is written by an African American woman or because it manipulates language and dramatic forms that necessitate a move away from patriarchal paradigms but also because it considers the question of the survival of Black Man from a womanist perspective. Black Man's survival is integrally connected to Black Woman, as the survival of both is to the larger African American community. Parks takes the opportunity to construct a female subject position within the destructive historical and discursive context of violence upon black "flesh." Representations of the black male body in pain predominate in the play, while such female characters as Black Woman with Fried Drumstick are represented as the nurturers and sustainers who heal broken bodies. Black Woman with Fried Drumstick resists the framework of racial violence, handles the neighbors, kills hens, cooks, feeds, informs, and keeps the faith. A motherlike figure, she is constructed as a powerful female under the extreme circumstances of slavery and its aftermath. When Black Man arrives with a tree branch still tied to the noose around his neck, Black Woman says: "Your days work aint like any others day work; you bring your tree branch home. Let me loosen thuh tie let me loosen thuh necklace let me loosen up thuh noose that stringed him up let me leave thuh tree branch be. Let me rub your wrists." Within the context of a lynching occurring "among . . . picnic baskets," Parks's dramatization transforms the conventional female domestic sphere (89). Parks's work exemplifies what Tate calls the "gendered literary strategies of social intervention" in which "domesticity becomes a site of female political negotiation, and the heroine a self-authorized political agent" (21). Since "female slaves had only slight biological claim on the institution of motherhood and about as much social claim on that of womanhood as a brood mare, sow, ewe, or cow" the appropriation of black female domesticity can be construed as a radical act (25). Parks's assertion of Black Woman's domesticity depicts, as Tate writes, "freedom not simply as an escape from the political condition of slavery but as the gaining of access to the social institutions of motherhood, family, and home" (32). Parks sustains an ambiguity as to whether Black Woman is wife, mother, or a nurturing nonrelative of Black Man, allowing Black Woman to be read as a representative, even archetypal, female. Out of necessity, poor families often share beds, and terms of affection and endearment are exchanged between individuals regardless of blood relations. In light of slavery's denial of formal kinship relations, the particulars of blood, legal, or sacramental relationships are of lesser importance than the actions of love and healing carried out between individuals to ensure their survival. Their supportive relationship, however, falls within what Ann duCille terms the "coupling convention" (14). DuCille identifies coupling as "the primary signifiers of freedom and humanity" for black female literary subjects, while noting that "critics have taken little note of this subversive, political use of the coupling convention" (19). Contrary to the discourse pathologizing the African American woman as a contemptuous matriarch, the play presents Black Woman as the foundational discursive matrix that ensures the survival of "Ours" (90).

Representations of black women's bodies are further complicated by the material realities of the female slave's function as not only the means of production through her slave labor but also the means of slave reproduction. Under conditions of domination, in which African bodies were constructed as property, gender roles for black men and women were effectively dismantled, along with kinship relations, language, name, and history. Spillers notes that "[u]nder these arrangements, the customary lexis of sexuality, including 'reproduction,' 'motherhood,' 'pleasure,' and 'desire' are thrown into unrelieved crisis" (67). The position of powerlessness in which the slave was placed calls for a reexamination of gender construction. Although Parks's construction of the black female person may appear problematic because of its emphasis on the role of nurturer and transmitter of history, culture, and language, it must be critiqued within the context of the material realities of reproduction and motherhood for female slaves.

The extreme conditions of slavery enacted a process of ungendering, since personhood and all the concomitant identity characteristics that definition entails are mutually exclusive to the state of being an object—in effect, a nonperson. As Spillers clarifies, "[b]ecause African-American women experienced uncertainty regarding their infants' lives in the historic situation, gendering, in its coeval reference to African-American women, *insinuates* an implicit and unresolved puzzle both within current feminist discourse *and* within those discursive communities that investigate the entire problematics of culture" (78). The recuperation of those roles for the African American female subject that feminism correctly construes as constricting signifies one way of approaching the restoration of expressions of female gendering that were denied during slavery. That is not to recommend the powerlessness and submissiveness of the Cult of True Womanhood to African American women but rather to explain the reasons for the centrality of nurturing roles in the creation of African American female characters in modern texts about slavery. Slavery's denial of the rights of motherhood to slave women resulted in a void that demands that the femininity of enslaved and non-enslaved women be explored differently because, however circumscribed, there were laws in place to protect the legitimacy of motherhood and rights of kinship to nonenslaved women. The rights of maternity—and paternity—were nonexistent for slaves.

Parks dramatizes the black female subject's cultural powers and how she used them to create a means of access that would allow her to enact the nurturing and kinship that were legally and socially denied to slaves. The black female body carries out the acts of nurturing, feeding, and soothing as radical acts within an expanded domestic sphere in which black gender relations, subjectivities, and self-affirmations resist hegemonic political, cultural, and social forces. Parks's representation of Black Man and Black Woman dramatizes the kind of relationship described by Tate: "Those held in slavery had their own intraracial relationships and social practices as adaptations to the brutality of this institution, relationships that maintained a veritable equality between the sexes [and] reflected the mutual respect that grew out of domestic and field labor and sharing of their common fate of racial oppression" (56). Because Parks presents these social practices via the black female body as well as being articulated by the black female subject, *The Death of the Last Black Man in the Whole Entire World* can be called a contemporary "domestic allegor[y] of uniquely black *and* female political desire" and can be compared to works Tate describes as "allegories of racial and sexual liberation, as plots of self-definition, self-individuation, indeed as quests that privilege an exploration of the black-female desiring subject" (95).

The play's Overture introduces the first death of Black Man within the context of European expansion, colonization, and the Middle Passage. When the character Black Man With Watermelon says, "[t]he black man moves his hands," the character Queen corrects him by asserting: "Not yet. Let Queen-then-Pharaoh Hetshepsut tell you when" (82). African American history begins, therefore, with pre-Columbian Africa, and Queen is the one who can "tell you when." It is she who tells the true African story: "Before Columbus thuh worl usta be *roun* they put uh /d/ on thuh end of roun making round. Thusly they set in motion thuh end. Without that /d/ we coulda gone on spinnin fo ever. Thuh /d/ thing ended things ended" (83). In retelling the beginnings of African troubles and of the genocide in the New World, the Queen conveys and interprets African American history. The interpretive language of the play, therefore, has feminine origins, and the power of the word is central to the revision of African American history and to the possibilities for recuperating the self inherent in the telling. Language serves to critique paradigms of domination. The "/d/" is representative of the individualistic, European tradition that privileged rationalism over other modes of engaging reality and that labeled and categorized human cultures in a hierarchy that served to legitimate African slavery and colonialism on an international scale. The beginnings of the history of *The Death of the Last Black Man in the Whole Entire World* must therefore begin before slavery, when "world" was still "worl." Putting the "/d/" at the end represents the end of the non-European world as it was then known. As the character Before Columbus says about Europeans: "They thought the world was flat. They stayed at home. Them thinking the world was flat kept it roun. Figuring out the truth put them in their place and they scurried out to put us in ours" (83). The "/d/" at the end of the word represents the change in worldview and the creation of a discourse that fueled conquest, assigned human groups "their place," and made the bottom line the motivation for colonialism and expansionism. The female characters, Queen and Black Woman, are instrumental in emphasizing the importance of the word to the project of the recuperation of identity.

Via the reappropriation of signifiers, Parks uses one of the most effective avenues to representing black female discursive powers. By deconstructing language and manipulating signifiers, Parks transforms the black female body from the symbol of violence and objectification to the source of pleasure, survival, and nurturing relations between individuals within the larger African American community. The black female characters wield discursive power. They establish the times and places of the drama: "There are many ways to wait. One way uhwaited like this way. . . . Nothin tuh do but wait. What we never do but by bein be doin it" (92). This process begins in the play's Overture: "Yesterday today next summer tomorrow just uh moment uhgoh in 1317 dieded thuh last black man in thuh whole entire world" (82). When Black Man repeatedly experiences and survives death, he turns to Black Woman to restore and re-member him. Episodes of violence rupture Black Man's sense of self and seem to leave him confused. He repeatedly asks, "Who give birth to this? I wonder" and "Who gived birth tuh me I wonder?" It is Black Woman who nurses him with "cold compress then some hen. Lean back. You comed back. You got uhway. Knew you would. Hen?" (84). Through the powers of Black Woman—she "who knows"—Black Man and the African American community regenerate themselves. When Black Man, in his post-traumatic confusion, asks: "Was we green and stripe-dly when we first comed out?" Black Woman responds, "Uh huhn. Thuh features comes later. Later comes after now" (84). Parks establishes Black Woman as the principal authority not only on time and history but also on the development of the discursive subject through her particular knowledge of the black body and her ability to invert its stereotyped derogatory significations.

Parks's manipulations of the dramatic form on the level of structure, sustaining and gradually revealing the subtext as historical truth, also hinge on the subject position of the African American female, as embodied in the character of Black Woman . The play is divided into seven sections: Overture, Panel I: Thuh Holy Ghos, Panel II: First Chorus, Panel III: Thuh Lonesome 3some, Panel IV: Second Chorus, Panel V: In Thuh Garden of HooDoo It, and Final Chorus. Panels I, III, and V portray Black Man and Black Woman as the main characters on stage in the aftermath of Black Man's various escapes from death. In spite of the Christian titles of the play's panels, the content of the stories of Black Man and Black Woman are not accurately represented by these titles from the European religious tradition. The discontinuity Parks establishes between European-based title and African-based content creates a space in which the relationship between name and meaning is transformed. The "dislocation between text and image opens up a critical space" in which resistance to the hegemonic culture can take place (Franco 12). Parks constructs a self-representation of the black female body that manifests through speech acts the dissonance between name and meaning. By diminishing the traditional meaning of the external text and reconstituting the internal subtext, Parks simultaneously switches mythological systems, posits a criticism of the hegemonic symbolic order, and privileges the African American female subject position.

If, as Spillers proposes, the dominant discourse reports that the "Negro Family" has no "Father to speak of" and that "it is, surprisingly, the fault of the Daughter, or the female line," then Parks's play contests this "female . . . misnaming" by coupling Black Man and Black Woman as representative mother and father (66). The history of violence on the black body is clearly identified as the result of the "strange relations" with the white father. As Ham relates in his "Ham's Begotten Tree" speech: "Those strange relations between That thuh mother and Yuh Fathuh thuh son brought forth uh odd lot: called: Yes Massuh, Yes Missy, Yes Maam n Yes Suh Mistuh Suh. . . . (90). Black Man with Watermelon is lynched by his white father out of hatred and fear. If the story of slavery in the New World is one of miscegenation and its denial, then Black Man is persecuted by his cultural—and often biological—white father who is also his owner. Hence, as Spillers states, "the black American male embodies the *only* American community of males which has had the specific occasion to learn *who* the female is within itself, the infant child who bears the life against the could-be fateful gamble, against the odds of pulverization and murder, including her own. It is the heritage of the *mother* that the African-American male must regain as an aspect of his own personhood" (80). Parks posits that Black Man's occasion to "learn who the female is within" himself can be construed as an opportunity rather than a handicap, that by regaining "the heritage of the *mother*" he is neither emasculated nor feminized, but instead regains "an aspect of his own personhood."

With this in mind, the survival of Black Man depends on the subjectivity and will to power of Black Woman, in keeping with the womanist agenda that there cannot be liberation for self without liberation for the other. Parks emphasizes the intersection of race and gender supremacy, and posits that recognition of their juxtaposition in the African American experience is crucial to the project of generating a counterdiscourse. She establishes a force other than the patriarchal father to help the black male subject survive; that force is Black Woman and the discursive powers manifested through her black body. Since the white father is a product of Western patriarchy and is the agent responsible for the African American "crucifixion," Black Man can hardly find resurrection through the Judeo-Christian, European patriarchal father who bears the responsibility for his persecution. By telling the "truth" of history, Parks retells a contrapuntal story line that rejects European patriarchy—a story in which it is the relationship between Black Man and Black Woman that saves their humanity. When Black Man resurrects, his return is in the context of the actions taken by Black Woman and in her nurturing him back to health through the restorative forces she represents. He returns from his repeated deaths to her reassuring statement: "knew you would." Black Woman fulfills the roles necessary to survive the extreme circumstances of racial violence, whether it is as nurturer, guerrilla, activist, historian, or philosopher.

The richness of Parks's language is revealed in the play's ability to convey significance through multiple registers. On one level, Panel V: In thuh Garden of HooDoo It presents an indictment of the violence enacted on the black community; on another, it offers an antidote to the effects of that violence. The title of the panel also asks: who is responsible for the persecution of the African American community? Switching metaphysical and linguistic registers, Parks offers Panel V as a way to empower the black community. In the language of "early African-American religion with origins in West African spiritual life," "hoodoo" means "the spirit or essence of everything" as well as "magic" or "spell." Within this cultural context, "HooDoo It" becomes a directive to the African American community to use the "gift of hoodoo" to rectify the aggressors, begin the healing, and ensure the survival of the African American community (Major 240).[2] Parks's gift of hoodoo is language, which she uses to enunciate a self-representation that is black and female, replacing the "logic of binary opposition" with the "logic of coupling" (Hall, "New" 472). Parks's enunciation of African American identity recognizes that identity remains a process of negotiation in which the "hoodoo" of discourse must consistently intervene. A kind of hoodoo priestess with powerful incantations at her disposal, the black female subject that Parks represents is integral to the reconstruction and recuperation of the body and identity of the black male. It is the female characters, Queen and Black Woman, who bring Black Man back from the dead and re-member his body, asking "Why dieded he huh? Where he gonna go now that he done dieded? Where he gonna go tuh wash his hands?" (82).

The motif of the black characters moving their hands is repeated throughout the play. Hands are significant on several levels. Laura Doyle points out that because "the human sense of situatedness originates in an intimate relation with and orientation toward the body of another . . . [a]nother with hands . . . [t]he first 'place' we inhabit is, so to speak, a pair of hands. We are held in space by hands . . . typically those . . . have been a mother's or female mother figure's" (210). The hands of Black Man, isolated as they are from the rest of his fragmented body, also dramatize the separation from the mother, while representations of the black female characters' hands emphasize their recuperative force. As Queen describes it, "I left my mark on all I made. My son erased his mothers mark" (88). In the Overture, Black Man says, "The black man moves. His hands–" and Queen responds, "You are too young to move. Let me move it for you" (82), in a gesture that poignantly attempts to compensate for the loss experienced by both parent and child in the separation slavery forced upon them. Black female hands also represent the loss of communication and connection to homeland and kin. Queen tells that when she saw "Columbus comin . . . I waved my hands in warnin. You waved back. I aint seen you since" (93). Black female hands are the hands that hold, that wave, and that move in this work within the context of the self-representation of black female subjectivity.

Finally, it is Parks's hands that personify black female hands writing subjectivity into the history of African American intellectual production. The symbol of the objectified black female hands becomes the instrument for generating history, reestablishing connections, and empowering the African American subject. Hands are used for writing, and when Black Woman asks, "Where he gonna go tuh wash his hands?" All respond, "You should write that down. You should write that down and you should hide it under uh rock" (83). In this rhetorical gesture, Parks links the fragmented black female body, as represented by the hands isolated by slavery and representative of the tools of slave labor, to language. In the Overture, the character Yes and Greens Black-Eyed Peas Cornbread encourages the others:

> You should write that down because if you dont write it down then they will come along and tell the future that we did not exist. You should write it down and you should hide it under a rock. You should write down the past and you should write down the present and in what in the future you should write it down. It will be of us but you should mention them from time to time so that in the future when they come along and know that they exist. You should hide it all under a rock so that in the future when they come along they will say that the rock did not exist (83).

By representing black female hands as the means of communication via gesture and writing, Parks subverts the representation of the fragmented black body and re-presents the black female body as the discursive site of resistance

Black Woman describes her forms of resistance and action when Black Man was taken away to be executed. Her resistance included not following instructions and "knowing" that Black Man would escape:

> Comin for you. Came for you: that they done did. Comin for tuh
> take you. Told me tuh pack up your clothes. Told me tuh cut
> my bed in 2 from double tuh single. Cut off thuh bed-foot where
> your feets had rested. Told me tuh do that too. Burry your ring
> in his hidin spot under the porch! That they told me too to do.
> Didn't have uh ring so I didnt do diddly. They told and told
> and told: proper instructions for thuh burial proper attire for
> thuh mournin. They told and told and told: I didnt do squat.
> Awe on that. You comed back. You got uhway. Knew you would.
> Hen? (84)

Black Woman's refusal to follow the instructions that would further frag-
ment their lives, as represented by cutting the bed in two and by cutting off the "bed-foot," dramatizes her forms of resistance. "They" would
make her female person the instrument of additional fragmentation. The
black female body acts in ways that resist fragmentation, and Black
Woman refuses to participate in the violence, even symbolically, on black
flesh. When Black Man escapes by outrunning the forty-nine-foot extender
that was hooked up to the electric chair because there wasn't enough
"electric" in the town, Black Woman describes to him the actions she
took:

> Strutted down on up thuh road with my axe. By-my-self-with-
> my-axe. Got tuh thuh street top 93 dyin hen din hand. Dropped
> thuh axe. Tooked tuh stranglin. 93 dyin hen din hand with no
> heads let em loose tuh run down tuh towards home infront of
> me. Flipped thuh necks of thuh next 23 more odd. Slinged um
> over my shoulders. Hens of thuh neighbors now in my pots.
> Feathers of thuh hens of thuh neighbors stucked in our mattress.
> They told and told and told. On me. Huh. Awe on that. Hen?
> You got hway. Knew you would. (84)

By way of explanation she tells him that she "[k]new you will wanted
uh good big hen dinner in waitin. Every hen on the block" (84). Her actions can be read on multiple levels. She is not just making dinner for
her man but destroying the property of the people whose instructions
she had refused to carry out, as well as engaging her representative black
female body in active resistance. Not only does she not do what "they"
tell her to do, she proceeds instead to do the telling herself.

On another level, Parks is re-creating an African-based mythological and cultural context for Black Woman's actions by invoking the symbol of the ax. The ax is the symbol of Shango, a Yoruba god. According
to Gary Edwards and John Mason, "Shango is instant illumination and

retribution . . . just as lightning illuminates the night by allowing one to
see in a flash. . . . Lightning also symbolizes his tongue, and it is his
tongue which distinguishes the truth and the lie" (42). In another scene,
Black Woman explains that "[t]huh lights dimmed in thats what saved
you. Lightnin comed down zappin trees from thuh sky. You got uhway"
(89). Under the Yoruba pantheon, while particular gods may be associated with one or multiple sexes, they cross gender categories when "possessing" humans. Black Woman then, in employing the ax, calls down
the power of the male thunder god. Indeed, it is lightning hitting the
tree that saves Black Man at one point, thereby permitting a turn in the
course of events. If the objectification and animalization of slavery dismantled gender roles, Parks has Black Woman manipulate the ambivalence of gender constructions to her advantage. Black Woman is
represented as accessing the power of the male god and using a symbolically male tool, the axe. As a representative black woman, she tells
the story of African American subjectivity, using her "tongue" to distinguish the "truth and the lie," thereby discursively transforming the
objectified black female body. Much like Pheoby in Zora Neale Hurston's
Their Eyes Were Watching God, who is the audience, confidante, and
interpreter that facilitates the development of Janie's identity through
storytelling, Black Woman bears witness to Black Man, to the African
American community, and to the theater audience. In the shared exchange
between Black Man and Black Woman, history is learned, identity is asserted, and language is manipulated to enact and describe resistance.
Parks figures the discursive black female tongue as the symbolic lightning of language, as the female linguistic force that broke the tree branch
still attached to Black Man's neck and which also brought the rain and
eventual abundance. In the context of this discursive power, it is Black
Woman who keeps the faith and who confirms Black Man's resurrections
with her affirmations, "Knew you would."

Parks's use of the tongue as a symbol accentuates that there is an
integral relationship in this play between orality as language and orality as a mechanism of incorporation. Parks has described the relationship between language and incorporation in the theater by stating that
"in drama, language is taken from the world, refigured, and set on the
page, then taken from the page, refigured, and set loose in the world
again" (Solomon 75). Black Woman's suggestion that eating something
will make it your own corroborates that incorporation is an important
part of access to power. Orality offers an important mechanism for interacting with the world, internalizing phenomena, and even devouring
one's enemies. In addition to the obvious oral forms that constitute theater, turning phenomena into a word (whether spoken or written) makes

it possible to "digest" the experience, to drink it in, to absorb it, and thereby to take control of it. Incorporation makes phenomena one's own and allows one to redirect its energies. That is why the directive to "write it down" is repeated throughout the play. Incorporation is at the core of language and writing and bodily sustenance. Black Woman's actions reveal the multifarious uses of orality. Within the context of his existential anxiety, Black Man asks: "Melon mine?–. Dont look like me." Black Woman's response is: "Gobble it up and it will be" (84). Besides using the lightning of language to set the world right, a mouth can tell the true story, satisfy hungers, and assert identity by incorporation while reversing the image of a black female body from degenerated object to a means of resistance. The play displays an acute awareness of the relationship between identity and language. Incorporation is part of the process of displacing meaning, of the refiguring mechanism that mediates between language that is "set on the page" and language that is "set loose in the world."

The Chorus confirms that the true African American experience "must be *written down*," emphasizing that it was through the black female body that incorporation and refiguration occurred. The play's message that "it must be written down" is a proposal of how a community can consume the modern world and its media technology. If, as Antonio Gramsci proposes, "human nature is the totality of historically determined social relations" and therefore hegemony is the process of continuously mediating forces, then the play dislocates signifiers on the level of the text and thereby contests and negotiates hegemonic forces (133). Hence, when Black Man asks: "The black man bursts into flames. Whose fault is it?" All are able to reply: "Ain't mines" (83). The Chorus instructs the community to use writing to re-member the black body. Among the survival tactics shared is "You should write that down and you should hide it under uh rock." Yes and Greens asks: "Did you write it down? On uh little slip uh paper stick thuh slip in thuh river afore you slip in that way you keep your clothes dry, man." Prunes and Prisms also asks: "Aintcha heard uh that trick?" (86). Not only are these instructions for rescuing and surviving history, but placing a piece of paper into a body of water is part of making a ritual offering, reinforcing the community's belief systems. Writing, represented by "uh little slip uh paper," substitutes for the usual sacrifices of foodstuffs. Writing becomes the glue that bonds the community and contributes to the subject's agency within the stream of intellectual production. Parks thereby extends the representation of orality into the arena of discourse, encouraging the creation of a counternarrative.

Given that orality is central to transformation, it seems only natural that food should be so often represented in the play. Witt has written that the association of African American women with food "is fundamental to the ongoing production of U.S. subjectivities and U.S. national culture" and that food has been "central to much of contemporary black women writers' work" (7, 24). Parks makes symbolic use of food, and more than half of the play's characters bear the names of foods: Black Man with Watermelon, Black Woman with Fried Drumstick, Lots of Grease and Lots of Pork, Yes and Greens Black-Eyed Peas Cornbread, Ham, and Prunes and Prisms. Food is rich in social and cultural associations especially since, as Witt points out, soul food "aficionados and abstainers alike often betrayed a profound and seemingly unconscious ambivalence toward the cuisine that they associated with black slavery, black poverty, and black Christianity" (80). Parks takes advantage of the symbolic potential of food. For example, the character Ham serves multiple duty as a part of the Southern menu, as a biblical figure, as a human body part, and as a referent to black music and culture.[3] Parks manipulates the multiple notions of associating the character Ham with objectified black body parts and uses Ham as a referent to the mythology of the sexualized black body. Food has also served as a powerful metaphor for re-membering the African American cultural body and its history. In *Ma Rainey's Black Bottom*, August Wilson plays with the notion of the United States as a melting pot in which African Americans are the leftovers:

> Everybody comes from different places. . . . Soonawhile they began to make one big stew. You had the carrots, the peas, and potatoes and whatnot over here. And over there you had the meat, the nuts, the okra, corn . . . and then you mix it up and let it cook right through . . . then . . . you got a stew. . . . You take and make your history with that stew. . . . Your history's over and you done ate the stew. But you look around and you see some carrots over here, some potatoes over there. . . . So what you got? You got some leftovers and you can't do nothing with it. You already making you another history. . . . See, we's the leftovers. The colored man is the leftovers. (57)

In her play, Parks constructs a black female body that is symbolically associated with food to different ends. The associations once again provide Black Woman, as discursive subject, an opportunity to challenge the "impassable symbolic boundaries between racially constructed categories" and to construct an alternative meaning, a meaning that can be constitutive of black identity (Hall, "New" 445). Black Man with Watermelon and Black Woman with Fried Drumstick manage to survive because they carry their "food" with them. Not only physically essential for human survival, food also serves as a familiar cultural marker. Food can be used as a device in ritual—when offered to an ancestor or when ingested as part of a sacrament. Parks uses food as a powerful metaphoric tool for restoring what has been ruptured on the physical, social, cultural, and linguistic levels. She maximizes food and all its nutritive forces as a vigorous element in re-membering the black body. To borrow terms from Wilson's Ma Rainey, not only will "leftovers" keep you alive, but with them you can "make another history."

The power of symbolic language regarding food is constitutive not only of history but of ontology. Melons are associated with the black body in a talk Black Man and Black Woman have about being:

BLACK MAN: I:be. You:is. It: be . . . Melon. Melon. Melon: mines.
I remember all my lookuhlikes. . . .

BLACK WOMAN: Gnaw on this then swallow it down. Youll have
your fill then we'll put you in your suit coat.

BLACK MAN: Thuh suit coat I picked out? Thuh stripely one?
HA! . . . Thuh stripely one with thuh fancy patch pockets! (92)

This revised repetition of image and language explains an earlier association with watermelons in which Black Man asks: "Was we green and stripe-dly when we first comed out?" (84). In a word play involving the slang word "juice" for electricity and watermelon "juices," Black Man relates his body to the fruit:

BLACK WOMAN: They juiced you some, huh?

BLACK MAN: Just a squirt. Sweetheart. . . . Flip on up thuh go
switch. Huh! Juice begins its course. . . . Jump-juice meets me-
mine juices. . . . (85)

This close symbolic association between food and self allows Parks to write a counternarrative to the dismembering one of slavery and its aftermath. If the black body can be symbolized as "fruit" only in its dismemberment (recalling Billie Holiday's song "Strange Fruit"), then the symbol's traditional ties to abundance, nature, and regeneration are being repressed. The black body may be conventionally represented as the object of violence, of being "juiced," but Black Woman insists that the black body also means something else. Thus she instructs him to "swallow it down," to "have your fill," in order to re-dress Black Man, as it were, in his "suit" that, while familiar, signifies a totally different meaning and context. *This* "stripely" suit is something *he* picked out, something he clearly expresses pleasure in. Without negating the fact that the black body has been presented as the sign of "strange fruit," Parks re-presents it as a sign of regeneration, of fulfillment, of pleasure.

Food is most often associated with cornucopia and bounty. By foregrounding the regenerative forces of the natural world—like the mysterious proliferation of watermelons—Black Man can thrive in spite of repeated near deaths. Like hens that still give eggs after having their necks wrung, and still sprout feathers after having been fried, Black Man lives. The discursive identification of the black body with food transforms both into metaphors for bounty that go beyond the binary representations of the black female body as the stereotyped site of sustenance or pollution. The "spring-time" and abundance that Parks dramatizes has a restorative effect, as Black Man realizes with some surprise: "My hands are on my wrists. Arms on elbows. Looks: old fashioned. Nothing fancy there. Toes curl up not down. My feets-now clean. Still got all my teeth. Re-member me" (92–93). If reproduction was made unbearable for slave women because the system of slavery transformed motherhood into the reproduction of nonpersons or objects of slavery (as Toni Morrison's novel *Beloved* dramatizes in her story about Sethe), then Parks's association of the black female body and her subjectivity with food's nature takes a step toward restoring the joy, hope, and nurturance that fecundity can represent.

Black Man and Black Woman express wonderment at the abundance at their feet in spite of their lives having being tormented by violence. Black Man exclaims: "Our crops have prospered. Must uh rained why aint that somethin . . . " (88). Black Woman, again with the authority of knowledge, explains: "Winter pro-cessin back tuh back with spring-time" (93). There is humor even amidst the violence: "Our one melon has given intuh 3 . . . 3 August hams out uh my hands now surroundin me an is all of um mines? . . . wrung thuh necks of them hens and they still give eggs. . . . Still sproutin feathers even after they fried. Huh: like you too" (89). Clearly there is evidence of hoodoo power at work. The subtext of regeneration in the final panels of this play accentuates fecundity: in the multiplying watermelons, the nurturing, the re-membering, springtime, and the physical pleasures Black Man and Black Woman come to enjoy. As Black Woman clearly states, "Must be nature" (93). The body's dependent relationship to food makes the latter an ingenious symbol for recovery because food is tied in with the cycles of nature and bodily production. Like the proliferation of watermelons and regeneration of chickens, black men and women continue to survive in spite of death and violence. The bounty may seem incomprehensible but is nonetheless represented as part of a powerful discursive force, as the result of Parks's manipulation of signifiers and their content and meanings. Hélène Cixous reminds us that the material presence of the body is a necessary condition of the circumstance in pain and in performance (547). Parks manipulates the necessity of the material presence of the black body to place it in the circumstance of pleasure. In the last scene of the play, Black Man "remembers what I likes." The bounty of "SPRING-TIME" is accompanied by a reacquaintance with physical pleasure, with what one "likes." In Parks's play, the desires of Black Man and Black Woman "exceed . . . sexual pleasure to become consummate self-affirmation, a confirming life force charged with transformative power" (Tate 105).

The Death of the Last Black Man in the Whole Entire World offers an opportunity for theater to retell the African American history of the pain of the "theft of the body" while re-membering the black body. Against the dramatization of repeated assaults on Black Man in his quest for social equality, Parks re-presents Black Woman as the discursively constructed black female body through whom the perpetually fragmented black male body is re-membered. While the play and its title apparently foreground the black male body, in fact it is the female body manifested in speech acts that transforms the narrative of "flesh" into a subject positionality that proves integral to constructing an integrative discursive body. Parks, as an African American writer, reverses the deteriorative effects of slavery by discursively constructing Black Woman who, while recuperating the body of Black Man within a politicized domestic sphere, is also herself discursively reconstructing black female subjectivity. Parks reconstructs black womanhood "in an enlarged intraracial domesticity as the signifier for enlightened, politicized black self-authority, self-interest, and self-development" (Tate 132). Parks makes use of deconstructed language and dramatic form to contest dominant discourses that have pathologized the black body and to present a counternarrative of the black body as the source of restorative abundance. As a result of these uses of language and dramatic structure, at the end of the play, in the presence of the Figures that comprise the African American community, Black Man and Black Woman recite their body parts and their attachment to each other. Black Man can say that he still "has all his teeth," and Black Woman can exclaim, "I'm still here" (91). The last words of the play instruct "hold it." Does this refer to "holding it" in the body of the text? Does writing operate as the modern propioceptors of the body of cultural memory? Compared to images of loss and dismemberment, such as the hair loss in Adrienne Kennedy's plays, Parks's images posit the re-membering aspects of language through her representations of the black female body. By re-membering the black body, Parks transforms language into the vehicle through which the black female subject not merely survives, but thrives.

NOTES

1. I refer to the 1990 published version of the play. A somewhat different version was later published in Mahone 240–70.
2. Reed wrote in the introduction to *19 Necromancers from Now* that: "Sometimes I feel that the condition of the Afro-American writer in this country is so strange that one has to go to the supernatural for an analogy. Manipulation of the word has always been related in the mind to manipulation of nature. One utters a few words and stones roll aside, the dead are raised and the river beds emptied of their contents" (xix). Parks's uses of time, hoodoo, African-based characters, and dramatic structure merit a comparison to Reed's Hoodoo aesthetics. See also Reed's poem "Neo-HooDoo Manifesto" in his 1972 collection *Conjure.*
3. See Major's definition: "Hambone. n. (1890s–1940s) probably a reference to the human thigh and the hip; word used in children's jingles ('Hambone, Hambone, where you been?'); from the late nineteenth century through the thirties, an all-purpose metaphor for black cultural experience; variously known to refer to rhythm, the penis, hard times." Also, "Hams n. (1930s–1940s) human legs." "Ham n. (1700s–1940s) in Christianity, Noah considered Ham the ancient ancestor of black people; picked up from white use" (220).

WORKS CITED

Carby, Hazel V. "Policing the Black Woman's Body in an Urban Context." *Critical Inquiry* 18 (Summer 1992): 738–55.

Christian, Barbara. "Gloria Naylor's Geography: Community, Class and Patriarchy in *The Women of Brewster Place* and *Linden Hills*." *Reading Black, Reading Feminist.* Ed. Henry Louis Gates Jr. New York: Penguin, 1990. 348–73.

Cixous, Hélène. "Aller à la mer." *Modern Drama* 27.4 (Dec.1984): 546–48.

Doyle, Laura. *Bordering on the Body: The Racial Matrix of Modern Fiction and Culture.* New York: Oxford UP, 1994.

duCille, Ann. *The Coupling Convention: Sex, Text, and Tradition in Black Women's Fiction.* New York: Oxford UP, 1993.

Edwards, Gary, and John Mason. *Black Gods—Orisa Studies in the New World.* New York: Thoruba Theological Archministry, 1985.

Franco, Jean. "What's in a Name? Popular Culture Theories and Their Limitations." *Studies in Latin American Popular Culture* 1 (1982): 5–14.

Gramsci, Antonio. "The Modern Prince." *Selections from the Prison Notebooks of Antonio Gramsci.* Ed. Quintin Hoare and Geoffrey Nowell Smith. New York: International, 1971. 123–202.

Hall, Stuart. "Cultural Identity and Diaspora." *Identity: Community, Culture, Difference.* Ed. Jonathan Rutherford. London: Lawrence, 1990. 222–37.

———. "New Ethnicities." *Stuart Hall: Critical Dialogues in Cultural Studies.* Ed. David Horley and Kuan-Hsing Chen. New York: Routledge, 1996. 441–49.

Herbert, Bob. "The Black Man Is in Terrible Trouble. Whose Problem Is That?" *New York Times Magazine* 4 Dec. 1994: 72–110.

Herring, Cedric, ed. *African Americans and the Public Agenda: The Paradoxes of Public Policy.* Thousand Oaks: Sage, 1997.

hooks, bell. *Talking Back: Thinking Feminist, Thinking Black.* Boston: South End, 1989.

Kelly, Kevin. "The Astonishing Power of 'Last Black Man.'" *Boston Globe* 14 Feb. 1992: 37.

Mahone, Syndè, ed. *Moon Marked and Touched by the Sun: Plays by African American Women.* New York: Theatre Communications Group, 1994.

Major, Clarence, ed. *Juba to Jive: A Dictionary of African-American Slang.* New York: Penguin, 1994.

Moynihan, Daniel Patrick. *The Negro Family: A Case for National Action.* Washington, D.C.: Government Printing Office, 1965.

Parks, Suzan-Lori. "The Death of the Last Black Man in the Whole Entire World." *Theater* (Summer/Fall 1990): 82–94.

Reed, Ishmael. *Conjure: Selected Poems, 1963–1970.* Boston: U of Massachusetts P, 1972.

———. *19 Necromancers from Now.* New York: Doubleday, 1970.

Rev. of *It Shall Be Named*, by Renée Cox. *Black Male: Representations of Masculinity in Contemporary American Art.* New York: Whitney Museum, 1994.

Solomon, Alisa. "'Signifying on the Signifyin': The Plays of Suzan-Lori Parks." *Theater* (Summer/Fall 1990): 73–80.

Spillers, Hortense J. "Mama's Baby, Papa's Maybe: An American Grammar Book." *Diacritics* (Summer 1987): 65–81.

Tate, Claudia. *Domestic Allegories of Political Desire: The Black Heroine's Text at the Turn of the Century.* New York: Oxford UP, 1992.

Wahl, Grant, and L. Jon Wertheim. "Paternity," *Sports Illustrated* 4 May 1998: 62–71.

Wallace, Michelle. *Black Macho and the Myth of the Superwoman.* New York: Verso, 1991.

White, Deborah Gray. *"Ar'n't I a Woman?: Female Slaves in the Plantation South.* New York: Norton, 1985.

Wilson, August. *Ma Rainey's Black Bottom.* New York: Plume, 1985.

Witt, Doris. *Black Hunger: Food and the Politics of U.S. Identity.* New York: Oxford UP, 1999.

DORIS WITT

Detecting Bodies

BarbaraNeely's Domestic Sleuth and the Trope of the (In)visible Woman

*It is sometimes advantageous to be unseen, al-
though it is most often rather wearing on the
nerves.*

—Ralph Ellison, *Invisible Man*

In 1992 African American writer BarbaraNeely published *Blanche on the Lam*, an award-winning first
novel in what has since become a popular detective fiction series.[1] The
eponymous protagonist, ironically named Blanche White, is a dark-
skinned, heavyset, natural-haired, forty-something African American
woman who has chosen to work as a domestic servant rather than become a nurse. *Blanche on the Lam* begins with Blanche being sentenced
to thirty days in a North Carolina jail for bouncing a check. Understandably upset by the prospect of spending a month behind bars—"a jail cell
was cruel and unusual punishment for a person who panicked in slow
elevators" (1)—Blanche avails herself of an opportunity to flee. Taking
refuge as the temporary servant for a wealthy white family, she quickly
becomes drawn into a perilous situation involving inheritance fraud and
murder. Two subsequent installments in the series—*Blanche among the
Talented Tenth* (1994) and *Blanche Cleans Up* (1998)—find Blanche having left North Carolina for Boston and using "hush" money from the white
family to send her niece and nephew to a private school. In *Blanche
among the Talented Tenth* she unravels the causes of two deaths among
members of the black bourgeoisie who vacation on the coast of Maine,
and in *Blanche Cleans Up* she investigates the mysterious murders of
persons connected to a conservative white male politician who is cam-
paigning for governor of Massachusetts.

My initial interest in Neely actually stemmed not from a particular fascination with detective fiction but rather from research I had been doing on black women's labor as domestic servants. No sooner had I seen a review of *Blanche on the Lam*, consequently, than I was off to the bookstore. Since then I have broadened my reading to encompass numerous contemporary African American women detective fiction writers. At the time, however, I construed Blanche primarily as a legacy of Mildred, the protagonist of newspaper columns Alice Childress published during the 1950s under the satiric title "Like One of the Family."[2] The columns (and an eventual book compilation) take the form of conversations engaged in by Mildred, who works in service, with her friend Marge—though the reader hears only Mildred's end of the dialogue. Like Mildred, Blanche is highly critical of the exploitation of domestic servants. Both are well aware that they are treated by their employers like anything but "one of the family."[3] But whereas Mildred focuses her commentary mostly on workplace dynamics and racial politics, Neely presents Blanche as constantly interpreting the meaning of a wide range of physical traits and practices, including skin tone, hairstyle, body shape, fashion choices, speech patterns, eating habits, and reproductive decisions. In fact, one might argue that the detective work Blanche undertakes is very centrally a decoding of contemporary United States body politics, as inflected by sexuality, gender, ethnicity, race, class, age, and (dis)ability. The reader is expected to bring to the novels some preexisting awareness of the interpretive possibilities encoded in these modes of human differentiation. Yet, along with Blanche, the reader is also instructed in the limitations of her or his preconceptions.

In the current cultural climate in the United States—when constructivist discourses of the body compete for mainstream acceptance with resurgent biological essentialism, when efforts to redress ongoing collective discrimination against women and nonwhites are being countered by conservative claims of reverse discrimination, and when a revival of black nationalism has helped further marginalize black feminist perspectives from their already precarious position in the public domain—Neely's portrayal of both Blanche's body and Blanche's efforts to decipher others' bodies becomes particularly fascinating. Blanche prides herself on being open-minded, but her psychic well-being, professional success, and, at times, physical survival require her to form speedy judgments about her employers, coworkers, and acquaintances, as well as about their attitudes toward her. In such situations—which have, of course, historically required subordinated groups in general to become adept at the work of detection—bodily clues always matter. Moreover, in keeping with another of the most salient experiences of African American life and enduring tropes of African American literature, Blanche herself shifts continually between the poles of invisibility and visibility. Treated as non-existent in some contexts, she is the object of intense scrutiny in others. Stephen Soitos has explained that other African American writers preceded Neely in conjoining this experience/trope of invisibility, which has had special resonance for those women of color who work in domestic service, with the genre of detective fiction, which has historically valorized stealth.[4] But as I will attempt to demonstrate through a discussion focusing primarily on Neely's first two novels, the Blanche series is still unique. It has provided not just an important corrective to a literary genre that was overdetermined by the early 1990s to privilege the urban male-oriented noir writings of Walter Mosley but also a compelling exploration of why African American women's pursuit of social justice has, especially given the complexities of identity politics in this same period, necessitated a sometimes contradictory politicization of the body.

Invisibility, Passing, and Disability:
Blanche on the Lam

Like myself, scholars of detective fiction have tended to perceive Neely as more invested in issues surrounding black culture and cultural difference than crime. Soitos claims that while "murder and blackmail provide the motivations for plot development" in *Blanche among the Talented Tenth*, the story itself "has more to do with social frictions among African Americans presented in an insular and intense environment" (232). Similarly, Kimberly Dilley cites Neely's observation that "she came to the mystery novel in part because . . . she could use the mystery element to engage the reader in subjects they would not necessarily read about otherwise" (128). Hence, there is some justification for my perception that the question of "who done it" does not necessarily seem central to the reader's experience of Neely's novels. At the same time, Neely also indicated to Dilley that she was consciously interested in expanding the parameters of detective fiction to include more African American writers and protagonists (99). To appreciate fully the import of Neely's work, consequently, one needs to have at least a basic understanding of how the Blanche series might be contextualized vis-à-vis the genre of detective fiction.[5]

In choosing to focus on Neely as an alternative to the "boys in the 'hood" fixation of much early 1990s United States popular culture—a fixation that contributed to the enthusiastic reception of Mosley's Easy Rawlins and his loyal, if violent, friend Mouse—my aim is not to imply that other contemporary black women mystery writers such as Delores Komo, Nikki Baker, Eleanor Taylor Bland, Valerie Wilson Wesley, Terris

McMahan Grimes, Grace F. Edwards, and Lisa Saxton have not also been creating important counterhegemonic representations. In many ways, in fact, their novels are more successful than the Blanche series in addressing the diversity of contemporary African American urban life—as evidenced by stories featuring struggling private investigators in St. Louis and Newark, a lesbian investment banker in Chicago, a widowed police detective in the Chicago suburbs, a "buppie" state employee in Sacramento, a former police officer turned sociology student in New York City, and two mismatched wives of professional baseball players in Washington, D.C.[6] My concern, rather, is that the existing scholarly literature on detective fiction includes extended treatment neither of how African American women mystery writers have used the genre to engage in debates over the human body nor of the historical circumstances that have helped shape their representations. After reading this scholarship, moreover, one is left with the assumption that, as a popular genre, detective fiction does not warrant the careful textual scrutiny commonly given modernist and other high culture texts—Ralph Ellison's famous novel *Invisible Man* certainly among them.[7]

Vision—seeing and being seen—is central to my attempts to address these critical lacunae for the obvious reason that it serves as a nexus where the social history of black women's invisible labor as domestic servants intersects with the generic history of the private eye. In his study of domestic labor in the United States at the turn of the century, David Katzman observes: "One peculiar and most degrading aspect of domestic service was the requisite of invisibility. The ideal servant as servant (as opposed to servant as a status symbol for the employer) would be invisible and silent, responsive to demands but deaf to gossip, household chatter, and conflicts, attentive to the needs of mistress and master but blind to their faults, sensitive to the moods and whims of those around them but undemanding of family warmth, love, or security" (188). Sociologist Judith Rollins provides ample evidence that such treatment has continued well into the twentieth century. Rollins worked as a domestic for several months during the early 1980s in preparation for writing a study of employer/servant relationships. She describes herself as "surprised at how much rather personal information [her employers] exposed" in her presence (208). After having forced herself to remain silent while working in one kitchen, even though she knew the answer to a question her employers were discussing, Rollins concludes: "This situation was the most peculiar feeling of the day: being there and not being there" (209).

Neely portrays Blanche as meeting with, but also resisting, comparable expectations. In *Blanche Cleans Up*, for example, while serving drinks at a fund-raising event for Allister Brindle's political campaign, Blanche overhears a black minister promise to bring out the inner-city vote for the right-wing gubernatorial candidate:

> Brindle set his glass on the mantle over the fireplace. "Now, about the election." He gave Samuelson's shoulder a little shake. "I really need your help in Roxbury, Maurice."
>
> "Not to worry, not to worry," Samuelson assured him. "Aunt Jemima and Uncle Ben know which side their bread is buttered on. And if they don't, it's my job to tell them." (16)

Outraged, Blanche attempts to remain calm and quiet, in keeping with the code of invisibility for her job, but "before she could stop herself, she turned abruptly and jabbed a sharp elbow into Samuelson's lower spine, knocking him off balance and splashing whatever he was drinking onto his shirt. Uncle Ben and Aunt Jemima that, you butt-sucking maggot!" (16).

At the same time, it is worth noting that Blanche has decided to help serve hors d'oeuvres during the event because she is nosy: "Curiosity—disguised as helping Carrie hand around the canapés—carried Blanche into the library where the guests had gathered for drinks before lunch" (14). This is an exemplary moment where Neely brings the history of black women's invisible labor as domestic servants to bear on the genre of the detective novel and vice versa. The fiction of the servant's invisibility provides an ideal cover for prying eyes.[8] Blanche frequently takes advantage of this fiction and, once she has begun her investigations in earnest, is actually frustrated when her employers "see" her. Thus Neely notes that while Blanche is serving coffee to Brindle and his campaign manager on the morning after a videotape turns up missing—serving coffee, that is, precisely because she hopes to find out what the videotape contains—Brindle "stopped talking when Blanche approached the table. He watched her without a word while she served the coffee. Blanche never looked directly at him, but she could feel his suspicion like a hungry hound sniffing at her ankles" (104–05). Whereas previously Blanche had been invisible to his eyes, hereafter in the novel Brindle watches her almost as closely as she watches him. Because the observer/observed binary is fluid and reversible, furthermore, Blanche often uses the tools of her job as a cover in case she is found in a part of a home where her presence would draw attention: "She lugged the vacuum and a bucket holding a feather duster, furniture polish, chamois, sponge, spray cleaner, and a long-handled brush up the back stairs. She had no intention of using all of these items, but it looked good to have them" (*Blanche on the Lam* 82).

Neely's nuanced treatment of the politics of visibility in the servant/
employer relationship finds an analogue in recent academic studies of
performance as a strategy for disrupting the disciplinary matrix of the
gaze. In *Unmarked*, for example, Peggy Phelan mounts a critique of visibility politics. Noting that many progressive social movements associated with identity have attempted to render the bodies of socially
disempowered groups visible, she insists that we need to be cognizant
of the contradictory underpinnings of the desire to be seen, as well as
its political risks. "Identity," Phelan writes in addressing the first concern, "is perceptible only through a relation to an other—which is to
say, it is a form of both resisting and claiming the other. . . . Taking the
visual world in is a process of loss: learning to see is training careful
blindness" (13). Human visual perception, in other words, is no more
natural than the framing done by a film director; in the process of constructing a visible world, we construct an invisible world as well. As
the Blanche series repeatedly illustrates, members of socially privileged
classes teach themselves not to see domestic servants, and the servants
themselves can help to ensure that they remain unseen—for instance,
by wearing the required uniform or having in their possession the expected tools of their trade. Neely's portrayal of Blanche also clearly reflects, however, what Phelan describes as the fundamental hazard that
underwrites visibility's lure: "Visibility . . . summons surveillance and
the law; it provokes voyeurism, fetishism, the colonial/imperial appetite for possession. Yet it retains a certain political appeal" (6). The entire plot of *Blanche on the Lam* is predicated on Blanche's decision to
accept a temporary position as a servant in order to escape the surveillance of the law. Nonetheless, when she realizes that her new employer,
like one of her predecessors, cannot "stand to see the help in regular
clothes," Blanche concludes that the woman's fear was that others would
"mistake them for human beings" (12). Even when actively wielding the
servant's invisibility as a tactic of resistance to a racist legal system,
Blanche still bristles at the dehumanization of being unseen.

What makes the Blanche series so challenging, therefore, is not just
Neely's appropriation for detective fiction of the traditional invisibility/
visibility binary operative in domestic labor but also the way that she
continually reconfigures that binary's resonance so as to draw the reader's
attention to its instability, historical and cultural contingency, and political ambiguity. At the same time, Neely does not simply dismiss
biological (or naturalizing) discourses of vision and identity. Rather, it
seems to me that she has negotiated a position that allows simultaneously
for biological and constructivist interpretations because both have provided strategies of resistance to the dominant culture and because she

wants her readers to understand the benefits and drawbacks of each option.[9] To support this claim, I will take as my focal point Neely's treatment of two characters in *Blanche on the Lam*: Aunt Emmeline and Mumsfield. Writing in an era when blood has been in many ways deprived of its former association with race, Neely uses these characters to transform the standard passing narrative that prevailed around 1900 into a commentary on the ramifications for African American women of United States society's more recent fascination with genetic determinism.

In *Blanche on the Lam*, shortly after beginning work for a wealthy white couple, Grace and Everett, Blanche realizes that they are out to deprive Grace's cousin Mumsfield of his inheritance from his Aunt Emmeline. When we first meet Aunt Emmeline, Neely describes her as having "dirty white sausage curls which bobbed gently, like the head of the felt and plaster hound dog in the back window of Blanche's cousin Buddy's car" (31). Subsequently, Blanche makes another mental note about Emmeline's appearance, deciding that she "looked like a drunken Little Orphan Annie at eighty, with her frizzy yellow-white hair and blank, watery eyes" (41). Neely reinvokes this specific analogy shortly thereafter, when describing the scene in which Blanche is asked to witness the revision of Emmeline's will, but she makes one important alteration. We are told that Emmeline's "blue satin bed jacket was trimmed with white lace. A matching cap covered her Little Orphan Annie Afro" (53). At this point, in keeping with standard conventions of detective fiction that allow the reader access to all the clues available to the fictional sleuth (even while ideally necessitating that the sleuth still remain one step ahead), the attentive reader might begin to suspect that the woman is "actually" black.

This possibility is particularly accessible to readers already familiar with the concept of passing. This concept has received renewed scholarly attention in recent years, in part because it lends credence to constructivist treatments of race. Earlier in this century these instabilities surrounding the meaning of race emerged in discourses of blood: many whites (and others) fretted that black racial identity was not necessarily visible, that colored blood might be undetectable to the eye. Hazel Carby has argued that in late-nineteenth-century African American literature the figure of the mulatto/a often functioned to foreground the reality of racial intermingling that undermined the fiction of racial segregation (*Reconstructing* 89).[10] Certainly this is one of the functions fulfilled by Mosley's deployment of the thematics of passing in *Devil in a Blue Dress*—namely in the scene in which Mouse reveals to Easy that the visually white Daphne Monet possesses black blood (200). It is

important to bear in mind, however, that Neely works a significant variation on this plot in *Blanche on the Lam*. The woman portraying Aunt
Emmeline is engaged in an act of double passing, since not only is she
not white but (again in keeping with a common plot device of detective
fiction) she also turns out not to be the real Aunt Emmeline.

Neely's decision to portray only the impostor as black does perhaps
mute the potential for *Blanche on the Lam* to follow *Devil in a Blue Dress*
in exposing the fictive foundations of contemporary white society's ongoing investments in racial purity: after all, the reader is given no reason to suspect that colored blood courses through the veins of the real
Aunt Emmeline or her relatives. Yet Neely still manages to use her passing
plot to call into question the validity of biologized narratives of racial
recognition. That is, according to the ideology of passing, it was commonly assumed that members of the in-group would recognize their own.
Neely has Grace acknowledge this belief after Blanche has finally realized that the woman she has understood to be Aunt Emmeline is an impostor. While expressing to Blanche her surprise that the African
American gardener, Nate, had recognized the woman impersonating Aunt
Emmeline, Grace muses: "They say you people always know one of your
own, no matter how light-skinned. But she was so white . . . " (194).
Blanche ponders to herself in response: "The idea that all black people
recognized each other, no matter how diluted their African blood, ap-
pealed to Blanche, but she was proof it wasn't so. It certainly hadn't occurred to her that there was any ancestral connection between her and
that old drunk" (194–95). Readers who had already deduced that the
"Little Orphan Annie Afro" was proof of the impostor's blackness are
thus forced to question their presuppositions about the relationship
among vision, human embodiment, and racial identity.

Yet since Neely portrays Blanche as only reluctantly distancing herself from such narratives of biologized "blood" recognition, it should
come as no surprise that she also allows Blanche to register something
unusual about Emmeline's appearance. During the night after she has
witnessed the alteration of the will, Blanche dreams that "she was chasing
a blood-red bus down a long, narrow highway and was in turn being
chased by Mumsfield. . . . Instead of her own hair, big, fat gray sausage
curls flopped about on her head" (60–61). One might speculate that the
"sausage curls" have indeed made visible (to Blanche) the invisible truth
of the imposter's black blood. As a result, Neely enables her readers to
choose between two very different models for conceptualizing the body
politics of *Blanche on the Lam*, one that allows for the possibility that
racial difference is always perceptibly inscribed on the body (in this case,
via hair) and another that implies that it is not. Arguably, though, Neely

subordinates the latter reading to the former when she notes that Aunt Emmeline is suspicious of Blanche's sleuthing tendencies from the outset. "Don't give me that 'brought you some dinner' crap, gal. I know they sent you here to spy on me!" Aunt Emmeline pronounces (42). It does, this scene would appear to imply, finally take a black woman to know a black woman, for none of the other characters in the novel readily perceive that there might be more to Blanche than meets the eye.

None, that is, except Mumsfield. If Blanche feels no "ancestral connection" between herself and the woman impersonating Aunt Emmeline, she does, to her chagrin, feel a bond with the wealthy white male heir. His eventual appearance in her dream is hardly surprising since Blanche has anticipated Mumsfield's entrance into the kitchen before she has even met him. Her first impression is of "a short, plump young man with almond-shaped eyes. . . . His whole body was round, from the dome of his balding head . . . to his rounded shoulders, baby paunch, and round-toed Buster Brown shoes" (22–23). Having at first mistaken him for a "[c]onceited chauffeur" because he proudly informs her that he is "very good with automobiles" (23), Blanche soon begins drawing comparisons between him and a child she knows who has Down syndrome. She subsequently queries Grace and learns that Mumsfield was born with a genetic variation of Down syndrome known as mosaicism.

Mosaicism is understood to differ from Down syndrome in that it "results from the failure of the chromosome to divide not *before* fertilization but immediately *after*, during the early stages of cell division in embryogeny" (Bérubé 21). What this means is that a person with mosaicism possesses a mixed set of genes—some containing the "normal" twenty-three paired chromosomes and some containing the extra chromosome understood to characterize Down syndrome. Through her deployment of this particular variation in *Blanche on the Lam*, Neely is able to establish a connection between racial passing and what one might call genetic hybridity.[11] Like Aunt Emmeline, Mumsfield exists in the liminal space between two recognized social groups. Aunt Emmeline's visible whiteness renders her not normatively black; her "black" blood renders her not legitimately white. Similarly, Mumsfield's "normal" chromosomes render him, in Grace's accounting, "not as bad" as someone who has full-fledged Down syndrome: "Retarded educable, they call it. . . . [H]e's quite smart in some ways" (70). Yet finally Mumsfield's "normal" cells are not sufficient to outweigh the aberrant ones and remove the qualifier "retarded."

By the early 1990s, the prevailing models of racial difference had long since begun to substitute chromosomes for blood. In this respect, Neely's decision to combine the passing and mosaicism plots might be read as an affirmation of the common poststructuralist critique of scientific claims to objectivity. If science follows culture, and if Western culture has historically been constituted via racism, then we need to be no less suspicious of current scientific discourse about genes than we are about former scientific discourse about blood.[12] From the vantage point of the present moment, moreover, it is even tempting to see *Blanche on the Lam* as foreshadowing the 1994 publication of *The Bell Curve*, Richard Herrnstein and Charles Murray's notorious book arguing that intelligence is (at least in part) quantifiable, genetically determined, and linked to race and ethnicity. Brought forward in this context, Neely's treatment of the issue of Mumsfield's educational ability in *Blanche on the Lam* could be read as a displacement of ongoing debates surrounding African American intelligence. Neely takes such pains to draw the reader's attention to physical similarities between Blanche and Mumsfield—their shared gap teeth and surplus body fat, most notably—that the reader would almost be remiss in refusing to recognize the analogy.

In addition to depicting Blanche and Mumsfield as converging in bodily appearance, another important strategy through which Neely encourages the reader to construe Mumsfield's mosaicism as existing on a continuum with black female difference is by portraying Blanche as feeling, against her will, a psychic connection with him:

> This thing with him was beyond her Approaching Employer Warning Sense, which alerted her to the slightest rustling or clinking of a nearing employer. This was more like the way she always knew when her mother was around, or Ardell, or which one of the children was about to fling open the door and bound through the house. This ability to sense Mumsfield's approach was of the same nature but different. What made it different was the fact that she didn't know this white boy and didn't appreciate having him on her frequency. (45)

As her concern for Mumsfield continues, Blanche wonders whether she would "always find some reason—retardation, blindness, sheer incompetence—to nurture people who had been raised to believe she had no other purpose in life than to be their 'girl' . . . Had the slavers stamped mammyism into her genes when they raped her greatgrandmothers? If they had, she was determined to prove the power of will over blood" (182). In Blanche's musings here, the prevailing twentieth-century strands of biological determinism—genes and blood—have become interchangeable. Regardless of which strand one invokes, Blanche affirms her belief that biology is not destiny, that human beings can be reduced to neither their genetic nor blood makeup.

Given her commitment to resisting ideologies of biological determinism, Blanche is particularly chagrined to realize that, notwithstanding
her efforts to treat Mumsfield as she would any wealthy white employer,
"she too had fallen into the trap of not really listening to what he was
saying" (177). This meditation eventually results in Blanche's conclusion that Mumsfield's "Down syndrome made him as recognizably different from the people who ran and owned the world as she. It was this
similarity that made him visible to her inner eye and eligible for her
concern" (214). Shortly after having staked out what had appeared to
be a constructivist attitude toward biological science—an affirmation of
"will" over "blood"—Blanche finally justifies her emotional investments
in Mumsfield by accepting the empirical reality of his disability and accordingly designating him an honorary black woman. From this perspective, Mumsfield's genetic difference from normative bourgeois white
masculinity renders him, paradoxically, invisible just like Blanche and
thus deserving of being registered by her "sixth sense."[13] Accordingly,
just after Blanche finally comprehends the import of Mumsfield's assertion that Aunt Emmeline "never talked to you, Blanche"—that is, Blanche
has spoken only with the impostor—Neely writes: "Blanche turned her
head and stared out the window while she worked what Mumsfield had
just told her into the mosaic of what she already knew" (177). Obviously
an overdetermined word choice in this context, "mosaic" might be read
as a trope for the multiple and sometimes inconsistent ways of knowing the human body that Blanche mobilizes in her quest to establish a
counterhegemonic mode of existence as a working-class black woman
in a bourgeois white man's world.[14]

Of course, construing Neely's motives in this fashion does not ob-
viate the need to ask whether drawing such an analogy between race
and "retardation" (or, more broadly, disability) is politically justifiable.
This question carries particular resonance for a discussion of Neely since
African American women helped pave the way for current recognition
of the limitations of analogical thinking—namely, that it tends to elide
the existence of those who inhabit both sides of a given equation.[15]
Viewed from this perspective, Blanche's attempt to interpret Mumsfield's
situation using an interpretive framework that she has developed to explain her own experience of social subordination as a working-class black
woman needs to be viewed with some skepticism on the part of the
reader. In what specific ways is discrimination against those with
disabilities comparable to and divergent from discrimination based upon
race, gender, and/or class? And how, under this model, would one
theorize the status of persons of color who have disabilities? Clearly, then,
there are problems with Blanche's epiphany about Mumsfield.

Yet it would surely be wrong to dismiss Neely's efforts to explore the congruencies between race and disability—especially since she published *Blanche on the Lam* in the wake of the passage of the Americans with Disabilities Act of 1990. As Rosemarie Garland Thomson has explained:

> after identifying disability as an "impairment that substantially limits one or more of the major life activities," the law concedes that being legally disabled is also a matter of "being regarded as having such an impairment." Essential but implicit to this definition is that both "impairment" and "limits" depend on comparing individual bodies with unstated but determining norms, a hypothetical set of guidelines for corporeal form and function arising from cultural expectations about how human beings should look and act. (6–7)

Blanche's willingness to view Mumsfield from both biologizing and constructivist perspectives, as well as her eventual conclusion that he occupies a position in society analogous to that of black women, might be construed as Neely's way of affirming the efforts of disability rights activists to adopt the politically productive—if still, as in Phelan's account, flawed—oppositional model of identity politics in challenging the privileging of "normate" lives, needs, and bodies.[16]

Moreover, because African American women have themselves been excluded from normative human subject positions by virtue of their real and perceived differences from (bourgeois) white men, they, too, are symbolically configured as "disabled," even if they are otherwise ablebodied. Thomson has demonstrated in her own efforts to reconceptualize disability as a minority identity rather than a physical pathology that African American women writers such as Ann Petry and Toni Morrison have frequently represented characters with disabilities—particularly black women—in a way that "insists upon and celebrates physical difference" (105). By refusing to render nonnormative bodies invisible, these writers "repudiate such cultural master narratives as normalcy, wholeness, and the feminine ideal" (105). The question Thomson's approach raises, though, is whether bringing black female bodies as a collective into the *discursive* realm of disability tends to elide the *material* heterogeneity of those bodies—as manifested by differences in shape/size, hairstyle/texture, skin color, age, and so forth. This question underwrites, in part, my inquiries into Neely's representation of Blanche's own body in the series' second novel.

Visibility, Colorism, and Carnival:
Blanche among the Talented Tenth

Even as *Blanche on the Lam* adapts the conventions of detective fiction to work variations on the theme of the black servant's invisibility in white households, by foregrounding the instabilities in Blanche's own status as a perceiving subject, Neely also repeatedly asks her readers to envision Blanche as the object of the gaze.[17] Shortly after Blanche flees the courthouse at the outset of *Blanche on the Lam*, for example, Neely describes her protagonist as "a stout woman" who "didn't consider herself fat," though "she did admit to having big bones and hips. And breasts and forearms to match, when it came right down to it. Only her legs were on the smallish side" (6, 7). Subsequently, we learn that Blanche has not processed her hair since switching to a natural twenty years previously and that she is dark-skinned. In a key series of binaries through which hegemonic United States body politics are (despite the successes of the Black Power mantra "Black Is Beautiful") still articulated—fat/thin, kinky/straight, dark/light—Blanche has gotten the devalued end of the deal. Rather than lessening her appeal as a protagonist, however, Blanche's physical appearance is clearly both intriguing and (ideologically) attractive to Neely's readership. "Blanche is ample-figured and smart," notes a reviewer of *Blanche on the Lam* in *Essence* magazine (Washington); others refer to her as "[q]ueen-sized" (DeCandido) and as a "dark-skinned domestic-by-choice who suffers much humor because of her name . . . " (Harris, Rev. 143).

Preoccupation with Blanche's body has been even more apparent in the remarks of nonprofessional reviewers. Most memorably, a reader who identifies herself as "the daughter of a domestic worker" posted the following comment on Amazon's website for *Blanche Cleans Up*:

> I'm ecstatic that Neely has done something quite revolutionary: She has given us a bright-colors-wearin', eggplant-black, size sixteen sista with a head full of natural hair and a sense of entitlement to match it all. At last, at last.
>
> In a literary world where women authors of color still create main characters who look nothing like their African selves; in a music world where pop stars croon to video stars who look nothing like any woman in their family; in a glamour industry where ethnic clones of Barbie still rule, what a daring and refreshing change. (Texas)[18]

Such an assertion would tend to suggest that the popularity of the Blanche series is inextricable, especially for African American women readers, from its protagonist's physical embodiment. Indeed, the intensity of this psychic investment is perhaps best illustrated by the recognition that Blanche does not even actually possess all of the traits that are attributed to her. For example, although in *Blanche among the Talented Tenth* Neely does portray Blanche as offering sympathy to a black woman who is ridiculed for wearing "loud" clothing, nowhere in the series are we given to understand that Blanche herself typically wears "bright colors."[19]

To understand Blanche's appeal, one thing we need to bear in mind is that the meaning of bodily markers such as weight or skin color takes on different configurations in the series depending on the context. In *Blanche on the Lam*, the main binary through which the body politics operate is black versus white—especially working-class black women (represented by Blanche and, provisionally, the rotund Mumsfield) versus bourgeois white women (represented by the slender but aging Grace).[20] Neely might be said to have appropriated the classic mistress/servant dynamic promoted most memorably by Hollywood films, a dynamic that required black actresses who performed as movie maids, such as Louise Beavers, to maintain fat bodies in keeping with the prevailing stereotype of mammy (Bogle 62–63). But rather than contesting this history by creating a size-eight protagonist, Neely instead invests the stereotype with new meaning.[21] To focus only on such interracial dynamics, however, is to flatten out important nuances in Neely's representation of contemporary United States body politics. In particular, doing so can lead one to ignore the substantial intraracial fissures that structure the Blanche series, fissures that are most fully realized in *Blanche among the Talented Tenth*. Whereas *Blanche on the Lam* offers the reader only scattered glimpses of Blanche interacting with other African Americans, mostly via telephone, *Blanche among the Talented Tenth* explores Blanche's hypervisibility once she enters the world of wealthy blacks. In her first novel Neely uses Blanche's body to critique white female models of beauty, but in her second novel she begins waging a campaign to affirm the desirability of dark skin, natural hair, and large size. The main target of her wrath, though, is the presumed devaluation of these features by socioeconomically privileged African Americans.

The premise of *Blanche among the Talented Tenth* is that Blanche's niece, Taifa, and nephew, Malik, whom she is raising at the request of her late sister, have been invited to spend the summer at Amber Cove, the vacation home of two of their classmates. Blanche agrees to oversee all four children while the parents of Taifa and Malik's friends spend time alone. After arriving, she learns that Faith, an unpopular resident of the resort, has recently died in a suspicious accident; shortly thereafter another resident commits suicide. Yet even as Blanche becomes involved in a quest to understand the story behind each death, she also grows preoccupied with decoding the motives of her new suitor, the light-skinned, old-monied Robert Stuart (a.k.a. Stu). In developing this novel, Neely caters to readers who have some knowledge of African American history. The book's title alludes to the early-twentieth-century idea, propagated most famously by W.E.B. Du Bois, that a small percentage of educated African Americans should be the advance guard in the movement for racial equality.[22] By the early 1990s, in the midst of growing fissures between African Americans who had entered the professional classes in the wake of post-1960s social reform movements and those who remained disenfranchised, black intellectuals such as Henry Louis Gates Jr. and Cornel West were positioning themselves as heirs to the mantle of the Talented Tenth—even though Du Bois himself had abandoned this concept after growing disillusioned with both the United States and the economic system of capitalism.[23]

Of course, long before Gates and West achieved public notice, economically successful African Americans had been scripted as the black bourgeoisie and dismissed with contempt by sociologist E. Franklin Frazier for unquestioningly mimicking white middle-class mores. Although Frazier did comment in his 1957 study on what he perceived as a tendency among middle-class black women "to put on . . . weight" (222), he does not generally dwell on the appearance of black bourgeois bodies. Anyone familiar with African American cultural history is aware, however, that the black middle class has long been associated with specific regulatory practices of the body: naturally "good" or artificially straightened hair; naturally light or artificially lightened skin; and, currently at least, a slender physique. During the era of the Talented Tenth's first reign, Wallace Thurman had most famously led the way in exposing the "secret" of intraracial colorism. His 1929 Harlem Renaissance novel *The Blacker the Berry* depicts the trials of a woman whose obsession with her dark skin exacerbates her very real experience of discrimination in what Zora Neale Hurston contemporaneously labeled a "color struck" society. Like Thurman and Hurston before her and many other black artists since, Neely critiques the problematically masculinist, as well as elitist, Talented Tenth ideology of racial uplift by demonstrating how intraracial class conflicts have been articulated via regulatory practices of the female body. [24]

In the largely white context of *Blanche on the Lam*, Blanche poses little threat to a woman such as Grace because the uniform she is forced to wear operates mainly to reinforce a distinction that our existing cultural codes allow us to recognize as already visibly inscribed on Blanche via her large butt, dark skin, kinky hair, and gap teeth. In *Blanche among the Talented Tenth*, by contrast, these same features render Blanche much more of a disruption to African Americans whose aim is to disassociate themselves from the working class. Thus, shortly after arriving at Amber Cove, Blanche finds herself contemplating

> the close relationship between light skin and wealth—hadn't she read somewhere that light-skinned blacks made a dollar for every seventy-three cents dark-skinned blacks made? . . . So folks here could dis her on two counts. She'd already discovered she couldn't pass for white, even in her imagination and she'd been around the well-to-do long enough to know that there weren't enough expensive clothes in the world to help her pass for money. It wasn't simply how a person dressed or talked that marked them, but how long they could sit without fidgeting and how easily they assumed they were at the top of whatever pecking order might be in place—traits that came from at least three generations of never having to be concerned about survival, and never coming in contact with need. (21)

These musings evoke Richard Dyer's argument that "[m]uch of the cultural history of the past few centuries has been concerned with finding ways of making sense of the body, while disguising the fact that its predominant use has been as the labour of the majority in the interests of the few" (138). Blanche perceives that the black bourgeoisie, like its white counterpart, would prefer not to be reminded that its lifestyle is made possible by the laboring masses. But this desire to naturalize class inequality is even more complicated for African Americans than for European Americans. As Carby has explained, middle-class blacks live a "contradictory existence" because they define themselves against the working class even as the concept of "The Race" forces them to pursue solidarity with all African Americans regardless of class position ("Policing" 746).

Accordingly, in *Blanche among the Talented Tenth*, Blanche is made aware of the disruption she poses to Amber Cove society from the moment she first enters the inn's main lobby. Neely carefully delineates the undisguised disdain with which she is treated by the desk clerk, Arthur Hill. After having stared at Blanche's "unprocessed hair," Hill "placed his hands on the counter, leaned slightly forward and played his eyes over her luggage, shoes, and clothes in a way that said who made her clothes and how well she'd whitified her hair were major issues for him. In the case of someone as black as her, were her clothes and the condition of her hair even more important to him? Something had to compensate" (15–16). Himself only a fantasized member of the bourgeoisie

that employs him, Hill takes umbrage at Blanche's audacity in presenting herself as a guest of Amber Cove because her appearance denatural-
izes the association between class status and physical embodiment, thus
forcing him to acknowledge his own conflicted loyalties. Admittedly,
however, Neely's description of this particular encounter only imperfectly
illustrates my claim inasmuch as Blanche's body size does not appear
to be an issue. In Blanche's reading of his thought processes, Hill is concerned primarily with her hair, color, and clothing, and this portrayal
seems noteworthy given the way that the novel's opening paragraph calls
attention to Blanche's "substantial" behind.

Subsequent scenes in the novel also suggest that hairstyle/texture
and skin color function for Blanche as markers of black bourgeois aspi-
ration toward whiteness in a way that weight does not. For instance,
when Blanche accidentally bumps into Veronica Tatterson, causing her
to drop a hair-straightening product, Neely's description of Blanche's
perception of Veronica contains a telling omission:

> With her sandy blond hair and old ivory skin, Blanche had
> thought the woman was white; a closer look revealed that some
> of that lack of color was due to skillfully applied makeup that
> made her face a shade or two lighter than her arms. She had
> the kind of wavy and shoulder length, kink-free hair many little
> black girls would kill their Barbie dolls for, even today. But ap-
> parently she was getting some help with that. . . . Poor thing, she
> thought. At the same time, she wanted to laugh at this silly
> woman made uncomfortable because someone she didn't know
> now knew she used chemicals to give her hair that white-girl
> look. (19–20)

At stake here is not the size and shape of Veronica's body but instead
Blanche's discovery that Veronica uses cosmetics and chemicals to make
her skin appear lighter and her hair straighter.

To pursue the question of what it means for both the intraracial class
politics and the detective plot of *Blanche among the Talented Tenth* that
the thematics of hair texture, skin color, and body shape are not always
articulated in a parallel fashion, I will first consider in greater detail
Neely's treatment of hair and color. In the two passages that I have just
quoted, Blanche equates straightened hair with a desire to emulate
whiteness—hence, her subsequent delight in seeing Veronica's prospec-
tive daughter-in-law, Tina, who not only is very black, but whose
"[d]readlocks hung to her shoulders" (67). Blanche is drawn to Tina before she has even met her because she presumes that her dreadlocks must
reflect racial self-affirmation. Such a perception runs counter, however,

to recent scholarly work on the politics of black hairstyles. For example, Kobena Mercer has argued that practices such as straightening hair do not transparently reflect a desire to be white, that, if "*de-psychologize[d]*" and recontextualized as "a popular *art form* articulating a variety of aesthetic 'solutions' to a range of 'problems' created by ideologies of race and racism" (100, 101), these practices can be understood to function as a mode of black cultural affirmation.[25] Yet even though Blanche herself subsequently responds to Malik's expressed desire to grow dreadlocks by pondering with disdain the image of "bunches of boys in dreds with their pants hanging off their butts rapping about what bitches black women were" (152), Neely still does not allow Blanche consciously to consider alternative possibilities for interpreting the meaning of what she perceives as "whitified" hairstyles.

Just as Blanche associates straightened hair with black racial self-disavowal, she generally perceives light-skinned African Americans to be less truly black than dark-skinned African Americans. When she walks into the dining room at Amber Cove a day after arriving, Blanche immediately notices that she is the only dark-skinned person in the room. Realizing with shock that everyone is staring at her, she quickly takes stock of the workers and members whom she has encountered thus far and is "pleased to find the humor in being the only guest present with any true color" (40). Whereas in *Blanche on the Lam* Neely had gone out of her way to complicate the connection between skin color and racial identity, in *Blanche among the Talented Tenth* her efforts to critique intraracial colorism lead her to provide Blanche with a less flexible model. In keeping with the dialectical pattern that we have seen before, however, Neely complicates this issue by including the scene in which Blanche mistakes Veronica for a white woman and also an exchange in which Stu explains how he was rejected by his father for being light skinned: "All my life he was saying things like, 'Boy! Why don't you get some sun,' or 'Boy, you don't have as much color as a vanilla shake!'" (179). Angry at Stu because he has earlier revealed dismay at her choice of profession, Blanche remains silent while thinking to herself, "Another variation on the color fuck-up" (179). Using this technique, Neely offers the reader access to multiple models for construing the relation between skin color and racial identity/authenticity even as she insists that, while colorism may exact a psychological toll on light- as well as dark-skinned blacks, the latter group also pays a financial toll.

Of course, Blanche's own immediate attraction to Stu—at first sight, she thinks to herself that "he probably gets anonymous pussy in the mail" (34)—would tend to suggest that she herself is not entirely immune to desire for "blue-green eyes," hair with "just a hint of wave," and skin the color of "milk with a dollop of coffee, instead of the other way around" (34). But Neely disavows Blanche's participation in what might be termed a form of intraracial "jungle fever" by indicating that the "physical attributes" of Stu that infatuate Blanche are not his hair and color but rather his "big hands with long, graceful fingers and the kind of lean hips that promised one of those pert, kissable behinds" (35). This depiction of Blanche's fantasy about Stu's buttocks is especially note-worthy not only because Blanche's own "size-sixteen" behind seems so symbolically important to *Blanche among the Talented Tenth* but also because body size and shape operate in the novel as a strategy for articulating intraracial class conflicts in a fashion that diverges from the way hair and color operate.

Perhaps most significantly, Neely frequently invokes Blanche's "big butt" as a synecdoche for black bourgeois attraction to the black work-ing class that it simultaneously others.[26] This desire is structured along a heterosexualized binary, primarily via the relationship between Blanche and Stu. Blanche's musings about Stu's motives in courting her offer an astute explication of this dynamic:

> She knew she was attractive to the kind of black men whose African memory was strong enough for them to associate a big butt black black [sic] woman with abundance and a smooth com-fortable ride, men who liked women who ate hearty and laughed out loud. Mostly they were men who worked with their hands at jobs not designed to be enjoyed. So they let their cars and clothes and personal styles describe who they were instead of their job in the sanitation department, or as a bag handler at the airport, or hotel doorman. . . . Stu wasn't that kind of man. He didn't act like one and he certainly didn't live like one. . . . And then there were his looks. He wouldn't be the first light-skinned man who'd thought her blackness meant an automatic trip to paradise in gratitude for his willingness to screw someone as black as her. . . . (56–57)

Once again refusing to locate herself solely in the camp of either bio-logical determinism or social constructionism, Neely allows the reader two divergent possibilities for construing the import of Blanche's body shape for Stu and other African American men. Whereas the allusion to "African memory" invokes a naturalized conception of black American men as sharing a collective, even atavistic, racial investment in what one might term the "Hottentot Venus" figuration of black female bod-ies, the remainder of the passage rescripts this claim in terms of the historically contingent realities of working-class black male economic disenfranchisement and light-skinned black male exploitation of colorism's disparate impact on black women.[27]

Intriguingly, moreover, Stu's fascination with Blanche's body turns out to be intricately connected to his emergence as the villain of the novel's detective plot. As a result, Blanche's efforts to decode the body politics of her romantic relationship with him eventually become inextricable from her efforts to decode the mystery of the deaths at Amber Cove. During Stu's confession scene toward the end of *Blanche among the Talented Tenth*, we learn that, while serving in the military during the Black Power era two decades earlier, he had fallen in love with and later married a "beautiful" Vietnamese woman, Thuy Duong. But after Stu's father threatens to disinherit him if he marries "outside the race" (217), Stu decides not to inform his parents that he and Thuy have already wed. Angry at Stu's cowardice, Thuy abandons him and takes up a new life in Philadelphia's Chinatown using the name Susan Moon. Stu locates her and attempts to rekindle the relationship, but she dies in his arms. Afraid of being charged with murder, Stu abandons her body in a dumpster. When Faith eventually steals an anklet that Stu had purchased for Thuy as a gesture of reconciliation, the plot is set in motion that leads to Stu's exposure.

The significance of Stu's marital history for the body politics of *Blanche among the Talented Tenth* becomes apparent when Stu explains to Blanche why he had failed to anticipate his father's response to Thuy. She was "[s]o delicate," he recollects, "I knew Dad would love her, even if she wasn't black" (217). Whereas previously the reader might have been able to construe Blanche as paranoid in her inability to believe that Stu's attraction to her is motivated by more than a desire to experience the thrill of sexual "slumming," after receiving this information we are left with little choice but to interpret Stu's courtship as a form of (posthumous) revenge against his color-struck father. With her big butt, black skin, gap teeth, and kinky hair, Blanche embodies in fetishistic excess all the features that the "delicate" Thuy had lacked. Yet it also seems possible that Neely wishes the reader to interpret Thuy's own adoption of the name Moon to have been a joke as well—and not only for its obvious pun on the Moonies and attendant anxieties regarding the "yellow peril."[28] To "moon" someone, after all, is to expose one's buttocks, and the most common stereotypes of Asian women include the possession of neither a "big butt" nor its earthy promise of "abundance and a smooth comfortable ride." Furthermore, since the Moon as a "heavenly body" is commonly gendered as passively feminine, Thuy's new surname also parodies the cultural construction of Asian women as, unlike black women, accepting of male domination. Quite the contrary, Thuy and

Blanche both refuse to condone black patriarchal regulation of women's bodies. Yet Blanche herself goes farther by appropriating the masculine prerogative of physical revenge. After hearing Stu's confession, she puts "the force of all her rage and betrayal, the weight of her entire frame behind the fist she [drives] into his stomach. Air whooshed out of him as though he were a released balloon" (219).

Construing Neely's deployment of "butts" and "Moon" as a multivalent joke might ultimately help explain not only how the mystery plot of *Blanche among the Talented Tenth* is connected to the novel's body politics but also why body size and weight often seem to function for Blanche as a counterpoint to, rather than merely an extension of, color and hair obsessions. Throughout the novel, Neely adopts precisely the analytic model that Mercer has critiqued in that she carefully psychologizes black fixation on hair texture and skin color through an extended portrayal of Blanche's thought processes as she ponders their meaning for African Americans. But her treatment of Blanche's weight, by contrast, often veers toward what Mikhail Bakhtin has described as the "carnivalesque"—utopian moments when bourgeois bodily norms are disrupted by what he labels the intrusion of the "grotesque" body. When Blanche uses "the weight of her entire frame" to punch Stu, for example, the air that "whooshed" out of him might be understood as an eruption of the grotesque, albeit an aptly vacuous eruption in that it presumably represents the deflation of his (overinflated) ego. Although Bakhtin explicitly associates the grotesque body with the working class, one can readily infer from his arguments that "negroes" and women exemplify a grotesque aesthetic more readily than do whites and men (230, 240).[29]

Far from wishing to represent herself in terms of the classical model that functions for Bakhtin as the grotesque's constitutive opposite, however, Blanche often deploys her bodily functions as a strategy of resistance. For instance, at the outset of *Blanche on the Lam* she uses her need to "ease her bowels" as an excuse to delay being taken to jail. When the matron responds to the sound and/or smell of Blanche's excretions by announcing in a "disgusted tone" that she will wait outside (3), a situation is created that enables Blanche to flee. Neely also portrays Blanche as invoking grotesque bodily functions as an analogy for the skin and hair obsessions of middle-class African Americans, particularly women. Most memorably, when she knocks the shopping bag containing hair-straightening chemicals from Veronica's arms, Blanche thinks to herself that Veronica "looked as though Blanche had caught her farting at the dinner table" (19). Blanche is trying to negotiate a position that resists both white and middle-class black constructions of working-class African American women. The difficulty in this pursuit is that an action that might be construed as resistant in the context of black interclass dynamics will often seem far less effectively counterhegemonic if undertaken in the context of white/black interracial dynamics. Blanche herself makes an effort, after all, to relieve herself "with as little noise as possible" when in the company of the white matron so as not to reinforce the woman's racist assumptions about black bodies (2).

In concluding her discussion of Ann Petry's use of grotesque iconography to portray a character with a disability, Mrs. Hedges, in *The Street*, Thomson expresses concern that "[a]estheticizing disability as the grotesque tends to preclude analysis of how those representations support or challenge the sociopolitical relations that make disability a form of cultural otherness" (112). While affirming Thomson's analysis with respect to the long history of problematic representations of subjects with disabilities, I would also argue that Neely's deployment of a muted form of grotesque iconography in *Blanche among the Talented Tenth* actually helps de-aestheticize and de-psychologize our perception of black women's bodies in a way that forces us to recognize the body as a political—if also politically contradictory—site. On the one hand, Blanche's relatively rigid interpretation of hair straightening and skin bleaching suggests that regulatory practices of the body have intrinsic meanings, that those practices can be construed as politically reactionary or resistant without reference to the context in which they take place. Yet her more flexible attitude toward the functions of the grotesque body forces the reader to recognize, on the other hand, that context always matters, indeed that because we live in multiple contexts simultaneously, any given practice must be subjected to multiple sets of interpretations. In the transition from the interracial conflicts of *Blanche on the Lam* to the intraracial dynamics of *Blanche among the Talented Tenth*, Neely pushes her readers to understand why our efforts to "decode" the meaning of body politics are often undermined by our failure to perceive that bodily practices are always shaped by and usually respond to numerous sociocultural imperatives at once.

Having said that, I should acknowledge that an extended treatment of this topic would need to go much farther than I have in exploring the nature of actual reader responses to the Blanche series so as to understand its popularity. In what ways, for example, do the responses of white readers differ from those of black readers? In what ways do the responses of middle-class black women differ from those of working-class black women? Do women of color who possess light skin, slender physiques, and/or straightened hair find the same pleasure in the Blanche series as do women whose bodies more nearly approximate that of Blanche? To what extent, moreover, does Neely's privileging of working-class black female identity tend to reinforce in problematic ways the re-flexive hostility toward the black middle class evidenced elsewhere in African American literature, as well as in popular culture more broadly? How can one separate the useful aspects of Neely's critique of the ex-ploitation of working-class labor/bodies under capitalism from her por-trayal of middle-class African Americans as less "authentically" black than working-class African Americans? My generally positive response to Neely's fiction has not been intended as a means of avoiding these obviously thorny questions. Rather, I hope my discussion of Neely's tex-tual strategies for negotiating the politics of the body might serve as a contribution toward opening up discussion of such broader concerns.[30]

Conclusion

In her most recent novel, *Blanche Cleans Up*, Neely further complicates her tactics for appropriating the detective novel by portraying Blanche as she moves between black working-class and white upper-class culture. Neely raises the stakes by constructing a highly topical plot requiring Blanche to question her perceptions of normative sexuality and lesbian/gay bodies, as well as black motherhood and re-productive rights. As a result, the body politics in the Blanche series as a whole are destabilized once again. Although space limitations prevent me from discussing *Blanche Cleans Up* at greater length, some of the arguments I have made about the body politics of Neely's first two nov-els might also be applicable to this more recent work. At the very least one would need to interrogate closely Neely's decision to incorporate a child sexual abuse subplot into the novel given the efforts of conserva-tive political groups in recent years to equate homosexuality with pe-dophilia. Neely clearly intends *Blanche Cleans Up* as an affirmation of African American lesbian and gay sexuality. Yet the proximity of these two plots creates the potential for slippage between politically resistant and politically reactionary readings.

What strikes me as most important about the series, finally, is that Neely depicts Blanche as a working-class black woman who not only has developed a commitment to social justice because of her own expe-riences of oppression but who also is willing to acknowledge the limi-tations of her experience-based perceptions. Blanche knows that her interpretive framework can be flawed, and she is usually confident enough to admit when she has been wrong. Thus, in future installments of the series, Neely might well choose to have Blanche revisit her feel-ings about Mumsfield and conclude that his "recognizable difference" does not render him "similar" to herself in the way that she construes him at the end of *Blanche on the Lam*. And, though admittedly unlikely, it is also not entirely impossible that Blanche could end up straightening her hair. The series is so valuable, it seems to me, precisely because of such apparent gaps in its epistemological and political outlook. Far from deriving straightforward directives for how to theorize the contradictions of the human body, readers instead are able to learn, along with Blanche, how to meet the paradoxical but surely unavoidable challenge of simultaneously trusting—and distrusting—our "natural" perceptions of the world.

NOTES

I am grateful to Andrew Garland for help with the research for this essay and to Vanessa Dickerson, Mike Bennett, Corey Creekmur, Teresa Mangum, Bluford Adams, and an anonymous reader for their insightful responses to various drafts.

1. The author spells her name without a space between "Barbara" and "Neely." The popularity of a given author is always hard to assess, but Amazon.com sales rankings consistently indicate that the Blanche books have been among the most sought-after of detective novels written by black women. In addition, in her chapter on amateur sleuths in women's detective fiction, Dilley discusses Neely as one of five representative contemporary authors and says that her choices are a function of their popularity, as ascertained by "numerous conversations with readers at book signings and mystery conventions; award nominations from critics, peers, and readers; and the suggestions of a mystery bookseller in Dallas, Texas" (xii).

2. Harris, whose pathbreaking book *From Mammies to Militants* first explored the thematics of domestic service in African American literature, has also made the connection between Childress and Neely. Childress's columns might be seen as a womanist response to Langston Hughes's popular "Simple" stories, featuring black "everyman" Jesse B. Semple.

3. See Childress for a vivid example of how Mildred explains to one of her employers precisely why the "like one of the family" language is problematic.

4. Soitos cites Hopkins's portrayal of Venus in *Hagar's Daughter* (1901–02) as the earliest example of the use of the trope of invisibility in black detective fiction. Since Soitos also considers *Hagar's Daughter* to be the first black detective novel, his reading situates a black maid as the originary black amateur sleuth.

5. On the issue of why Neely's first novel was marketed as detective fiction, see Stanton.

6. Soitos says that Komo's 1988 novel *Clio Browne* was the first detective novel by an African American woman published since *Hagar's Daughter* (see note 4) and thus also the most immediate precursor for Neely's Blanche series (228–30). Other black women who have been publishing detective fiction since the mid-1990s include Penny Mickelbury, Chassie West, Nora DeLoach, and Judith Smith-Levin. Neely's influence is evident on many of these writers, for instance, in the marketing of Grimes's protagonist as a "size[-]sixteen buppie" (*Somebody*, jacket copy). See Woods for further information on these authors. In this context I should also mention Colson Whitehead, whose first novel introduces African American elevator inspector Lila Mae Watson in a story that parodies, while also transcending, hard-boiled detective fiction. Finally, one might compare Neely's novels to a series by Kathy Hogan

Trocheck featuring Callahan Garrity, a white licensed private investigator who runs her own cleaning business. For the reader's convenience, my Works Cited includes listings for all of these authors, as well as for Mosley's Easy Rawlins novels.

7. Soitos is an exception to this claim since he does offer detailed readings of (mostly male) authors such as Chester Himes and Ishmael Reed. For informative if brief discussions of Neely that contextualize her work in different ways, see Soitos 179, 225, and 230; Dilley 8–9, 98–99, 103, 110–13, 116, 125–28, and 138; and Willen, especially 48–50. Although Walton and Jones do not discuss Neely in *Detective Agency*—presumably because the Blanche series lacks the urban/noir settings associated with the hard-boiled detective fiction that constitutes their book's main focus—they do include helpful analysis of the writings of Bland and Wesley. See especially 160–62. By contrast, Klein's classic study *The Woman Detective* includes disturbingly little mention of detective fiction by women of color, even in the revised 1995 edition.

8. Komo treats the same theme when she writes of Clio's memories of posing as a domestic servant (9). Similarly, Mosley's Easy disguises himself as the janitor of buildings that he actually owns (see, for example, *A Red Death* 1–4).

9. Spivak's well-known argument for "strategic essentialism" might be invoked here as a way of theorizing Neely's undertaking. See Spivak's essay "Subaltern Studies: Deconstructing Historiography" in *In Other Worlds*, especially 205–07.

10. For other informative perspectives on passing, see the essays in Ginsberg.

11. Bhabha's discussion of hybridity as a rupture in the production of colonial discourse/power has influenced my decision to invoke the term in this context (173).

12. See Gossett for a classic history of the evolution of ideologies of "race" in the United States and Hubbard for a critique of genetics from the perspective of a trained scientist. Excellent work on the intersections of race and science can also be found in both Harding (*Is Science Multicultural?* and *The "Racial" Economy*) and Ross.

13. See Willen 49 for a divergent interpretation of Blanche's attitude toward Mumsfield.

14. That is, the usage is overdetermined in that it links the genetic explanation of Mumsfield's disability with the process by which detectives piece together clues.

15. See Piercy 482 for the most infamous example from second-wave white feminism: the "woman as nigger" analogy. For black feminist critiques of analogical thinking, see the anthology edited by Hull, Scott, and Smith.

16. "Normate" is Thomson's coinage for those who label some bodies deviant in order to construct themselves as nondisabled, and therefore representative, human subjects (8).

17. Mulvey has developed perhaps the most famous theorization of the gendered gaze. For discussions of the gaze that foreground race as well as gender, see Gaines and also Mercer's two-part essay "Reading Racial Fetishism" from *Welcome to the Jungle*.

18. Similarly, another reader observes on the same site that "you can't help but feel kinship with Blanche[,] who is appealingly human and well fleshed out. No pun intended" (Alabama).

19. One might also contextualize the affirmation of Blanche's body as a manifestation of black women's resistance to bourgeois norms vis-à-vis the reception of the 1995 film version of Terry McMillan's novel *Waiting to Exhale*.

Like the novel, the film portrays four financially successful black women. But the actresses' bodies are nonetheless deployed in a fashion that constructs a class-inflected hierarchy among their characters. Of course, it is Gloria (Loretta Devine) who finally gets the guy, in a scene memorialized among some of the film's black women viewers by the chant "Go, Glo. Go, Glo": as the camera follows her from behind, Gloria crosses the street under the gaze of her kind and gentle new neighbor, a widower played by Gregory Hines (De Witt 25). One might be tempted to read this scene—and the celebratory response of these viewers to it—as Gloria's triumph over the slender women whose bodies function to secure them a position among the black upper classes in a way that the zaftig black woman's body never will (DeWitt 25).

20. Neely's description of Blanche's encounter with Grace clearly relies on the reader's perception that signs of aging, such as wrinkles, are undesirable. For excellent analyses of aging as a mode of body differentiation, see Woodward and Featherstone and Wernick.

21. For insightful discussions of black women and body size, see Bordo and Thompson.

22. For more on the concept of the Talented Tenth, see Du Bois 319–66 and Childs.

23. Gates has declared himself a supporter of capitalism (Slaughter 32), but West professes democratic socialism even as he famously suggested in the early 1990s that black "nihilism" was more of a concern than black economic disempowerment (9–29).

24. See Gaines on the conservative underpinnings of the ideology of racial uplift and Carby (*Race Men* 9–41) on the antifeminist implications of efforts by scholars such as West to "embody" Du Bois's legacy.

25. See Mercer's essay "Black Hair/Style Politics" in *Welcome to the Jungle*. For other takes on the politics of hair, see Caldwell, Davis, Grayson, Jones (273–306), and especially Rooks.

26. For a fuller discussion of this process of attraction/repulsion between the black middle and working classes as it is inflected by black women's history of domestic servitude, see my reading of Gloria Naylor's novel *Linden Hills* (204–10).

27. On the Hottentot Venus, see Gilman. On colorism's ramifications for black women, see Russell, Wilson, and Hall.

28. These anxieties increased in the wake of the fall of Saigon in 1975, after which large numbers of Vietnamese "boat people" began immigrating to the United States, but one should note that United States immigration policies had already been relaxed a decade earlier.

29. Neely's depiction of Blanche as she ponders Veronica's embarrassment at having her "beauty" secrets discovered is an excellent example of this technique. "Us and our hair, [Blanche] mumbled as she smeared lotion over her ample thighs and buttocks, it's as deep as our color stuff. Her stomach reminded her that she hadn't had any breakfast" (63). Blanche psychologizes hair and color, but her own growling stomach functions instead as an intrusion of the grotesque.

30. Bobo provides a wonderful scholarly precedent for such inquiries.

WORKS CITED

Alabama reader. Review of *Blanche Cleans Up*, by BarbaraNeely. Online posting. 6 Sept. 1998. Customer Comments. Amazon.com.

Baker, Nikki. *In the Game*. Tallahassee: Naiad, 1991.

———. *The Lavender House Murder*. Tallahassee: Naiad, 1992.

———. *Long Goodbyes*. Tallahassee: Naiad, 1993.

Bakhtin, Mikhail. *Rabelais and His World*. Trans. Helene Iswolsky. Bloomington: Indiana UP, 1984.

Bérubé, Michael. *Life as We Know It: A Father, a Family, and an Exceptional Child*. New York: Pantheon, 1996.

Bhabha, Homi K. "Signs Taken for Wonders: Questions of Ambivalence and Authority under a Tree outside Delhi, May 1817." Gates 163–84.

Bland, Eleanor Taylor. *Dead Time*. New York: St. Martin's, 1992.

———. *Done Wrong*. New York: St. Martin's, 1995.

———. *Gone Quiet*. New York: Signet-Penguin, 1994.

———. *Keep Still*. New York: St. Martin's, 1996.

———. *See No Evil*. New York: St. Martin's, 1998.

———. *Slow Burn*. New York: St. Martin's, 1993.

———. *Tell No Tales*. New York: St. Martin's, 1999.

Bobo, Jacqueline. *Black Women as Cultural Readers*. New York: Columbia UP, 1995.

Bogle, Donald. *Toms, Coons, Mulattoes, Mammies, and Bucks: An Interpretive History of Blacks in American Films*. Expanded ed. New York: Continuum, 1991.

Bordo, Susan. "Reading the Slender Body." *Unbearable Weight: Feminism, Western Culture, and the Body*. Berkeley: U of California P, 1993. 185–212.

Caldwell, Paulette. "A Hair Piece: Perspectives on the Intersection of Race and Gender." *Critical Race Feminism: A Reader*. Ed. Adriene Katherine Wing. New York: NYU P, 1997. 297–305.

Carby, Hazel. "Policing the Black Woman's Body in an Urban Context." *Critical Inquiry* 18.4 (Summer 1992): 738–55.

———. *Race Men*. Cambridge: Harvard UP, 1998.

———. *Reconstructing Womanhood: The Emergence of the Afro-American Woman Novelist*. New York: Oxford UP, 1987.

Childress, Alice. *Like One of the Family: Conversations from a Domestic's Life*. Boston: Beacon, 1986.

Childs, John Brown. "Afro-American Intellectuals and the People's Culture." *Journal of Theory and Society* 13 (1984): 69–90.

Davis, Angela. "Afro Images: Politics, Fashion, and Nostalgia." *Picturing Us: African American Identity in Photography*. Ed. Deborah Willis. New York: New, 1994. 171–79.

DeCandido, GraceAnne A. Rev. of *Blanche Cleans Up*, by BarbaraNeely. *Booklist* 94.14 (15 Mar. 1998): 1206.

DeLoach, Nora. *Mama Stalks the Past*. New York: Bantam, 1997.

De Witt, Karen. "For Black Women, a Movie Stirs Breathless Excitement." *New York Times* 31 Dec. 1995, nat. ed., sec. I: 1+.

Dilley, Kimberley J. *Busybodies, Meddlers, and Snoops: The Female Hero in Contemporary Women's Mysteries*. Westport: Greenwood, 1998.

Du Bois, W.E.B. *W.E.B. Du Bois: A Reader*. Ed. David Levering Lewis. New York: Holt, 1995.

Dyer, Richard. *Heavenly Bodies: Film Stars and Society*. New York: St. Martin's, 1986.

Edwards, Grace F. *If I Should Die*. New York: Doubleday, 1997.

———. *No Time to Die*. New York: Doubleday, 1999.

———. *A Toast Before Dying*. New York: Doubleday, 1998.

Ellison, Ralph. *Invisible Man*. New York: Vintage-Random, 1995.

Featherstone, Mike, and Andrew Wernick. *Images of Aging: Cultural Representations of Later Life*. New York: Routledge, 1995.

Frazier, E. Franklin. *Black Bourgeoisie*. 1957. Rpt. New York: Free-Simon, 1997.

Gaines, Jane. "White Privilege and Looking Relations: Race and Gender in Feminist Film Theory." *Cultural Critique* 4 (Fall 1986): 59–79.

Gaines, Kevin. *Uplifting the Race: Black Leadership, Politics, and Culture in the Twentieth Century*. Chapel Hill: U of North Carolina P, 1996.

Gates, Henry Louis, Jr., ed. *"Race," Writing, and Difference*. Chicago: U of Chicago P, 1985.

Gilman, Sander L. "Black Bodies, White Bodies: Toward an Iconography of Female Sexuality in Late Nineteenth-Century Art, Medicine, and Literature." Gates 223–61.

Ginsberg, Elaine, ed. *Passing and the Fictions of Identity*. Durham: Duke UP, 1996

Gossett, Thomas. *Race: The History of an Idea in America*. New ed. New York: Oxford UP, 1997.

Grayson, Deborah. "Is It Fake? Black Women's Hair as Spectacle and Spec(tac)ular." *Camera Obscura* 36 (1995): 13–30.

Grimes, Terris McMahan. *Blood Will Tell*. New York: Signet, 1997.

———. *Somebody Else's Child*. New York: Onyx, 1996.

Harding, Sandra. *Is Science Multicultural? Postcolonialisms, Feminisms, and Epistemologies*. Bloomington: Indiana UP, 1998.

———, ed. *The "Racial" Economy of Science*. Bloomington: Indiana UP, 1993.

Harris, Trudier. *From Mammies to Militants: Domestics in Black American Literature*. Philadelphia: Temple UP, 1982.

———. Rev. of *Blanche on the Lam*, by BarbaraNeely. *Obsidian* II 7.1–2 (Spring–Summer 1992): 143–46.

Herrnstein, Richard J., and Charles Murray. *The Bell Curve: Intelligence and Class Structure in American Life*. New York: Free, 1994.

Hopkins, Pauline. *Hagar's Daughter*. Rpt. in *The Magazine Novels of Pauline Hopkins*. Ed. Hazel Carby. New York: Oxford UP, 1988. 1–284.

Hubbard, Ruth. *Profitable Promises: Essays on Women, Science, and Health*. Monroe: Common Courage, 1995.

Hull, Gloria, Patricia Bell Scott, and Barbara Smith, eds. *All the Women Are White, All the Blacks Are Men, but Some of Us Are Brave: Black Women's Studies*. New York: Feminist, 1982.

Hurston, Zora Neale. *Color Struck*. *The Portable Harlem Renaissance Reader*. Ed. David Levering Lewis. New York: Viking-Penguin, 1994. 699–715.

Jones, Lisa. *Bulletproof Diva: Tales of Race, Sex, and Hair*. New York: Anchor-Doubleday, 1995.

Katzman, David M. *Seven Days a Week: Women and Domestic Service in Industrializing America*. Urbana: U of Illinois P, 1981.

Klein, Kathleen Gregory. *The Woman Detective: Gender and Genre*. 2nd ed. Urbana: U of Chicago P, 1995.

Komo, Delores. *Clio Browne: Private Investigator*. Freedom: Crossing, 1988.

McMillan, Terry. *Waiting to Exhale*. New York: Viking, 1992.

Mercer, Kobena. *Welcome to the Jungle: New Positions in Black Cultural Studies*. New York: Routledge, 1994.

Mickelbury, Penny. *Keeping Secrets*. Tallahassee: Naiad, 1994.

———. *Night Songs*. Tallahassee: Naiad, 1995.

———. *One Must Wait*. New York: Simon, 1998.

———. *Where to Choose*. New York: Simon, 1999.

Mosley, Walter. *Always Outnumbered, Always Outgunned*. New York: Norton, 1998.

———. *Black Betty*. New York: Norton, 1994.

———. *Devil in a Blue Dress*. New York: Norton, 1990.

————. *Gone Fishin'*. New York: Norton, 1997.

————. *A Little Yellow Dog*. New York: Norton, 1996.

————. *A Red Death*. New York: Norton, 1991.

————. *White Butterfly*. New York: Norton, 1992.

Mulvey, Laura. *Visual and Other Pleasures*. Bloomington: Indiana UP, 1989.

Neely, Barbara. *Blanche among the Talented Tenth*. New York: Penguin, 1994.

————. *Blanche Cleans Up*. New York: Viking-Penguin, 1998.

————. *Blanche on the Lam*. New York: Penguin, 1992.

Petry, Ann. *The Street*. Boston: Houghton, 1946.

Phelan, Peggy. *Unmarked: The Politics of Performance*. New York: Routledge, 1993.

Piercy, Marge. "The Grand Coolie Damn." *Sisterhood is Powerful: An Anthology of Writings from the Women's Liberation Movement*. Ed. Robin Morgan. New York: Vintage, 1970. 473–92.

Rollins, Judith. *Between Women: Domestics and Their Employers*. Philadelphia: Temple UP, 1985.

Rooks, Noliwe M. *Hair Raising: Beauty, Culture, and African American Women*. New Brunswick: Rutgers UP, 1996.

Ross, Andrew, ed. *Science Wars*. Durham: Duke UP, 1996.

Russell, Kathy, Midge Wilson, and Ronald Hall. *The Color Complex: The Politics of Skin Color among African Americans*. New York: Anchor-Doubleday, 1993.

Saxton, Lisa. *Caught in a Rundown*. New York: Scribner's, 1997.

Slaughter, Jane. "Henry Louis Gates Jr." Interview. *Progressive* 62.1 (Jan. 1998): 30–32.

Smith-Levin, Judith. *Do Not Go Gently*. New York: Harper, 1996.

————. *The Hoodoo Man*. New York: Ballantine, 1998.

Soitos, Stephen F. *The Blues Detective: A Study of African American Detective Fiction*. Amherst: U of Massachusetts P, 1996.

Spivak, Gayatri. *In Other Worlds: Essays in Cultural Politics*. New York: Methuen, 1987.

Stanton, Junious R. "Author Uses Mystery Genre to Examine Race and Class." *Los Angeles Sentinel* 18 Nov. 1998: B4. Ethnic NewsWatch. www.softlineweb.com/ethnicw

Texas reader. Rev. of *Blanche Cleans Up*, by BarbaraNeely. Online posting.7 March 1998. Customer Comments. Amazon.com. 1996–98.

Thompson, Becky W. *A Hunger So Wide and So Deep: American Women Speak Out on Eating Problems*. Minneapolis: U of Minnesota P, 1994.

Thomson, Rosemarie Garland. *Extraordinary Bodies: Figuring Physical Disability in American Culture and Literature*. New York: Columbia UP, 1997.

Thurman, Wallace. *The Blacker the Berry*. New York: Collier-Macmillan, 1970.

Trocheck, Kathy Hogan. *Every Crooked Nanny*. New York: Harper, 1992.

————. *Happy Never After*. New York: Harper, 1995.

————. *Heart Trouble*. New York: Harper, 1996.

————. *Homemade Sin*. New York: Harper, 1994.

————. *Midnight Clear*. New York: Harper, 1998.

————. *Strange Brew*. New York: Harper, 1997.

————. *To Live and Die in Dixie*. New York: Harper, 1993.

Walton, Priscilla L., and Manina Jones. *Detective Agency: Women Rewriting the Hard-Boiled Tradition*. Berkeley: U of California P, 1999.

Washington, Elsie. "Book Marks." Rev. of *Blanche on the Lam*, by BarbaraNeely. *Essence* Apr. 1992: 54.

Wesley, Valerie Wilson. *Ain't Nobody's Business If I Do*. New York: Avon, 1999.

————. *Devil's Gonna Get Him*. New York: Putnam's, 1995.

———. *Easier to Kill*. New York: Putnam's, 1998.

———. *No Hiding Place*. New York: Putnam's, 1997

———. *When Death Comes Stealing*. New York: Putnam's, 1994.

———. *Where Evil Sleeps*. New York: Putnam's, 1996.

West, Chassie. *Loss of Innocence*. New York: Harper, 1997.

———. *Sunrise*. New York: Harper, 1994.

West, Cornel. *Race Matters*. Boston: Beacon, 1993.

Whitehead, Colson. *The Intuitionist*. New York: Anchor, 1999.

Willen, Margaret M. "Saying Ourselves: Women of Color Writing Detective Fiction." *Clues: A Journal of Detection* 18.2 (Fall–Winter 1997): 43–57.

Witt, Doris. *Black Hunger: Food and the Politics of U.S. Identity*. New York: Oxford UP, 1999.

Woods, Paula L. "Sleuthing Sisters Write the Book on Murder." *Emerge* 8.7 (31 May 1997): 62. Ethnic NewsWatch. www.softlineweb.com/ethnicw

Woodward, Kathleen. "Instant Repulsion: Decrepitude, the Mirror Stage, and the Literary Imagination." *Kenyon Review* 5 (Fall 1983): 43–66.

———. "Youthfulness as Masquerade." *Discourse* 11.1 (Fall–Winter 1988–89): 119–42.

VANESSA D. DICKERSON

Summoning SomeBody

The Flesh Made Word in Toni Morrison's Fiction

Quiet as it is kept, the black female body is a hot thing.[1] White men have secretly reveled in it, not only buying, selling, and raping it but also assuaging the need and desire for mother's milk with it. Black men have agonized over it, wanting to beat, bruise, possess, forsake, protect, and love it. White women have adored it for the relief it afforded from wifely, maternal, and household duties; for the beauty it gave them; for the femininity of which it assured them both in the dreadful and frightening "tangle of braids" and in the deep rich timbre of voice that underscored what has been identified, by contrast, as the charm of the white woman's voice—"sibilance, a mild lisp, a gentle stammer" (Brownmiller 59, 116). For white men a site of political empowerment; for black males a source of being, love, and shame; for white women a source of, among other things, freedom and aestheticization—the body of the black female matters deeply. Used to extend the life, health, and desirability of others, the black female body is more than a prosthesis, however. It is the cultural linchpin Hortense Spillers describes as a necessary signifier: "a meeting ground of investments and privations in the national treasury of rhetorical wealth. My country needs me, and if I were not here, I would have to be invented" (454). Still for all the wealth it provides, the body is not saved. Neither precious nor privileged, it is problematic.

Historically relegated to the auction block instead of the pedestal, the black female body has been constructed as the ugly end of a wearisome

Western dialectic: not sacred but profane, not angelic but demonic, not fair lady but ugly darky. Along with her male counterpart, the black woman has belonged to one of those races "perceived as more animal-like and less god-like" (Spelman 127). In short, the black female body has been anti-Victorian as it has not shared the "impenetrable mystery" (Michie 7), the immutability, the immanence assigned to women in such nineteenth-century conventions as the Angel in the House or the Cult of True Womanhood. Linked instead to a knowable corporeality and to reproduction, the black female body has not been interiorized as ideal but localized as thing. Consciously and unconsciously made to experience her body as the damned and notorious device of someone else's construction, the black woman has not simply accepted or come to terms with the way the Western world has smudged, smeared, and cast out her body in representations of expediency instead of truth, representations meant not so much to faithfully describe reality as to secure the status quo. As the essays in this volume attest, under these circumstances, every venue of self-representation, whether on the stage or the film set, in the bedroom or the kitchen, in a nightclub or a department store—becomes instrumental in the recovery of the maligned black female body.

One of the most powerful and successful reappropriators of black representation is Toni Morrison. In her earliest novels, *The Bluest Eye* (1970) and *Sula* (1973), as well as in her Nobel Prize–winning *Beloved* (1987), Morrison writes narratives that recuperate the reviled and colonized "flesh/body" (Spelman 459). Though the female protagonists in these novels are, as Morrison says of the character Pecola in her afterword to *The Bluest Eye*, "unique" not "representative," they share "aspects of . . . woundability," as their bodies, like their lives, tend to be "dismissed, trivialized, misread" (210, 216). Each of these protagonists comes to terms with a racialized "somatophobia" (Spelman 126)—a social disdain for the black body—through a mental and spiritual invention involving a shift of the body into textual ambiguity: the text itself performs a recovery of sorts. More specifically, in a moment of self-reflexivity during which the black body transcends what Paul Jay has called the "exigencies of narrative art" (16), the flesh is made word as Morrison moves her female protagonist into a liminal space such as illness or the otherworldly.[2] Here the body can become a reference for the larger black community, serving as a historical or remembered site of love, compassion, and understanding.

While *The Bluest Eye*, *Sula*, and *Beloved* all crescendo in singular moments during which the discursive and material body conjoin in the flesh made word, each novel concerns itself with a different aspect of bodily representation. Thus *The Bluest Eye* features the complexity and problematics of visualizaton. The black female body is unseen because it is socially constructed as a body not worth the effort of seeing. Such invisibility proves, of course, damaging and denigrating. Yet all too often when the black female body is looked upon or made the object of the gaze, the body is still perceived as unworthy, if not worthless. Invisibility itself, then, may understandably become a cloak preferable to the nakedness and exposure of visibility. In *Sula*, Morrison is not so much concerned with the cloaking and decloaking of the body as with its discovery. Morrison creates in Sula a protagonist bent upon the aesthetic exploration of her own body and the body of others. Instead of erasing herself, as Pecola seeks to do in *The Bluest Eye*, Sula determines to paint herself in bold strokes and, in doing so, to know, if not celebrate, the amazements of the flesh. Morrison takes this amazement of the black female body to a different level in *Beloved*, where issues of invisibility, visibility, and discovery are subsumed in the historical recovery of the body. Sethe's encounter with the ghost of her baby girl signifies beyond the private, the personal, and the individual; the resurrected body of Sethe's girl-child turns out to be a personal and communal healing of historical wounds. In each of these novels, Morrison summons us to the validation of the black female body.

The Visibly Invisible Body

In *The Bluest Eye*, Morrison's protagonist, twelve-year-old Pecola Breedlove, is granted no physical presence, let alone beauty, in the visual and textual registers of social prospects. Billboards, television, candy wrappers, drinking cups, magazines, newspapers, even the grade school primers that constitute the child's first official and systemic encounter with language and norms—all of these document the story of a beauty that resides in an omnipresent white female body and, by indirection, of a beautylessness assigned to the hardly visible black female body. Pecola lives practically without a reflection in the world at that critical point in her life—puberty—when "[a]dolescents . . . look for themselves in mirrors not only in private but also in public and in groups" (La Belle 4). Heir to the Breedloves' close-set small eyes, high cheekbones, "low irregular hairlines," "[k]een but crooked noses," and "shapely lips" (*Bluest* 38, 39) wherever Pecola looks, she tends to find what Patricia Williams describes as the obliteration of the body.[3] Pecola is without "normal," acceptable form in a world that makes the physical features of the Greta Garbos, Shirley Temples, and Ginger Rogerses the referents of a "fearful symmetry."[4] The dissonance between Pecola's self and the images society holds up to her as ideal results in a split between what Jenijoy La Belle, in her study of the looking glass, would term her "psychological presence and her physical body"(3). In *The Bluest Eye*, this culturally mandated fracture is the impetus for what Pecola experiences as disintegration or self-erasure:

> "Please, God," she whispered into the palm of her hand. "Please make me disappear." She squeezed her eyes shut. Little parts of her body faded away. Now slowly, now with a rush. Slowly again. Her fingers went, one by one; then her arms disappeared all the way to the elbow. Her feet now. Yes, that was good. The legs all at once. It was hardest above the thighs. She had to be real still and pull. Her stomach would not go. But finally it, too, went away. Then her chest, her neck. The face was hard, too. Almost done, almost. Only her tight, tight eyes were left. They were always left. (45)

The pain-tightened eyes remain witness to the horror—a society in which the white female body can evoke the freshness of milk, the sweetness of candy, prized baby dolls, and the glamour of movie stardom, while the black female body can only conjure images of dandelion weeds, cracks in the sidewalk, and brood mares.

Already "a minority in both caste and class" (17), Pecola cannot even take pride in the only thing she can own—her body. For with few exceptions, others confirm the undesirability of her person. Thus the "fifty-two-year-old white immigrant storekeeper" Yacobowski sees neither the face nor the body of Pecola when she visits his store to buy candy. A new arrival to America, soon to be assimilated, Yacobowski has learned how not to see the body of the young black girl whose people for over two hundred years have been a constitutive but unaccepted force in America: "Nothing in his life even suggested that the feat was possible, not to say desirable or necessary" (48). The black schoolboys who do see Pecola identify her as the dark and ugly foil of Maureen Peale, a "high-yellow dream child" (62); they fire insults at her, hoping to discharge and shift onto her, if only briefly, "their contempt for their own blackness" (65). Geraldine, a self-styled "colored" girl wary of "niggers" and the "dreadful funkiness" of life, actually looks into Pecola's eyes to find her worst nightmare: matted and plaited hair, the girdleless body that signifies filth and poverty (87, 83). She sees a "nasty little black bitch" (92), the kind of child she wishes her young son, Junior, to avoid. Pecola is damaged, as Morrison herself comments in the afterword to the novel, by the "internalization of assumptions of immutable inferiority originating in an outside gaze" (210).

It is Pauline Breedlove, Pecola's mother, who delivers the most blistering rejection of Pecola's body when Pecola enters the home of Pauline's

employers, the Fishers, and knocks over a deep-dish cobbler, splatter-
ing hot juice on her own legs, the Fishers' floor, and the little Fisher
girl's dress. Although Pecola's is "the body in pain," to borrow Elaine
Scarry's expression, Pauline identifies with the blonde child, rushing
at Pecola with words "hotter and darker than the smoking berries" to
slap her down to the floor and into the hot pie juice, then hastening to
the Fisher child, "hushing and soothing the tears of the little pink-and-
yellow girl" (109).[5] In Pauline's eyes, the little Fisher girl possesses the
delicate, fragile, neat body—the elevated body she must keep clean and
stress-free—while Pecola has the durable, expendable, clumsy body—
the prone body that may be subjected to burns, slaps, and the burden of
someone else's filth: a "laundry bag, heavy with [the] dirty "wet clothes"
of the Fishers (109). Unlike the body of the Fisher girl, which receives
no concrete physical description, Pecola's is given a solidity and reality
that brings it more sympathetically near. Nevertheless, while the narrative represents Pecola's body as the real, embraceable body and the Fisher
girl's as the specterized and distant body, Pecola's is socially assaulted,
the Fisher girl's held dear. To put it another way, the white child's body
is what Mary Douglas in *Purity and Danger* would identify as the tidy
body, the one associated with culture and civilization; Pecola's is the
unruly body, the polluted or polluting body associated with nature (Butler
128–31).

In her role as the Fishers' household servant, Pauline Breedlove views
Pecola's body in a way similar to Yacobowski's. She completely separates herself from her child. Just as Yacobowski does "not waste the effort of a glance" at Pecola, Pauline does not bother to look at her
daughter's wounded body. Yacobowski does not see Pecola because "for
him there is nothing to see"(48). Pauline, however, does not see Pecola
because the body of her child has been supplanted at the movie the-
aters, on the billboards, and in the magazines by versions of the little
Fisher girl. In fact, Pauline—or Polly, as she is called only in the Fisher
household—is unable to see Pecola because she cannot bear to see herself. As the Fisher's maid, Pauline behaves in a way not only reminiscent of Yacobowski but also, more significantly, of Junior's mother,
Geraldine, the sanitizer. Though Pauline does not refer to Pecola as a
"nasty little black bitch," she is obviously distressed by the mess her
daughter has made and feels the child's presence is invasive. Mammylike,
her role as caretaker of the white child disables her as black mother.

Morrison suggests that the society in which the black female child
in the Western world comes of age problematizes the relation between
the black mother and the body of her black female child. Thus, when
Pecola is born, Pauline begins to distance herself from her child's body,

identifying it as another strike against her own self, since the issue of her body cannot approximate the likes of Shirley Temple or the pink-and-yellow Fisher girl. Although Pauline "used to like to watch" her baby girl who, after all, "caught on fast" and was "a right smart baby," she "knowed she was ugly. Head full of pretty hair, but Lord she was ugly" (125, 126). Even Mrs. McTeer, the narrator Claudia's mother who graciously and temporarily takes Pecola into her home when the Breedloves are evicted, indicates that the body of the black female child is a potential site of messiness and nastiness that troubles. When her own child gets sick and throws up on the bed in the "old, cold, and green" McTeer home with its kerosene lamps and drafty, rag-stuffed windows, Mrs. McTeer is upset. "You think I got time for nothing but washing up your puke," she grumbles to her sweaty, feverish child for whom she feels "[l]ove, thick and dark as Alaga syrup" (11, 12). Mrs. McTeer may not be on guard against the funkiness of life, but she is wary of wildness or forwardness. She moves quickly to snuff out any unseemly behavior when a neighboring white child, Rosemary, accuses Claudia and her sister, Frieda, of "playing nasty" in the alley (30). After a cursory glance and no interrogation, Mrs. McTeer whips the girls in her determination that they will not "be nasty," that they will not engage in any sexual activities or explorations. It is only after she discovers that Frieda has been trying to attend to Pecola's menstrual flow that Mrs. McTeer reassures the young girls, pulling them into the warmth of a conciliatory embrace and ending Pecola's introduction to menstruation with the "music" of her laughter (32).

Although Mrs. McTeer does what Geraldine would never do—she takes Pecola into her home—she clearly experiences Pecola's body as economically and morally intrusive. Claudia remembers the "fussing soliloquies" to which Pecola, Frieda, and she were subjected because Pecola drank so much milk. Mrs. McTeer wonders whether she is "suppose to be running . . . a charity ward," whether she is "sup*posed* to have nothing," and whether "[f]olks just spend all their time trying to figure out ways to send *me* to the poorhouse" (24). Although this surrogate mother for Pecola is "willing to do what I can for folks," she, as a mother who is struggling to provide for her own girl-children, feels the weight of Pecola's body (25).

Interestingly enough, while Pauline Breedlove and the other black mothers—Mrs. McTeer and Geraldine—find Pecola's body, indeed the pubescent black female body, a source of anxiety, the three black whores—China, Poland, and Miss Marie, the Maginot Line—react differently to Pecola. As women whose professional names identify their bodies as territories and landmarks, as bodies "selling hot pussy," to borrow bell hooks's expression—these "mothers," Pecola feels, "do not despise her" (51).

The narrative strikingly represents these three characters as radical black women who do not fit traditional accounts of the fallen woman (the good-hearted prostitute, the young girl gone astray, or the hardened criminal) and who do not obsess about ideal bodies. In the business of abusing more than servicing male bodies ("all were inadequate and weak, all came under their jaundiced eyes and were the recipients of their disinterested wrath" [56]), these characters are depicted as timeless—forever ironing, forever singing, forever curling hair—and threateningly free: they are "gargoyles" and "harridans," old, ill-tempered, harrowing creatures who are disturbingly "merry" and "amused by a long-ago time of ignorance" (55). Eternally involved in cosmetic preparations, these women, who trade insults about each other's bodies, are ultimately not invested in the damaging social prescriptions for beauty. Talk of being overweight and skinny or of having bandy legs gets "breez[ily] and rough[ly]" dismissed with laughter: "Don't worry 'bout them bandy legs. That's the first thing they [male clients] push aside. All three of the women laughed" (52). Because they inhabit a place in which they can subvert the external gaze or turn it against the gazer (China, for example, deploys her ability to create, fabricate, and makeup hairstyles, mouths, and eyebrows not so much to please or win the approval of, as to mount an assault on male consumers), they are neither defined by that gaze nor take it as their guide: the three prostitutes are not critical of or troubled by Pecola's body. Still, their freedom or irreverence does no more to build Pecola's esteem for her body than her mother's rejection does to undermine it. Unfortunately, even for the whores, the love Pecola so desperately needs to hear about is either unspeakable or spoken through fable.[6]

When the mothers fail to redeem Pecola's body, she turns to the fathers, Cholly Breedlove and Soaphead Church, whose contact proves equivocal if not utterly destructive. "Overwhelmed" by social dissatisfaction with her body, Pecola is drawn to the promises of Soaphead Church: "If you are overcome with trouble and conditions that are not natural, I can remove them; Overcome Spells, Bad Luck, and Evil Influences," Soaphead Church declares. "Remember, I am a true Spiritualist and Psychic Reader, born with power, and I will help you. Satisfaction in one visit. . . . Satisfaction guaranteed" (173). By the time Pecola hands herself over to the ministrations of the color-struck pedophile Elihue Micah Whitcomb, alias Soaphead Church, her body is in triple jeopardy, for she is not only an "ugly" black female child, but a pregnant black female, soon to be, like her mother, one of "these here women," according to the white male physician, "who you don't have any trouble with" because "[t]hey deliver right away and with no pain" (124–25). Not only is Pecola pregnant, but she carries her father's child. Her father, Cholly, in a misbegotten act of love and powerlessness, rapes an already devastated body, divesting it of purity, if not innocence. No longer merely a site of ugliness, Pecola's body has become a vessel of sin. Now "pitifully unattractive," Pecola is desperately in need of the miracle Soaphead Church offers (173).

While Soaphead Church, obsessed with the European body, takes credit for helping Pecola realize her dreams of having blue eyes, Pecola ultimately revises herself by entering a twilight zone of being. Her body, which has been the vortex of a hateful social prejudice and a devastating paternal love, is reinscribed in a self-reflexive dialogue of italicized and roman print that constitutes a fleshing out of double consciousness. In the end, two Pecolas exist linguistically, or at least the two voices of one Pecola who is transformed into the possessor of a pair of blue eyes that are only visible to the imaginary friend who is "*[r]ight after her* [Pecola's] *very eyes*" (196). Pecola retreats or advances into a delusion that allows her to represent herself—if not to the world, then to her own self—as someone special and, by Western standards, pretty. In the end, Pecola is only able to recover her person, to carry on with her life, in the odd, catlike hybridization of blue eyes in a black face.[7] Pitted against a society that has invested so heavily in the denial of black female pulchritude and living among family members unable to love or to protect themselves, let alone Pecola, from the ruinous onslaught of what Morrison aptly terms "disqualifying metaphors" (216), Pecola finds it hard "to come clean" (Spillers 454). Her recovery proves at best equivocal, as she is unable to get clear of all the ways in which society has misnamed, misused, and sullied the black female body. Even rescripted somewhere between the straight bold lines of roman (regular/normal) and the maddeningly thin lines of italic (irregular/different) print, Pecola, Morrison suggests, can know no real peace. Taunted by the insinuations of her imaginary or autobiographical friend, Pecola worries that her blue eyes are not the bluest eyes, and she is plagued by memories of how her father violated her: "A little black girl yearns for the blue eyes of a little white girl, and the horror at the heart of her yearning is exceeded only by the evil of fulfillment" (*Bluest,* 204). The body Pecola recovers is disabled, given over as it is to "birdlike gestures," to "a mere picking and plucking" that reveal how "the damage done was total" (205, 204).

Problematic as Pecola's mental improvisation is, it is yet the basis for a belated insight when Claudia recognizes that Pecola had a beauty that "was hers first . . . which she gave to us." Claudia understands how

Pecola's body had became a cultural dump, the site of "all of our waste which we dumped on her." For Claudia, Pecola serves as a meaningful reminder of accountability; out of the "waste and beauty" of Pecola's person grows Claudia's insight into how the society, her community, and she herself create, sustain, use, and crucify each other (205). In the end, Pecola gives us all not just sad (that is, blue) eyes but, more specifically, the bluest eye. This is to say that by the end of the novel readers are left with a "common vision (suggested by 'one eye')" (McDowell 106) of how we all fail in our responsibility to little black girls with dark brown eyes.

The Aesthetics of Body Exploration

If *The Bluest Eye* is about a black female determined to change her body, then *Sula* is about a black female determined to keep and to explore hers. In the process of keeping and exploring, Sula leaves a chimerical, if not indecipherable, mark on a narrative replete with bodies—the body of a "headless soldier" that "ran on, with energy and grace, ignoring altogether the drip and slide of brain tissue down its back" (8); the body of the young boy Chicken Little, who slips from Sula's hands into the river where he drowns; the bodies pied-pipered into excavation tunnels where they meet death in a slide of mud and melting ice on National Suicide Day; the body of Cecile Sabat lying in state in her "Frenchified shotgun" home in New Orleans (24). In the text, nasty and violent things happen to bodies: they are drowned, exploded, burned, cut, broken, drugged, and constipated.

As violent as these phenomena are, another less visible violence also figures in the text. This latter violence occurs because a number of bodies, especially those of women, get shaped in the service of patriarchy. Thus while Shadrack, who goes off to fight in World War I, and Plum, who later fights in World War II, both put their bodies at risk fighting someone else's war, the Wright [right] women put their bodies at risk of mutual and self-abuse by conforming to someone else's ideal, specifically to the dichotomous roles males have constructed for women. Helene Wright's mother is a "Creole whore" (17), what Michie would call "a cipher of *male* lust" (61).[8] Helene Wright, a paragon of respectability, relates to her own and to other black female bodies with a kind of Victorian unease or shame. She is ashamed of her Creole mother and so dissatisfied with the shape of her own daughter Nel's nose that she has the child pull and pluck at her broad nose to reshape it. Interestingly enough, the body of the respectable Helene herself is reduced to a bonelessness and spinelessness associated with custard when she smiles "dazzlingly and coquettishly at the salmon-colored face of the [train] conductor" (21) who verbally disrespects and abuses her. Later, when Nel grows up and becomes Nel Greene, she puts her body at the disposal of her husband, Jude, whose manhood is affirmed by sex and children: as Jude's wife, Nel will hide "his raveling edges . . . shore him up." Without Nel, Jude "was a waiter hanging around a kitchen like a woman. With her he was head of a household pinned to an unsatisfactory job out of necessity. The two of them together would make one Jude" (83).

Unlike the Wright women, who obsess over what is right for their bodies, the women in the Peace household are not only more comfortable and at peace with their bodies, they are also aware of the power of their bodies. Most notable is the fact that the Peace women engage in "manlove" (41) not manservice. Although, they enjoy men and would rather have them near than far, the Peace women tend not to relinquish control of their bodies to men or to spend time thinking of ways to manipulate their bodies to appear more attractive to men. Sula's mother, Hannah, for instance, "who simply refused to live without the attention of a man . . . mostly the husbands of her friends and neighbors," finishes whatever she is doing, and "rippling with sex" without so much as a "pat of the hair, or a rush to change clothes or a quick application of paint" takes aside her lover for lovemaking in the cellar, pantry, parlor, or even her bedroom (42–43). As Barbara Christian contends, "Far from being the seductress traditionally dressed in red, who manipulates men to her own ends," Hannah has "funky elegance" and "remains independent in her self" (80).

While it is Hannah who best demonstrates that she is at peace with her body, that she does not have to be "resolved to be on guard—always" (22), it is Eva who best exemplifies a sense of her body's power. Thus Eva Peace—Sula's strong, feisty grandmother—gives up a leg to a train to manipulate the insurance system and thereby feed her starving children, effectively making, as critic Barbara Hill Rigney asserts, a "statement indicting poverty and the conditions of life for black women"(25). Later, Eva, who ends her son's heroin-induced misery by setting him afire, hurls her crippled body out of a window to save her child Hannah who catches fire while canning food and "putting up for a winter they [the citizens of Medallion] understood so well" (75). Eva literally and figuratively uses her body as a shield to protect her children from the economic, even cosmic, onslaught they face. Her acts may not be the typical maternal sacrifices; however, they do reveal a radical maternity determined to combat the misery of children beset by poverty, drug abuse, and violence. The mother's very body can sometimes be the only insurance policy the black child has in this world of Medallions.

In Medallion, Sula is somebody potent, dangerous, and different. As a child, her play is not like anybody else's. When she picks Chicken Little up and spins him around, she at first is intent upon affording him a childhood pleasure; however, when he slips from her hands into the water, Sula's fear and agitation are qualified by the pleasure she takes in watching his body fall into and be covered up by the water. As her best friend, Nel, later realizes, it had "felt so good to see him fall," it had been a "joyful stimulation" (170). Sula's gaze is not like anybody else's. Her interest is piqued, for instance, when Hannah's body catches fire. Sula watches her mother bubble, blister, boil, and cook "not because she was paralyzed, but because she was interested" (78). She has, Nel observes, "an odd way of looking at things" (104).

Sula also has an odd way of confronting the young white boys who harass Nel after school. When Sula squats in the dirt road before the white boys, pulls out a paring knife and "slash[es] off on the tip" (54) of her own finger, this act, which recalls Eva's amputated leg and anticipates Sethe's decapitation of her own child in *Beloved*, constitutes a declaration of Sula's refusal to be a colonized body, to be a body without prerogatives. Cutting off her finger, Sula makes a statement about owning her own body and her capacity to act upon the bodies of those who would assault it: "her voice was quiet. 'If I can do that to myself, what you suppose I'll do to you?'" (54–55).

Sula's very coming and going are unlike anyone else's. After Nel's wedding, Sula, "a slim figure in blue," struts away only to appear ten years later, "accompanied by a plague of robins" (85, 89). Upon her return from college, Sula does not use language like anybody else in Medallion. Thus Nel is soothed by her friend's "lovely college words like *aesthetic* or *rapport*" (105). Nel also finds that Sula's betrayal is not like anyone else's. When Nel catches Sula in a sexual posture with her husband Jude, what Nel sees indicates that indeed Sula is beyond any hackneyed arrangement of bodies, any traditional notion of friendship: "They had been down on all fours naked, not touching except their lips. . . . Nibbling at each other, not even touching, not even looking at each other" (105).

Even Sula's "manlove" is unlike any other. Thus she, or so the community rumors, does the unthinkable and sleeps with white men. When she at long last allows a man, the "golden-eyed" Ajax, to come "regularly" to talk and to make her feel "the drift of her flesh toward the high silence of orgasm," Sula does not "dwell" so much on Ajax's "wand-lean body," on the ripple of his muscles, or on the bulge of thighs as she does on a metaphorical descent into or a rubbing, scraping, and chiseling away at the body of her lover (125, 130). Linguistically, Sula converts Ajax's body into precious materials such as gold leaf and alabaster, imagining the layers she must penetrate if she is to locate his soul. Her speculations about her union with Ajax do not take her on that fabled trajectory toward the heavens but on a dark earthbound path to primal mud: *"I will water your soul, keep it rich and moist. But how much? How much water to keep the loam moist? And how much loam will I need to keep my water still? And when do the two make mud?"* (131). In this "prose poem," as McDowell (108) terms it, although Sula begins "to discover what possession was" (*Sula* 131), her desire remains unconventional because it is not based on the need to own, trap, or use but to explore. "It's just as well he left, " she concludes when Ajax abandons her. "Soon I would have torn the flesh from his face just to see if I was right about the gold and nobody would have understood that kind of curiosity"(136).

Sula herself is a curiosity, a body that can bewitch or be a witch by virtue of its idiosyncrasy, by virtue of its agency to construct what bell hooks identifies in her essay "Revolutionary Black Women" as "a radical subjectivity" (46). Unlike the historical black female body that has been sacrificed to the greed and narcissism of another race, Sula's body will not be the object of confinement, limitation, and clichés that not only "deny the concept of individual or nonnormative bodily experience and purge the deviant woman from representability" but also "eras[e] the potential for adventure" (Michie 89).[9] When Sula goes away to college then returns to Medallion, she returns to live the life of an irrepressible jazz body, one given to variation and experiment. She is, much like Cholly Breedlove, a dangerously free agent who can only be deciphered in the head of a musician. Just as Cholly does not conform to notions of the ideal father, so Sula does not conform to the role of the ideal woman. In fact, she all but mounts a personal campaign against the imposition of Victorian definitions of woman as pure, chaste, and domestic. Her body is not elevated through the Victorian triad of disuse, denial, and inexperience. She seeks no marriage; she claims no virginity; she proves no nurturer. Sula rejects domestication of her body. Instead, she is set upon reveling in a body that is, after all, phenomenal, or so the mercurial birthmark above her eye suggests.

A sign in one of Nathaniel Hawthorne's best-known short stories of defect, flaw, stigma, imperfection, degradation, of a darkness besmirching the snowy complexion of the fastidious Aylmer's beautiful wife, Georgiana, the birthmark proves in Morrison's novel to be a less objectionable mark. Instead of a blemish to be removed or erased, on the body of the eponymous Sula the birthmark is a text to be read and understood. Not only a physical site of hyperpigmentation but also an ontological site of hyperblackness, Sula's birthmark—variously perceived as "stemmed

rose," "rose mark," "scary black thing," "copperhead," "rattlesnake,"
"Hannah's ashes," and "tadpole"—makes legible her community's need
to express its own sense of hyperdisplacement, its sense of being much
like the place it inhabits, the Bottom, torn "from . . . roots," moved out,
"leveled," "raze[d]," and "pr[ied] loose"(52, 96, 97–98, 103, 104, 114,
156, 3). The birthmark extending from Sula's eyelid to her eyebrow speaks
to what Sula both is and may become—roach, bitch, witch, friend—and
also serves as a page or screen where others can set down or project their
own fears (copperhead, scary black things) or their own desire (rose).
The mark above Sula's eye underscores what Nel identifies as Sula's ability to allow self-expression in others: "Talking to Sula had always been
a conversation with herself . . . Sula never competed; she simply helped
others define themselves. Other people seemed to turn their volume on
and up when Sula was in the room" (95). Of course, the birthmark is
neither rose nor copperhead nor scary black thing; rather, it is all of these,
but it is especially the tadpole, an emblem of the constant evolution and
transformation that are tied into growth and survival. Sula's birthmark
is the signature of a body "double-dutched," extra, complex, a site of
multiplicity, mystery, and "the changing same."[10]

Death itself affords Sula yet another venue by which to explore the
body, as Sula's dying proves as peculiar as her birthmark. Having observed directly and indirectly the ways in which black bodies slip away—
or are thrown away, washed up, burned up, and drowned—Sula becomes
what so many before her have been: the body in pain. Burning up in a
fever that takes her out of this life as effectively as the flames that en-
gulfed her mother and her uncle Plum, Sula physically connects with
one of the defining experiences of the Bottom where blacks, forced
into absurd and cramped spaces, have to look for "a little comfort
somewhere . . . somehow" (4–5), where unbeknownst to the whites the
"adult pain . . . [of black people] rested somewhere under the eyelids,
somewhere under their head rags and soft felt hats, somewhere in the
palm of the hand, somewhere behind the frayed lapels, somewhere in
the sinew's curve" (4). Sula, too, experiences pain, but she suffers with
a difference, as the interlude of her illness becomes an opportunity to
test the limits of her body. Concentrating on the "pain [that] took hold,"
Sula analyzes "the wires of liquid pain" that loop through her body,
"identifying them as waves, hammerstrokes, razor edges or small explo-
sions" (148). Even the heightened bodily experience of pain cannot fix
or transfix Sula, who eventually feels more boredom than agony: "Soon
even the variety of the pain bored her and there was nothing to do" (148).
Sula lies in "weary anticipation" of "termination" and the "unassailable
finality" of death (149, 148); however, Morrison questions this finality,

giving Sula a postmortem textual resilience. Sula notices that she is no longer breathing, "her heart had stopped completely . . . she was not breathing because she didn't have to. Her body did not need oxygen. She was dead" (149). At this point, novelistic representation is destabilized as realistic narrative slips into a narrative metaspace. Morrison compositionally moves physical being into present being, narrativizing beyond the body. To put it another way, Morrison textually extends Sula's body, relocating it, bringing it out of the lacuna to which the word "dead" would normally have consigned Sula. With two more sentences, Morrison writes through the textual gap, linguistically recovering Sula's bodily senses and her mind, keeping her present, revealed, on stage: "Sula felt her face smiling. 'Well, I'll be damned,' she thought, 'it didn't even hurt. Wait'll I tell Nel'"(149). In a textual reinscription reminiscent of Pecola in *The Bluest Eye*, and anticipatory of the ghost in *Beloved*, Sula enters a liminal space in which her body is written into ambiguity, particularly when she smiles, an act that blurs the boundaries between the flesh and consciousness: the now-dead Sula can still feel her face smiling.

Bell hooks bemoans the fact that Sula, a character engaged in the construction of a radical black female subjectivity, proves "not self-actualized enough to stay alive." Incapable of being one of "those black women who survives," Sula, by hooks's account, is found sorely wanting: she is "not a triumphant figure" (48). Morrison, however, portrays Sula as one who dies yet at the same time as one who has no ending. Sula's smile signals some kind of success or victory that she cannot wait to share. It may well be that, as hooks declares, "Sula . . . has no conscious politics, [and] never links her struggle to be self-defining with the collective plight of black women" (48), but Sula's desire to "tell Nel" is a statement of sisterhood, if not revolution at some grand level. In fact, Sula's determination to "tell Nel" is best understood as intimate politics, a personally nuanced politics. Though Sula's life and passing will not directly bring about revolution, it will bring about gradual change in the community. When Nel finally realizes her love for Sula, whose stubborn subjectivity enriched Nel's own life, Nel is in a position at the end of the novel to pass Sula on like so many "dandelion spores in the breeze"(174). Even a life lived on one's own terms makes a difference ultimately, if not immediately. So Sula herself recognized: "Oh, they'll love me alright. It will take time, but they'll love me" (145). We are left with the possibility that the community that does "gather at the river" to witness Sula's "death" will not only know peace and turmoil but will also come together. As for Nel, she learns solidarity when, twenty-five years after Sula's passing, she stands before Sula's tombstone and identifies Sula Peace and the other Peaces as the word made flesh, supreme expressions of desire. The Peaces buried in the graveyard "were not dead people. They were words. Not even words. Wishes, longing" (171). Leaving "the colored part of the cemetery" (173), Nel has her deepest and near-revolutionary insight into her own true longing: she had loved her friend with a love that "had no bottom and . . . no top" (174); she realizes she had loved Sula always.

Summoning the Historical Body

While Morrison's *Sula* ends near a tombstone, her *Beloved* begins with one. However, the body inscribed on the headstone—that emblem of the flesh made word—initially proves no site of understanding but of spite and misunderstanding. Beloved, a one-year-old child whose mother, Sethe, has cut its throat to spare it from the evils of slavery, returns to haunt "the gray and white house on Bluestone Road" as an angry, venomous spirit. The women in the house, Sethe and her daughter, Denver, summon the "outraged" spirit back into their world (4). When "the one word that mattered" (5)—"Beloved"—gets fleshed out, it appears as a "fully dressed woman" who walks "out of the water" with "new skin, lineless and smooth, including the knuckles of the hand" (50). Her child miraculously resurrected, Sethe henceforth spends her time proving her love and remembering that she killed her child to save it from victimization by a system in which black bodies "were moved around like checkers . . . rented out, loaned out, bought up, brought back, stored up, mortgaged, won, stolen or seized" (23).

Beloved's return is a return to the mother, one of the child's primary sources of sustenance and reference.[11] When Beloved returns, she comes back to see Sethe's face, to experience the flesh. She returns with the wide-open eyes and the demanding mouth of the nursing child. She returns with a thirst for her mother's milk and a hunger for Sethe's body that conjure up ideas of vampirism and cannibalism: "Sethe was licked, tasted, eaten by Beloved's eyes" (57). So strong is Beloved's hunger that Sethe begins to waste away with Beloved's need: "The flesh between [Denver's] mother's forefinger and thumb was a china silk and there wasn't a piece of clothing in the house that didn't sag on her" (239). Sethe grows "smaller" as Beloved sucks at Sethe's life, "swell[ing] up with it [growing] taller on it" (250). Beloved's prodigious appetite and burgeoning body do not signal the "fallen nature, indelicacy or promiscuity" of those Victorian women who figure in Michie's study of the flesh made word (12–29). This is not a sex or a hate thing; it is a love thing. Beloved does consume Sethe, battening off her. Yet Beloved's hunger is not initially the savage cannibalism of the "people who chewed up her life and spit it out like a fish bone" (*Beloved* 177); it is particularly not the cannibalism of the three grown white men who steal Sethe's milk, two of them sucking at her lactating breast while one records the encounter. It is the cannibalism, if you will, of the child with its powerful and instinctive desire for nurturance, orientation, and love.

One of the most important manifestations of a fulfilling and orienting love becomes talk. Denver, who is herself eager to talk to Beloved, to have "sweet, crazy conversations full of half sentences, daydreams and misunderstandings," notices "how greedy [Beloved] was to hear Sethe talk" (67, 63). Words are food to the child Sethe recovers: talking "became a way to feed her. . . . Sethe learned the profound satisfaction Beloved got from storytelling" (58). Thus the discursive engagement between Sethe and Beloved is life-giving; Sethe narrates Beloved into being, and the stories simultaneously revitalize Sethe, who, in seeking to forget the pain of slavery, has dulled her own feelings: "[E]very mention of her past life hurt. Everything in it was painful or lost. . . . But, as she began telling about the earrings, she found herself wanting to, liking it" (58). Beloved's insistence that Sethe "tell me" is not only a request that Sethe recount the personal history Beloved has missed but also a demand that Sethe recall and acknowledge the communal history that accounts for Sethe's decision to kill her beloved baby girl. In other words, the power of narrative enables Sethe to compose herself and to make intelligible her desperate act.

Indeed, Beloved's hunger itself seems, if not desperate, then "somehow excessive" (Rody 93). Her hunger finally announces so much more than the hunger of any one female or any one individual. Beloved's abnormal attachment to and hunger for her mother is indicative of and perhaps synonymous with the angst of separation and disorientation of a whole people who were torn from their homeland, deprived of dignity and substance in a world that made of them provisional bodies, if not indeed ghosts. To put it another way, Beloved's hunger is diasporic: her hunger and need are great enough to express the need of the whole race brought across the water by "the men without skin" (*Beloved* 210), men who at their will separated men and women, parents and children, sisters and brothers, while they chained the living to the dead.[12] Appearing at 124 Bluestone ill and disoriented, with only the clothes on her back, with no knowledge of her people and little if any knowledge of where she had come from, Beloved represents the body of the Middle Passage that is not to be forgotten: the black body stripped of family, name, language, and homeland, forced into small, "unlivable" spaces (198).[13] Socially, politically, and economically denuded, Middle Passage blacks were bereft of practically everything except their bodies, which, in that twelve-to-twenty-week passage, were laid waste by hunger and disease, filth and death, as well as brutal mistreatment.[14] Brought to the shores of America, the Middle Passage body became the slave body atomized by white oppression—backs to be flayed (whites use a whip to plant a scar like a chokecherry tree on Sethe's back); palms, shoulders, and ribs to be branded (Sethe's mother has a circle and a cross branded underneath her breast); necks to be put into nooses; mouths to be filled with bits (one of the former Sweet Home slaves, Sethe's lover, Paul D, is made to plow with a bit in his mouth); wombs to produce more human stock. Broken and fragmented, blacks found it as hard as Beloved did to maintain wholeness: "It is difficult keeping her head on her neck, her legs attached to her hips when she is by herself. Among the things she could not remember was when she first knew that she could wake up any day and find herself in pieces" (133).

The black body all in pieces constituted, as Sethe and Baby Suggs both knew, flesh subject to the most destructive legacies of all—self-hatred. When the white schoolteacher enters Sethe's yard to take her children and herself back into slavery, it is not only Sethe's memory of white physical assault on the black body but also of the more insidious assault of self-hatred that is uppermost in Sethe's mind. With a stroke of the blade, Sethe mercifully spares her baby girl, so she believes, from the flayings, brandings, noosings, and shacklings, as well as from the horrible and haunting knowledge "[t]hat anybody white could take your whole self for anything that came to mind. Not just work, kill or maim you, but dirty you. Dirty you so bad you couldn't like yourself anymore. Dirty you so bad you forgot who were and couldn't think it up" (251).

Whereas Sethe acts to spare the body from history, Beloved acts upon her desire to have a history through the body. When Beloved returns, then, she gives a special meaning to Baby Suggs's plea for the recovery of the body, for Beloved comes back because she needs somebody to love her unloved flesh. It is a love of the flesh that Sethe's mother-in-law, holy woman, and "doer of the word," Baby Suggs, had preached before her own death and the reincarnation of Beloved:[15]

> Here . . . in this here place, we flesh; flesh that weeps, laughs; flesh that dances on bare feet in grass. Love it. Love it hard. Yonder they do not love your flesh. They despise it. They don't love your eyes; they'd just as soon pick em out. No more do they love the skin on your back. Yonder they flay it. And O my people they do not love your hands. Those they only use, tie, bind, chop off and leave empty. Love your hands! Love them. Raise them up and kiss them. Touch others with them, pat them together, stroke them on your face 'cause they don't love that either. *You*

got to love it, *you*! And no, they ain't in love with your mouth. Yonder, out there, they will see it broken and break it again. What you say out of it they will not heed. What you scream from it they do not hear. What you put into it to nourish your body they will snatch away and give you leavins instead. No, they don't love your mouth. *You* got to love it. This is flesh I'm talking about here. Flesh that needs to be loved. (88)

While Baby Suggs's litany of body parts recalls Pecola's naming of the fingers, arms, feet, legs, thighs, stomach, neck, and eyes the young girl strains to dissolve and make disappear, Baby Suggs does not propose self-effacement; rather, she exhorts her listeners to engage in a communal reclamation of the black body that has been stolen, used, and disgraced.

To the extent that Beloved and Sethe are able to love each other's bodies, they restore each other; however, when the two women exclude those around them (Beloved moves Paul D out of the house; Sethe and Beloved "cut Denver out of the games" [239]) and when Beloved begins to supplant and possess her mother—taking her mother's lover to bed; dressing in Sethe's clothes; imitating Sethe's speech, laughter, and mannerisms; appropriating her mother's flesh in a reverse pregnancy that makes Beloved the mother figure and Sethe the child—they suffer from a surfeit of what critic Claudia Tate would call "unsocialized desire" (9) that ultimately requires the intervention of others. At the end of the novel, thirty neighborhood black women who have shunned Sethe and 124 Bluestone come to rescue a Sethe "locked in a love that wore everybody out," locked in a love that tried Sethe's mind and body as she "was worn down, speckled, dying, spinning, changing shapes and generally bedeviled" (243, 255). The black women get together to save Sethe from the beloved, from the flesh that is whipping her, from an unmediated past. In the thirty praying and singing black exorcists, Sethe sees "loving faces before her" (262). Beloved, who has been the occasion for the gathering, gets translated into ambiguity as the flesh she has assumed becomes word or, more precisely, hearsay and speculation. No one can say what happens to the body called Beloved: "first they saw it and then they didn't," and one little boy claims he "saw, cutting through the woods, a naked woman with fish for hair" (267). Though Beloved's body is physically absented, her name and memory are present in the mouths and memory of the community—"the text does not give up Beloved" (Rody 112).[16] She is, as surely as Sula is, "lift[e]d . . . into language" (Scarry, *Literature* xv); she becomes folklore.

Like Pecola's and Sula's before her, Beloved's body becomes a summons to community. When the thirty black women—alerted by the Bowdin's black servant, Janey, and led by one of Sethe's black neighbors, Ella—approach Sethe's house to cast out Beloved, they not only understand how everyone is responsible for doing what they can to undo each other's hurt and wrong, they also understand how Sethe's condition speaks to their own. They see their own pasts in Sethe's suffering. Thus Ella recalls that she, too, "had been beaten every way but down. She remembered the bottom teeth she had lost to the brake and the scars from the bell were thick as rope around her waist. She had delivered, but would not nurse, a hairy white thing, fathered by 'the lowest yet'" (258–59). These mothers, daughters, sisters, and wives who share through their bodies some of the same insults, abuse, and misinterpretations also recognize how they themselves are implicated in Sethe's pain: they had avoided, if not envied, the women at 124 Bluestone. They see that just as Sethe did not come to her suffering alone, she cannot get beyond it alone. Just as she cannot raise a child alone, she cannot finally negotiate the past that Beloved embodies alone. Beloved, Pecola, and Sula in their unique movements between the word and the flesh ultimately force a realization, whether immediate or belated, that the heart of the community—a collective identification that can take us back to unspoken understanding ("In the beginning there were no words. In the beginning was the sound, and they all knew what that sound sounded like" [259])— is indeed the prize. In coming to terms with the mistreatment of their bodies, Pecola, Sula, Beloved, and Sethe teach us that recovery is finally not something we do alone; recovery is something we do for each other.

NOTES

I would like to thank the committee for faculty development and Neil Abraham, vice president for Academic Affairs, at DePauw University for allotting me time and money necessary for the revision of this essay and the completion of this volume. I want especially to thank Michael Bennett, who has not only been instrumental in making this volume happen but just plain inspirational.

1. I imitate and borrow from Morrison's *Sula* (103, 92) and *Beloved* (213) in this paragraph.
2. I borrow this trope from Michie's book. In *The Flesh Made Word*, Michie focuses mainly on the representation of white Victorian women. The language used to describe the flesh of the white female is no doubt as limiting, clichéd, and paradoxical as Michie contends; however, that language, at its Victorian best, still describes "a physically beautiful [white] heroine" (5). Traditionally, and especially during the Victorian period, where the black woman's body meets language, there is not only limitation and cliché but also demonization and disqualification.

3. Law professor Williams writes in *The Alchemy of Race* about how her students in the margins of their notebooks unconsciously and consciously deface her, exaggerating the features that make her black: "They see my brown face and they draw lines enlarging the lips and coloring in 'black frizzy hair.' They add 'red eyes, to give . . . a demonic look.' In the margins of their notebooks, I am obliterated" (115).

4. I take this expression from the title of Frye's famous study of William Blake.

5. Pecola is one instance of the black child robbed of the affirmation of the caretakers of her body. She is one example of the black child whose need for his or her mother is sacrificed to the white child's pleasure or comfort in a mammy. The novel's narrator, Claudia, deplores this hateful, if not criminal, appropriation in her reference to Shirley Temple and Bojangles when she announces, "I hated Shirley. Not because she was cute, but because she danced with Bojangles, who was *my* friend, *my* uncle, *my* daddy, and who ought to have been soft-shoeing it and chuckling with me. Instead he was enjoying, sharing, giving a lovely dance thing with one of those little white girls whose socks never slid down under their heels" (19). The little white girls (and boys) take to themselves relations, reflections, experiences, and feelings that ought rightfully belong to the Claudias and Pecolas of the world.

6. Black mothers in the novel have trouble expressing their love in words. Pauline favors the white child over her own Pecola, and it is only the little Fisher girl and her family that refer to Pauline with familiarity, if not affection, as "Polly." Pecola addresses her mother as "Mrs. Breedlove," a term of formality and distance, not endearment. Mrs. McTeer proves just as formidable a mother. When she takes care of her sick daughter, Claudia, she manipulates the girl's body with a roughness and anger that some readers may interpret as unloving. However, Claudia comes to understand that the pain she experienced when her mother fussed about her sickness was really "a productive and fructifying pain. Love, thick and dark as Alaga syrup, eased up into that cracked window. I could smell it—taste it—sweet, musty, with an edge of wintergreen in its base—everywhere in that house" (12). These women never speak of their love; nonetheless, it does not mean the love is not present. Only Miss Marie speaks of her "fabled love for Dewey Prince," but when Pecola asks for more details about the place children might have in that love ("You and Dewey Prince have any children, Miss Marie?"), Miss Marie "fidget[s]," "pick[s] her teeth," and does not "want to talk anymore" (56, 57).

7. Morrison recalls a young black girl in elementary school who wanted blue eyes and her sense of being "violently repelled by what I imagined she would look like if she had her wish" (*Bluest* 209). In the novel, Pecola has a harrowing encounter with a black cat that belongs to Geraldine, a "colored" woman who seeks to dissociate herself from "niggers" (87). After Pecola recovers from having the cat thrown, clawing and scratching, into her face, "[t]he blue eyes in the black face held her" (90).

8. Michie goes on to describe a whore, specifically Dante Rosetti's prostitute, Jenny, as "a reflection of other people's desires, a blank page on which a series of men can write their narratives of her significance" (61). While, as I indicate, Michie's characterization of the prostitute may very aptly describe the Creole whore in *Sula*, I hesitate to postulate that Helene's mother is a complete "cipher." Morrison is quite capable of creating whores who reverse this assessment of the negated or blank woman, whores such as the three merry harridans in *The Bluest Eye* who make ciphers of men. Then, too, Morrison suggests that it is Helen Wright who stifles herself by becoming a "reflection" of Victorian convention and respectability.

9. Michie very shrewdly observes of cliché that "it defines and perpetuates an unceasingly iterable notion of 'woman'; all women are alike, all replaceable" (89). This is true up to the point that race is introduced. At this point, it is clear that all women are not alike, that, according to European standards, black women cannot replace white women: the two are not interchangeable. Black women are confronted, then, with the cliché within the cliché.
10. The term "double-dutched" is taken from Lee's *Granny Midwives*; the phrase "the changing same" is from McDowell's book. McDowell—who also speaks to the birthmark as a sign of fluidity, of resistance to stasis, of a "SELF as perpetually [the tadpole suggests] in process"—recognizes the shifts in viewer perspectives but focuses more on how those perspectives on the birthmark define Sula's "multiple identity" (105). McDowell does not consider how the birthmark serves the community.
11. In her study of folklore in Morrison's fiction, Harris also argues that Beloved wants a mother: "Her desire is for a mother, and she will have that mother even if it means killing her in the process of claiming her" (160). I take this idea farther in my emphasis on the mother as an ontological and historical point of reference for the child.
12. In a powerfully conceived essay in which she recognizes how Morrison's novel is "involved in the project of reclaiming or recovering [slave] bodies in narrative for posterity," Smith comments that "in addition to her feelings and desires from the grave, Beloved seems also to have become one, in death with the black and angry dead who suffered through the Middle Passage" (351).
13. On 29 October 1998 at the Midwest Faculty Seminar held at the University of Chicago, Morrison observed that the culture has no memory of the Middle Passage, that it is not, for instance, in the songs, and "it never survived in the lore . . . except in the naming."
14. Later in the eighteenth and nineteenth centuries, the Middle Passage crossing took about five to eight weeks.
15. Baby Suggs is a fictional character who fits the profile of those women who are the subject of Peterson's work, *"Doers of the Word."* She is much like that "older generation of women," including Sojourner Truth and Jarena Lee, who "chose to enter . . . the clearing, the site of religious evangelical activities that had been unleashed by the Second Great Awakening and drew the powerless—women, blacks, rural folk, and all those dislocated by the economic upheaval of the Jacksonian market revolution—to religion as a source of power" (18). Only when Baby Suggs draws blacks to the clearing, which Peterson identifies as a "liminal space," she draws them to a religion of the body.
16. I here enlist the support of Smith, who shrewdly and rightly contends that "Beloved's existence is predicated upon a communal memory of her; she dissolves when they forget and swallow her all away. And yet in her very dissolution and absence, in the communal denial of her existence, she remains present. The narrator here again locates her in a prelinguistic moment. Dependent upon the recognition of others, Beloved exists nevertheless and as well in the spaces prior to their acknowledgement of her" (352).

WORKS CITED

Brownmiller, Susan. *Femininity*. New York: Simon, 1984.
Butler, Judith. *Gender Trouble: Feminism and the Subversion of Identity*. New York: Routledge, 1990.
Christian, Barbara. "The Contemporary Fables of Toni Morrison." Gates and Appiah 59–99.

Frye, Northrup. *Fearful Symmetry: A Study of William Blake*. 1947. Princeton: Princeton UP, 1974.

Gates, Henry Louis, Jr., and K. A. Appiah, eds. *Toni Morrison: Critical Perspectives Past and Present*. New York: Amistad, 1993.

Harris, Trudier. *Fiction and Folklore: The Novels of Toni Morrison*. Knoxville: U of Tennessee P, 1991.

Hawthorne, Nathaniel. "The Birth-Mark." *Selected Tales and Sketches*. Ed. Michael J. Colacurcio. New York: Penguin, 1987.

hooks, bell. *Black Looks: Race and Representation*. Boston: South End, 1992.

Jay, Paul. *Being in the Text: Self-Representation from Wordsworth to Roland Barthes*. Ithaca: Cornel UP, 1984.

La Belle, Jenijoy. *Herself Beheld: The Literature of the Looking Glass*. Ithaca: Cornell UP, 1988.

Lee, Valerie. *Granny Midwives and Black Women Writers: Double-Dutched Readings*. New York: Routledge, 1996.

McDowell, Deborah E. *"The Changing Same": Black Women's Literature, Criticism, and Theory*. Bloomington: Indiana UP, 1995.

Michie, Helena. *The Flesh Made Word: Female Figures and Women's Bodies*. New York: Oxford UP, 1987.

Morrison, Toni. *Beloved*. 1987. New York: Plume, 1988.

———. *The Bluest Eye*. 1970. New York: Plume, 1994.

———. *Sula*. 1973. New York: Plume, 1982.

Peterson, Carla L. *"Doers of the Word": African-American Women Speakers and Writers in the North (1830–1880)*. New York: Oxford UP, 1995.

Rigney, Barbara Hill. *The Voices of Toni Morrison*. Columbus: Ohio State UP, 1991.

Rody, Caroline. "Toni Morrison's *Beloved*: History, 'Rememory' and a 'Clamor for a kiss.'" *American Literary History* 7.1 (1995): 92–119.

Scarry, Elaine. *The Body in Pain: The Making and Unmaking of the World*. New York: Oxford UP, 1985.

———, ed. *Literature and the Body: Essays on Populations and Persons*. Baltimore: Johns Hopkins UP, 1988.

Smith, Valerie. "'Circling the Subject': History and Narrative in *Beloved*." Gates and Appiah 342–55.

Spelman, Elizabeth V. *Inessential Woman: Problems of Exclusion in Feminist Thought*. Boston: Beacon, 1988.

Spillers, Hortense J. "Mama's Baby, Papa's Maybe: An American Grammar Book." *Within the Circle: An Anthology of African American Literary Criticism from the Harlem Renaissance to the Present*. Ed. Angelyn Mitchell. Durham: Duke UP, 1994.

Tate, Claudia. *Psychoanalysis and Black Novels: Desire and the Protocols of Race*. New York: Oxford UP, 1998.

Williams, Patricia J. *The Alchemy of Race and Rights: Diary of a Law Professor*. Cambridge: Harvard UP, 1991.

PART III

Recovering

MARGARET K. BASS

On Being a Fat Black Girl in a Fat-Hating Culture

For the most part I use the word fat because it tells it like it is. Words like heavy and large and stout are euphemisms, and I feel there is no point in dodging the issue. I like the term fat, and I think other people will like it, too, once its pejorative connotation is removed.

—Theodore Isaac Rubin, *Alive and Fat and Thinning in America*

Charles Davis called me nearly twenty-five years after we had been classmates from fourth through sixth grades at Darnell Cookman Elementary School, one of the "colored" elementary schools in Jacksonville, Florida, where my family had moved from Pittsburgh. After the initial shock the segregated South gave my nine-year-old sensibility, on most days I didn't think about it. I lived in an entirely black world then, and I only thought about white people when the inevitable racist event occurred.

My parents prepared me well for our move to the South. I recall the hours and days my parents, and particularly my mother, sat and detailed very explicitly the horror of Jim Crow and racial segregation. My precocious, unruly brother and I had to be schooled in the ways of the South. The rules for boys were more consequential; their lives were often at stake.

I survived that confusing and painful period of my life never understanding racism or Jim Crow but rebelling against it in my own childlike way whenever an opportunity arose. When scolded by a department store clerk for drinking water out of the "white" fountain, my brother and I would feign ignorance and declare: "We thought the 'c' word stood for cola and the 'w' word stood for water. We don't want to drink cola. It's not good for us." Worked every time! Nothing about those rules made sense to me, and so my mother found herself, time and time again, "explaining" things for which there are no explanations.

The most remarkable thing about that experience is that I came out of it unscathed. Jim Crow neither lowered my self-esteem nor crushed my spirit. When I asked why we "Negroes" were treated so badly, my mother told me that it had nothing to do with us. Racism and segregation were not our fault—there were mean and unreasonable people in the world who believed for some peculiar reason that "Negroes" were inferior to whites. "That's not true, darling. There is nothing wrong with you. You are beautiful. You come from a long line of proud people, so you must be proud as well." And then came stories about the many brilliant black men and women who had proven white supremacists wrong.

Because of my caring and conscientious parents, I have never felt one moment's shame about my Africanness. I glory in my kinky hair, wide nose, full lips, and creamy brown skin. I can even appreciate my big butt, but that ends the appreciation for my body. I am repulsed by the rest of me.

No one prepared me for living life as a fat person. As I look back through time at childhood photos, I am astonished to see my "chubby" child body. I have vivid memories of treks to the "Chubby Shoppe" at Sears Roebuck or J. C. Penney's to buy clothes for me. My mom and I, frustrated by the limited supply and "ugly" clothes for fat girls, felt none of the joy mothers and little daughters were supposed to feel on shopping sprees. "I get tired of shopping for you in these places," my mother said. "Other mothers can buy pretty clothes for their daughters; there are no pretty clothes for fat girls." No one prepared me for living as a fat person. I remember no tender moments, me on Mom's knee, with gentle discussions about how the thin or near-thin world treats fat people. That world—those jeering hordes—is colorless in the mind of the fat person. It represents one huge, disapproving, scornful eye. Geneen Roth echoes the lesson I learned very young: "In our culture it's unacceptable to be fat, which makes it seem self-destructive to continue to be overweight. Fat is regarded as a deviation from the norm; it is considered ugly, unfeminine, offensive, even disgusting. Fat sticks out; it is unavoidable, apparent" (34).

I remember my father's confirmation of that collective cultural attitude when he sat on the side of the bed in undershorts, a T-shirt, and my mother's wide-brimmed hat, mocking her, chanting "Two-ton Tony" at her while my brother and I squealed with laughter and my mother cried. She was fat then—weighed well over two hundred pounds—but not even her own experience of a fat person's misery inspired her to tell me what was in store for me. Perhaps I was too young to understand the depth of her own sadness and shame, but I remember years of watching her count calories and eat dry toast and hard-boiled eggs. One of my mother's proudest moments was the day she celebrated one of her many big weight losses by buying herself an Oleg Cassini dress from one of the swankiest department stores in Jacksonville. My brother, Danny, and I called it her rug dress, for the material felt like the plush pile of the best carpet one could buy. The dress was beige with a collarless neckline; it had two pieces of material that dropped from the neckline and crossed each other, stopping just at her breasts. Size ten. Mom bought a beige hat to match her dress. The hat had feathers that lay neatly across her forehead like carefully combed bangs. "Two-ton Tony" had been buried somewhere under all that dry toast, and my new, improved, and much smaller mother emerged. That day, and all the days my mother wore that dress, were among her happiest.

It did not occur to my mother to talk to her chubby daughter about her anguish or her struggle to make her body thin. It did not occur to my mother to ask her chubby daughter, who hated gym class, to join her in her daily exercise regimen. These omissions had nothing to do with neglect. My mother's mind was on other things—her efforts and energies focused on shielding me from the physical and psychic dangers all around me in the Jim Crow South.

My parents, like the nation, were so completely consumed by the issue of race that it became their sole obsession. They had to protect us from an uncaring and mean world. But for me, the world was mean in another way. My classmates and friends did not taunt and torment me because I was black; they tormented me because I was fat and vulnerable.

I did not enter this world knowing that I was a fat girl. Like Sally Tisdale, "I'm not sure when the word 'fat' first sounded pejorative to me, or when I first applied it to myself" (414), but I think I did not know I was fat until I was in the fourth grade of a segregated school in Jacksonville. I have known it ever since.

Charles Davis called to explain the years of tremendous cruelty I suffered from a group of children whom I wanted to befriend. They were mostly boys—names I can still remember thirty-five years after the fact: Donald Mulberry, Giradeau Nesbit. Charles's call came from nowhere, from some pang of guilt or shame that made him recall those awful days: "I've talked to the guys about what we did to you since we've been adults. None of us can figure out why we treated you so badly, but we're all sorry. I am so sorry, Margaret." I did not question Charles's motivation.

I felt no victory, sought no revenge. There was only the comfort of know-ing that I hadn't made it up. It had happened just as I'd remembered.

I still hurt from that long-ago childhood time. I ache with the memory of the complete rejection and unceasing abuse that I suffered every single day, many times a day. One of the boys would pass by my desk and hit or kick me, or they would all gather on the schoolyard at recess and yell "You big, fat, blowed-up hog!" as my other classmates laughed with relief, grateful not to be the target of the boys' meanness. Sometimes the boys formed a circle around me and punched and poked and taunted until I'd ball up my fist and swing my arms in search of a target—any mouth or nose. I wanted to hit them in some tender place. I wanted to draw blood. I wanted to make them cry.

Donald, Charles, and Giradeau never, ever referred to me by name. There was never a time when they'd forget themselves and be kind or even civil to me. I don't think they even saw me as a person just like them. I was just a blob, a fat nothing, a grade school version of my father's "Two-ton Tony." I wonder why my fifty-year-old self still remembers this time so vividly, why these forty-year-old memories make me cry. Geneen Roth, in *Feeding the Hungry Heart*, tells me that it is not unusual to re-call, vividly and painfully, such childhood cruelty. Recounting her own childhood experience she says: "Shocked at the cruelty, I was nevertheless convinced of its truth. Even now, sixteen years later, it is painful to recall, so painful that this is the first time I have talked about it" (59).

Fat silences. Fat makes you alone and lonely even when you're nine or ten. The truth of it shames you; you do not tell when people hurt you. You are ashamed to admit that you are fat—ashamed to be fat—so you do not tell unless you find someone who cares and understands. I still do not know why I chose Mrs. L. P. Jones (God rest her soul) as the one person with whom I would share my sorrow. Perhaps it was because she was our teacher; she saw and heard what was going on. Perhaps it was because I thought she liked me in some particular way. Mrs. Jones was tall and stately, always impeccably dressed. Her hair was carefully pressed and curled. We never saw the nappy edges around her dark brown forehead and temples or the telltale "kitchen" at the back of her neck that signaled time had passed for an appointment at the beauty shop for a hot comb and curl. I loved her because she was kind to me. She spoke my name softly and without derision, and I'm sure she told me at least once that I was a "nice girl." So I wrote Mrs. Jones a letter in which I described my miserable little life: "I wish I could run away to a land where fat girls are loved. I wish my classmates liked me. I wish I could feel happy sometime."

Mrs. Jones taught me what the word "betrayal" meant. I felt it long before I could define it in words as she gathered my classmates round her desk and mocked me, reading my letter to them. "Listen to this, class. Just listen to what this silly Margaret Bass has written to me. 'Dear Mrs. Jones, . . . '" She leaned back in the chair in which she sat. She had a wide, almost salacious grin on her face, loving the prospect of the pleasure she was about to experience. I can still hear the tone of her voice, see the expression on her face at that moment. I can still hear their laughter (and hers). I see my nine-year-old head buried in my hands, lying on my desk. I see that little girl crying mournfully—ashamed, humiliated, violated, and hurt. This is a story I have not told before.

> I was a fat child; not obese, but fat enough not to be able to climb the ropes in gym class when everyone was watching. Fat enough not to feel accepted, not to like my body, and never to have boyfriends (Fraser 169).

I began this essay by talking about how my parents prepared me to live life fully despite discrimination and oppression—how they taught me to be proud although the world outside said I had no right or reason to be. My parents did a great job. I am a proud African American woman, an overachiever who takes nothing about her life for granted. I am me, but I am also representative of a people, and I am ever mindful of the ways in which my behaviors and actions have reverberations beyond my own life. My students, for the most part, do not understand this way of thinking about the self. "You're just you," they say. "You aren't responsible for other black people." We come from different worlds, they and I. I did not grow up thinking of myself as separate from my community, and in my mind that community is poor, or just escaping from poor, and black and southern and deeply religious. I achieved for me, but I also achieved for them—my people, my community—and I still do.

What I am trying to say here is what I have said before: racism did not kill my young spirit or make me dislike myself. I have never shed one tear or suffered one moment of shame because I was born black. I refused to let racism degrade or humiliate me. Armed against this oppression, why was I so ill-equipped to handle the discrimination I experienced as a fat child? Racism and Jim Crow were socially acceptable, just as fat prejudice was and is now, but racism and Jim Crow never touched my self-image. If anything, they made me love my African self more. Why is the woman I have become so completely shaped by my experience of fat prejudice? "Because," my friend Barbara tells me, "with fat there is the element of will. You are black because you have to be— you can't change that, but the culture says you are fat because you want to be." There is a way in which Susan Bordo's research in *Unbearable*

Weight seems to corroborate Barbara's suggestion. Bordo says obesity can be seen as "an extreme capacity to capitulate to desire" (201). And while I believe Barbara and Susan Bordo when they say that our culture deems fat as some reflection of desire, specifically the desire to eat too much or "pig out," I would suggest that this idea represents a complete misunderstanding of the emotional, psychological, and physical underpinnings of fatness. My friend David reminds me of this. "Aren't there other reasons why people are fat, Margaret? Don't genetic strain and metabolisms differ? Doesn't our need to turn fat into a moral issue suggest that the culture needs a scapegoat, a people toward whom we can be overtly prejudiced?" I am relieved when David tells me these things I already know, but these are things I cannot say about fat. This culture does not permit those of us with fat bodies to represent or characterize our fat. We may explain, apologize, or do whatever we can to rid ourselves of fat, but we must tolerate the representations and meanings of fat imposed on us by our society. David's comments and my refusal to address them in my own words in my own essay about fat, reveal just how much fat silences. There are limits to what fat people can say about fat, for what we *do* say we say to compensate for our weak will and lack of discipline and self-control. If we suggest that genetics and metabolism or the human need to label a despised other are the real issues, we do so to absolve ourselves of responsibility for our miserable condition. So when my thin friend David utters these words, I am grateful for his voice and his understanding.

I have not maintained my childhood obsession or misery about my weight throughout my life. There have actually been times that I have liked my body—for example, during the years I taught high school in rural Mississippi. In that small, mostly black town of working-class folks, sharing meals was at the center of community life. Weddings, funerals, revivals—every event was followed by a huge community meal where nearly every woman brought a dish of her specialty. There was a competition of sorts: "Was Miss Quillie's potato pie better than Miss Willie Mae's?" No person was more appreciated than the one who ate heartily and unabashedly complimented the cooks on their culinary creations, and no person could do that better than I.

I have been overweight for most of my life, but its significance has waxed and waned depending on the environment in which I lived. Those good people in Pinola, Mississippi, loved me as I loved them. They thought I was beautiful. "You's a good lookin' gal. Healthy. Got flesh. Chile, you sho' is fine." They thought their food was the only gift they had to give. They do not know how deeply grateful I remain for their acceptance and appreciation of my body.

Unlike many fat people, I have not been a compulsive dieter. I have been committed to eating healthily, for the most part, and from time to time I have been a faithful exerciser. I have been various weights near thin, but not quite. I have mostly been content to let my weight go its own way—doing whatever it wants. While I have always been acutely conscious of my "weight problem," because I have always been teased by various relatives and friends, I have only recently begun to experience some of that misery that the nine-year-old me suffered all those years ago. I have learned to hate my fat body.

> Research studies conducted in the late 1980's and 1990's confirm that the Cult of Thinness is spreading beyond the white middle class. Eating disorders have reportedly increased among the American black population. One researcher speculated that "increasing affluence among some blacks, and thus their access to traditional white middle class values, and the homogenization of life style and priorities, perhaps as a result of the increasing influence of the media, have finally penetrated the black culture; the young black female (and perhaps the male) is getting fatter and is becoming more concerned about her fatness." The problem appears particularly acute among persons of color who are upwardly mobile. (Hesse-Biber 109)

I attribute my relapse to my movement into the white middle-class world that forces me, again, to be conscious of myself in two competing ways. My African Americanness is purportedly revered and welcomed by my colleagues at a mostly white university that "values diversity." I am the embodiment of racial diversity and because I am like them in so many ways, I am easily assimilable. My greatest asset is my use of language. I can talk. I "speak so well," and while I may sound black, I do not (unless I want to) "talk black" in meetings, classrooms, or other more formal settings. They can count on me.

My fat belies my new "white" middle-class status, and I am keenly aware of that each time I enter a room and survey the body types. (And yes, I find great comfort in finding another fat, or fatter, woman in the room.) My foreignness is apparent every time I am invited to "do lunch" and I find that no one ever eats but me. The current trend seems to be ordering appetizers rather than meals. "Oh, I'm so hungry. I think I'll have one of these delicious appetizers!" "And?" I ask. "Oh Margaret, that's enough for me. I'll be just stuffed when I eat all this." I watch the waiter place a salad plate before my friend. There are two leaves of lettuce, three olives, and a sliver of chicken breast. "Girl," she says, "I've been waiting for this treat all day," and I wonder where the food is and what the treat is, and I'm convinced that eating at all is the treat. And so my friends order their "treats," and I order my meal. Shame creeps from my belly to my face as I am forced to admit that I eat meals—big meals by appetizer standards, and I am fat. I am the one who should order the appetizer, for I am the only fat one in the bunch. The source of my problem lies in front of me on that big plate. As my friends and I begin our meal, somewhere between bites one and three, one woman sighs and suggests that she ate a "huge breakfast" and is simply not hungry. The others, one by one, "get full." I do not, and I do not believe them either. They are not full, but they are not fat. They do not "capitulate to desire." After the meal, mine is the only clean plate. My clean plate indicates some moral failing that is at the root of all obesity. The value of membership in the "clean plate brigade," as my parents used to call it, has fallen sharply in the last decades.

I find that many white women talk about eating and not eating and too little eating and too much eating all the time, and many thin people speak negatively about weight and gaining weight and being too fat without even giving a thought to the fat person next to whom they stand. Americans can talk about weight and fat people freely, without censorship or disapproval, because everyone knows that it is wrong and bad and undisciplined and greedy and gluttonous to be fat. We also know that to be fat is not to be representatively middle class:

> Corpulence went out of middle-class vogue at the end of the century . . . excess body weight came to be seen as reflecting moral or personal inadequacy, or lack of will. These associations are possible only in a culture of overabundance—that is, in a society in which those who control the production of "culture" have more than enough to eat. The moral requirement to diet depends on the material preconditions that make the choice to diet an option and the possibility of personal 'excess' a reality. (Bordo 192)

According to Bordo, I either live in the wrong century or have assimilated (but not quite) into the wrong socioeconomic milieu.

Just a few years ago, I could crawl into my racial cocoon when the subjects of weight, fat, health, and diet came up in conversations. Back then, African American adults seemed much more accepting of fat people than either my childhood classmates or my present colleagues. Aside from some "good-hearted" teasing, I did not feel the discrimination or exclusion that I now feel as a fat person. I guess my generation lived with fat parents, grandparents, siblings, and relatives of every sort. Obesity was prevalent among African Americans, so fat stood out less than it does now. Fat was common, natural, and often admired. Shar-lene Hesse-Biber says the "'Cult of Thinness' primarily occurs in wealthy Western societies among white, upper-middle-class educated fe-males. . . . The excessive pursuit of thinness has been rare among people of color in the United States (e.g. Blacks and Latinos)" (108). So years ago I'd laugh insincerely and defensively and talk about "these middle-class white women and their obsessions with body and food," but Bordo tells us that things have changed: "Many cultures, clearly, have revered expansiveness in women's bodies and appetites; some still do. But in the 1980's and 1990's an increasingly universal equation of slenderness with beauty and success has rendered the competing claims of cultural diversity even feebler" (102).

Now not even blackness provides that comfortable space that it once claimed for a fat black girl, and perhaps that space never existed beyond the kitchen of some mythical grandmotherly type who just "loves to cook and watch people enjoy my food. Y'all leave the chile alone. She's alright. Let her enjoy herself." Of this figure, Marvalene H. Styles says:

> Even when she prepares meals as a way of making a living she takes pride in watching her consumers literally gorge themselves until the fatty tissue forms and finds a permanent resting and growing place. Plumpness is a symbol of the wonderful job which she is performing. . . . A big body to the Black woman rep-resents health and prosperity. . . . Bigness represents health and prosperity, but in America thinness is beautiful. (163)

While I would be the first to dismiss the sweeping generalizations that Styles makes about the black "cook" and other black women, the cook (who is always she) is a figure many African Americans of my gen-eration would recognize. She is our mother or grandmother or dear family friend, and she believes that her meals are a gift to us—that the weight we carry often signifies that we have "made it." We no longer live in various states of deprivation. We do not look like "starving Africans." We can buy food. We can eat. One of the greatest privileges and plea-sures that my graduation from college afforded me was my ability to buy anything I wanted to eat. My job and my paycheck suggested that there was one kind of deprivation that I did not have to suffer any longer. I could eat three meals a day. I could buy food, and buy I did. The gro-cery store is still my favorite place to go. During those early years of living on my own, I would spend hours in the grocery store browsing in much the same way that I do in the library—looking at foods I'd never tasted or heard of, feeling the containers, reading their labels, and imag-ining hidden delights! My greatest desire was to taste a T-bone steak, and for months I ate a "good" steak of some variety every day. As I reflect on Bordo's work, I wonder, given our history in this nation, if many African Americans are not a century or more "behind" white American culture in relation to weight—if corpulence remained in vogue well into the twentieth century for many of us, particularly those of us who are new to the middle class. If that is so, it is not surprising that at the start of the new century we would catch up with the "Cult of Thinness" as we catch up with other aspects of middle-classness, like having access to better health care.

My mother would say, "we've always been middle class," and I think she is right. I guess I have always believed myself to be middle class, but even this term was not part of my vocabulary before my initiation into the academy. My brother and I went to the library every week; we read lots of books. My mother took us to plays and museums and planetariums and concerts. I saw both Marian Anderson and Paul Robeson when I was a child. I suppose I was middle class, but it doesn't seem to be the kind of middle-classness that white America defines. The African American middle class I knew, and know for the most part, bears little resemblance to the middle class in which I now live. Mine was a middle class without money. I have been hungry and suffered from malnutrition. I have lacked proper clothing and shoes. I have only nineteen teeth because my parents could not afford dental care. I have gone without certain "necessities," but my values have always been middle class. My mother, after all, loves opera and still has Kobbe's *Opera Book* on her bookshelf in her government-subsidized apartment.

Such was the way, I guess, of much of the black middle class of my youth. Thus we were and were not middle class, and many, many members of my immediate community were working class, so the black cook figures prominently in my life as one who provided food, sustenance, nurturing, and comfort.

I feel some great pride myself when my guests "pig out" on one of my high-cholesterol, high-caloric and -fat, southern soul meals. Do I wish them dead? No. Do I wish them fat? Of course not. What I delight in is the expression of appreciation for my cultural heritage, although most of my present friends (who are, by the way, white) would say that the food I serve is "bad" for us. Their appreciation for my meals confirms that even they think "bad" tastes good.

I cannot win this war between American culture and my body, so "America," which usually means middle-class, mostly white America, wins; it wins in the interest of health. The nation and the medical profession have determined that what many black and poor folks and southerners eat is unhealthy food, food that no one should eat. But the nation doesn't often stop to realize the significance of food to culture and identity. And yes, I know about the rates of kidney and heart disease, hypertension and diabetes, among African Americans in this nation, but those facts have little to do with the emotional significance and impact of telling a group of people that the staple foods and dishes that define and distinguish their culture from "mainstream" America are taboo. At least African American nutritionists and chefs respect our traditions by developing "healthy" soul food recipes, but I still like the "bad" stuff. And I, in all my middle-class awareness, should know better. No way should I eat "that stuff." Well, I do know better. I know that fatback in collard greens isn't good for me, but, no matter how I try, I cannot convince myself that fatback in greens tastes bad; I know better.

> The obese embody resistance to cultural norms . . . the obese—
> particularly those who claim to be happy although overweight—
> are perceived as not playing by the rules at all. If the rest of us
> are struggling to be acceptable and "normal," we cannot allow
> them to get away with it; they must be put in their place, be
> humiliated and defeated. (Bordo 203)

I am defeated. I am humiliated and put in my place, and as I write I marvel at how closely related this language is to the language of racism. My racial self would never allow this, but my fat self concedes, gives up. I don't think any middle-class person, woman, in this country can be fat and happy. Despite the worthy efforts of fat acceptance crusaders, I don't believe they've made a dent in this culture's prejudice against fat people. Oh, you can love your life, have a great job and great friends, a wonderful marriage or partnership, but fat and happy? Not likely. Ask Jenny Craig, The Diet Center, Weight Watchers, Overeater's Anonymous. Consider the hundreds of women who would rather expose themselves to the risks of dangerous drugs than to be fat. Middle-class America, black and white, won't let you be fat and happy, and I resent it. I resent the ways in which I feel compelled to capitulate to someone else's standard of health and beauty. There are actually studies that suggest one can be fat and healthy.

When I first lived and worked among the white middle class, my fat represented resistance to cultural norms, and even as I write this I envision a reader scornfully suggesting that I use this reason as an excuse for my obesity. I have given up so much to enter and live in this white world; my fat and my food seem to be all that I have left that reminds me of a world that never was. For as I write, I remember that I began this essay with the story of my childhood in the late 1950s and early 1960s. No white middle-class world was calling me a "fat blowed-up hog."

Among colleagues and professionals I must own this fat, and now it ain't black to be fat. This fat, my fat, might actually belie the representation of Africanness free from past stereotypes that I strive to uphold. My fat signifies the perpetuation of a stereotype. Intellectually I have the right stuff; grammatically I have the right stuff. I drink espresso and latte (still hate wine and beer though), and I know which forks and spoons to use at a formal dinner. But I look like "mammy" without her bandanna.

Self-loathing? Of course it is. If I hated my racial self, I would be the subject of all kinds of studies—pitied by blacks and whites alike. But this is different; I *should* hate my fat. Maybe I'll be led to get up off my "lard ass" and do something "about myself," but nothing is as simple as it seems. One loses more than fat when one loses.

WORKS CITED

Bordo, Susan. *Unbearable Weight: Feminism, Western Culture, and the Body.* Berkeley: U of California P, 1993.

Fraser, Laura. ""Self-Hate and Rejection." *Feeding the Hungry Heart.* Ed. Geneen Roth. New York: Plume, 1993. 168–71.

Hesse-Biber, Sharlene. *Am I Thin Enough Yet?* New York: Oxford UP, 1996.

Roth, Geneen, ed. *Feeding the Hungry Heart.* New York: Plume, 1993.

Rubin, Theodore Isaac. *Alive and Fat and Thinning in America.* New York: Coward, 1978.

Styles, Marvalene H. "Soul, Black Women and Food." *A Woman's Conflict.* Ed. Jane Rachael Kaplan. Englewood Cliffs: Prentice, 1980. 161–76.

Tisdale, Sally. "A Weight That Women Carry." *The Writer's Presence.* Ed. Donald McQuade and Robert Atwan. Boston: Bedford, 1997. 413–22.

MARK WINOKUR

Body and Soul
Identifying (with) the Black Lesbian Body in Cheryl Dunye's Watermelon Woman

Researchers on the subject of black lesbian-directed films will not find many primary texts or much significant criticism.[1] Though a broadening body of queer criticism and a goodly amount of race and gender criticism has proliferated through the 1990s—prompting Lynda Goldstein to observe in "Queer Bodies of Knowledge" that "queer studies has reached critical mass in the gay nineties"—little of this criticism has been devoted to African American lesbian filmmakers. Citing very few lesbians of color, even B. Ruby Rich devoted the bulk of her 1991 discussion on black queer representation to white filmmakers Lizzie Borden, Sheila McLaughlin, and Gus Van Sant. More recently, the bulk of David Van Leer's excellent and comprehensively titled "Visible Silence: Spectatorship in Black Gay and Lesbian Films," though mentioning Cheryl Dunye and other lesbian filmmakers, is devoted to readings of the films of Marlon Riggs (157–82). Fabienne Worth locates this lacuna in the lesbian academic community itself: "Difficulties are compounded . . . by the divide between white/academic/standard/ and (paradoxically?) lesbians on the one hand and activist/artist/ vernacular/gays of color on the other, signaling even then the absence of a lesbian of color . . . " (8). The present work, therefore, is about a genuinely new field of critical archaeology: black lesbian filmmaking. As such, it is specifically a reading of the possibilities of the field through one film's account of the black lesbian body and voice: Cheryl Dunye's *The Watermelon Woman.*

Though *The Watermelon Woman* is a good place to begin for several reasons—it is a feature-length film seen by a relatively broad audience, it is widely available on video, the director is committed to the project of representation of black lesbianism—my principal reason for choosing this text is that the critic's work has been in some sense anticipated in the film itself. As one of the chief producers of these new primary texts, Dunye explicitly discusses in *The Watermelon Woman* the absence of a history for which she would like to be the heir: the "herstory" of black lesbian filmmaking. She has thus oddly given us a primary text whose fantasy archaeology preempts any critique and history of itself. As she says about her own work: "*The Watermelon Woman* came from the real lack of any information about the lesbian and film history of African American women. . . . Since it wasn't happening, I invented it" (69). Dunye is accomplishing in *The Watermelon Woman* what both queer and race critics demand as primary goals of contemporary texts: on the one hand recuperating history, while on the other postulating that historical repression renders full recuperation impossible. Dunye accomplishes both tasks by inventing a history that she then acknowledges as invention. The artifice allows for the self-reflexive investigation of black and interracial Hollywood and Philadelphia culture and history, while simultaneously critiquing a mainstream culture that has tended to exclude both blacks and queers, to erase the record of their existence.[2] More important than her investigation of any particular history, however, is the lesbian anti-oedipal paradigm Dunye establishes in which the historical and the psychological are conflated—along with history and fiction, the body and the voice—through the enactment of Kaja Silverman's elaboration of the "negative Oedipus complex," which defines a filmed relationship between the feminine voice and body. This paradigm allows Dunye to circumvent white patriarchal repression in a series of representations dependent on a redefined relationship between the bodies of the historicized black mother and daughter. Dunye weds the problematized voice of the daughter/filmmaker to the reenvisioned body of the mammy/spectacle.

At the simplest narrative level, the film is about a black lesbian filmmaker named Cheryl—played by Dunye herself—attempting to recoup black lesbian history through the making of a documentary about an obscure actress referred to as the Watermelon Woman, who is identified with roles as a filmic mammy and whose rich private (homo)sexuality belied her public persona. After telling us that the actress known as the Watermelon Woman—Fae Richards—was "the most beautiful black mammy" in Hollywood, the director-within-the-film cuts to a shot of Fae in *Plantation Memories*, an imaginary 1930s "plantation" film like *Jezebel*

(1938) or *Gone with the Wind* (1939), in which Fae comforts a southern belle—presumably the slave's mistress—with the hope that her man will return. Dunye's simple assertion that this mammy figure is "beautiful" opposes the implicit (yet dominant) body criticism by filmmakers and critics like Marlon Riggs, who asserts that the body of the mammy is always grossly overweight in order to render her harmlessly asexual for a Jim Crow–era audience that requires that feminine beauty be concentrated in the white mistress.[3] At a certain level, the asexuality of the mammy's body reinforces the sense that miscegenation could not have occurred between the slaveowner and the slave woman. In an interview later in the film, Camille Paglia overtly critiques this critique of the mammy. She sees the body of the mammy as goddesslike, similar to the body type of the Italian women from whom she herself derives and in marked contrast to white middle-class feminism, which for her is characterized by "anorexia and bulimia." (The film briefly cuts from Paglia to three skinny white students, perhaps also lesbian, whose ignorance of Fae Richards is comic: they think she is a blaxploitation heroine.) But while Paglia generally identifies the mammy as sexual, Dunye specifically suggests that, in her relationship to the white mistress, she also connotes lesbian desire.

Dunye's text progresses and regresses, back and forth between a heavily mediated and a putatively unmediated lesbian body. The film moves from stereotypical images of the mammy to the self-acknowledged lesbian body of Dunye herself, in the process initiating the audience into a world of representation of which it might otherwise have no experience. At the same time, and unlike other films that contain an otherwise more overt treatment of the lesbian body, it does not disavow that earlier vision of the mammy, seeking rather to find strategies for acknowledging a relation between an earlier "sister" (and, as we shall see, "mother") and her contemporary avatar.

In the sense that it refuses to repudiate the history it examines, the film has much in common with Woody Allen's *Zelig* (1983) as an exploration of the relationship between ethnic history and the personal, the body. *Zelig* and *The Watermelon Woman* both contain metanarratives, fictional histories reinforced by fake interviews with "real" personages (for example, Saul Bellow in *Zelig* and Camille Paglia in *The Watermelon Woman*) and fake aged photographs, film stills, and film sequences. Both films revolve around explorations of ethnicity through a figure whose body is also problematic, though the films' explorations take place in different registers. In *Zelig* the problem is the representation of male Jewish assimilation, projected through the mysteriously metamorphosing body of the eponymous hero. In *The Watermelon Woman* the problem is the representation of the representability of the black lesbian body. One body disappears; the other (rather like the victims of the last Argentine military coup) is "disappeared." The body of the eponymous heroine does not metamorphose as does Zelig's; rather, the interpretation of that body changes, both through the interpretation of her biographer, Cheryl, and in Dunye's interpretation of that character as an archetype to be acknowledged, admired, built on, and differed from.

The most important similarity between the two films, however, also points to the most significant difference. In both films, the director plays the central character. But, while Allen plays the putatively historical object of scrutiny, Zelig, Dunye plays the director of the documentary within the film's diegesis. Dunye's dual roles as director of both the fiction feature film and the nonfiction documentary biographer within the film invite the audience to consider Dunye's body as both subject and object, thus problematizing this binary opposition altogether.

Dunye's representation of black lesbianism in the film simultaneously deproblematizes and reproblematizes self-representation. Dunye is extremely comfortable narrativizing her own life, as she does in most of her earlier short "Dunyementaries." Interspersing the narrative are shots of Dunye simply sitting in front of the camera in medium shot, speaking in metanarrative fashion about the activities going on in the film. We shall have occasion to return to these shots because they are so unusual, so against the classical Hollywood norm, and because, as a motif, they constitute a principal structuring agent for the film. She is also comfortable with her own on-camera nudity and sex scenes. There is not the same need to separate the public and private that informs the works of auteurs from Dorothy Arzner to Sheila McCarthy, who make films about themselves but who are not themselves featured.[4] Arzner critics like Judith Mayne and Alexander Doty can make only tenuous and arguable connections between Arzner's private self-representation and the representations of the masculine feminine of her films. Critics need not play the traditional game that Doty calls "guess who's lesbian, gay, or bisexual" (43).

Dunye's self-representations are much more like those of pioneering lesbian filmmaker Barbara Hammer, who is also her own main topic of filming. Both are explicitly interested in the body of the lesbian self; both represent lesbian desire. Further, like Hammer (and other lesbian filmmakers), Dunye is not afraid to be critical of a certain feminism sometimes referred to by gay and lesbian critics as "legislating politically and sexually correct behavior and . . . policing lesbian erotic identity" (Worth 6). However, though quintessentially self-referential, Hammer's films do not as a rule contain those metanarrative moments evident in Dunye's films, which remind one of nothing so much as the narrative technique in even earlier experiments like *Citizen Kane* (1941) or *Masculin/Feminin* (1966). Just as important, Dunye attempts to reinscribe the lesbian body back into narrative—back into a history—while Hammer's films are more separatist, more explicitly avant-garde in their complete dismissal of this narrative enterprise.

Dunye's narrative is achieved at the cost of a certain audience anxiety about the relationship between character and filmmaker. When we encounter Dunye near the beginning of the film in a medium shot, the filmmaker is seated in front of a still camera in a way that renders ambiguous whether we are seeing her in character as "Cheryl" or as the director, Dunye. The subject of Dunye's monologue is crucial in understanding this ambiguity. She asserts about Fae Richards that "Girlfriend had it goin' on. . . . I'm going to make a movie about her. . . . Something in the way she looks and moves is serious, is interesting." We are to understand that Fae is expressly sexual and, at least in Cheryl's mind, possibly lesbian as well. Later in the film, at the point of discovery, Cheryl exclaims, "Can you believe it? Fae is a sapphic sister, a bull-dyker, a lesbian. Oh my gosh I knew something was up when I saw *Plantation Memories*. I guess we had a thing or two in common, Miss Richards: the women and movies." What is important about this way of introducing Fae is that her ambiguous identity is somehow bound up with the ambiguity in Dunye's identity, as if the integration of Fae's history within the context of the history of black lesbianism and Cheryl's own life is a necessary precondition for the integration of the filmmaker and her on-screen persona, of the filmmaker and the possibility of making films. This ambiguity in persona is so pronounced during those moments when Dunye—either in full front one-shot or behind the camera in voice-over narration—interprets the story-thus-far, that through the remainder of this essay I shall have to refer to this narrator as a third persona, almost an additional character. I shall refer not only to Cheryl (the character's last name is not even given in the final credits) and Dunye (the director) but also to Cheryl/Dunye, the narrator whose identity we shall come to understand as the film's principal structuring device. While Cheryl attempts to establish her identity as a black lesbian filmmaker through an identification with Fae, Dunye is attempting to integrate or reconstitute Cheryl/Dunye—an identity split by the traditional distinction between actor and director—as Cheryl Dunye. While Cheryl establishes a historical subjectivity for black lesbianism denied by racial repression, Dunye establishes a private lesbian subjectivity denied by classical Hollywood repression. While Cheryl's filmmaking difficulties—the opposition from her friend and her lover, the paucity of filmmaking resources—

represent Dunye's psychoanalytic "vicissitudes," the presence of Dunye's body before the camera, like the story itself, "invites us," as bell hooks suggests in another context, "to consider the production of history as a cultural text, a narrative uncovering of repressed or forgotten memory" (94). Dunye inserts her own body into the narrative in order to inscribe and integrate herself into a history she is thus problematizing, at the same time insisting on the mutual identification of the vicissitudes of the body and the psyche.

One sees Dunye attempting this integration and inscription in her earlier films. For example, the narrative structure of *She Don't Fade* (1991) is similar to that of *The Watermelon Woman* in that the filmmaker spends considerable time narrating the story of the lead character she plays, sitting in front of the camera and interrupting the diegesis in the same way Cheryl/Dunye does in the later film. In her first appearance as the narrator of *She Don't Fade*, Dunye makes an extremely interesting rhetorical transformation. She begins by discussing her character's professional life in the third person: "Shae's twenty-nine years old. She recently broke up with a lover about a year ago. Around that time she started her own vending business, which is really really good." However, at the point at which she begins discussing Shae's relationships with women, the narration becomes first person: "It was good to do that at that time because it got me into myself when I had been in relationships with women consecutive. The last one was three years; the one before that was so many years. I'd been going out with women pretty much as a livelihood for a while." Dunye's ambiguous rhetoric suggests her ambivalence in the director's relationship to her on-screen persona. The split in the filmmaker's on- and behind-camera personae has to do with the split between professional and passional identities, between voice and body. While American work culture takes this rupture as an ideological given—necessary, for example, to homogenize an incredibly heterogeneous workforce—Dunye's work tends to bring that split back into prominence, acknowledging a need to heal this rupture between professional vocalization and passional embodiment. The inclusion of the director's body highlights the fact that the black woman's body traditionally speaks for something else not seen: ideology, patriarchy, and so forth. Dunye's body speaks for itself.

The difficulty with reading *The Watermelon Woman* as a problem in self-integration is that within the narrative we do not understand why Cheryl and Dunye are not *already* integrated. Already lesbian-identified, Cheryl does not have to confront the problem of coming out of the closet in this film (or in most of her short films). She has a circle of friends on whom she can rely, and her relationship with her mother seems, for the most part, fairly easygoing. The only serious relational problem with which we are presented—the only issue of real indecisiveness—is her brief love affair with a white woman, Diana. A sort of Heisenberg relational principle operates here: one can have either a narrating voice or a narrated body, but not both.

The problem is not so much the character's sexuality, precisely, as it is representing a hitherto unrepresentably "fleshed out" black lesbian sensibility and sexuality. The self-reflexivity of black lesbian films tends to provide an explanation for the subject's lesbianism. Often separating the authorial voice and the image represented after the manner of documentaries, several important films by prominent lesbian directors—*Tomboy* (1997), *Frankie and Jocie* (1994), and *I Never Danced the Way Girls Were Supposed To* (1992)—are often narrated texts; authorial voice reduces character autonomy via narration. This dynamic occurs in part because of the usual economic constraints placed on truly independent filmmakers who, for the sake of saying as much as possible in a limited amount of time, must say rather than show. These are important founding texts in the representation of the lesbian body, but, because they are specifically about that, they often (like documentaries) read like etiologies of lesbianism: the need for explanation and justification is strongly visible. Body is subordinated to voice. In these films the black lesbian body tends to be defined in the negative, in its opposition to the straight body or to the definitions imposed on the lesbian. Occasionally, such definitions are even acknowledged as sufficient. *Tomboy* keeps referring back to computer-generated definitions of the word "tomboy," as if trying to find one that works. At the end of the film the narrator reads a final definition: "Tomboyism: a wholesome delight in rushing about at full speed, playing at active games, climbing trees, rowing boats, and making mudpies. 1876, *The Oxford English Dictionary*." The narrator gains authority via reference to one of the very tools patriarchy uses to determine social legitimacy.

In contrast, Dunye's black woman's body has no etiology as such, so it is almost utterly different from traditional representations of such bodies, in both film and literature—say in its avatars in such works as *Beloved* and *The Color Purple* (both the literary and film versions), as well as in most queer representations. The difference lies in the fact that, despite their problems, her bodies are self-determining rather than victimized. They are neither colonized nor orientalized in the usual scripts. By this I mean more than simply that her heroines/her selves make choices; we also see the process through which such choices—mainly about love objects—are made. The peculiar authorial presence suggests that bodies narrate themselves. Often those choices are so unlike the usual filmic mainstream narrative of the black woman that they must in fact be carefully "read" because they do not offer themselves as simple choices but rather as the products of a series of arcane or obscure personal discriminations. Though the relationship between Cheryl and her white lover ends, we are never shown its erosion. We are left to infer from the self-reflexivity of the photography of Cheryl and Diana watching the "race film" that its ending was dependent both on Cheryl's dedication to her project and on Diana's history of colonizing her black lovers. We have to read the reason, which has to do with the nature of desire, not with historical determinancy. Rather than submit herself to the script of history, Cheryl/Dunye creates a new script for a new history.[5]

In contrast to the attempt to find an etiology for lesbianism, Dunye's project detaches the body of the black lesbian from the body of history about it. She does this by sinking, as it were, into the belly of the beast: the white lover who in *The Watermelon Woman* orientalizes the black lesbian body as simply an object of desire. In fact, several instances of interracial lesbian desire are interwoven in *The Watermelon Woman*: Fae Richards as the Watermelon Woman and her *Plantation Memories* mistress; Fae and Martha Page, her director (iconically and ironically, a sort of Dorothy Arzner figure); Fae and the mulatto in a clip from a "race film" in which both star; Cheryl and Fae; Cheryl and Diana; Diana and her previous black lovers (even the black manager of the video store in which Cheryl works hits on Diana); and Camille Paglia and her romanticized black goddess. The film suggests a flirtation between Cheryl and Annie Heath, a coworker. Even a "race film" sequence starring Fae, in which she and a mulatto friend are fighting, is photographed in intimate proxemics. And implicitly, according to critics like Lynda Goldstein ("Getting"), Cheryl/Dunye is carrying on an affair with her white lesbian audience. Most of these relationships are either implied (the mistress and her mammy) or historically repressed (Page and Richards). The relationship between mistress and mammy fits the orientalist dynamic, Linda Nochlin observes, in which "the conjunction of black and white, or dark and light female bodies, whether naked or in the guise of mistress and maidservant, traditionally signified lesbianism" (126).

Though not interested in lesbian etiology, Dunye does explore the relationship between desire, history, and repression in her examination of interracial attraction. Essentially, she represents the black body as the site of contesting discourses of desire: black lesbian self-expression against white liberal orientalization, being the body against having the body. Significantly, the white body is never a field of contestation; only black bodies are forced into object position. Though curious, the black lover is never seeking the experience of whiteness but rather something relational.

Such desire is explicated most completely in *The Watermelon Woman* and *The Potluck and the Passion* (1993). In both films desire is defined as the black lover's attempting (unsuccessfully) to be ahistorical, while the white lover is embroiled in her desire for a black experience rather than for the particular other with whom she finds herself. In *The Watermelon Woman*, especially, "black-on-white" lesbianism is defined in historical terms, a parallel erected between the relationship Fae carries on with her white director/lover and the relationship between Cheryl and Diana, whose name suggests an even earlier history: the classical Greek (white) goddess of the hunt, associated with the erotic while not herself a desiring subject. The white goddess stands for knowledge of Eros divorced from desire, a position valorized in Western culture but criticized when held by the film's white lover.

The film contains more subtle devices through which the interracial relationship is historically critiqued. After the first moment in which we see Diana seducing Cheryl, the film cuts to a clip from a "race film" starring Fae, who at that moment is criticizing a friend for trying to pass by wearing too much white powder. Again, the black body is the object of visual examination. When the film cuts back to Diana and Cheryl, the camera slowly tracks back to reveal that they are both on a bed watching the film on television. Cheryl is visibly uncomfortable in a way that Diana is not, feeling that she is being "set up," which is to say objectified. Still, Diana's seduction of Cheryl takes place, at which point the film cuts back to the film/video, where Fae slaps the mulatto. Later, as if to reinforce the connection between Diana and an oppressive past, we discover that her father was in the diplomatic corps. Diana was born in Jamaica and "traveled everywhere." She is thus connected to imperialism, or at least to neocolonialism. Further, Diana knows someone who knows the Page family, the pseudopatrician clan of Fae's sexually exploitative lover/director.

Diana's past suggests that even white resistance to racism is not a ticket to understanding or black acceptance. Though Diana does not exploit her paramour within the parameters of her father's neocolonialist paradigm, she inherits a fascination with the notion of "the black as other" that, even at its most benign, is an insufficient response to black lesbian privateness, given that Dunye's enterprise is to "normalize" the black lesbian, to evade the consequences of racial otherness. Diana's admission that she has had three (male) black lovers evokes from Cheryl not gratitude at the breadth of Diana's acceptance of black culture and community but the response that Diana is a "mess."

Diana and Cheryl watching the clip together constitutes a fascinating example of self-reflexivity because it is oddly reminiscent of other

such moments in the history of the classical Hollywood style that confront an unknowing audience with the paradoxical sense of seeming to
be on the inside of the joke while actually being outside. (I am thinking
of "backstage musicals," which, like *The Watermelon Woman*, decep-
tively promise the audience a glimpse of how spectacles are *really* staged.)
While an anonymous white audience may feel a sense of solidarity with
Cheryl's and Fae's characters against Diana and the anonymous passing
actress, the real identification should be with the latter two, for that audience is also passing at this moment, allowed the same temporary and
ambiguous "in" as Diana. In other words, a white audience adopts the
black body as its own for a while. But this audience is being excoriated
at the same moment Fae slaps the passing actress. And, if the audience
identifies with Diana, it is identifying with someone who is, as mentioned, exploitative and, ultimately, rejected. (As if finally rejecting any
possible white identification with black filmmakers, we are told by Fae's
long-term black lover, June, that Martha Page was "one mean and ugly
woman." She intimates that Fae's entry into film was dependent on Page's
casting couch.)

Identification is further complicated because we are also at a loss
to know with whom in the Cheryl/Dunye dichotomy we are supposed
to identify. Cheryl's body is cross-referenced with Fae's: while Cheryl
is shot in such a way as to valorize her and Diana's coupling—the lovemaking is soft-core, all close-ups of breasts and tongues—the historical
contextualization of the "race film" reminds us that Dunye is filming
herself at a particular historical moment, that she represents history as
well as herself. Cheryl's body repeats Fae's history, but Dunye's directorial "voice" constitutes the black lesbian gloss on that history. This film
history includes *Imitation of Life* (1934 and 1959) and *Pinky* (1949), Hollywood films that also speak to the ambivalence of cross-racial desire
through young black women ostracized for conflating desire with attraction to the racial other—women whose black bodies are the fields of contestation. Dunye must walk a fine line between dismissing such desire
for specific reasons of body politics and dismissing it in the blanket manner of historically white and male Hollywood's denial of black female
desire itself. Again, in writing a history that does not exist, Cheryl/Dunye
must find a way of representing desire that valorizes the romance of the
color difference incorporated in the film's soft-core photography of Diana's
and Cheryl's lovemaking while rejecting the historical orientalization of
the racial other's body. By filming a history that does not exist, Dunye
is in effect recovering the body despised by history. In including the de-
eroticizing "race film" as part of the foreplay between Cheryl and Diana,
she is denying the potential eroticization of the lovemaking sequence

between black and white bodies. (Elsewhere, Camille Paglia's rave against white, anorexic feminism is itself undercut by the visual cues of Paglia's whiteness and thinness, as if her own attempt at solidarity is merely another version of the racial tourist's identification with the other.)

Lynda Goldstein is one of the few critics who speak to the phenomenon of white lesbian audiences viewing black lesbian films, championing the dynamic under the rubric of "tourism." She asserts that gay and lesbian film festivals offer a context for white lesbians to have their consciousness raised as tourists of black lesbian films; thus she finds that white lesbians constitute a benign audience:

> [W]hite lesbians who "get into" these [black lesbian] shorts do
> so within a viewing community founded on a deeply entwined
> relationship between (inter)racial erotics and politics. Pleasur-
> ably implicating white lesbian viewers in this relationship while
> highlighting their whiteness (often by exclusion), the texts con-
> struct a . . . celebratory borderland in which race and queerness
> are simultaneously eroticized and politicized. ("Getting" 177)

But Goldstein's unproblematized reading of white lesbians as tourists of black lesbian life is troubling, given tourism's history as an economic consequence of imperialism and colonialism. The equation between sex, tourism, and the orientalized body in its present form is traceable at least back to the 1930s, which is to say the last great moment of European imperialism. It is on display, for example, in a white gay "cruiser's" (read: sexual tourist's) work: Cole Porter's "All of You," in which the singer/ wooer asserts that "I'd like to take a tour of you." The other's body becomes a trope for Western imperialism. (Porter covertly exploits oriental- ized sexual difference in even more famous tunes: "Like the beat beat beat of the tom-tom, when the mighty jungle roars," in his suggestively titled "Night and Day," and "do do that voodoo that you do so well" in "You Do Something to Me.") In short, tourism is historically hegemonic; it is about the politically neutralized, aestheticized othered body. It al- lows one the feeling of knowing a culture but at a distance, a knowl- edge of the art without a sense of the colonized anxiety from which it derives. In defining white audiences as benignly tourist, the critic simply reproduces the tendency of Hollywood to define the black queer experience through white directors (as in Steven Spielberg's *The Color Purple* [1985]), simply replacing the interpreter-as-director by an interpreter-as-critic.

Dunye's covertly delightful resistance to a simply benign reading of her films is evident in her reversal of focus from the body of the black woman to a problematizing of the white body. Dunye mentions her confusion at the white lesbian use of the expression "vanilla sex" to describe sex without toys because, in the black lesbian community, the same expression means sex with white women. (The metaphor is further extended in *The Watermelon Woman* when Cheryl's critical friend, Tamara, suggests that Diana is simply into "chocolate.") In a kind of displacement of the usual vision of the black lesbian body, which in primary and critical texts has been the most absent presence in mainstream cinema, the white woman is the absent toy while the black woman is the player (both in the hermeneutic sense of playing as a culturally vital game and in the related, black colloquial sense of manipulating someone, as in "don't play me like that").

One sees this displacement at work in *The Watermelon Woman* in the portrayal of the white lovers, who are in fact played by their black lovers in both ways. (In the "race film," the passing mulatto is of course "playing" white in still another sense.) The narrative suggests that the aggressor—the player—is Diana, the huntress. Cheryl is the distinctly uncomfortable character, playing the mediator between her lover and her jealous black friend, Tamara. But if Cheryl is uncomfortable, Dunye is not. She creates the video screen version of the "race film" and the strategy—rejection—that Cheryl will ultimately employ to resolve the problem of Diana. Cheryl's discomfort can be seen as a native's feeling of victimization by the tourist, but it may also be an awareness of the foreshadowing that the video clip within the film suggests. It is in fact Diana who is trapped between Dunye the director and Cheryl—the former creates and the latter enacts the scenario by which the goddess is exorcised. Diana is trapped between the past—her parents' colonialist history and the roughly simultaneous past of Fae Richards—and the black queer present in the form of Cheryl/Dunye, who is perfectly aware of that past and refuses to be exploited by it, even in a simple act of tourism.

This entrapment of the white character by the two personae of the same person—Cheryl/Dunye—suggests less the dynamic of tourism and more a connection to the two-faced "Signifyin' Monkey" about which Henry Louis Gates Jr. writes. This Signifyin' is also a kind of game playing, of the slave in relation to his or her master; the slave says one thing and means another, seems to agree with and obey the master while at the same time behaving in an insubordinate manner. For Dunye, however, the two behaviors are now distributed between two personae: the director and the character. The trick is to create out of these two personae one whole body undefined by white hegemony:

Represented as a process, Cheryl's coming out also means becoming "Cheryl," the central character in what the maker has termed her "Dunyementaries." This character is a vehicle for an ongoing, conventionally autobiographical plot . . . as well as for restructuring and calling into question the subjective realities of that plot. (Fuchs 197)

The white audience is itself "played," made to believe in a racial détente in the first half of the film that is subverted in the second half, during which Diana's orientalized relation to the racial other is subverted, the relationship itself ended by the nearly colonized Cheryl.

My only point of divergence from Cynthia Fuchs's argument is that, while she describes the "Dunyementaries" as a fashionably postmodern, destabilized vision of the self, and by implication of the body, I believe that the texts represent a desire for wholeness, a desire to unite the director and the character—voice and body—in each text and that the destabilization in Cheryl/Dunye works to that end. The refusal of stereotypical identities, even if those identities are modern, is not the same as the refusal of identity. At one point Cheryl criticizes one of her black dates as "heavy femme Afrocentric" but only to define herself against that definition. She goes out of her way to make certain that, though history and representation are uncertain variables, she is not: "Hi, I'm Cheryl and I'm a filmmaker. . . . I'm working on being a filmmaker. The problem is I don't know what to make a film on." Identity as a confused filmmaker is not the same as a confused identity.

This minor departure from Fuchs, however, marks an important split between her argument and the kind of experimental film Kaja Silverman describes in *The Acoustic Mirror*. At first glance, Silverman's relevance to black lesbian cinema is at best obscure. Her examples from feminist countercinema are always about the woman director's questioning of the narrative voice-over—a masculine domain which, in the classical Hollywood cinema, almost always reinforces the subjectivity of men while objectifying women. Most of Silverman's countercinematic examples have to do with the creation of voice-overs that seek to recover a feminist critical heterogeneity in the narrating voice. Alternatively, the factor complicating the gender discussion in Dunye's films is, of course, race. While for Silverman the theoretical problem for women is to create a subjectivity that overcomes the objectification of the (implicitly heterosexual) feminine voice in the classical Hollywood style, for Dunye the problem of the black lesbian is to enter representation at all. While for Silverman's filmmakers, it is important to alienate the woman's voice from its body, in Dunye's films it becomes important to find a structure that consolidates the black lesbian body and voice. Though Silverman mentions one filmmaker interested in race and class, her argument is only incidentally concerned with these issues. Her discussion of Patricia Gruben's *Sifted Evidence* (1981) is largely about the orientalizing tendency of the film-maker, even if it is in some measure a critique of that tendency. In contrast, Dunye's films are constructed by a sensibility refusing to be orientalized by a pervasive internal (and internalized) colonialism.

However, though Silverman is interested in race only as a sidebar, her psychoanalytics of a feminist countercinema can be extremely useful in reading black lesbian cinema. In a crucial section of *The Acoustic Mirror* (the section in which she derives the name for the book in the demeanor of the mother), Silverman discusses the way in which traditional psychoanalysis partitions the female child's initial identification with and desire for her parents' bodies.[6] If identification goes to the mother and desire to the father, the child is heterosexual; if identification and desire are reversed, then the child is lesbian (150). Silverman then posits a countermodel in which an open feminine sexuality presents itself a moment after the mirror stage but before or beside the oedipal stage in the "negative Oedipus complex," a psychic moment that "turns upon *not only desire for the mother, but identification with her*" (149, my emphasis). This moment, in which femininity "is at least in part an identification with activity" (153), exists in opposition to normative cultural imperatives that femininity be passive. Though Silverman is primarily interested in women's voices (and who narrates or is narrated is as important in Dunye's work as in the work of the feminist avant-gardists whom Silverman discusses), one may also discuss the way in which this alternative identification is also played out in terms of body surfaces: color, shape, and so forth. Dunye creates a representation of the negative oedipal stage of both identification with and desire for the body of the black lesbian mother.

At the simplest level, the narrative would seem explicitly to contradict this notion of identification and desire. The narrative brings Cheryl back to her mother's house in order to derive clues about the fate of Fae Richards. But though Cheryl seems at first superficially like an infant for whom the mother is omnipotent and omniscient, that relationship is quickly exploded. In a voice-over, Cheryl initially asserts that "My mother was the first person I called up because I knew she'd have something to say about the Watermelon Woman." But her mother, Irene Dunye, proves an inadequate if suggestive source of information. She even denies having asserted that she knew anything about Fae. Photographically, Cheryl is not seen in the same frame as Irene, as if further to deny identification between Irene's physical presence and her own. (Tamara's mother also gives Cheryl a false lead: the card of a "race film" collector, who turns out to be more than mildly gynephobic.) This failure to find

an adequate imago in the "actual" mother is, however, simply a restate-
ment of the problem as diegesis rather than an admission of its insolu-
bility. Silverman discusses the effects of the Oedipus complex on the
woman's sense of the maternal:

> the real force of the hostility which she directs against herself
> after the conclusion of the negative Oedipus complex has more
> to do with the devaluation of the original erotic object [the
> mother] than with anything else. In effect the female subject is
> punishing the mother (and consequently herself) for being in-
> ferior and insufficient, unworthy of love. (158)

The "reconstruction of the negative Oedipus complex" (159)—the creation of a benign relationship to the maternal and hence to the self—to
which Silverman looks for a cure will be in the realm of the imaginary
rather than in any literal attempt to value the mother.

Cheryl's self-avowed enterprise is to find a historical someone with
whom she can identify, an enabling feminine body-imago, the other/self
who enables the restoration of the negative oedipal complex at the level
of visual (self-)representation. As Cheryl/Dunye asserts:

> what she means to me, a twenty-five-year-old black woman
> [is] . . . hope, it means inspiration, it means possibility, it means
> history. And most importantly what I understand is that I'm the
> one who's gonna say I am a black lesbian filmmaker who's just
> beginning, but I'm gonna say a lot more and have a lot more
> work to do.

In pursuing Fae Richards, she is attempting to render the mammy as the
enabling maternal. In Fae, however, she also discovers a physical object of desire and so an awareness of her own body as historically desirable. She creates a black lesbian body in order to recover her own.
Though probably a bit older, Fae is roughly contemporary to Irene, whose
acquaintances had seen and fought over Fae at the kinds of clubs that
Irene also inhabited. While the character of the Watermelon Woman is
used within the film as a counter to the usual observations about the
filmic mammy's sexual unattractiveness, Lisa Marie Bronson as Fae is
slim and otherwise physically attractive by Cheryl's standards. Fae
is as slim as Cheryl's white love object, Diana, and, more important, as
Cheryl herself. Fae simply does not look like Hattie McDaniels or Louise
Beavers, despite the mammy kerchief and dress. (It is the sexually and
politically up-front friend, Tamara, who has Louise Beavers's body type.)
Fae is chronologically the mother and iconically the lover. For Cheryl,
in the only segment of *Plantation Memories* we are shown (three times),

Fae, "the most beautiful black mammy," "had it goin' on." The latter expression especially connotes both admiration and desire. Further, Cheryl and Fae are filmically identified in several ways throughout the film. When Dunye first shows us the clip from *Plantation Memories*, she does not crosscut between Cheryl/Dunye and the clip. Rather, she pans back and forth between the video monitor and the character. Later, when she shows the clip again, it is in the frame with Cheryl/Dunye. Another sequence in which Cheryl/Dunye researches Fae at the library begins with a close-up in which the narrator's face is obscured—replaced—by black-and-white studio photographs of 1930s black actresses. Finally, near the end of the film, home-movie shots of an older Fae are crosscut with similarly "amateurish" Steadicam shots of Cheryl. The crosscuts are not motivated by the story, which does not require Cheryl. Instead, they suggest that Fae's history is being ordered or reimagined by Cheryl/Dunye in such a way that Dunye is granting the physical, photographic maternal/erotic identification with Fae that she is denying Irene.

Even the names of the Watermelon Woman suggest the same ambiguity about and layering in gender and racial identity I have found in the name Cheryl/Dunye. As Cheryl/Dunye describes a discomfort with identity, so part of her project is to discover the identity of the eponymous heroine: "Her name: the Watermelon Woman. That's right, Watermelon Woman. Is Watermelon Woman her first name, her last name, or is it her whole name?" Only gradually does Cheryl/Dunye discover, first, that the Watermelon Woman's stage name was Fae Richards and then that her birth name was Faith Richardson. (Only in a throwaway line and during the final credits do we discover that even the character in *Plantation Memories* probably has a name: Elsie.) We are to infer that, in adopting a film career, Fae Richards jettisoned the component of her surname that suggested a patriarchal history: "son." The replacement of Faith with Fae suggests, via a pun between Fae and fey, homosexuality and, via the sonic similarity between Fae and ofay, the theme of interracial desire.

Cheryl/Dunye is de-siring desire, looking at a historical representation for an object of desire that also returns us to the mother, who is after all the first body of study—the first body of evidence—in any personal history. The film brilliantly folds the psychoanalytic and the social into the physical and iconic in a way unlike any of the films Silverman discusses. It is the historical dimension that prevents the film from falling into the clinical "melancholia" about which Silverman speaks and into which several of her filmic examples, implicitly or explicitly, fall—a state in which "the female subject is punishing the other (and consequently herself) for being inferior and insufficient, unworthy of love" (158).[7] Moreover, just as the fictional Cheryl is conflated with the nonfictional Dunye, so Cheryl's/Dunye's refusal to distinguish between nonfiction documentary and fiction film folds historical black lesbianism into the psychological. All the history we get is filtered through the consciousness of Cheryl, who is in some sense always speaking to her directorial avatar. The political is filtered through the created mother now, not through patriarchy, which has itself been effaced—as patriarchy itself erases alternative racial and gender histories.

Fae's embodiment of the maternal is further complicated because, again, it involves a model of interracial desire. This model would seem to contradict the identification of Fae as the primary erotic object. In *Plantation Memories*, the Watermelon Woman comforts her white mistress for four of the six shots in a sequence that lasts forty seconds, in intimate full or close-up two-shots, significantly lacking the "third element," the absent white male lover. Through most of the sequence, Fae caresses the tears from the face of her mistress. We begin to sense that, as well as representing it, Cheryl/Dunye is ambiguously seeking a model for interracial desire that precedes her affair with Diana, as if what attracts her about the sequence (regardless of her assertion about her affair with the white Diana that she has "never done anything like this before") is the way in which, despite its racism, it is at least an expression of interracial affection between two women as much as it is a simple representation of Fae. Put another way, it is as if she is looking for a model of interracial desire detached from the (tourist's) baggage of history, a model in which color can be sexually other—erotic—without being orientalized, in which the black woman is equal in and out of bed rather than the abject other of the white woman.

But while the possibility of interracial desire is not rejected (Cheryl does not indicate at the end of the film that she will no longer engage in cross-racial relationships), Cheryl does not remain with Diana. It is as if the historical tourist's baggage Diana carries prohibits the possibility of the racial erotics the film desires. The white tourist's body defines Cheryl by contrast, not through affirmation and personal integration. The rejection of the interracial relationship occurs at the same moment as the realization of Cheryl's relationship with Fae. The patriarchal model of interracial desire is rejected in favor of an erotic identification with an older black lesbian. (The declaration of the end of the relationship with Diana and the reading of June's letter asserting the need for black lesbian self-affirmation are contiguous in the film.) In the moment at the very end of the film when Cheryl articulates the denial of her identity as Diana's lover ("Diana and I aren't Diana and I anymore"), Cheryl/Dunye simultaneously accomplishes her film and introduces the documentary

Cheryl has made, which appears in the final credits, as if both the affair and its end are events that enable the beginning of the project at hand. That project has been only in part the making of the documentary. More important, it has been the integration through affirmation of Cheryl/Dunye as Cheryl Dunye, filmmaker, who, on introducing both the final credits of the Dunye film and Cheryl's documentary, asserts: "I am a black lesbian filmmaker who's just beginning, but I'm gonna say a lot more and have a lot more work to do." The confusion that characterized her similar assertion at the beginning of the film is replaced by a certainty that sexual and professional identities—body and voice—are synchronous if not identical.

Because of Diana's white patriarchal past, Cheryl's rejection of Diana represents the refusal of the father and of patriarchy as, respectively, personal and historical erotic objects within the traditional Freudian oedipal model. In the rejection of Diana, the white father—who is explicitly absent here in the same way that the black lesbian is always only explicitly absent—is finally excluded from the libidinal economy of the film. (The film is structurally already de-sired: there is only one significant male character, and he is black and gay.) In part because Diana's sexuality, though lesbian, is identified as patriarchal in its neocolonial aspect and in part because Cheryl's sexuality is bound up with her search for the eroticized maternal body, racial desire is gendered in a recognizably dualistic way but with a twist. While the traditional dichotomous associations in which blackness is feminized and whiteness masculinized are observed, the valence of these associations is reversed: the black maternal feminine is valorized at the expense of the white patriarchal masculine. Needless to say, it is not the traditionally hypocritical valorization of the usual stereotypes (mammies and Uncle Toms incorporating the Twainian virtue of servitude or the Faulknerian virtue of endurance). Black femininity is defined not by the absence of the phallus but in the presence of maternal plenitude in the black woman.

Where is black maternal plenitude evidenced in the film? How is it exhibited, represented? There are a number of moments of discovery and self-discovery in the film, moments in which Cheryl/Dunye becomes aware of a useful history in a way that elicits an otherwise inexplicable *jouissance* and an identification of the integrity of the character. These moments cut away from the diegesis; instead of furthering the narrative, they tend to be associated in some way with Fae. But for the fact that they are single shots, one might almost call them instances of thematic montage. For example, after her discovery that Fae and she have much in common, and after a few photographs of Fae with her director/lover, the film cuts to a marvelously open, high-key, full shot of Cheryl/Dunye on her roof, wearing sunglasses, a short-sleeve Hawaiian shirt, and casual pants. Standing on a bench, she is dancing in slow motion, as if savoring the pleasure of the identificatory moment. At another moment, Cheryl's indistinguishability from Fae becomes an instance of plenitude: her parroting of Fae's performance as the Watermelon Woman, in which we hear the voice of Fae but see center screen the self-pleasuring karaoke performance of Cheryl/Dunye (a performance repeated in the final credits). Though it is still unclear who this persona is—whether we are to understand her as Cheryl or, because these moments do not fit comfortably in the film's diegesis, as Dunye—the audience forgets the discomfort with the body of the black woman in front of the camera that constituted both Cheryl and Dunye at the beginning of the film. It has been effaced by the identification of Fae/Cheryl. Even the fact that the character is to some undefinable degree outside the narrative is no longer a source of discomfort. The identificatory plenitude of the black maternal body is indexed in the visible *jouissance* of her dancing daughter's body.

The notion that femininity "is at least in part an identification with activity" (Silverman 153) is present in Cheryl's/Dunye's identification of her vocation with the women in her life: she eroticizes filmmaking as a lesbian activity. In speaking about Fae's sexuality she asserts that "I guess we had a thing or two in common, Miss Richards: the women and movies." She discusses her progress on the documentary through a pun about mutual orgasms: "this film project . . . is finally *coming together*: Hollywood, the Watermelon Woman, Fae Richards, and [pause] Diana" (my emphasis).

At a structural level, the plenitude of the negative Oedipus complex is represented in those moments during which Cheryl speaks directly and self-reflexively to us from the screen, in all those moments during which we do not know whether we are hearing the character or the director, when in fact the distinction between the fictional character and the creating sensibility is collapsed. Of course, as the inclusion of the karaoke sequence in the final credits indicates, these moments are understood as plenitudinous only retrospectively, at the very end of the film, as periods of self-reflexivity on the part of the audience. This self-reflexivity presents maternal plenitude as the possibility of alternative forms of representation only after the audience has itself gone through the process of maternal self-creation. "Cheryl/Dunye" describes the process of an identity formation that evades white patriarchal Hollywood formulations of black femininity and in so doing provides representations that will paradoxically generate audience anxiety in the creation of ambiguities to which audiences of Hollywood films—even of many avant-garde lesbian films (those films, for example, that provide the certainty offered by etiologies of lesbianism)—are unaccustomed. The confusion about the identity of Cheryl/Dunye is the necessary precondition for other textual ambiguities: audience identifications with particular characters, the collapse of history into fiction, and the inability to identify against whom irony is directed. Ambiguity about who is behind/in front of the camera fits into the libidinal economy of the negative oedipal complex because it erases the distinctions between wanting and wanting to be like, desiring and identifying, body and voice.

Cheryl in front of Dunye's camera is not mirror phase but premirror because she is not coercive but open. (The negative vision of the mirror stage posited by Silverman [and Lacan], so familiar in noir films from *Citizen Kane* (1941) to *Vertigo* (1958), is vestigially present in *The Watermelon Woman* in the "race film" Diana and Cheryl watch together, which mirrors the relationship between Diana and Cheryl. The characters in the 1930s clip are even themselves placed in front of a mirror.) On the one hand, Cheryl becomes the "daughter" of Dunye because she is created by her, in the traditional way in which artifacts are conceived to be the offspring of their artificers. She is the ideal creation: a daughter who affirms the mother's own independent existence through the attempt to reconstitute the mother's past. But as herself the created artifact, Cheryl is also the enabling mother of Dunye, in the same way that Fae, as the artifact of Cheryl, is the latter's enabling mother. Both artifacts allow for Dunye to create the text of *The Watermelon Woman*. More important, in those scenes of Cheryl/Dunye, both are the same, not distinguished, as in the moment before the mirror stage in which the mother's and child's bodies are indistinguishable to the child. Again, these moments of character instability, when the audience cannot tell the identity of Cheryl/Dunye, are retrospective moments in search of identity stability—the site of Silverman's negative Oedipus complex. Most importantly, the audience is gently placed in an identificatory position opposite the ones usually encouraged in the classical Hollywood style (in which the consciousness of the filmmaking process and consequently the desire of the filmmaker are effaced): consciousness of and identification with the filmmaker as desiring subject. In short, if we are wondering—as the entire film has suggested we do—about Dunye's subjectivity, we are to some degree identifying with her, which is to say we desire Cheryl, a black lesbian in search of a grounded black lesbian identity.

In fact, once we understand that the merging of Cheryl and Dunye is the point of the film, we recognize that this merging is thematized and reiterated at several levels. For example, Cheryl is herself conflated not only with Dunye and with Fae but with June, Fae's life partner after

Martha Page and consequently another mother figure. Though June dies just before Cheryl meets her (thus elevating her, like Fae, into the realm of the imaginary), Cheryl receives a letter about Fae from her. In a voice-over, Cheryl begins reading the letter. Then both June and Cheryl read until June's voice takes over alone. The lesbian mother finally narrates her own story, if only for a moment.

In the end, the psychoanalytic model offered by Silverman is racially inflected in *The Watermelon Woman* by the film's identifying the beloved and lost black mother (Fae) with the adult Cheryl "through a *revival or reconstruction* of the negative Oedipus complex" (159, my emphasis). The film's largest diegetic function is to find value in the image of the black lesbian body erased, in both history and the psyche, by white patriarchy. In other words, the film imagines and plays out the moment at which alternative identities like black lesbianism become possible.[8] The diegesis of *The Watermelon Woman*, as in other Dunye films, takes Silverman's thesis seriously, allowing Dunye to re-create the negative Oedipus complex in the relationship between Cheryl and Fae. The way Cheryl describes and historicizes Fae coincides with the way Dunye anatomizes Cheryl, so that Cheryl's avowal of interest in Fae works simultaneously as an assertion of self-discovery. Getting back to the mother coincides with recovering the self: "I think I've figured out what my project's goin' to be on: I'm going to make a movie about her. I'm gonna find out what her real name is, who she was and is, everything I can find out about her."

NOTES

1. As a consequence, the following film and video distributors deserve not only my deepest gratitude for their help and advice, but the thanks of the critical community for keeping the films in this field in circulation: Julie Whang and Erica Vogt at Women Make Movies, Desi del Valle at Frameline, and David Kolow and Dorothy Thigpen at Third World Newsreel. I would also like to thank Mike Peyton for advice and for helping to track down some of the films.
2. This enterprise is in some sense like the postmodern endeavors of writers like Don DeLillo and Umberto Eco, who are also interested in absent or repressed histories. However, the aura of paranoia and horror that invests such texts as DeLillo's *Libra* and Eco's *Foucault's Pendulum* is absent because, as we shall see, Dunye's texts are not so much about the patriarchal mechanisms that repress history (which in her work are more or less taken for granted) as they are about providing a racial and feminine alternative.
3. See, for example, Riggs's *Ethnic Notions* (1987).
4. Regarding Arzner, see "Female Authorship Reconsidered"in Mayne 89–123.
5. Dunye provides a moment in the film that might stand for her separation from one normative avant-garde. When Tamara wants to provide some "urban realism" for a wedding video they are shooting to raise money, Cheryl asserts that she is uninterested in this enterprise.

6. The negative Oedipus complex constitutes a moment that Silverman ambiguously associates with Lacan's mirror stage itself: "The child gropes its way toward identity by incorporating the mother's facial expressions, sounds, and movements, not just before that mythical moment at which it first catches sight of its own reflection, but afterwards, as it begins to assimilate the system of language" (150).

7. Though several of Silverman's examples—like Sally Potter's *The Gold Diggers* (1984)—are supposed to suggest a positive countercinema, her assumption throughout is that "[w]ithin that variety of feminist film practice which is characterized by a similar theoretical sophistication . . . the female voice is often shown to coexist with the female body only at the price of its own impoverishment and entrapment" (141).

8. In this regard, Silverman explains that "the lost object is not so much surrendered as relocated within the subject's own self. . . . Freud explains that the reproaches which the melancholic seems to direct against him- or herself are in fact directed against the once-loved object which he or she has internalized" (157).

WORKS CITED

Doty, Alexander. "Whose Text is it Anyway?: Queer Cultures, Queer *Auteurs*, and Queer Authorship." *Quarterly Review of Film and Video* 15.1 (1993): 41–54.

Fuchs, Cynthia. "'Hard to Believe': Reality Anxieties in *Without You I'm Nothing, Paris Is Burning*, and 'Dunyementaries.'" Holmlund and Fuchs 190–206.

Gates, Henry Louis, Jr. *The Signifyin' Monkey: A Theory of African-American Literary Criticism.* New York: Oxford UP, 1988.

Goldstein, Lynda. "Getting into Lesbian Shorts: White Spectators and Performative Documentaries by Makers of Color." Holmlund and Fuchs 175–89.

———. "Queer Bodies of Knowledge: Constructing Lesbian and Gay Studies." *Postmodern Culture* 4.2 (Jan. 1994). *http://muse.jhu.edu/journals/postmodern_culture/v004/4.2r_goldstein.html.*

Holmlund, Chris, and Cynthia Fuchs, eds. *Between the Sheets, In the Streets: Queer, Lesbian, Gay Documentary.* Minneapolis: U of Minnesota P, 1997.

hooks, bell. *Art on My Mind: Visual Politics.* New York: New, 1995.

Mayne, Judith. *The Woman at the Keyhole: Feminism and Women's Cinema.* Bloomington: Indiana UP, 1990.

Nochlin, Linda. "The Imaginary Orient." *Art in America* (May 1983): 126.

Rich, B. Ruby. "When Difference Is (More Than) Skin Deep." *Queer Looks: Perspectives on Lesbian and Gay Film and Video.* Ed. Martha Gever, John Greyson, and Pratibha Parmar. New York: Routledge, 1993. 318–39.

Silverman, Kaja. *The Acoustic Mirror: The Female Voice in Psychoanalysis and Cinema.* Bloomington: Indiana UP, 1988.

Van Leer, David. "Visible Silence: Spectatorship in Black Gay and Lesbian Films." *Representing Blackness: Issues in Film and Video.* Ed. Valerie Smith. New Brunswick: Rutgers UP, 1997. 157–82.

Worth, Fabienne. "Of Gayzes and Bodies: A Bibliographical Essay on Queer Theory, Psychoanalysis and Archeology." *Quarterly Review of Film and Video* 15.1 (1993): 1–13.

JACQUELINE E. BRADY

Pumping Iron with Resistance

Carla Dunlap's Victorious Body

In a famous speech delivered in 1851 at the Akron Women's Rights Convention, Sojourner Truth urged her audience to behold her body. "Look at me," she is said to have demanded, "Look at my arm! I have ploughed and planted and gathered into barns, and no man could head me! And ain't I a woman? I could work as much and eat as much—when I could get it—and bear the lash as well! And ain't I a woman?" (Painter 94).[1] Truth's strategy of resistance here involves actively making a spectacle of her body's power in order to demonstrate that she is indeed equal to men. Through the articulation and display of her comparable capacity, in fact necessity, to labor, to consume, and to produce, she levels the sexes and drives home the then highly controversial point that African American women, similar to African American men, deserved the right of suffrage. Following this line of argument, she continues to locate the issue of equality in her body but adjusts her comparative technique by likening herself, in the following line, to white women: "I have borne thirteen children out with my mother's grief, none but Jesus heard me!"(95)

A century and a half later, we see that Truth's apparently emancipatory maneuver—her self-spectaclization of bodily might—unfortunately adopts some of the hegemonic discourses that she strove to resist. In her self-professed embodiment of physical powers, she catches herself up in at least two of the oppressive discourses prominent in the middle of the nineteenth century. She frames herself as the "primitive other" whose body, marked by muscular mass and unbreakable stamina (presumably from abiding the rigors of outdoor life), stands in stark contrast to the "civilized" man of the marketplace and his preciously domestic Victorian lady. Then, with her second equalizing tactic, the mention of her reproductive status and identification with motherhood, she embeds herself in the patriarchal tradition of "true womanhood," positioning herself within the subjectivities of babymaking and mothering.[2]

It is easy to critique Truth's powerful oration for recuperating the very structures that it intended to reject. Time and time again, today's seemingly defiant practice of women's bodybuilding has come under the same criticism.[3] Now retired from professional bodybuilding, African American Carla Dunlap, a former Ms. Olympia, can be seen as following in Sojourner Truth's groundbreaking, if toe-stubbing, footsteps. Spearheading women's entry into the almost exclusively male territory of bodybuilding in the early 1980s, Dunlap, like Truth, embodied resistance as she took to competitive bodybuilding stages, spotlighting her physical prowess. Also similar to Truth, Dunlap's body, specifically as it is represented in the bodybuilding cult film *Pumping Iron II: The Women*, can be read as the site of struggle between hegemonic and marginal discourses. As an African American female bodybuilder, Dunlap conveys a staunch opposition to the Victorian culture of feminine frailty, as well as its contemporary manifestation of, in Kim Chernin's words, a "tyranny of slendernesss."[4] At the same time, however, she physically emblematizes the notion of the erotic and exotic other currently surviving in the commodity culture's call to celebrate difference.

In a critique of *Pumping Iron II*, George Butler's unique docudrama of the Caesars Palace World Cup Championship for women bodybuilders, Anne Balsamo laments what she perceives as the eventual victory of the dominant culture's gender ideology. Rebuking the film for its limited focus on Dunlap, the only black competitor and the actual contest winner, Balsamo argues that "while these representations highlight the athletic capabilities and power of the female body, they also show the ways in which that power is symbolically recuperated to a dominant cultural order through the sexualization of the bodies of athletic stars" (41).

Along with Balsamo and many others, I see the body as an emblem of our locatedness in time and space, always indicating the salient ideological tensions belonging to a specific historical moment. In this way, the body resembles Mikhail Bakhtin's sign, which in Kathleen Rowe's explanation is "dynamically charged with social meaning and dialogic struggle" but also laden with "intertextual traces of earlier use, earlier struggles" (51). All too frequently the site of the body reflects an acquiescence to or internalization of the normalizing processes of hegemonic culture, thereby promulgating a multitude of what Michel Foucault has so aptly labeled as "docile bodies" ("Docile" 179–87). "This docility," explains Elizabeth Grosz, "no longer functions primarily by external regulation, supervision, and constraint, as Foucault claimed, but is rather the consequence of endlessly more intensified self-regulation, self-management, and self-control" (*Space* 2).

On one hand, the bodybuilding discipline can readily be seen as a normalizing practice that participates in the production of such docile bodies. The symmetrically built, perfectly muscular physique toward which bodybuilders aspire is a white androcentric body—a hopeful totalizing principle ensuring the erasure of any gendered and phenotypical codes that suggest a less powerful historical materiality. In this way, bodybuilding offers to its practitioners the promise of capitalist mass production. Like Henry Ford's factory system, bodybuilding claims that the standardized model can be yours if you honor the rules, work efficiently, and consume effectively. By following the steps of a rigid program, bodybuilders' daily lives become a calendar of body controls. They change diet and workout according to the competition season. They chart their weeks by an exacting workout schedule and then break their hours into separate exercises. They measure out their days into five or six meals and their meals into strict percentages of proteins, carbohydrates, and fats. Furthermore, in the highly systematized process of working out, bodybuilders internalize the factory's mechanisms of surveillance. Surrounded by mirrors, they scrutinize their own work, reprimanding themselves for unfinished projects (underdeveloped muscle); chiding themselves for failed tasks (not lifting a target weight); and docking themselves of food if they appear less than hard-bodied. Constructing a machinelike body system of part, sinew, and striation, which they then hold out for display, bodybuilders transform organic movement into static information. In this way they build, in Foucault's words, docile and knowable bodies ("Means" 190).

On the other hand, professional female bodybuilders, with their huge muscular proportions, do not fit into standardized molds so easily. Against the notion of docility, Pamela Moore argues persuasively that female bodybuilders interrupt investigative knowledge by calling attention to their bodily surfaces. According to Moore, their "no secrets" policy of showing skin and sinew redirects the gaze away from the interiorized zone of the "natural feminine" body. Instead of the mysterious contours of an internal "Womanly Nature," female bodybuilders highlight the external body as a highly visible artifice, repelling intrusive examination ("Feminist" 76). Like the drag queen's performance, this form of self-representation that playfully reveals its own constructedness resists he-gemonic neutralization. Moore's reading of built female bodies cautions us against a feminism that blames all styles of female body display for colluding with the dominant culture's tendency to make women visible in problematic ways.

In my observation of and participation in this activity, female body-builders certainly do partake in a docile behavior of extreme self-regulation. Precisely because theirs is a discipline hyperfocused on surfaces, they fret about body-fat levels and worry about physical ap-pearances in ways one could hardly see as alternative. But however docile and serious their means, their ends, as Moore suggests, are often some-thing different. Oversized muscles on women arise as ironic and dis-concerting constructions because they highlight the female body as a zone of contesting cultural definitions. Muscles, when built to the size of Bev Francis's in *Pumping Iron II*, make it difficult for dominant cultural mechanisms to neutralize or naturalize the female body. The "pumped" chests and dented buttocks of female bodybuilders do not "still appear as tits and ass" in the way that Chris Holmlund claims they do (95).

Yet given the docile properties of the bodybuilding practice, what hope does an African American female such as Dunlap have in success-fully dismantling its normalizing devices? Furthermore, in an era wherein representations of marginal bodies are often overdetermined by a pow-erful media with the aid of enchanting technologies, must the act of vo-litional self-representation always be contained by the dominant culture? Or can we conceive of a mass cultural form focusing on the specular black female body, be it the self-made body of the bodybuilding prac-tice or the filmic body of the documentary movie, capable of negotiat-ing the complexities of Dunlap's subjectivities and thus fitted for the expression of an African American female cultural identity? In other words, are women, specifically black women, doomed even in moments of self-representation to remain, as Linda Frost suggests, "beautifully caged" (260).

Against Balsamo's rather bleak view that today's mediated represen-tations of African American athletic women hopelessly fail in their at-tempts to defy the dominant culture, I propose a rereading of *Pumping Iron II* that recovers Dunlap's body in a posture of possible opposit-ionality. Reexamined as a palimpsest of historical traces, Dunlap's body evinces a complicated layering and intricate interweaving of multiple discursive lines. Oftentimes, as Balsamo and others have suggested, these discourses crystallize into unfortunate dominant cultural formations. It is my contention, however, that sometimes Dunlap's spectacularly mus-cular, technologically mediated, African American female body can shift its discursive shape. Invoking a rhetoric of feminism that reaches back to Sojourner Truth and a history of black women's health activism that stretches "from the Progressive Era to the New Deal and on into the Civil Rights era" (S. Smith 15), Dunlap can transform into a more powerful critical communal body. Therein lies what bell hooks would deem a "radical position of tranformational feminism," which she describes as "that political movement which most radically addresses the person—the personal—citing the need for transformation of self, relationships, so that we might be better able to act in a revolutionary manner, challenging and resisting domination, transforming the world outside of the self" (22).

Dunlap's "transformational" body, as it emerges in the film *Pumping Iron II*, is a specifically rich site of investigation not only because it is already doubly marginalized, as a black and feminine body, and mediated through documentary filmic technologies but also because it is willfully "self-made" into a muscular body through the arduous discipline of bodybuilding. The activity of bodybuilding, as several critics have noted, fits well into Foucault's definition of "a technology of the self"—a practice that produces ways of seeing and knowing one's self in the world. As such, bodybuilding is bound up in a process of self-production that simultaneously defines and delimits the bodybuilder, much in the same way that masks and tattoos both hide and reveal an identity. One objection leveled at the practice of female bodybuilding reproaches it as an activity that, like anorexia, mistakenly and dangerously situates subjectivity in the fleshly body, thereby reducing definitions of femininity to the body's surface form.[5] Leslie Heywood counters this criticism with her view that female bodybuilding participates in a "third wave gender activism." She contends that, "on an individual level, one woman at a time, women change how they see themselves and their position in relations to the larger world, and how they are seen by others" (57). For better or for worse then, this technology's slippage between body and self emerges plainly in *Pumping Iron II* when one female bodybuilder, shown soaping her sculpted torso in the shower, declares, "I feel I'm trying to find a new me. A new me is growing out of all these muscles."

Contradicting the more skeptical view of women who "work out" and "pump iron," I hope to illuminate women's bodybuilding by borrowing Elsbeth Probyn's surprising model of anorexia as a practice that helps women negotiate the network of discourses producing the female body (201–12). Hence, Dunlap's discipline of bodybuilding, like Probyn's own practice of starving, can be understood as an "embodied strategy" enabling a "small movement across the discourses of the current period"

(206). Adjusting my lens to female bodybuilding, I follow Probyn's intentions when she writes:

> I wish merely to point to ways of conceptualizing practices (such as anorexia) that avoid the perils of a dichotomous argument of either strict interpellation or full human agency. The site of anorexia shows up the entanglement of discourses and articulations of any particular time, and leads us to consider how the meanings we live with, the significance of our selves, are produced intertextually across a range of discourses. In this manner the anorexic's strategy serves to disturb the nexus of ideologies which seek to contain women. (206)

More specifically, for purposes of this discussion, I want to show that Dunlap's marginal body in *Pumping Iron II* injects a wedge into the narrative line of white female bodybuilders. Partly owing to its status as an oddity, her body widens the nexus of struggling meanings in the built female body and opens a communal space that provides a site for feminist discussion. Guided by her as a critical communal black body, the female bodybuilders of *Pumping Iron II* can resist normative discourse through the self-reflexive practice of questioning gender constructs.

Women's Bodybuilding: Tracing Oppression and Transgression

Female bodybuilding is commonly seen as transgressive because it involves an active and intentional reconstruction of the body to highlight and enhance the muscular system. A woman who takes up such a practice appears to fly in the face of several of the long-held dictums of American society. At the same time, however, the woman bodybuilder situates herself in a vast network of popular medico-scientific discourses proliferating in America, like a flu bacteria, since the health-happy, recreation-giddy Progressive era—a time when Theodore Roosevelt, in light of a boom in factory growth, a rise in scientific experts, and a swell in urban centers, encouraged families to "advance the American race" (read: white middle class) by partaking in health-promoting activities.

Indeed, women bodybuilders share with men bodybuilders an obsession with bodily largesse. Plagued with what in the popular rhetoric of pathological disease is being called a disorder of "biggerexia," an unremitting desire for size, these women shirk the still shockingly commonplace Darwinian principle of sexual dimorphism, which in its most general formulation holds that, by virtue of the "natural order of things," men are big while women are little. This watered-down version of Victorian biology, with its vogue for hierarchical categorization, derives from a framework of industry systems and the economic principle of the division of labor (Russett 132). In this Victorian logic, higher-ranking organisms, such as human bodies and Northern European races, were thought to work perfectly by distributing several different tasks among their many separate components. In contrast, lower order creatures, like amoeba, worked imperfectly because their simple structures performed all functions. Cynthia Eagle Russett effectively shows how these scientific notions contributed to the Victorian concept of a "complementary" division between the sexes—the public male work of production and the domestic female work of reproduction (146). In the Victorian romance of complementary difference, male and female bodies were thought to mirror these divisions, fitting properly together like two interlocking parts.

Darwinian biology told a slightly different story when it came to the non-European races. Opposite of the suitably divided structures of the Victorian white middle class, non-white races, wherein men and women both labored outside the home, were viewed as primitive one-unit formations and thus deemed inferior species. However dangerous in practice this racist logic is, it nevertheless allowed black female bodies to function actively, as Truth claims hers does, in a manner more similar to black male bodies. At the risk of reducing many different black communities into one monolithic construct, I will offer that perhaps one upshot of this Victorian discourse can be seen even now in African American culture's generally greater acceptance of body mass in females.[6] Deidre Johnson-Cane, African American powerlifting champion and coauthor of *The Complete Idiot's Guide to Weight Training*, admitted that when her body was transforming in the early stages of her weightlifting career, her family and community appeared less concerned with the potentially subversive steel-hard armor of muscle she was amassing than with the curvy carapace of body fat she was losing.

Within the community of females who pump iron, white and black female bodybuilders, bound up in separate processes of self-representation—negotiating different discourses that link them to different subjectivities—experience the exhibition of the body differently. This is another way of positing a black feminist agenda that, in Valerie Smith's description, "proceeds from the assumption that black women experience a unique form of oppression in discursive and nondiscursive practices because they are victims at once of sexism, racism, and by extension classism" (47). Susan Willis's discussion of transformer toys, with its critique of the function of transformation and self-transformation as elements in the serial commodification of capitalism, can help us examine the process of self-representation operating for female bodybuilders and understand how it signifies differently for black and white women. Willis's analysis is a specifically appropriate place to begin because feminism and bodybuilding constantly call on the language of self-transformation and also because the transformer toy was the new best-seller when *Pumping Iron II* was being made. Willis critiques transformers as plastic embodiments of a facile transformation process wherein the early form is erased and replaced by a new one rather than built up progressively ("Shop" 188). This transformed form is not only erased but also raced in that it takes place within the "zone of contention where the terms of cultural definition have been largely determined by the white male-dominated system of capitalist production" (194). Ultimately, Willis asserts, "[t]he transformers are so closely associated with high-tech capitalism that they offer little opening [out of this white male-dominated 'zone of contention'] other than the ambiguity over appropriation versus assimilation" (194). And so the transformations are appropriated or assimilated by a white male-dominated form.

Likewise, many commentators have observed that the ur-figure of the bodybuilding discipline is a de-eroticized assertion of phallic puissance encased in a white androcentric form. As white female bodybuilders fit themselves into this model by adding on layers of muscle, they build on to their identities in the outlines of this form. Coding and coating themselves with an armature of power, these female bodybuilders become ideal warrior women. Meanwhile, by Willis's reasoning, black female bodybuilders seem to break down their racialized subjectivities and replace them with deracinated ones. In this way they become commodified replicas of a white supermodel. Simplifying this logic a bit: white females, seen as defining their bodies in a white male model, gain new meaning as forms of power; antithetically, black females, understood as defining their bodies in the white male model, lose the original meaning of their cultural identities.

Because this discipline hinges on transforming the organic body into a machine-body, all bodybuilders de-root themselves from some portion of their historical materiality. In other words, the project of bodybuilding is fundamentally utopian, based on the notion of assembling disordered flesh into perfect symmetrical form. I am not certain, however, that any bodybuilder's process of transformation through excision can successfully produce a closed-circuit negative imprint as Willis might suggest. Black or white, bodies always disappoint. When applied to bodybuilding, her reasoning generates many more questions around the issue of a stable racial model. Don't the self-reconstructions of black female bodybuilders also give them power? Can their transformation into a white male body type really be so complete? Is the black body so easily effaced? If so, what does this say about the relationship between black cultural identity and the body? In what contexts can blackness still be seen? The critique that ends by dismissing black female bodybuilders as white male replicants needs to probe the gym-built blank body further for the racially specific discursive layers that resurface or never fully disappear.

Bodybuilding in general, as in its depiction in *Pumping Iron II*, can be faulted for espousing a transformer philosophy of change that ignores the bumpier navigation of racial tensions. However, it is also possible to see bodybuilding as a practice that momentarily levels various power positions, so that in the group effort of building up the body (which always entails the humanizing experience of pain) differences come into play in less tension-producing ways. With cheaper fees, serious bodybuilding gyms generally attract a diverse mix of working-class and lower-income members, as opposed to the more homogeneous health and fitness spas that cater to the white middle and upper classes. In these hardcore gyms, bodybuilders of different races, genders, and sexualities come together with the similar purpose of training their bodies. As opposed to Willis's notion of a transformer gadget, bodybuilding gyms more closely resemble Mary Louise Pratt's description of a "Contact Zone," wherein the relations among the various unequal bodies are treated "in terms of copresence, interaction, interlocking understandings and practices" (441). The softening of tensions necessary for this array of different bodies to work in such close physical proximity, not their erasure, can lend itself to a learning atmosphere, much like the inner-city college classroom Pratt describes.

Outside of the bodybuilding gym in the harsh world of glaring economic inequalities, clear cultural discriminations, and gaping gender divides, all females are potential victims of rape; however, female bodybuilders confound this assumption because beyond their overtly subversive display of gargantuan muscularity lies the terrifyingly deviant reality of physical power. Catherine Mackinnon contends that "[i]t's threatening to one's takeability, one's rapeability, one's femininity to be strong and physically self-possessed. To be able to resist rape, not to communicate rapeability with one's body, to hold one's body for uses and meaning other than that can transform what being a woman means" (122). Female bodybuilders go about the process of re-creating their bodies into visible bulwarks by actually enacting this power. They repeatedly lift enormous amounts of weight, endure extreme mental and physical pain, and undergo rigorous challenges of both diet and cardiovascular workout in order to produce a fortified body. While male bodybuilders frequently have the reputation of being total aerobic weaklings and high-voiced, incompetent street fighters (Fussell 43–60), women bodybuilders are often feared for their power. Promoting this belief, some have recuperated the strong woman act, adding on to their already superhuman training routines with showy feats of strength, such as squashing a football between their thighs. Dunlap, for example, has one stunning publicity photo in which she holds her white husband like a surfboard high above her head. If we recognize the history of the African American female body as one of repeated rape by white male culture—first by the system of slavery that institutionalized actual rapes, then by the medical establishments that enforced sterilizations, and now by a capitalist system that commodifies the body and bars access to control over the means of production—then this photograph is a provocative display of physical role reversals. With Dunlap, in the words of bodybuilders, "large and in charge" of her white husband, the photograph gives us a hopeful message of what is possible. In light of the fact that Dunlap now operates her own gym, this image also signals a mode of access to the media forms that shape the African American female body in the popular imagination. Self-built and now self-made, Dunlap the business owner has gained more control over her self-representations.

These "strongwoman acts" also remind us that bodybuilding has its historical roots in the sideshow, where muscles were originally signs of cultural deviance.[7] Early muscle-men and muscle-women—such as Sandow "the magnificent" and Sandwina, a strongwoman and feminist activist who changed her name to piggyback on Sandow's international popularity—actually did travel the country under the big top as "freaks." To be sure, the current underworld of professional bodybuilding, steeped as it is in the hedonistic consumption of anabolic steroids and tradition of bizarre bodily rituals, produces human curiosities. Men and women who inject cancer-causing monkey hormones—or, worse, hormones drawn from human cadavers—perform a death-defying act (albeit backstage) that perhaps outshines that of the freak-show snake handler or sword swallower. In gyms across America one can still hear serious bodybuilders aspire to the honorable state of "freakiness." With this said, the "grotesque" muscles of female bodybuilders make them counternormative not because, as is commonly assumed, built women look like "men" but rather because they resemble monstrous male bodybuilders.[8]

A discussion of the sideshow is particularly salient because there, in addition to the birth of American bodybuilding, we can locate the early "sexualization" and "freakification" of the displayed bodies of women of color. Ethnological show business in America and Europe regularly made curiosities out of ethnically and racially other humans—Amazons, Eskimos, Africans, Indians—enhancing the perception of their strangeness by exhibiting them in exotic clothing and with backdrops that depicted primitive jungle scenes. Those human spectacles purportedly retrieved from the "dangerous" and distant reaches of the "dark continent" drew some of the largest crowds. During the nineteenth century, through the institution of the traveling freak show, the bodies of women of color appeared in the form of two different figures which, in turn, permeated American and European cultural imaginations.[9]

The first and probably better known of these two types of ethnological oddities was that of the "sexualized primitive," embodied by Saartjie Baartman. Baartman, a San woman from Africa, was famous for her case of steatopygia, an unusually enlarged buttocks. Jokingly billed as the Hottentot Venus, Baartman was framed in the freak show as the bodily antithesis of the classic goddess. Portrayed as an animal, she toured Europe in a cage with a keeper who would hit her with a switch and invite audience members to touch her derriere. In 1810 the *London Times* reported that "[t]he Hottentot was produced like a wild beast, and ordered to move backwards and forwards, and come out and go into her cage, more like a bear on a chain than a human being." To further underscore her wildness and opposition to Victorian concepts of beauty, she was often exhibited wearing nude-colored clothing, tribal face paint, and exotic headdresses. Additionally, she was displayed smoking and carrying weapons, activities that highlighted her difference by linking her to the traditional behavior of men.

With her voluptuous body parts and alleged animal-like mental faculties, Baartman was used to epitomize an overabundant sexuality that, according to Sander Gilman, "serve[d] as the central image for the black female throughout the nineteenth century" (235). When Baartman died at the young age of twenty-five, her body was dissected by the famous French naturalist Baron Georges Cuvier, who placed her among the lowest order of human beings, comparing her to a monkey and orangutan. Literally setting this crude stereotype of black femininity in stone, Cuvier made plastic casts of Baartman's body, waxen molds of her genitals (one which remained on display at the Musée de l'Homme in Paris until 1982), and detailed diagrams of her labia.

A second sideshow figure seemed to fare better than the Hottentot Venus. In contrast to Baartman's show as the "savagely sexualized" woman, the Circassian maiden, frequently a light-skinned and probably racially mixed woman, paradoxically combined erotic femininity with chaste Victorian womanhood. According to Frost, "The Circassian Beauty becomes an overdetermined signifier of the dominant cultural concerns of Victorian America, embodying notions of colonial ambition and

Orientalism, the superiority of the United States and Manifest Destiny, the position of women within Victorian America and the cult of True Womanhood, the purity of the White race and the sexualization of the African American woman" (250). Zalumma, Fatima, Zumigo, Komel, and Zoe were the exotic names of young women, all with signature bushy hairstyles, displayed in freak shows for their beauty and recent refinement in the face of a former slave status (20). Unlike the brute and primitivist imagery associated with the caged Hottentot Venus, the maiden beauties were often portrayed in delicate settings and interior spaces. In some postcard photographs, the maidens lounge freely among tropical plants in risqué postures and silky boudoir clothing. In other scenes, they wear the formal attire of the chaste Victorian lady.

The prototype for this maiden figure is Barnum's Zalumma of Circassia. Advertised as a slave maiden, Zalumma, according to the great circus owner, was saved from the evil clutches of a Turkish harem (other sources say she was actually an immigrant settled in New Jersey). As the sideshow story goes, Zalumma allegedly hailed from the Caucasus, an area in the Black Sea region of Turkey, which legendarily boasts the purest of white blood: hence, the term Caucasian, still in use today. In a tremendous act of Victorian chivalry, Barnum's scout discovers, rescues, frees, hires, educates, and converts Zalumma.[10] Thus, with an odd twist of American marketplace logic, women of probable immigrant status like Zalumma or apparent mixed-race women like Zumigo who played sideshow Circassians were paid to embody unsullied whiteness and American virtue. While Baartman represented the grotesque excess of a helplessly primitive African body, Zalumma and her many imitators symbolized the admirable moderation of a recently civilized and Americanized mind: big top advertisements emphasized their education and articulation; their performances included demonstrations of their intelligence; one maiden was even said to be published. The description by Lieutenant Murray of Maiden Komel conveys her in glorious Victorian detail:

> She possessed all that soft delicacy of appearance that reminds the sterner sex how frail and dependent is woman, while she bore in her face that sweet and winning expression of intellect, that, in other climes more favored by civilization, and where cultivation adds so much to the charms of her sex, would alone have marked her as beautiful. (15–16)

Fragments of these two nineteenth-century stereotypes stay problematically lodged in the popular memory today. The culmination of the carryover from the days of the Hottentot Venus and Circassian maiden is the tendency, still strong in media treatments of African American athletes, to reduce the black female body to erotic, exotic other. With her straightened hair and streamlined body, in *Pumping Iron II* Dunlap exhibits neither of the aforementioned physical trademarks but manifests instead a physique molded into the shape of classical sculpture, a timeless construct of power. Despite these missing racial codes, Dunlap nevertheless slips into both stereotypical subject positions in two scenes that are noticeable because, as power operates from above, they frame her as a "performative body" in atypical moments of physical activity without speech. Yet, as power also operates from below, these scenes merely mediate Dunlap's own physical artifices, her stylistic choices, her preferences of expression, and her bodily construction and revelation through activities. At her pick, for instance, Dunlap's posing routine opens and closes to a jungle soundtrack with blaring elephant noises and roaring tiger sounds that call to mind the primitivist scenarios framing Baartman. Meanwhile, her movements imitate that of a hunted animal. Similarly, in a tranquil swimming pool scene, Dunlap, with the polished allure of the Circassian maiden, practices her water ballet among Grecian patterned tiles that recall Western antiquity. Here, camera close-ups help to fetishize her body by highlighting the lovely swanlike movements of her willowy limbs.

Pumping White Women's Bodies

Pumping Iron II: The Women is the "sister" version of the original *Pumping Iron*, a movie that charts out a battle of muscularity and masculinity between bodybuilding icons Arnold Schwarzenegger and Lou Ferrigno. A widely acclaimed hit among bodybuilding enthusiasts since its release in 1985, the sequel pretends to chronicle the story of the 1983 Caesars Palace World Cup Championship for women bodybuilders, all the while maintaining the facade of "live news" through devices of documentary realism, such as "soft peddling questions and answers" (R. Moore 126), off-screen voice interviews, improvised conversations, and candid camera moments. In so doing, *Pumping Iron II* reconstructs the event into a narrative about the current state of the white female body, where long-standing notions of a natural feminine physique must now vie against a recent fascination with a technological gender-bending body. It is a story, according to the videocassette sleeve, of "blood, sweat, and beauty."

Positing this agenda straightaway, the movie opens with a view of a western mountainscape, then cuts abruptly to a shot of a tanning bed. While a woman lies there in protective goggles, looking like some sort of alien cyborg, the music of a techno-pop song chants out the lyrics: "I am the future / beyond your dreams / I am the beauty / look at me / future sex / I've the muscles / future sex / I've got the motions / future sex / I've got the body." Certainly, after this entry into the narrative through the juxtaposition of opening images—the natural sublime and then the technological sublime—both shot in eerie blue hues, "look" is what the viewer does, moving back and forth with the pseudo-documentary's corresponding binary of two female body types: the natural feminine and the technological transgressive.

In order to foreground the struggle of these two monolithic discourses, the scope of the movie narrows a more complicated view of the larger bodybuilding competition with its subtle array of body differences into a glaring match between two competitors who represent opposite extremes. Disregarding the known competition results, Butler retrospectively contrives a somewhat bitter battle between the third-place and eighth-place finalists. Rachel McLish, on the one hand, is portrayed as a glamour-girl bodybuilder with small, round, and fleshy musculature. Bev Francis, on the other hand, with enormous angular muscles, minimal subcutaneous body fat, and superhuman physical power, is depicted as a masculinized machine-body. The movie continuously reinforces their oppositionality, probing the ground between the binary of natural feminine and technological transgressive white women's bodies as it develops separate subnarratives about four competitors within the larger drama of the Francis/McLish face off. Their physical dissimilarity comes into sharpest focus in a crucial moment during the competition's pose down when the judges ask them both to step forward and flex side by side. As McLish gyrates her petite torso, wiggling her "washboard abs" and Francis contracts her massive upper body, wielding her "big gun" biceps, one competitor comments to another, "Strange comparisons. Total opposites."

Pumping Iron II consistently positions McLish as a sexualized "feminine" body. With her financially endorsable and more traditionally female looks, McLish embodies the naturalized commodity. From the opening scenes of her at a photo shoot bedecked in a feathery headdress and heavy gold necklace, to views of her sunbathing poolside with her boyfriend, McLish is represented as a "girly girl" who uniformly buttresses the golden rules of gender-discriminatory male dominance. Because she adheres to hegemonic normalizing principles and embraces her assigned category of the "feminine" so skillfully, declaring in her book that "Flex Appeal Is Sex Appeal," McLish reaps the benefit of popularity among the competition judges as well as the bodybuilding media. When asked by a coach if the past year's commercial publicity has softened her, she proudly admits to being a "really strong powder puff."

Further elaborating on this oxymoronic conception of herself, McLish unabashedly idolizes Wonderwoman, whose "perfect waist," "tiny little legs," and large chest smack of the sexy pinup girls who are hardly wondrous for their strength. Moreover, ever the self-monitoring primper, in the precontest preparation, after other contestants are shown lifting weights in order to gorge their muscles, McLish looks in the mirror and worries about her hair: "Does my hair look ok?" she asks her boyfriend-trainer, adding, "I think the hair is just as important as the body, sometimes more." Suitably, her acts of resistance, embarrassingly recuperative of dominant cultural values, are failed attempts to skirt competition rules by wearing unacceptably ornate and padded bikinis.

In "The Social Construction of Gender" Judith Lorber avows that "[b]odies differ in many ways physiologically, but they are completely transformed by social practices to fit into the salient categories of a society, the most pervasive of which are 'female' and 'male' and 'women' and 'men'" (34). *Pumping Iron II* proves Lorber's point by choosing not to complicate Rachel McLish's feminine body with the fact of her Native American ethnicity. Similarly, the messy particulars of Bev Francis's working-class background and Australian nationality are overlooked by the filmmaker who slots her into the category of the masculine body. Not surprisingly, Dunlap's racial difference and cultural identity also go unremarked. Her feminist defiance, however, counteracts the erasing technique of the film's narrative. In one illuminating scene, Dunlap hands her posing bikini to a table of scrutinizing judges and states, "I'm normal," as if assimilation were as easy as wearing the right thing. Her body language, however, has a much different message. With an irreverent tone of voice and a sarcastic smile, Dunlap resonates as a shape-changing trickster figure who warns: "These are not my rules, but I'll play your way for now."

In *Pumping Iron II*, Francis's body is configured as the polar opposite of McLish's. The movie works to reinforce her in this antithetical role as a futuristic transgressive body type with superhuman powers. She is first revealed to the viewer, for example, with Spiderman-like abilities, scaling the walls of a hotel. In clear contrast to McLish's bathing-suit poses, the second shot of Francis shows her at a weight-lifting meet in her native country of Australia. A hulking frame in tube socks, she squats and grunts in order to successfully deadlift 510 pounds. After winning her lifting rounds, she poses her Herculean muscularity before the competition audience. This scene, paralleling McLish's posing for a photographer in feathery regalia, has Francis similarly placed as the object of the gaze. If, however, McLish is a fitness magazine's spectacle of feminine beauty, then Francis is a weight-lifting competition's specter of the grotesque. Likened by a trainer to a "monster unchained," Francis blurs the boundaries between human/machine/ man/woman. To emphasize this point, the director punctuates his filmic narrative with outdoor shots of androgynous half animal-half human sculptures.

In contrast to McLish, who dauntlessly endorses bodybuilding's homogenizing tendencies, Francis audaciously aims to break ground by defying establishment categories. Against McLish's fierce competitiveness and "ladylike" posturing, the down-to-earth Francis horses around in front of her family, hamming it up in a playful routine that parodies the sex-gender binary system. With her bulbous hamstrings, Francis first mimics several demure centerfold poses, then shifts to ridicule the old male bodybuilders, saving "an Arnold as Mr. Universe" for her finale. On a more serious note, seeing herself as a "pioneer" of the new woman's body, Francis performs her posing routine to the futuristic music of the movie *2001: A Space Odyssey*. "I wanna really shake people," she admits; "I wanna show 'em that people can really develop muscle and still look like a woman." Indeed, on account of her colossal development, Francis stands apart from all of the other competitors. This point comes to light, literally, in a backlit shot of the final line up of fifteen women competitors, where only Francis can be distinguished from the row of silhouetted bodies. For her unique muscularity and braveness, she garners audience adoration: they cheer heavily when she strikes poses and boo loudly when she takes eighth place.

To some degree all works can be analyzed by their audience reception. Having watched this movie over the past couple of years with many different types of women, admittedly most with feminist inclinations, I am struck by how consistent their reactions are to both McLish and Francis. The responses to McLish have been unflaggingly negative, as female watchers cannot seem to get past her vapid sniveling to appreciate her glamorous body. Also without fail, Francis gets points for her likeable character yet penalized for her oversized body. If these are at all typical of a general reception to this movie in the wider female population, then they scream out with a need for alternative self-representations that transcend the monolith of girl-woman/macho-woman. Dunlap's escape of this undesirable binary trap is expressed by the fact that she is perpetually seen as the most admirable character. Strong, smart, and a good sportswoman, she is a hopeful beacon and welcomed interloper in this formidable tale of two white female bodies. Her appearance not only articulates the objectionable quality of this binary but also shows that it will never be dismantled if the process of transformation stops at technologies of the self.

Carla Dunlap's Victory

In *Black Skin, White Masks* Frantz Fanon asserts that the meaning of the "black body" can only be understood in relation to the "white body" (225). In other words, according to Fanon, white culture defines blackness and vice versa. Into this agonistic scene of competitive white women's bodies in *Pumping Iron II* enters the only African American competitor, Carla Dunlap, who disrupts the narrative line by taking first place. Gloria Steinem, touting Francis as the triumphantly transgressive body type, calls the fact of Dunlap's top placement "a clear compromise" (104). Steinem, in her shortsightedness, ignores Francis's problematic reinscription of hegemonic constructs and overlooks Dunlap's winning physical composition, her more even proportions and more symmetrical lines. (By bodybuilding standards, Francis lacks the development in her shoulders and legs necessary to balance out her large back and chest.) From her feminist point of view, Steinem easily sees through the naturalization of McLish's feminized body. Indeed, Steinem admits that Dunlap's black body presents a challenge to the competition judges (103). Steinem proceeds, however, to neutralize Dunlap's body by mapping it as the safe middle ground—the de-raced zone of Woman with a capital W—between two white female bodies. Her cursory treatment of race and blind spot regarding the complexity of Dunlap's African American subjectivity constitute a mistake that is not uncommon among white feminists who gloss over important issues of difference while stressing the similarity of women's oppression. Here Steinem evinces a cultural bias and misses Dunlap's most revolutionary achievement.

Beyond her prize-winning physicality, Dunlap's even bigger victory lies in her little-glorified position as a critically resistant, female communal body. In his article, "A Phenomenology of the Black Body," Charles Johnson writes:

> In an amazing and revolutionary feat of cultural reconstruction, contemporary black women have made dominant the profile of the female body as first and foremost, spiritual: a communal-body of politically progressive, long suffering women who are responsible, hard working, and compassionate, who support each other in all ways, protect and nurture their children and live meaningful lives without black male assistance. (134)

Johnson's description of the black female body most certainly applies to Dunlap's in *Pumping Iron II.* Although her story is relegated to subnarrative status, Dunlap is immediately outstanding as the only competitor of the film's overall narrative focus not shown in connection with a boyfriend or male trainer. On the contrary, the movie introduces us to her among her all-female family, grilling-out at her home in New Jersey. In comparison to the initial glimpses of McLish and Francis, which position them, respectively, as silent-passive and silent-active objects of the gaze, Dunlap comes to us as a subject in critical dialogue who speaks her mind amid the supportive female circle of her mother and sister, anticipating the commotion that Francis's new body type will undoubtedly cause. From this moment on, the director positions her as the commentator in the documentary. Like a camera, Dunlap can pan in to focus closely on the current event, pan back a bit to survey the scene of women's bodybuilding, or pull even farther back to open her scope onto the broader perspective of how women's bodies are constructed. By allowing her this perspective, which links her to the eyes and thus to thought in the classic mind/body dualism of Western philosophy, the director lessens the danger that Dunlap will be absorbed by a racist framework that can shrink black females into fetishized bodies.

Additionally, as the narrative mounts in a crescendo toward the date of the competition, both McLish and Francis are revealed in increasingly more dependent postures, turning to their male training companions for help and approval. Meanwhile, the depiction of Dunlap has her pulling into Las Vegas, the land of showgirls, in the driver's seat of a convertible. Behind the wheel with her all-women posse, Dunlap resembles early-twentieth-century American feminists who embraced the automobile as a symbol of mobility and independence.[11] The birth of the bodybuilding practice in America at the beginning of the twentieth century coincides with the rise of Ford factoryism, and clearly their processes of systematized body work closely resemble one another. With that said, this scene of Dunlap driving takes her out of the assembly line worker position and places her in the upwardly mobile seat of the middle-class consumer. It is an image that strongly contrasts with the introductory figure of the sleeping cyborg who is enclosed in the coffinlike structure of a tanning bed. Noticeably, it marks Dunlap's different position from the working-class stations of the other competitors. The representation of Dunlap's arrival in a car with her female family suggests that the active consumption of some technologies can help to take you places. This scene also shows, however, that you must keep your eyes open, include your community, and carry your historical roots with you. The importance of family history in the process of self-representation of the black female body is also demonstrated later, during the contest posing rounds, when in shot/reverse-shot mode the camera zooms in on Dunlap on stage then switches to a close-up of her mother's loving smile, reinforcing the notion of their familial reciprocity and connection.

In "The Ideal of Community and the Politics of Difference," Iris Marion Young critiques small-group collectivities such as the one formed in *Pumping Iron II* by Dunlap's all-black, all-female family. According to Young, these groups can be faulted for trying to seal themselves off from the differences of others into an airtight totality of similarity. "The richness, creativity, diversity, and potential of a society," claims Young, "expand with growth in the scope and means of its media, linking persons across time and distance" (314). If, by virtue of its mediated representation through the documentary form, Dunlap's family is pried open to face the wider web of female bodybuilders, then Dunlap throws it fully open. Extending her sisterly harmony outside of her immediate family to the other competitors, Dunlap is repeatedly pictured in moments of supportive exchange. Whether it is taking time out to talk with McLish after her hysterical meltdown or hugging the other finalists instead of receiving her own first-place award, Dunlap's sense of community overrides her penchant for competition. Even in the midst of the final judging rounds, when she is summoned to pose off against Francis, Dunlap does not jockey for position or "flex and fight," as McLish does, for the spotlight. On the contrary, she watches her stage-mate to ensure that they move in unison, their body movements smooth and synchronized, like those of paired figure skaters.

Even more hopefully, *Pumping Iron II* contains several promising scenes where Dunlap gathers with the other women contestants in a collectivity to critically examine gender issues, as in a feminist consciousness-raising session. In *Talking Back: Thinking Feminist/Thinking Black*, bell hooks discusses the potential of such small-group gatherings:

> Small groups of people coming together to engage in feminist discussion, in dialectical struggle make a space where "the personal is political" as a starting point for education for critical consciousness can be extended to include politicization of the self that focuses on creating understanding ways sex, race, and class together determine our individual lot and our collective experience. . . . All efforts at self-transformation challenge us to engage in ongoing, critical self-examination and reflection about feminist practice, about how we live in the world. This individual commitment, when coupled with engagement in collective discussion, provides a space for critical feedback which strengthens our efforts to change and make ourselves new. It is in this commitment to feminist principles in our words and deeds that the hope of feminist revolution lies. (25)

Carrying on the long tradition of the African American Feminist Health

Campaign, with its enduring sentiment of empowerment through care for the body and lasting skepticism of the male medical establishment, these filmic moments reveal a community of women who come together in showers, whirlpools, and massage rooms to nurture, transform, and restore their bodies. Thoroughly integrated into these sensuous activities of "care for the self" are intelligent conversations about the feminine body. In one such scene, a bodybuilding competitor, in rejecting the predominant myth of a "natural femininity," reminds the other female bodybuilders, "Don't forget we are talking about a developed shape, a created shape, not God's given body." In another scene where Dunlap and Francis talk during massages, Dunlap makes this critical observation of normative constructs:

> If we are that shallow in our relationships to people and if femininity only depends on having muscles or not having muscles, what happens to someone who, let's say, has to have a mastectomy? . . . It's a slap in the face to women because women come in all shapes and sizes, and yet so few of our images are accepted . . . and it's not real.

These scenes also remind us that the middle-class African American female body connects to a rich history of grassroots organization and health activism. Susan Smith explains that in the Progressive Era middle-class black women, borrowing the eugenic language of racial evolution, "asserted that their class, as well as their gender, made them uniquely fitted to bring about salvation of the race" (18). With the Darwinian discourse of social advancement, they not only went about the process of spreading health but also worked to pluck the black female body from the Victorian racist setting of the sexualized other. Just as these black female activists subverted hegemonic culture from within its discursive confines, so, too, does Dunlap launch her attack from behind enemy lines.

In spite of the problematic ways in which this black first-prize winner is rendered subordinate to the story of white women's bodies, *Pumping Iron II* represents Dunlap as the prevailing leader of this critical women's small-group collectivity that engages in dialogical self-reflexive considerations of representations of self and body. This becomes most apparent when Dunlap, with the confidence of a champion, speaks for all the women contestants during a meeting with the judges from the International Federation of Bodybuilders (IFBB). "We need to define feminine as it applies to our sport," states Dunlap, calling the judges to task. "If we are not accepting passivity as the basis of the definition of femininity, then we've got to put a parameter around the word." Because this movie was partly made in order to sell female bodybuilding and because many of the IFBB judges are financially involved in the gym industry and therefore invested in watching the female ranks grow, Dunlap's revolt does more than simply question language constructs. By interrupting the meaning-making process of white male capitalist culture, Dunlap slows down their whole production process. Her interrogation tells them and us that she will not be transformed into a hegemonic structure so easily. Furthermore, her tactic demonstrates to the other female competitors and to female viewers that the "smart bomb," if you will, of a successfully transformational attack needs to be dropped on rule-making procedures. In this way, her questions work to alter the judges' policies and thereby Dunlap actually transforms them, much as her black female forbearers (from Sojourner Truth to Rosa Parks and beyond) challenged the broader legislative policies that still control women's bodies.

Dunlap's winning acumen, along with the cohesion of the women competitors, shines brilliantly against the dull and fragmented group of IFBB judges, who in a comic display of male hysteria and impotence talk over each other, fall asleep during performances, have difficulty adding up score points, and follow reductionist gender formulas. In a manner exemplary of what Mary Belenky et al. have described as didactic talk typical to men's ways of knowing (144–46), one judge responds to Dunlap's helpful request for a definition by referring to the first line in the rule book, which enables him to support this evasive answer: It is women's bodybuilding, so the contestants need to look like women. To this Dunlap, in a smartly resistant posture, shakes her head with frustrated disapproval and retorts, "We all have our ideas of femininity."

While Dunlap and the judge do not directly treat the topic of race, her comments and posture clearly point to the tensions inherent in differences. With regard to racial difference, *Pumping Iron II* can be faulted for a myopia, similar to Steinem's, that sees only the monolith of the Female Body rather than a diversity of female bodies. This problem points to the precarious position that females of color occupy as their success turns on their ability to penetrate the largely white male commercial industry of bodybuilding. Heywood helps explain the apparent contradiction of Dunlap's silence regarding issues of race. "Activist strategies," writes Heywood, "if they are to succeed in bringing about widespread change, must above all be marketable, salable to the very groups of people who would conceivably mobilize to bring about change" (57). Similar to lesbian rock singers who will, as Pratibha Parmar's documentary *Righteous Babes* shows, sing out their feminism but hush up their sexuality, black female bodybuilders, such as Carla Dunlap and Lenda Murray, teeter dangerously on a marginal precipice. The hard cold fact is that their livelihood as bodybuilders depends largely on company endorsements and commercial work. Severing their ties to the other female bodybuilders who anchor them, albeit to a white female space, might just mean a long hard fall from the grace of the bodybuilding industry.

It is important to note, however, that Dunlap's critical communal resistance, her transformational feminism, cannot be inscribed on the specular body in quite the same way that Francis's techno-masculine power and McLish's natural femininity can. This problem is endemic to the discursive limitations of technologies of the self, such as body-building. Andrew Ross finds a similar obstacle in the New Age move-ment: "Any secular end to the process of personal transformation depends upon the naive assumption that changing the self will change the world, an equation that might point to the lack of available languages for link-ing subjectivity with larger social or structural change" (68). *Pumping Iron II* shows that the most resistant expression an individual gym-built female body can do is show off an artificial structure. Dunlap's message is that a more significant transformation must occur in a community that opens itself up to differences and actively challenges the discursive con-structs as well as the legislative practices of the presiding powers. Only then, as Dunlap implies, will the self-representations of black women be capable of creating new bodies.

In this light, we can reinterpret the opening image of the tanning cyborg, its skin color reflecting the electric blue light that beats down on, up through, and across its muscular body. In a bikini, it is clearly gendered as a woman, but other identifying signposts of race, class, age, and nationality have been erased by our contemporary technologies of the body—the practice of bodybuilding, the strategies of diet and supple-mentation, the use of a tanning machine, the process of filmmaking. This representation of a cyborgian future-sex forecasts a world where varia-tion, most conspicuously racial difference, is elided. As an introductory scene, it also foreshadows the failures of *Pumping Iron II* specifically, and women's bodybuilding more generally, in accepting the complex ar-ray of distinctions in women's subject-positions and in the subsequent codings of those positionalities on the body. Even Carla Dunlap, for all her critical communal commentary, leaves out an examination of racial constructs. Finally, *Pumping II*'s cyborg is a spookily accurate premoni-tion of the direction that women's bodybuilding has taken over the past ten years, a course of massive techno-bodies leaving McLish's "natural body" behind at the beauty contest/fitness show.

As the movie focuses on the cyborg image, cuts to more active fe-male bodies, and then returns to the tanning bed, the encased resting body changes from McLish's to that of other competitors. Transforming cyborg-style is as simple as hitting a switch. A final close-up on this body reveals, by the curve of her cheek, that it might be Carla Dunlap. Yet far from Donna Harraway's utopian cyborg that delights in the dizzying dance of a world without borders, this Dunlapian cyborg is resting with her eyes shut, contained by the technologies in which she has embedded herself. The limiting discourses that illuminate her, reflecting on her specular body, are as close as the ceiling of ultraviolet rays in front of her face. Hope does not lie here in the solitary and unquestioning consumption of technologies of the gendered body. Potential does lie, however, in the substantial gap in the tanning-bed walls, somewhere in nexus of social relations and technologies, where Dunlap becomes not beautifully contained but triumphantly communal.

NOTES

1. As Painter notes in her biography of Truth, it is highly unlikely that Truth said these exact words (164–78); however, even the more historically accurate account of Truth's speech makes it clear that, whatever her words, she certainly engaged in a comparison of her bodily strength with that of a man.
2. See Shuttleworth for a fuller discussion of Victorian discourses and constructions of feminine bodies.
3. See, for example, Messner and Therberge.
4. See Chernin's analysis of the oppressive obsession with female slenderness.
5. See Grosz on the phenomenon of the body as written surface.
6. Margaret Bass's essay in this volume demonstrates the degree to which black women have become the targets of a fat-hating, disciplining gaze. I maintain, however, that the black female somatic ideal is generally a healthier model because it complies more readily to the physical proportions and fat levels of the organic female body.
7. See Fussell on this aspect of the history of bodybuilding.
8. See Bolin's study of competitive bodybuilders and the relationship between consumption patterns and self-image.
9. This section on the history of women of color in freak shows draws on the work of Gilman, Lindfors, and Frost.
10. For more on Barnum's relationship with Zalumma, see his autobiography.
11. As a tangential historical point, sports officials at the start of the twentieth century were outraged when cross-dressing athlete Eleanor Randolph Sears was caught driving.

WORKS CITED

Bakhtin, Mikhail. *Rabelais and His World.* Trans. Helene Iswolsky. Bloomington: Indiana UP, 1984.

Balsamo, Anne. *Technologies of the Gendered Body: Reading Cyborg Women.* Durham: Duke UP, 1988.

Barnum, P. T. *Struggles and Triumphs; or Forty Years' Recollections of P. T. Barnum, Written by Himself.* Buffalo, 1875.

Bartholomae, David, and Anthony Petrosky eds. *Ways of Reading: An Anthology for Writers.* 3rd ed. Boston: St. Martin's, 1993.

Belenky, Mary Field, et al. *Women's Ways of Knowing: The Development of Self, Voice, and Mind.* New York: Harper, 1986.

Bolin, Ann. "Flex Appeal, Food, and Fat: Competitive Bodybuilding, Gender, and Diet." *Play and Culture* 5.4 (1992): 381–82.

Bordo, Susan. "Reading the Male Body." Goldstein 265–306.

———. "Reading the Slender Body." Jacobus, Keller, and Shuttleworth 83–112.

Cahn, Susan K. *Coming On Strong: Gender and Sexuality in Twentieth-Century Women's Sport.* New York: Free, 1994.

Chernin, Kim. *Obsession: Reflections on the Tyranny of Slenderness.* New York: Harper, 1981.

Dickerson, Debra. "Not So Black-and-White." *Allure* Sept. 1997: 138–41.

Douglas, Mary. *Natural Symbols.* New York: Pantheon, 1982.

duCille, Ann. *Skin Trade.* Cambridge: Harvard UP, 1996.

Dutton, Kenneth. *The Perfectible Body: The Western Ideal of Male Physical Development.* New York: Continuum, 1995.

Fanon, Frantz. *Black Skin, White Masks.* New York: Grove, 1967.

Faurshou, Gail. "Fashion and the Cultural Logic of Postmodernity." Kroker and Kroker 78–93.

Foucault, Michel. *Discipline and Punish.* New York: Vintage, 1979.

———. "Docile Bodies." *The Foucault Reader.* Ed. Paul Rabinow. New York: Pantheon, 1984. 179–87.

———. "The Means of Correct Training." *The Foucault Reader* 188–205.

———. *Technologies of the Self: A Seminar with Michel Foucault.* Ed. Luther Martin, Huck Gutman, and Patrick Hutton. Amherst: U of Massachusetts P, 1988.

Frost, Linda. "The Circassian Beauty and the Circassian Slave: Gender, Imperialism, and American Popular Entertainment." Thomson 248–62.

Fussell, Sam. "Bodybuilder Americanus." Goldstein 43–60.

Gilman, Sander L. "Black Bodies, White Bodies: Toward an Iconography of Female Sexuality in Late Nineteenth-Century Art, Medicine, and Literature." *"Race," Writing, and Difference.* Ed. Henry Louis Gates Jr. Chicago: U of Chicago P, 1985. 223–61.

Goldstein, Laurence, ed. *The Male Body: Features, Destinies, Exposures.* Ann Arbor: U of Michigan P, 1994.

Grosz, Elizabeth. *Space, Time and Perversion: Essays on the Politics of Bodies.* New York: Routledge, 1995.

———. *Volatile Bodies: Toward a Corporeal Feminism.* Bloomington: Indiana UP, 1994.

Hargreaves, Jennifer. "Where's the Virtue? Where's the Grace? A Discussion of the Social Production of Gender through Sport." *Theory, Culture, and Society* 3.1 (1986): 109–21.

Harraway, Donna. *Modest Witness @ Second Millennium.Femaleman Meets OncoMouse.* New York: Routledge, 1997.

Heywood, Leslie. *Bodymakers: A Cultural Anatomy of Women's Body Building.* New Brunswick: Rutgers UP, 1998.

Holmlund, Chris. "Visible Difference and Flex Appeal: The Body, Sex, Sexuality, and Race in the *Pumping Iron* Films." P. Moore 87–102.

hooks, bell. *Talking Back: Thinking Feminist, Thinking Black.* Boston: South End, 1989.

Jacobus, Mary J., Evelyn K. Keller, and Sally S. Shuttleworth, eds. *Body/Politic: Women and the Discourses of Science.* New York: Routledge, 1990.

Johnson, Charles. "A Phenomenology of the Black Body." Goldstein 121–36.

Johnson-Cane, Deidre, Jonathan Cane, and Joe Glickman. *The Complete Idiot's Guide to Weight Training.* Indianapolis: Alpha, 2000.

Klein, Alan. *Little Big Men: Bodybuilding, Subculture, and Gender Construction.* Albany: U of New York P, 1991.

Kroker, Arthur, and Marilouise Kroker. *Body Invaders: Panic Sex in America.* New York: St. Martin's, 1987.

Lindfors, Berth. "Ethnological Show Business: Footlighting the Dark Continent." Thomson 207–18.

Lindsey, Cecile. "Bodybuilding: A Postmodern Freakshow." Thomson 356–67.

London Times 26 Nov. 1810: 3.

Lorber, Judith. "The Social Construction of Gender." Race, Class, and Gender in the United States. Ed. Paula S. Rothenberg. 4th ed. New York: St. Martin's, 1998. 33–45.

Mackinnon, Catharine. Feminism Unmodified. Cambridge: Harvard UP, 1987.

Messner, Michael. "Sport and Male Domination: The Female Athlete as Contested Terrain." Sociology of Sport Journal 5.3 (1989): 197–211.

Millingen, J. G. The Passions; or Mind and Matter, Illustrated by Considerations on Hereditary Insanity. London, 1848.

Moore, Pamela, ed. Building Bodies. New Brunswick: Rutgers UP, 1997.

———. "Feminist Bodybuilding, Sex, and the Interruption of Investigative Knowledge." Moore 74–86.

Moore, Rachel. "Marketing Alterity." Visualizing Theory: Selected Essays From V.A.R. 1990–1994. Ed. Lucien Taylor. New York: Routledge, 1994. 126–42.

Murray, Lieutenant. The Circassian Slave: or, the Sultan's Favorite: A Story of Constantinople and the Caucasus. Boston, 1851.

Painter, Nell Irvin. Sojourner Truth: A Life, a Symbol. New York: Norton, 1996.

Pratt, Mary Louise. "The Art of the Contact Zone." Bartholomae and Petrosky 441–55.

Probyn, Elsbeth. "The Anorexic Body." Kroker and Kroker 201–12.

Roberts, Dorothy. Killing the Black Body: Race, Reproduction, and the Meaning of Liberty. New York: Vintage, 1999.

Ross, Andrew. Strange Weather: Culture, Science and Technology in the Age of Limits. New York: Verso, 1991.

Rowe, Kathleen. "Studying Roseanne." Feminist Cultural Theory: Process and Production. Ed. Beverly Skeggs. Manchester: Manchester UP, 1995. 46–61.

Russett, Cynthia Eagle. Sexual Science: The Victorian Construction of Womanhood. Cambridge: Harvard UP, 1989.

Russo, Mary. "Female Grotesques: Carnival and Theory." Feminist Studies/Critical Studies. Ed. Teresa de Lauretis. Bloomington: Indiana UP, 1986. 13–20.

Schneir, Miriam, ed. Feminism: The Historical Writings. Rev. ed. New York: Vintage, 1994.

Shuttleworth, Sally. "Female Circulation: Medical Discourse and Popular Advertising in the Mid-Victorian Era." Jacobus, Keller, Shuttleworth 47–68.

Smith, Susan L. Sick and Tired of Being Sick and Tired: Black Women's Health Activism in America, 1890–1950. Philadelphia: U of Pennsylvania P, 1995.

Smith, Valerie. "Black Feminist Theory and the Representation of the Other." Wall 38–57.

Stein, Jane. Empowerment and Women's Health: Theory, Methods and Practice. London: Zed, 1997.

Steinem, Gloria. Moving Beyond Words/Age, Rage, Sex, Power, Money, Muscles: Breaking the Boundaries of Gender. New York: Touchstone, 1995.

Stockham, Alice B. Tokology: A Book for Every Woman. Chicago, 1886.

Telander, Rick. The Hundred Yard Lie. New York: Simon, 1989.

Theberge, Nancy. "Sport and Women's Empowerment." Women's Studies International Forum 10 (1987): 387–93.

Thomson, Rosemarie Garland, ed. Freakery: Cultural Spectacles of the Extraordinary Body. New York: New York UP, 1996.

Wall, Cheryl A., ed. Changing Our Own Words: Essays on Criticism, Theory, and Writing by Black Women. New Brunswick: Rutgers UP, 1989.

Wallechinsky, David. "Vaults, Leaps and Dashes: Women's Sports Go the Distance: A Tally." *New York Times Magazine* 23 June 1996: 46.

Willis, Susan. "I Shop Therefore I Am: Is There a Place for Afro-American Culture in Commodity Culture?" Wall 173–95.

———. "Work(ing) Out." Bartholomae and Petrosky 704–23.

Young, Iris Marion. "The Ideal of Community and the Politics of Difference." *Feminism/Postmodernism*. Ed. Linda Nicholson. New York: Routledge, 1990. 300–23.

NOLIWE ROOKS

PHOTOGRAPHS BY BILL GASKINS

Wearing Your Race Wrong

Hair, Drama, and a Politics of Representation for African American Women at Play on a Battlefield

The impulse for my beginning to think through the issues presented in this essay began with a little girl's tears. During the summer of 1996, I was giving a lecture at an African American book fair in Kansas City about the connections between race, body politics, and black hairstyles. My talk quickly evolved from a prepared paper into a heated exchange with audience members about the politics of black hair both within and outside of African American communities. Why did I think that hair had to mean anything at all? Why would I suggest that racial politics necessarily enter into meanings of and understandings about hairstyles? Was I trying to say that anyone who did not wear their hair in a way I liked was trying to be white, or ashamed of their black heritage? Did hair have to always mean the same thing to everyone? Who cared about the visual politics involved in looking at and interpreting a black body? Really, honestly, don't we have more important things to focus on and think about? It was a good discussion.

I was in the middle of explaining how they were absolutely right to question what could be seen as my attempt to romanticize and essentialize a so-called resistant black identity based solely on a chosen hairstyle. Indeed, I started to explain, a black scholar named Kobena Mercer had made a similar argument in "Black Hair/Style Politics." He warned against essentialized reductions that equate certain hairstyles with any type of overdetermined political meaning. The body, and by extension identity, he argues, is always shaped and socially constructed, and the attempt by scholars and intellectuals to reduce that shaping process to simple, reductionist oppositions between natural and straight hair as indicative of a radical or passive identity is a faulty enterprise (247–64).

I was just starting to show that I was talking about something different when a young woman in the front row raised her hand. She said she was twelve years old and a student at a local middle school. What she wanted to know was why her classmates made fun of her when she did not straighten her hair and why her teachers treated her differently when she wore her hair in an Afro. Most of all, she said, as tears slipped down her cheeks, she wanted to know what she was supposed to do or say to people who made her feel badly about herself. Both I and the other audience members told her that she had a right to be and appear in the world in any way that made her happy; that she should just feel good about herself and not worry about what anyone else thought about her; that these other people were just jealous. We all tried hard to put a smile on her little face and did all we could to convince her that she was a beautiful person who should be commended for even thinking about going against the crowd and styling her hair as she saw fit. In effect, in an effort to make her smile, we depoliticized the context about which she was speaking.

I think we tried to do a good thing for her. However, her tears and our response to them have stayed with me. I now wish I had merely told her that there have long been consequences both within and outside of African American communities for wearing one's race wrong and that hairstyles are often the means others use to determine whether we are wearing a right, or wrong, racial identity. That is to say, while we decided to focus on giving this little girl an understanding of the possibilities for a positive relationship to and with her body, we did not make quite clear that such understandings might not be endorsed by the larger culture. We offered her no way for negotiating the space between what we told her was her right to self adornment and her lived experience with the political realities of such adornment. We de-emphasized the connections she was attempting to make between hair, spectacle, and looking relations that are raced in their very nature. She understood the political nature of style and adornment to be about the power of the beholder (it mattered who was doing the looking and what their race was). We (I) overlooked these matters in an attempt to make her smile.

I have often wished that I had done better justice to the complexity of her analysis. More than giving her a reason to smile, I wish I had given

Figure 1. Tamara and Tireka, Easter Sunday, Baltimore, 1995.

her a way to understand how her individual present had everything to do with a collective past. I have wished that I had told her that the reaction others were having to her choice of hairstyle had everything to do with history made present and a past that was not.

At its core, what you have here is my attempt to answer a question a little girl once asked me.

Hair Dramas: An Introduction

> The body is a battleground whose self-determination has to be fought for. The metaphor of the body as a battleground, rather than postmodern playground, captures, as well, the practical difficulties involved in the political struggle to empower "difference."
> —Susan Bordo, *Unbearable Weight*

> The will to adorn is the second most notable characteristic in Negro expression. Perhaps his idea of ornament does not attempt to meet conventional standards, but it satisfies the soul of its creator.
> —Zora Neale Hurston, "Characteristics of Negro Expression"

In December 1996 a photograph titled "Tamara and Tireka" appeared in the *Chronicle of Higher Education*. Its appearance was not without drama. Quite a bit of tension was created among the editorial staff when an African American woman whose job it was to lay out the page for publication refused to do so. She accused the white editor of racism for wanting to publish the image and refused to speak with the artist, Bill Gaskins, about his work in general or this particular image of Tamara and Tireka, saying, "They're nothing but hoochie girls and that's not their real hair!"

In November 1998 a more public drama over hair and its meaning and relationship to African American identity erupted when a white elementary school teacher in Brooklyn was charged with racism, threatened with bodily harm, suspended, and subsequently reassigned to another school because she assigned a book entitled *Nappy Hair* for her students to read. While the book was supposed to build self-esteem in children with nappy hair, a group of black parents objected to the title, the illustrations, and the book's assumption that hair of that type could or should be seen as a positive ("Furor" A24).

This is an essay about black hair, drama, and the politics surrounding the self-representation of African American women who choose to adorn their bodies in certain ways. It takes as its starting point a belief that the body, while open to creative interpretations and in some respects willful self-creation, has "historically constituted both implicit and explicit contracts within our legal, political, and cultural systems" (Holloway 41). How African Americans have chosen to adorn our bodies has long been inextricably linked with how others perceive us to be wearing and performing our racial identity. It all depends on who is doing the looking.

In the first epigraph, Susan Bordo's assertion regarding the necessity of viewing the body as a battlefield, instead of a playground, functions as a warning against moves to discuss bodies without regard to the ways in which they are raced, gendered, and classed within the context of a dominant culture and power structure. In the second, Zora Neale Hurston proposes that we look at the adornment of black bodies as a notable (or essential) characteristic of "Negro" expression and, as such, disconnected from external pressures or prevailing standards. In one instance, racially inscribed and encoded bodies are held to be most usefully understood in a political context; in the other, we are urged to look upon their adornment as an unproblematic personal statement free from such considerations. This essay is an attempt to put these contradictory positions into a meaningful dialogue within the context of understanding how certain types of bodily adornment make it possible for others to perceive African Americans as wearing their race right, or wrong.

My earlier work on African American beauty culture explored the history of hair politics, hairstyles, and bodily representations in African American communities and looked at a static nineteenth-century dichotomy between the meanings of straight versus natural hairstyles (Rooks). In that work, I focused on those initial moments in the late nineteenth century when hair care and other beauty products marketed by African American women to other African American women became synonymous with a particular politics and identity. Here the question is how one juxtaposes the political and social realities of what certain bodies mean in public life and culture with the more playful desire to see bodily adornment as an expression of individual style?

The photographs in this essay are from a recent collection entitled *Good and Bad Hair: Photographs by Bill Gaskins.* On one level, the photographs in that work present readers/lookers with a variety of popular and personal approaches to wearing one's hair. On another, they isolate what amounts to a bold, assertive departure from the common definition of American beauty that excludes the physical features of many people of African descent. This narrow definition of beauty has created a race-based measurement for what is considered "good" and "bad" hair. These photographs identify African Americans from different regions of the United States who expressively symbolize their sense of self and often their sense of an African or black identity through their hair. Within this context, the image of Tamara and Tireka is a visual representation of the issues with which this essay is concerned—issues raised by the two epigraphs. This photograph can be read as an artistic diagram that shows how the historical, political, visual, and cultural overlap and interact. Alone, like most of the images in that volume, it serves as a visual representation of the Hurston quotation—the two young women look defiantly out at the world on an Easter Sunday morning. Their eyes gaze from under hair styled into playful yet soul-satisfying expression. They are adorned. However, the fact of and reasons for the drama generated at the *Chronicle of Higher Education* when the photograph was to appear in its pages shifts the meaning of the image to one that acknowledges Bordo's point. It is clear that if Tamara and Tireka are indeed using such types of adornment to play with their image and/or identity, they are at play on a battlefield.

This essay, in an attempt to narrow the distance between these two formulations of the meaning of African American bodies, puts visual representations of soul-satisfyingly adorned African American bodies in a sense-making dialogue with a discursive discussion of "embattled" African American bodies that struggle to empower difference. In order to understand the contours of public dramas and interactions involving African American women and hair (like the engagement over the book about nappy hair), I look at three "acts" in what I believe to be a larger

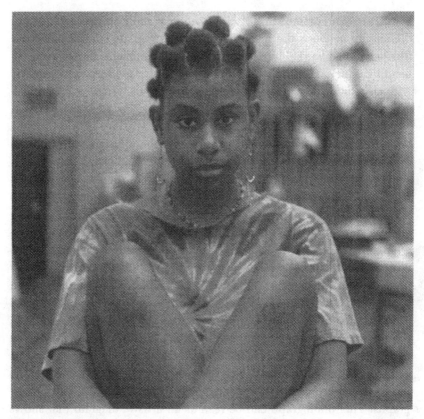

Figure 2. Jennifer, Baltimore, 1994.

drama involving race, hair, fashion, and identity played out in the cultural space of American newspapers during 1996 and 1997. By juxtaposing the visual with the discursive, I also seek to understand the political and social realities of what style means in relation to raced and gendered bodies in public life and culture. If the interactions discussed here are viewed as dramas (a condition, situation, or series of events involving interesting or intense conflicts of forces), then they define what happens when the specific understandings one group of people hold regarding the meaning of certain styles on a black female body come into conflict with individual understandings held by members of an outside group invested with the power and authority to bring those bodies and styles in line with what they believe to be acceptable. This essay explores what it means to wear one's race wrong while at play on a battlefield.

Act I

Late in 1996, a nine-year-old African American girl named Meghan Smith was a student in the third grade at Grace Christian School in Brandon, Florida. One day in December, she left home with her hair neatly braided in twelve cornrows that climbed up the curve of her head and were bunched in a ponytail at the crown and held in place by a little white barrette. When she arrived in her classroom, her teacher immediately sent her to the principal's office. The principal sent her home. Administrators at the school first informed her and then her parents that she was in violation of the school's dress code, which forbids "extreme" hairstyles that might distract the other students and disrupt learning. The school officials told her that her hairstyle clashed with the spiritual and educational mission of the school; they labeled her cornrows a fad and told her not to return to school until she changed the style ("Third-Grader's" 7–9b).

Although Meghan did not know it, her school forbade cornrows, dreadlocks, hair ornaments, and designs shaved into the hair. While offering no explanation for banning these particular hairstyles, school administrators decided that Meghan was attempting to make an undefined political or cultural statement with her hairstyle. Such statements, the school informed her, would not be tolerated. Because her parents had signed a contract that required them to pay for Meghan's schooling for the entire year whether or not she actually attended, they sent their daughter back the next day without braids. However, Meghan's father reported that he was having a hard time forgetting how his daughter cried when she was told that her hairstyle was extreme and he could not help feeling "deep and strong it's just not right" (7–9b).

Although Meghan's father is not reported as having explained exactly why he felt the school's strictures were not right, he does say that there is a cultural difference at work and that his child is being penalized for having a different type of hair. I would add that the problem is really the clash between the understandings of what hair signifies for Meghan's family and for the school administrators; by extension, it is also about the power of the administrators to enforce their understandings on Meghan without having to comprehend her position. For the administrators, Meghan's hairstyle triggered the enactment of a signification system that privileged her school community's belief that hairstyle functions most importantly to make a "statement." While hair is a genetically determined physical feature, just as importantly, its care and styling are quite clearly influenced by cultural concerns. What makes hair a unique and revealing "natural" feature in exploring the expressive culture (or will to adorn) of African Americans is the cultural value placed upon the ease with which it can be altered and a largely self-determined willingness and ability to do with it what one will: dread, cornrow, perm, dye, press. While some styling choices are born of a desire to look like somebody one admires or to adhere to a look desirable to some political or social position, hairstyles and the cultural interactions that produce them speak to a range of other concerns as well.

The significance of hair and its care in the experience of African American women can be examined through a number of sources: magazine advertisements, novels, films, photographs, the place of African American hair-care businesses in African American culture, among others. Within those cultural discourses, one does not have to look very far to discover the many reasons an African American father would feel "deep and strong" that denying his child access to such a style is wrong. This is especially true around the practice of braiding hair in African American culture and what and how it means for African American women. For example, in the late Sherley Anne Williams's novel *Dessa Rose*, the concluding scene involves the title character braiding her child's hair and "remembering" (weaving together strands of memories of) her life to that child. She says:

> I missed this when I was sold away from home . . . The way the womens in the Quarters used to would braid hair. Mothers would braid children heads—girl and boy—until they went into the field or for as long as they had them. This was one way we told who they peoples was, by how they hair was combed. . . . Child learn a lot of things setting between some grown person's legs, listening at grown peoples speak over they heads. This is where I learned to listen, right there between mammy's thighs, where I first learnted to speak, from listening at grown peoples talk. (234)

Children who are taught "between some grown person's legs" learn more than how to listen and speak. They also learn a way of looking at the world—a way of positioning their experiences in opposition or relation to those of the "dominant culture." They learn a history, which in many instances may ensure their survival. As a result, this scene in *Dessa Rose* highlights one of the truly important aspects of hair as it relates to African American culture: the act of styling hair as both a social and learning occasion.

A similar logic is operative in Karla Holloway's recollections of braiding her daughter's hair:

> When my daughter was a child, I braided her hair on the front porch. In twilight hours or warm summer mornings I worked intricately braided patterns into Ayana's hair, trying to capture some of that precious childhood time when my sisters and I

could not have been closer to our mother or grandmothers Celia and Marguerite than we were when they were braiding our hair. We sat propped between their strong legs, our shoulders leaning against their soft thighs, feeling touched and safe. Tenderheaded or not, those were times when our bodies and theirs, intimately intertwined and held by the web of their fingers and our hair, were sweetly cared for, and immeasurably valued. (70–71)

These same sentiments are again evident when Vera Smith—a young woman interviewed in a *Los Angeles Times* article on the relationship between braiders and their clients—discovered her knack for braiding in the second grade. She "was ecstatic when she made her first perfect cornrow and once word of her talent got around her Cincinnati Neighborhood, she spent weekends giggling and chatting as she plaited her sisters' hair, her friends' hair or her friends' sisters hair" ("Intricate" E1).

If within African American culture (literary and recollected), the act of braiding comes to symbolize closeness, comfort, and community, once the results of such practices came into public conflict with the dominant culture, the style came to construct the wearer (Meghan Smith) as operating outside of an acceptable history and tradition and marked her as unacceptably other. The school imposed an alternative meaning of braiding that erased any associative meanings of race constructed outside of the knowledge of the white school administrators. The space between understandings of Meghan's body as a battlefield and as something with which to exercise her "will to adorn" became contested territory. Her only option was surrender.

Act II

The same month, but hundreds of miles away from Meghan, two other African American girls surrendered to the authority of a dominant white culture to impose their understanding of race and racial identity as conveyed by a hairstyle within the public space of a junior high school. TaCara Nash (twelve years old) and Aqueellah Shareef (thirteen years old) were pulled out of their classrooms at Rickover Junior High School. In an effort to combat the possibility of gang activity, this suburban public school twenty-eight miles outside of Chicago, decided to ban braids, beads, cornrows, dreadlocks, hair coloring, designs shaved into the hair, and colored extensions. The two girls had both come to school that day with their hair in French Twists, and both sported zigzag parts. The styles the two young women wore that day were not covered by the ban, but school administrators believed that the zigzag

Figure 3. Carolyn, World African Hair, Braid, and Trade Show, Atlanta. 1997.

parts were close enough to the shaved-in designs that had been banned to ask the girls to leave school. Both returned the next day with their hair in different styles. They both were reported to have left the school in tears ("School's" E1).

Police officers who were asked to comment on this incident said that they had not found a correlation between certain hairstyles and gang activity. Administrators at the school, however, decided that there had to be such a connection. For them and the other members of the antigang task force, certain styles spoke volumes about the relationship between a student's style and their political, cultural, and social affiliations. In addressing the reasons for the ban on so many styles most commonly worn by African Americans, Thomas Ryan, superintendent of District 168, said the ban "has nothing to do with race or culture. It has to do with keeping our kids safe and preventing distractions in the classrooms" (E1).

Ryan does not go so far as to explain how particular styles, not proven to have any association with violent and/or criminal gang activity, could endanger students and disrupt learning. However, his actions would seem to denote the inability of a white administrator to imagine outside of dominant understandings of a limited range of possible identities for African Americans. Certain hairstyles denote an acceptable identity, others point to the possibility of an identity that cannot be tolerated. The offending styles, therefore, must be banished. It is not so much the hairstyles that are at issue here but rather the meaning of those styles when conflated with the meaning of an African American identity that is frightening to those who have the power to both discipline and punish. On a far too regular basis, that fright seems to express itself around the right of African Americans to adorn and represent their bodies in public places.

Entr'acte: Black Hair Means Drama— Legal and Other Matters

In the 1991 case of *Rogers v. American Airlines*, the federal court upheld the right of employers to prohibit the wearing of braided hairstyles in the workplace. Rogers had been fired from her job as a flight attendant because she chose to wear braids while working. Her supervisors believed that the style would frighten the passengers and demanded that she straighten her hair into a style they considered more presentable. While the court based its decision on the right of employers to have a say in the appearance/image they wanted to have portrayed, the plaintiff in that case, a black woman, argued that American Airlines' policy discriminated against her specifically as a black woman because she had a specific type of hair and, as a result, drew upon a wider range of styling choices in the presentation of an acceptable public identity. The court, choosing to base its decision principally on distinctions between biological and cultural conceptions of race, upheld her firing. Using much the same reasoning as Superintendent Ryan, they decided that the connection between race and cultural understandings of racial identity was not nearly as determining a factor in her lived experience as some sort of nondefined biological conception of race (Caldwell 268).

Although *Rogers* is the only reported decision that upholds the categorical exclusion of braided hairstyles, the prohibition of such styles in the workforce is both widespread and long-standing. In 1991 a group of African American women were fired for coming in to work with their hair in braids, and, more recently, in 1998 a black female employee who wore her hair in braids was fired from a Boston-area hotel for refusing to wear her hair in a more "acceptable," less ethnic style ("Natural" E1).

While those cases all involved some supposed right the employer had to make sure customers were happy and thereby protect corporate earnings, in the cases involving the previously mentioned schoolchildren, no such right of customer satisfaction was operative. In those instances, the drama revolved around the specter of a fear-inducing and disruptive conception of blackness. Therefore, the bodies remain, minus the hairstyles that might bespeak an alternative relationship to and understanding of black history and culture. The styles become "fugitive" when associated with a black body, and the possibility of "willful adornment" is kept in check by the possibility of capture in a trap of power relations, racial memories, and narrowly constructed identities. This is true because those in power can only imagine that such styles are making a statement relative to white culture. They cease to mean in any other context. In the meantime, the racial ideologies governing these "dramas" remain masked. There is, however, a very different set of interactions set in motion when these same styles are featured on a body that is marked and understood as white.

Act III

Three months after Meghan, TaCara and Aqueellah were asked to leave school, an article appeared announcing that cornrow braids were a crossover hit. It chronicled the surge among white women sporting the style. Madonna was spotted wearing cornrows, and the senior fashion editor at *YM* decided to start wearing the style after seeing a Calvin Klein advertisement the previous summer that featured a white woman with her hair cornrowed. As one fashion editor said, " I feel like Cher with my braids. I was mod chic. I was pretty groovy." The women interviewed for the article all reported that they like wearing their hair in braids and that they get lots of positive attention for having "discovered" a whole new world of beauty. They all located their initial exposure to the style within white culture and stated they first noticed braids to be attractive when worn on a white body ("Cornrow" G6).

How is it that women whose very image depends on making the "proper" kind of fashion statement can wear such hairstyles and African American children, for whom cornrows are a birthright, are sent home from school in tears for engaging in the same practice. That question leads us to many others. Depending upon the light that we shine, we are presented with a whole host of interactions, relationships, and issues: Is Naomi Campbell's decision to wear long blond wigs the same as these white women's decision to wear their hair in braids? Do we live in a historical period in which we have more important things to worry about than whether a few young black girls have to change their hair-

Figure 4. Kenny, Proud Lady Hair and Beauty Show, Chicago, 1994.

styles? Does anyone own beauty or particular hairstyles? Does it matter whether any of the people whose dramas I have described know the history of the hairstyles they choose to wear? Are Meghan's, Aqueelah's, or any black child's tears in any way relevant to an understanding of fashion, representation, bodies, and identity?

Questions about appropriation and hybridity are clearly evident in this third drama. Indeed, the belief that the fashion and style aspects of what is generally considered to be an African American community somehow bestow chic, cool, or "chosen" marginal status is not new. The difference here, however, is that hairstyles embraced by the dominant culture are no longer available to the styles' originators. None of the white women were asked to leave their place of employment and return reconfigured; none were fired or barred from the public eye. They were not hindered from nor punished for experimenting with varying forms of beauty. If certain styles construct African Americans as gang members, extreme or desirous of making some sort of political statement, those same styles denote risk-taking and an open mind when embraced by whites.

It is clear that American fashion is ready, willing, and able to absorb varying cultural markers (ethnic and otherwise). It acts, in a sense, as a bounty hunter, always on the lookout for renegade and retrograde statements that it can incorporate and contain. Once they are sported on the bodies of those seeking merely to obtain "fashion forward" status, hairstyles, clothing, and styling techniques tend to lose much of their power and cultural specificity while at the same time entangling the wearer in yet other levels of raced, classed, and gendered meanings. Indeed, as Leslie Rabine points out, "Women of fashion become the 'speaking' subjects of a symbolic system which inseparably entangles signs of oppression and liberation within the images of the fashionable feminine body" (60). Or as Kaja Silverman argues, fashion is a highly visible way of "acknowledging that its wearer's identity has been shaped by decades of representational activity and that no cultural project can ever 'start from zero'" (195). However, is it ever possible to center the effects of such practices on those whom fashion tracks down and delivers? In tracing the hidden genealogies of the hairstyles adopted by fashion "trendsetters" like Madonna, can we make sense out of and "recover" the bodies of fashion victims (like Meghan, TaCara, Aqueellah, and the young woman whose tears led to this essay) who are punished for wearing their race wrong in public?

Epilogue

> *I want to know my hair again, to own it, to delight in it again. To recall my earliest mirrored reflection when there was no beginning and I first knew that the person who laughed at me and cried with me and stuck out her tongue at me was me. I want to know my hair again, the way I knew it before I knew that my hair is me. Before I knew that the burden of beauty—or lack of it—for an entire race of people could be tied up with my hair and me.*
> —Paulette M. Caldwell, "Hair Piece"

My earlier work on beauty culture, bodies, and style explored the dichotomy between the meanings of straight versus natural hairstyles. I focused on those initial moments in the late nineteenth century when hair straightening became an option for large numbers of African Americans and on how that option became synonymous with a particular politic and meaning of identity and culture within African American communities. Here I am exploring subjects that, in a sense, were covered over or ignored in that earlier work. I am attempting to uncover, rather than re-cover, them. Specifically, I am interested in showing that, while hair may mean something particular within African American communities, once those understandings come into contact with the dominant culture, one may not be able to hold on to those original meanings. For me, this discussion is tightly connected to the body of a par-

Figure 5. Nicole, Baltimore, 1993.

ticular African American girl who cried because she couldn't figure out how to make her personal beliefs about what was appropriate for her body fit with what others told her they would prefer to see. The issues her questions raise, however, are not relevant only to her life.

In each of the newspaper articles discussed here, drama ensued when individuals and institutions within the dominant culture enforced their misinterpretations of African American culture, race, style, and fashion on African American bodies. Those misinterpretations functioned to banish the complex cultural meanings of hair and style held by African Americans. In the first two instances, school administrators made a clear and deliberate statement about the consequences of particular acts of self-adornment and the necessity for displaying an identity that was in line with their expectations. That those expectations might run exactly counter to the intent, history, and understanding of particular styles in African American culture was unimportant. As a result, at least three African American children and their families were instructed on the wages of difference and reminded that their bodies are far more than playgrounds. At the same time, however, an aspect of "fugitive" African American identity is evident. Taken together, the African Americans in these stories become one group of people attempting to escape another group who holds power over them. The children involved have learned an important lesson about how to be seen, by whom, and what the consequences are for not paying close attention when on the battlefield of self-representation.

The illustrations scattered throughout this essay function as examples of a range of African American fashion possibilities and alternatives that have thus far avoided capture or surrender. All of the subjects in the photographs are wearing their hair in what are often categorized as "aggressive" hairstyles. They would all most probably qualify as not acceptable in the public spaces of work or school. Two of the images picture women staring out into the world defiantly. Another pictures a woman looking out into the future. They all portray bodies adorned with self-pleasing, self-satisfying willfulness. None are sporting styles featured in mainstream fashion magazines, and all of the styles are associated most particularly with African American bodies and communities in various geographical regions. They function to remind us that even on a battlefield, beauty is primarily qualified by gender, raced when disqualified as beautiful, yet is always a joy to behold.

WORKS CITED

Benstock, Shari, and Suzanne Ferriss, eds. *On Fashion.* New Brunswick: Rutgers UP, 1994.

Bordo, Susan. *Unbearable Weight: Feminism, Western Culture, and the Body* Berkeley: U of California P, 1993.

Caldwell, Paulette M. "Hair Piece." *Critical Race Theory.* Ed. Richard Delgado. Philadelphia: Temple UP, 1995. 267–80.

"Cornrow Braids a Crossover Hit." *Kansas City Star* 5 Jan. 1997: G6.

"Furor over Book Brings Pain and Pride to Its Author." *New York Times* 25 Nov. 1998: A24.

Gaskins, Bill. *Good and Bad Hair: Photographs by Bill Gaskins.* New Brunswick: Rutgers UP, 1997.

Holloway, Karla F. C. *Codes of Conduct: Race Ethics and the Color of Our Character.* New Brunswick: Rutgers UP, 1995.

Hurston, Zora Neale. "Characteristics of Negro Expression." *Within the Circle: An Anthology of African American Literary Criticism from the Harlem Renaissance to the Present.* Ed. Angelyn Mitchell. Durham: Duke UP, 1994. 79–96.

"An Intricate Weave of Friendship and Art." *Los Angeles Times* 3 Apr. 1997: E1.

Mercer, Kobena. "Black Hair/Style Politics." *Out There: Marginalization and Contemporary Cultures.* Ed. Russell Ferguson et al. New York and Cambridge: New Museum of Contemporary Art and MIT P, 1992. 247–64.

"The Natural Look." *Los Angeles Times* 6 Aug. 1998: E1.

Rabine, Leslie. "A Woman's Two Bodies: Fashion Magazines, Consumerism, and Feminism." Benstock and Ferriss 59–75.

Rooks, Noliwe. *Hair Raising: Beauty, Culture and African American Women.* New Brunswick: Rutgers UP, 1996.

"School's Hairdo Ban Tangles with Ethnic Culture." *Chicago Tribune* 15 Nov. 1997: E1.

Silverman, Kaja. "Fragments of a Fashionable Discourse." Benstock and Ferriss
    183–96.
"Third-Grader's Braided Hair Sparks Cultural Dispute." *St. Petersburg Times* 9
    Dec. 1997: 7, 9B.
Williams, She   rley Anne. *Dessa Rose*. New York: Harcourt, 1984.

DEBORAH E, McDOWELL

Recovery Missions

Imaging the Body Ideals

This essay is dedicated to the memory of Sherley Anne Williams, who died July 1999 of uterine cancer, and who understood that the scars "writ about [our] privates" form a story we should tell.[1]

Wanted: A Body Not My Own

I confess. These days I envy Tina Turner's body and wish that mine looked more like hers. There. It's out. I've said it and violated and offended at one stroke several proprieties that women of a certain age and station are expected to observe. Shall I go on? I fantasize about occasions when I can sport one of Tina's flamboyant costumes: the toreador pants, the fire engine red slip dress with spaghetti straps that droop from the shoulder to expose a hint of cleavage; the silver-sequined mini-dress, the fish-net stockings that hussy up her legs (insured for several million dollars by Lloyd's of London, I am told). I dream of imitating her movements, the way her body rockets into motion, then claims every inch of the stage, the way it sweats and struts and gyrates, totally unbridled, seemingly free of all restraint.

This is the body I've never had, the clothing I've never worn, not even in my dreams, because my "physical education" outlawed all that. Like most girls I know who came of age in the Alabama of the 1950s, I was tutored to be strict and straitlaced, to be uncomfortable and guarded in my ungainly body, lest it be taken for one of those "loose," "wide open," "ever-ready" women with shameless "big-wheel" ways. Allegedly everybody "got a turn" at a "big wheel" woman. "You can see her coming," said my grandmother of one such woman, "can spot her by a mile." Her loud (meaning brightly colored), slithery clothing, the hips that rippled when she walked, signaled the sexual availability that brazenly flouted existing social codes.

Although I was born into the working class, mine was a disciplined, "mannered" bourgeois body-in-the-making, socialized to take its place among the ranks of "decent," "proper" women who would eventually represent the socio-cultural body; that is, who would be what was then called a "credit to the race." Cartwheels were forbidden, as were wide-legged seating postures or legs that crossed at the knee. Hips must not swivel when you walked. No movement, not even the faintest gesture, could call attention to what lay below the waist. But while the lofty work of building the ideal racial body proceeded on one front, body building of a "lower," more popular sort proceeded on another and was equally *de rigueur*.

After all, these were the days of padded bras and girdles, which I remember well. Called "foundation" garments, they were designed to do the impossible: transform flat-chested females with ironing-board butts into the fleshly Jezebels whose pictures were plastered on the cover of *Bronze Thrills*, a cheap drugstore romance magazine marketed to African American women. Its steamy scenes established one plain and painful truth: neither thrills nor romance awaited those readers who lacked the curves and cleavage that no prostheses could ever simulate. Back-page ads for WATE-ON, promising desired results in fourteen days, neither delivered on their promise nor made good on their money-back guarantees. And thus those, like myself, with razor-thin proportions, were left to dream of the "brick house" body, the ticket price of going-steady sweetheart rings.

The sounds and sayings of the black vernacular that rang throughout the quarters of the working class left no doubt about the desired black female body: flesh was voguishly delectable. "Nobody wants a bone but a dog," as was often heard or, when a "big-wheel" woman strutted by, "Jelly, jelly, jelly. Gotta be jelly 'cause jam don't shake thataway." In the lyrics of popular music, Otis Redding's "hip-shaking mamas" were desired over Joe Tex's woman with skinny legs. You will recall that in Tex's hit single, "Skinny Legs and All," he tries to auction off a skinny-legged woman to a horde of raucous men, but the end of the song finds him still without a single bidder. This pop hit rocked many a high school dance, and I was frequently the object of the tease, the "woman" no man wanted, presumably because my legs were skinny, too.

A few years later Joe Tex had changed his tune, recording a 1970s disco jam that superseded "Skinny Legs and All" titled "I Ain't Gon' Bump No More with No Big Fat Woman." "Somebody take her; I don't want her / Somebody take her; I don't need her. / Somebody take her;

she's too much for me" were the variations on the song's refrain, and its ending line–"It takes two hands to handle this woman"—echoed unmistakably the current Burger King jingle: "It takes two hands to handle a Whopper."

Why begin with this autobiographical prologue? Because, to quote Terry Eagleton, the body is a "stubbornly local phenomenon" (70) marked by its specific history, bound to its particular time and place. Body talk often departs from and ultimately reaches deeply personal stations, particularly the crowded stations of desire. Our "bodies" come into being and consciousness often at those privileged, sometimes pleasurable, but most often painful moments when our primordial desire to be desired is frustrated (or gratified) and our bodies take the credit or the blame. We tend to remember with stinging clarity the times when we discover that our finite, particular bodies meet or fail to meet some generalized aesthetic ideal, an ideal often molded from the matter of very specific bodies that set the shifting standards for the whole.

Joe Tex's "Skinny Legs and All" and "I Ain't Gon' Bump No More with No Big Fat Woman" constitute a double-sided coin engraved with the extremes of "not enough" on one side and "too much" on the other. And according to the fluctuating scales of physical desirability, I, like most African American women I know, have embodied, within the dominant cultural imaginary, both lack and excess (and excess as lack). We form, in sum, a negative but nonetheless powerful "positivist" ideal. Black female excess and appetite have been iconicized historically by the "big fat woman," from the Hottentot Venus to Hattie McDaniel to Oprah Winfrey. As Doris Smith Witt argues in her brilliant book *Black Hunger: Food and the Politics of U.S. Identity*, "the widespread conflation of African-American female bodies and fat" is a "central structuring dynamic of twentieth-century U.S. psychic, cultural, sociopolitical, and economic life" (189, 2). Thinness is prototypically embodied by the white woman. The famous bodice scene in *Gone with the Wind* is only one encapsulating instance. Mammy laces Scarlett while chastising her for failing to control her appetite, to "eat lak a bird." While Scarlett's seventeen-inch waist is one fetishized mark of her sexual desirability, Mammy's mammoth body has long since foreclosed on all of that. It's plain to see that she has helped herself to heaping plates of food, and even if Scarlett gorges—eventually—vowing never to be hungry again, her body never shows the signs of excess appetite, never bears the weight.

This collection makes a bold bid to leave this too too familiar history behind, in order to challenge the body of knowledge that has long constructed black women as simultaneously all bodies and nobodies, at once fully exposed and barely visible. Theirs, the editors declare, is a "recovery" mission grounded in black women's own representations. To excerpt their objectives: "This volume aims . . . to amplify the counterhegemonic discourse of African American women who attempt to recover their bodies," to "wrest control . . . away from the [discursive] distortions of others" and thereby "take back their selves." A tall order this, as well as a spectacular act of faith in the efficacy of discourse to meet and match, indeed to outmatch and overpower discourse; nevertheless, this collection proffers one example after another of black women who attempted nothing less.

The nineteenth century was a watershed era for black women's recovery of their bodies from discourses that functioned historically to consign them to the realm of the "serviceable corporeal," to summon Daphne Brooks's resonant turn of phrase in her essay here. From the poetry of Frances Ellen Watkins to the narratives of Harriet Wilson and Harriet Jacobs, that "recovery" lay in "decorporealizing" the body, making it symbolically disappear. According to Carla Peterson in *"Doers of the Word,"* for Wilson and Jacobs that disappearing act began with the "covering" of the pseudonym, through which both women "strove to resist bodily exposure, [to] veil not only their physical selves but also their interior lives." They demanded, adds Peterson, that their "fictional rather than their factual selves bear the physical and emotional brunt of both racial violence and the sexualized male gaze," thus deflecting their more common representation as "always . . . public and exposed" (152). "Uncovering" the body offered other black women of the era an alternative strategy of resistance anchored not in bodily coverage but in bodily exposure. In this way of reading, the body became the site of black women's subjection and, simultaneously, the route to their agency and liberation, their "recovery," if you will. To illustrate this paradox, more than one contributor turns to Sojourner Truth, an iconic figure in cultural studies on African American women and the body. Truth provides this collection a consistent point of affirmative reference and ligature functioning as both a bridge to the past as well as the illusion of its transcendence.

Brooks argues, for example, that by uncovering her breasts and arms Truth succeeded in "recovering" her body and overturning dominant cultural definitions of "womanhood" (and manhood), as well as in resisting the forced alienation from her body that slavery enforced. By turning her body into spectacle, in other words, Truth rescued it from "nineteenth-century proscriptions of racial and gender abjection." Such exposure amounted to an act of self-representation that liberated Truth from the imprisoning rhetorics of the day. Brooks bases her claims on "Ar'n't I a Woman?," the speech which Truth delivered at the 1851 Women's Rights Convention in Akron, Ohio.[2] This speech, like all others

Truth delivered, is known only through the reports and transcriptions of others.

Historian Nell Painter has done the most thorough scholarly job to date of sorting the myth and embellishment of "Ar'n't I a Woman?" from, as it were, plainer Truth. According to Painter, although at least four accounts of "Ar'n't I a Woman?" were reported in newspapers soon after the 1851 convention, it is actually the 1863 transcription by Frances Gage that has proved the most enduring. The "Sojourner Truth" of this version is the stuff of Gage's imagination, the product of her own needs and desires. Gage molded a body of Truth that she needed and that the age demanded: a body removed in its "masculine" ruggedness, removed in its "tremendous muscular power," from the ideals of delicate nineteenth-century white womanhood, another of the era's most sacred icons.

While it is impossible to ascertain just what Truth actually said in "Ar'n't I a Woman?" the speech has been appropriated, by black and white women alike, as an emblem of victimized and yet ultimately triumphant, or *recovered* black womanhood. As Painter notes, while the "angry, defiant character" of Gage's representation may well accord with twentieth-century terms and tastes, that character is far from being the sum of Sojourner Truth's complex parts. Although Truth was also known to be a woman defined largely by her evangelical preoccupations and frequently hobbled by a body often debilitated and worn, that image of Truth doesn't suit such tastes and thus gives way to an image represented exclusively by its strengths, by its powers of resistance, physical and verbal. But if Truth's "body" has been thoroughly appropriated and her "self-representation" accessible only through the mediating transcriptions of others, what is the body we have in Truth and what "self" does it, can it, represent?

Of course, neither of these questions should be taken to refer exclusively, or even primarily, to Sojourner Truth or to overlook her usefulness here as mere discursive figure. I am concerned, rather, with the vexing questions that Truth, as intellectual paradigm and property, raises about the operating logics, metaphors, and assumptions of this collection and of discourses on "the body" more generally. My concerns here spill outside the typical synoptic tendencies of an "Afterword" (you've read these essays, every one suggestive). Rather, I am stimulated by their broader implications to offer a roving set of meditations on the collection's conceptual backbones: black women's bodies, self-representation, and "recovery." I want especially to explore the multiple and distinctive valences of "recovery," but I am also concerned to inquire into the ways contemporary academics are writing about the body at this historical moment and unacknowledged, perhaps even unconscious "bodily" ideals.

What is the body we want? What is the body we need? What is the body we have? And can the three be reconciled? To what extent is the body we have realigned to meet the requirements of a standardized "ideal," and to what extent is this ideal sutured to the occular logics and obsessions of our culture and our age?

Intellectual Body Imaging

Throughout this collection, "self-representation" is structured in apposition to "recovering." Posited as a form of resistance and self-defense, "self-representation" supplants determinism with agency and thus makes for, enables, "recovery" of the body.

The contributors here fully understand and acknowledge collectively the inevitably partial ways in which they can "recover" or "claim" the body. They grasp and apply in different ways the commonplace insights of recent cultural criticism on the body:

1. The body is less a "being" than a malleable plastic surface infinitely shifting and culturally shaped. It has no "fixed, 'material' truth pre-existing its relations with the world and with others" (Jones 26).
2. The body is iterative, symbolic; flesh made word.
3. The body is a battleground, the site of cultural conflict and contestation in particular time and space. In other words, the concept of the body provides only the illusion of self-evidence, facticity, "thereness" for something fundamentally ephemeral, imaginary, something made in the image of particular social groups.

Academic cultural critics, while certainly not a homogeneous body, constitute one such social group. While those included here would readily acknowledge the fragility of their enterprise, their urge to fashion what I would call an "ideal body" for critical discourse is nonetheless apparent. Although this collection focuses on various bodies and their representations, from nineteenth-century "performance" poetry of abolitionism to late-twentieth-century body building, they meld, despite their variant shapes, into a single body "type." Taken together, the essays constitute a form of intellectual imaging, of body sculpting in the service of a broad discursive ideal. Not measured in proportions of breast to waist to hips, this idealized body emerges here, stacked for "resistance," "revision," "subversion," and "control."

Sojourner Truth is said to have demonstrated a "strategy of *resistance*" a "*revisionist* and transformative subjectivity"; Ada Isaacs Mencken, the "*subversive* power of bodily deeds." Frances Ellen Watkins attempted in her poetry to "transfigure the black woman's body from the locus of enslavement to a site of *resistance*." Pauline Hopkins's Winona is one who "*controls* how and by whom [her] body is seen or not seen." Suzan-Lori Parks transforms a black female body from "degenerated object to a means of *resistance*." Carla Dunlap and her cohorts in the world of body building seize the "vantage point of body control" (my emphasis).

One might read the penultimate essay on Carla Dunlap as the collection's home stretch, or borrowing from the essay's title, as its punctuating "victory." But over what has Dunlap been victorious, and what does she truly control? Such questions are not lost on Jacqueline Brady, the author of the Dunlap piece, who recognizes that the rock-hard, muscular, "pumped up" body of individual physique is powerless to control anything but itself and, at that, in palpably limited ways. Despite the women's muscular power, she continues, they still fail to alter or control the "external hierarchies or ideologies" that still bind their bodies, as it were. That uncontrollability, she concludes importantly, is rooted in the fact that transforming and "recovering" the body cannot end at the technologies of the self. Brady's insights, read backward, serve to temper the tones of affirmation and victory that ring throughout the collection, but I leave the volume with a set of lingering questions about its "body language," a language that centers so emphatically on control.

Perhaps assertions of control are never more strident and insistent than when control is plainly out of reach. Despite whatever isolated discursive interventions might be claimed, black women's *corporeal* bodies remain subject to subjection, subject to others' control. Not even Oprah Winfrey—arguably the most powerful woman in contemporary U.S. culture (as "power" is measured in yardsticks of wealth, celebrity, and influence)—controls either her body or its symbolization.

Contemplating Oprah provides an instructive take on this volume's organizing rubrics and mission statement. The editors are not amiss in observing that black women have historically been subjected to the "oppressive gaze of the dominant culture," which has "strip[ped] black female bodies of any cover." The language here—"stripped," "uncovered"—clearly evokes the history of black women's sexual subjection, their function as breeding machines birthing human chattel for plantation fields and auction blocks. But the tension between "covering" and "uncovering" before the camera, before the dominant culture's "oppressive gaze," becomes very complicated when Oprah is in view, for she speaks to nothing more profoundly than the body's frank unruliness, to its resistance to control. But she speaks more importantly to the complexities of self-representation, especially as it figures here as the route to "recovering" the body.

Oprah on the Carpet and on the Cover

I still can't believe I wasn't dreaming. I lay in bed dazed, disoriented, recovering from a hysterectomy, fingering the stitches from the purple scar running vertically down my belly, through the length of the umbilical line. Drifting in and out of consciousness, lamenting the bodies that would not be born of mine, I needed the distraction of television and hit the mark with the *Oprah Winfrey Show*. Oprah had invited twelve white women (there might have been ten? fifteen?) to her show to air their grievances, face to face, about her body's new shape and size. Invited in bloc, they gathered together to complain that Oprah's new body—toned, trim, outfitted in some form-fitting number—was not to their liking, was not, to their minds, a befitting form. She had temporarily disengaged from her iconic role, her corpulent body image, her audience's beau ideal.

It is certainly no secret that Oprah has long shown herself susceptible to the wishes and desires of her viewing public and has besides openly confessed to the unruly tendencies of the flesh as exhibited in her gaining and reducing form. Oprah, after all, has made her weight a national issue and obsession, a kind of national cause. After losing sixty-seven pounds in 1988, she dragged the equivalent amount of animal fat on stage in a red Flyer wagon. Standing triumphantly beside it, svelte in skintight size ten Calvin Kleins, she vowed never to be fat again. As we know, the skinny Oprah was short-lived. By 1992, the weight was back and then some.

That Oprah's heavy, more ample body was unifying, forging a connection between her and her viewers, was made crystal clear in that afternoon's segment, as woman after woman claimed to be alienated by Oprah's new look. She was clearly not "corporeal" enough. It should be noted that Oprah's judges ran the gamut of body types, from slender to plump, lumpish to lean, squat to statuesque, but not a one, in fact, obese. And yet the emotional needs of this Oprah-consuming public dared to demand that she gain weight again. Although this was a single episode and thus should not be overfreighted with meaning, it raises the question of whether black women can conceive of their own body images. According to the women featured on that episode, the answer is resoundingly, No!

Just why Oprah thought this dressing-down was deserving of a segment on national television I'll leave to others to decide, but the segment clearly suggested that Oprah's body wasn't hers to own, wasn't hers to shape. As Merrell Noden recently observed in *People Profiles Oprah Winfrey*, Oprah's openness with her audience "encourages some fans in the illusion that [she] is their possession. A stranger called out to her one day when she was out jogging. 'You'd better quit losing weight, because you're going to make the rest of us feel bad!'" Or, as a woman wrote in a letter to *Newsday*, "As a fat woman, I have attempted 64 different diets. Oprah was meant to be fat. She fasted her way down to a size eight. Will the real Oprah please come back to us?" (Noden, 105). The "real" Oprah is the fat Oprah, but in the eyes of the media culture that has long sought to control her image, even the "thin" Oprah was still, for some, too fat.

Sealing her image as media icon and possession, Oprah appeared on the cover of the August 26, 1989, edition of *TV Guide*, but, as was soon revealed, this was not the "real" Oprah, at least not from top to toe. The image featured Oprah's head and Ann-Margret's body. The magazine had concealed from Oprah its plans to do a body switch, which provoked her woeful observation: "I thought I looked pretty decent, but I guess the real me isn't good enough for *TV Guide*" (Bly 147).

Both Oprah and her fan above resort to the rhetoric of the "real," but Oprah has proven again and again the now axiomatic notion that ideas of the "real" are thoroughly dependent on representations. Oprah's appearance on the 9 October 1998 issue of *Vogue* magazine clearly bears this out. The feature coincided with the release of *Beloved*, the film adaptation of Toni Morrison's Pulitzer Prize–winning novel. Photographed in a strapless navy cashmere dress, Oprah strikes a glamorous, air-brushed seductive pose that mimics that of the classic odalisque. Reminiscent of Manet's *Olympia*, Oprah reposes on a chaise longue, and although, unlike Olympia, her body is not denuded, it is figuratively "nude" and eroticized in its accents and insignia. From her luxuriant, tumbling hair— mussed and tousled—and her pouty lips to her taut, toned arms that are braceleted and bare, Oprah is represented as sexually seductive and alluring. Against the "West's construction of not-white women as not-to-be-seen," Oprah lies recumbent, front and center, on the cover of the magazine (O'Grady 153).

I summon Manet's *Olympia* from among the range of possible examples of the odalisque in Western art, primarily because Oprah, as a black woman, has traded her expected marginalized "place" within that canvas and its symbologies. Clearly *not* Olympia's black maid, consigned to the peripheries of the frame, she is now the focal point, striking a voluptuous pose.

Interviewed for the cover story at the Four Seasons Hotel in Manhattan, Oprah was once again the heroine of a "rags-to-riches," "before and after" narrative of ascent and triumph, culminating here in *Vogue*. Significantly, Oprah's "transformation" from small-screen diva to "silver-screen queen" is telescoped most accessibly through the body. Asked by the interviewer whether she had ever dreamed of appearing on the cover of *Vogue*, Oprah quipped, "*Vogue* is the big house! Didn't think I'd be sittin' at that table!" She then recanted and allowed as how the fantasy of a *Vogue* photo shoot had in fact occurred to her during the filming of *Beloved*. She thought, "I would love more than anything to do a *Vogue* shoot with my girls [her costars in *Beloved*] and have us all dress the way we would have dressed had we not been slaves and had some money" (329).

That Oprah aspires, at least in *Vogue,* to represent the plantation mistress and member of the monied class constitutes a departure from the lives of the oppressed and abused black women she impersonated in the early years of her climb to fame. As a former classmate explained, most of the scripts she chose "were ones in which she was being beaten by a slave master . . . she would actually evoke that passion, that anger and bitterness as salt was poured in her wounds. It doesn't shock me that she has chosen the roles she has—*The Color Purple* and *Beloved*— showing the strength of women in desperate times" (Noden, 41).

While Oprah as Sethe continues this early penchant, the photo shoot of Oprah and her *Beloved* costars reflects anything but "women in desperate times." These are well-fed women, lolling in the lap of luxury. But viewed from another angle, they are, figuratively speaking, captives in the wild. Lounging on a lush, green Arcadian estate in Long Island, they are impeccably turned out in frivolous couture—bustles and bustiers, corsets and halters, full-skirted floor-length gowns of silk and satin stiffened and molded by stays. The shots are at once prim and provocative, decorous and dangerous. The women's pinched and corseted waists suggest spectral unruliness, excess appetite, all reined in and tied down to a stiff formality. And yet, peeping from above their wire-framed, push-up bras are the breasts, the cultural shorthand for women's sexual allure.

Modesty and sexual daring are in open conflict here, as Oprah attempts to navigate two distinct and racialized subject positions and symbologies, occupied prototypically by white and black women, respectively. Oprah has assumed here that her fantasy of inhabiting the big house, bedecked and bejeweled, would have been plainly out of reach in slavery times. But it bears remembering that, while the "big house" would certainly have been off limits, the finery was most certainly not. Available to slave women was a position between the mistress and the drudging slave, a position occupied by "Fancy" women and *gens de couleur*, who were sold to wealthy gentlemen in cities like Charleston, New Orleans, St. Louis, and Richmond. Frederick Law Olmsted wrote in "A Journey in the Seaboard Slave States" about the "Fancy Trade," the traffic in light-skinned black women for the express and exclusive purpose of prostitution and concubinage. These women were indeed outfitted in silks and satins and draped with jewels (Washington 59–60).

Oprah and her costars seem to be decked out for the ball, seem to have transcended a history of visual representation that bonds them to the subject bodies, but throughout her public life, Oprah has clearly embraced bondage of a different kind, enslavement to an aesthetic ideal of thinness, historically constructed as the obverse of black women's stereotypical contours. But interestingly enough, despite Oprah's requisite reduction for the *Vogue* cover spread, she is nevertheless reduced to that most synecdochical signature of the "black female" form: protuberant buttocks. Contrary to the contemporary "cover girl" image, embodied most frequently by a Caucasian, Oprah's cover shot displays no angularity, no jutting shoulder blades and rib cages, no pelvic boniness. Rather, she is pictured as if in "natural" bustle, her massive gluteal flesh thrusting out behind her. Further, in the inside shots, the elaborate clothing, which signaled in its historical moment the presence of an insubstantial female form, is thus ironic here, adding, symbolically, "flesh" on flesh.

Whatever the shape of her body, this is, in the wording of the story's title, "Oprah's Moment," her occasion to be Queen for a Day, complete with sapphires and diamonds and even a makeshift throne and symbolic court. That her on-the-cover moment required Oprah to shed twenty pounds was no great matter. Never shy to reveal the bodily editing she has had to repeatedly undergo before she could face the camera, Oprah recounts for Mike Wallace of *60 Minutes* the directives of the assistant news director during her early days on Baltimore television. "[He] came to me and said, 'Your hair's too long. It's too thick. Your eyes are too far apart. Your nose is too wide. Your chin is too wide. And you need to do something about it.'" But for the casting director of *The Color Purple,* less was not more, he advised, when he called to offer her the role of Sophia. "'I hear you're at a fat farm trying to lose weight. If you lose one pound you could lose this part.' So I stopped at Dairy Queen." Oprah also freely reveals how Jonathan Demme coaxed her into losing twenty pounds before the shooting of *Beloved.* "I go to his house, and he says, 'Listen, I love you, I love your body, but it's too big for this movie. You gotta wear the corsets, the big skirts—it's too big'" (Van Metter, 328)

In her nearly two-decades-long career before the camera, from television to silver screen, Oprah has seesawed between "too big" and not big enough and willingly subjected herself to the requirements of others' violent and exacting ideals. The caption of the *Vogue* cover— "OPRAH! A MAJOR MOVIE, AN AMAZING MAKEOVER"—cuts across her body and in blood red letters VOGUE cuts across her head, almost a coronation, but perhaps more aptly a figurative decapitation. It would be harsh to suggest that Oprah loses her head and pounds of her body to realize a fantasy of becoming Queen for a Day, for this is simply one photo opportunity that should not be seen as coinciding with Oprah's "self." As all her bodily "changes," both literal and metaphorical, have suggested, the body must be seen as multiple, protean, and capable, literally, of transformation into many different expressive "bodies." But be that as it may, what seems to find expression here leaves much to be desired.

While Oprah's pseudocoronation as *Vogue* "cover girl" shows her unabashedly the proverbial slave to her body, the photo shoot abolishes all signs of slavery. While the spread constitutes one part of the massive but ultimately ineffectual publicity campaign surrounding *Beloved*'s release as a film (it was a box-office failure), there is no trace of slavery here, not one film still of a barefoot, head-ragged woman in fraying homespun clothes, dragging her body like a feed sack or cotton bale. Absent is the familiar and obligatory lacerated back, bleeding from the overseer's lash. In other words, nothing here betokens slavery nor its bald outrages. Instead, we are treated to "period" clothes, props from the stage of a would-be costume drama. And standing in for or "representing" the body of the slave woman is the mistress—not the subject but the agent of bodily subjection.[3] Whose body is this? The subject position Oprah strikes seems willfully "white-washed" to a discourse of "the beautiful," within which, the photo spread suggests, a "black woman's" body cannot signify. This might qualify as "self-representation," but is it "recovery"? And must "recovery" be indentured to the visible body, to visual logic and its representations?

Compassing the Body

No set of meditations on black women and the body would be complete without a glance at Toni Morrison's corpus. Vanessa Dickerson does an excellent job here of reprising Morrison's insistent focus on the body. From *The Bluest Eye* to *Jazz*, Morrison offers up a view of the body identified not by its integrity but by its deformity and disfigurement, by its dismembered and misshapen parts: Pauline's foot, Eva's missing leg, Sula's birthmark, her self-mutilated finger, Golden Gray's missing arm, Dorcas's face marked and marred by hoof prints, Sethe's flagellated back and swollen feet, Paul D's mouth rubbed raw by the slaveholder's bit.

These repeated references to "missing parts," "lost limbs," and decomposing bodies combine to create the insistently mournful, elegiac quality of Morrison's work, as well as to contain, in compressed form, a philosophy of the body that extends its compass to its inside parts, both material and immaterial. Nowhere is Morrison's meditation on the body's inside parts more resonant and apparent than in *Beloved*. There, the limits of the body's meanings, as they might derive from the body's surface and tangibility, are repeatedly projected in bold relief. In *Beloved*, as throughout Morrison's corpus, the dispersed pieces of the body can only partly represent the "self" and are not reducible to the "self." In other words, body and self do not coincide; the body does not constitute the sum total of the self.

Morrison's entire corpus, beginning with *The Bluest Eye*, can be read as an extended meditation on the dangers and limits of idealizing the physical form. From work to work, she has dramatized the perils of color obsessions, of investments in all bodily ideals. She has shown the disparity between the body we have at any given moment and the body of our desires. Again and again, she establishes that flesh mortifies, that bodies exist fully and thoroughly in history, not in the timeless, motionless realm of cold ideals. Morrison's corpus encourages a view of the body not only as a mortifying, imperfectible organism, but also as a fundamentally elusive entity, an entity not fully graspable, at least through visual lenses and logics alone. In scene after scene, *Beloved* establishes that elusiveness, confronting the reader with a body that can't be fully seen and one that can only see *itself* in part.

Morrison's figurations of the body in *Beloved* might take us back to the paradigmatic body of this collection: Sojourner Truth. While Truth's breasts are her body's synecdoche, reading *Beloved* encourages us to ask what would change about Truth's body, what would alter our way of "knowing" Truth (and knowing the body's "truths," more generally), if we were "relieved of the weight of her breasts," as Sethe puts it (18)? What would change if we apprehended Truth's body not just through its surface but through the prism of its affects as well? To do so would broaden the analytical paradigm beyond the visual logic that dominates cultural studies of the body. Derived from the partly exposed "surface" of the body and its fetishized parts, this paradigm illuminates the discourse's ocular obsessions, its investments in the outer body, the body that can be seen and touched and felt, that can be anatomized, part by part.

As Sethe's story suggests, "recovering" the body requires attending to its inside parts, its buried zones. Grief, affect, the logos of emotion, constitute one buried zone of black women's "body studies," largely because the boundaries of the body are typically drawn around the surface of the skin. But while the skin encases, compasses the body, it does not constitute the body's total compass, is not its beginning and its end.

While recovering the emotions is an elusive prospect, in that emotions are difficult to materialize, the affective range is continuous with discourse on the body.

In the extant transcriptions of "Ar'n't I a Woman?" the language of veiled or muffled mourning runs throughout. In Gage's account, Truth laments: "I have borne thirteen chilren, and seen 'em mos' all sold off to slavery, and when I cried out with a mother's grief, none but Jesus heard me!" (200). Truth seems never to have reconciled herself to the loss of her children, and references to them figure throughout the life stories she dictated to others. That these cries originate in the body's "inside" parts, even if they are registered on its "outside" surface, suggests the importance of a view of the body that perceives the reciprocal relation between exterior and interior, between visible and invisible "matter," between the outside and the inside body.

References to "inside-ness" and "outside-ness," however, necessarily extend beyond the particulars of a single, corporeal frame, to embrace the body politic. Evaluating the state of black women's physical bodies within that larger social body remains among the most crucial and demanding body work to undertake. This brings us finally to the boundaries of the body that is this book. Let us return for the moment to the conceptual coordinates "recovery," "self-representation," and the "body."

Seeing Beyond the Breast: Another View of Recovery

Significantly, the majority of the bodies "recovered" here are clearly able-bodied, and the dominant critical concepts of this collection—resistance, revision, subversion, and control—seem implicitly structured to produce such strong and healthy discursive specimens. But no set of meditations on "recovering the body" with black women as its focus can fail to consider perhaps the most resonant and everyday meaning of "recovery": to regain a state of bodily health and wellness. If the headlines can be trusted, the state of black women's bodies gives great cause for alarm. Breast cancer is on the rise among African American women as are their mortality rates from the disease. Epidemic numbers of black women have hysterectomies because of rampant rates of fibroid tumors. According to a recent report, African American women are stricken with them at "two to five times the rate for White women, develop them earlier and have more severe symptoms" (Woods 52). The number of newly reported cases of AIDS shows equally epidemic rates among African American women. And these are just a few examples of a progressively worsening trend.

No one has written more trenchantly about black women, the body, and recovery than has Audre Lorde, who understood firsthand the dialectical connection between corporeal and corporate bodies. Lorde placed her body firmly on the line in everything she wrote, even and especially when it was being ravaged by breast cancer. Perhaps the most powerful and eloquent treatment of the disease can be found in *The Cancer Journals* (1980) and *A Burst of Light: Living with Cancer* (1988). In both texts Lorde subjects her body and its processes to the most exacting and unsparing scrutiny, while simultaneously waging a polemic against the "gross anatomy" of the corporate bodies—the medical establishment, American Cancer Society, National Cancer Institute—that mystify disease, as well as the social and environmental body that is its breeding ground.

The Cancer Journals begins with the frequently anthologized essay "The Transformation of Silence into Language and Action." While the stigma surrounding cancer in medical discourse has encouraged silence and secrecy in the sufferer, Lorde calls for ending silence, for making noise and acting up. Speaking out is prophylactic, silence, figured in the text as a choking weight, is death (23).

If illness begets metaphor, as Susan Sontag has established, *The Cancer Journals* bears her out, but Lorde seizes metaphors of illness to stigmatize neither disease nor patient, but to "wage war" on what she terms the "forces of death" (21). Military metaphors dominate the text, and Lorde likens herself repeatedly to a warrior, specifically to the Amazons of Dahomey, who supposedly cut off their right breasts to make themselves more effective archers. "I needed to . . . image myself as a *fighter resisting* rather than as a passive victim suffering," she writes, while challenging "every woman [to accept] a *militant* responsibility to involve herself actively in her own health" (73; my emphasis). The first essential step in the battle requires that women end the socialized alienation from their own bodies by giving themselves monthly breast exams. The next step is to arm themselves with information, however alarming. Page after page of *The Cancer Journals* provide then-current statistics on breast cancer: it is on the rise among women in America, its greatest incidence among women between the ages of forty and fifty-five; "of the women stricken, only 50 percent are still alive after three years" and only 30 percent if the woman is poor and black (62).

These last two sections of *The Cancer Journals* alternate between cry and battle cry, between journal entries recording the private pain—physical and psychic—of losing her breast and bulletins from the front, as it were. Lorde is battling the disease of cancer and fighting to preserve that self that is not merely physically defined. But she is fighting, as well, the discursive representations of cancer. Like Sontag's *Illness as Metaphor*, *The Cancer Journals* is both a polemic and an exhortation, a challenge to all those confronting the "forces of death" to reclaim the "language which has been made to work against us" (21, 22). Like Sontag, Lorde rejects the psychological theories of disease that hold patients responsible for their own illnesses and simultaneously renders them powerless to involve themselves in their own treatments and possible cures.

> The idea that the cancer patient should be made to feel guilty about having had cancer, as if in some way it were all her fault for not having been in the right psychological frame of mind at all times to prevent cancer, is a monstrous distortion of the idea that we can use our psychic strengths to help heal ourselves. . . . [This view] does nothing to encourage the mobilization of our psychic defenses against the very real forms of death which surround us. It is easier to demand happiness than to clean up the environment. . . . Let us seek "joy" rather than real food and clean air and a saner future on a livable earth. (74)

Lorde will not separate psyche from soma, inside from outside, her body from the social body. She reserves her most forceful attack for the American Cancer Society, the medical establishment, and the breast reconstruction industry, which together collaborate in reducing women merely to their bodies and, more reductive still, to mere objects for the fantasies and "comfort" of others.

In "Breast Cancer: Power vs. Prosthesis," Lorde exposes the crass materialism of the breast reconstruction industry, which conducts more research on breast reconstruction surgery than on "how to prevent the cancers that cost us our breasts and our lives" (68). She recounts her resistance to wearing a prosthesis. A detachable "part," the prosthesis is form without matter and, as Lorde argues, false breasts are the few among prosthetic devices designed "for appearance only, as if the only real function of women's breasts were to appear in a certain shape and size and symmetry to onlookers." This fixation on the cosmetic value of women's breasts is "merely a reflection of those attitudes within our society towards women in general as objectified and depersonalized sexual conveniences," programmed "to view [their] bodies only in terms of how they look and feel to others" (64).

Six years following her mastectomy, just before her fiftieth birthday, Lorde was diagnosed with liver cancer metasticized from her breast cancer. She discovered once again that the "'battle lines' were drawn . . . [over her] own body" and that medical specialists denied her the "simple claim to [its] . . . processes" (*Burst* 112). Defying the dictates of the medical profession, Lorde trusts her "original gut feeling that said, *Stay out of my body*" (130), and takes a strong hand in her own treatment. She chooses from an array of experimental, "alternative" therapies, including "creative visualization" of a war on cancer in which her diseased body is pitted against the most implacable, political foes. "Sometimes the wanton cells in my liver become Bull Conner and his police dogs completely smothered, rendered impotent in Birmingham, Alabama, by a mighty avalanche of young, determined Black marchers moving across him toward their future" (133).

Lorde's reference to Bull Connor here seems far from idly chosen, for as many have observed, segregation in the South was grounded in and on the body, anchored in the racialization of place, of caste and class. The black body was literally and materially a battleground throughout the segregated South, the ramparts of which Bull Conner and his minions violently defended with dogs, firehoses, billy clubs, and bombs. Lorde admonishes all "who live our battles in the flesh" to discover "ourselves as our strongest weapon in the most gallant struggle of our lives" (133).

Lorde, of course, ultimately lost her battle but, proverbially speaking, she didn't lose the war, including the war on discourse. Others are currently keeping her charge, continuing her drive to reconstruct black women's discursive bodies and to expose the threats to their material bodies. At no time has this task been more urgently needed than now, when black women's bodies are regularly figured as "diseased," and threatening, carriers of a range of "ills" that imperil the national body.

Body Race Reproduction

As Dorothy Roberts observes in *Killing the Black Body: Race, Reproduction, and the Meaning of Liberty*, poor black women have been fingered historically as "unfit" mothers and their reproductive lives routinely invaded, often against their will. This "institutionalized denial of reproductive freedom," notes Roberts, has uniquely marked black women's history in America—from slave masters' economic stake in their fertility to the "racist strains of early birth control policy to sterilization abuse of Black women during the 1960s and 1970s to the current campaign to inject Norplant and Depo-Provera in the arms of Black teenagers and welfare mothers" (4).

We can quickly lose sight of these material realities, as well as the ever-worsening socioenvironmental factors that place black women's health at great risk. The counterpart of these totalitarian abuses on black women's reproductive lives is the outright refusal, on the part of the medical profession, to provide their bodies the serious and specialized attention they deserve. Urgently needed is research into the ethnomedical aspects of their particular symptomologies. What Diane Price Herndl observes about the relative invisibility of accounts of African American women's health in nineteenth-century discourse—literary and medical alike–still obtains, to a large extent, today. The conclusion of medical science would seem to be that "black women never suffered any illness at all," even though it is well documented that they did, in fact, receive medical treatment (555–56), although "treatment" in this context seems an obscenely incongruous term. Significant among extant documents are those that establish the essential role black women's bodies played on the foundation of gynecology as a medical specialty. As Terri Kapsalis describes in her book *Public Privates*, during slavery, black women were routinely the objects of surgical experimentation. Indeed, she observes, the "speculum was 'discovered' in a slave woman's body," due largely, she infers, from the assumption that bonded women were "more suitable objects for speculum penetration and the physician's [probing] gaze" (32). Kapsalis rightly concludes that the reverberations of this early convergence of racism, slavery, and medical innovation can still be felt today. Although medical discourse neglects fully to register these echoes, they persistently affect the state of black women's health.

As Arthur Kleinman and Joan Kleinman observe, in a different context, understanding "how culture infolds into the body (and, reciprocally, how bodily processes outfold into social space)" is essential to the healing arts (710–11). Interestingly, the Kleinmans title their essay "How Bodies Remember," and although their study focuses on social memory and bodily experiences following China's Cultural Revolution, and thus cannot simply be transferred to this context, their findings contain some possible implications for the study of black women, the body, and recovery. As they note, "bodies transformed by political processes not only *represent* those processes, they *experience* them as the lived memory of transformed worlds. The experience is of memory processes sedimented in gait, posture, movement, and all the other corporal components which together realize cultural codes and social dynamics in everyday practices" (717).

The Kleinmans' observations stimulate me to raise questions perhaps impossible to address. What might contemporary black women's bodies "remember" about the possession of and assault on their bodies, on their reproductive systems? Can we speak of such things as deep "memory" of a system that claimed their bodies and the issue of their bodies in order to reproduce itself? Does that memory speak today in tumors on the uterine wall in numbers disproportionate to black women's representation in the general female population? Could these tumors constitute an unvoiced, unconscious response to the dangerous realities of supplying more bodies for a differently exploitative system to destroy? Such are bewildering questions, I'm well aware. Further, the statistics on fibroid tumors have their counterpart in equally escalating statistics on black teenage pregnancy.

Whether any of the preceding speculations could ever be advanced with a measure of authority is difficult to say, but an inquiry into the matter might begin with the concepts of "transgenerational haunting" or phantom, the revendent, the ghost (see Abraham and Torok), which Morrison dramatized so powerfully in *Beloved*. While *Beloved* explored the physic effects of slavery's ghost, Abraham and Torok theorized its physiological as well as its physic manifestations.

How is slavery "ghosted" in the bodies of contemporary African American women? Do they remember the children of their ancestors, whose personhood was institutionally nullified, whose labor could be extracted at great profit, who could be sold, at even greater profit, at a slave master's whim?

Obviously black women's children are not sold from them today, but we might ask nevertheless whether the reverberations of that system remain alive in different and contemporary forms. Black women's children, like black women themselves, are not bodies that matter. They remain vulnerable in a system, the economics of which still operates as the functional equivalent of "family separation" and which still places all black bodies at great risk.

Bodies In and Out of Time

We can quickly lose sight of these sobering material realities and their ever-widening distance from the discursive triumphs we are eager to exclaim. To repeat, if any group has had need historically of resisting and revising, subverting and controlling their bodies and their body images, black women have, for our bodies have never been our bodies; our "selves" have never been our selves. And thus to produce a collection devoted to exploring the deeds that black women themselves have done—as subjects, as agents—in the name and for the sake of recovering and controlling their own bodies as discursive entities, is much to be applauded. While such work can profitably continue, it must keep pace and commerce with the bodies that fail to represent, the bodies that fail to take control, the bodies that fail to be recovered. "Recover" obviously implies, plays on ideas of lost and found, but it also plays on ideas of burial and reburial, of covering that which is perhaps difficult to see. Such veiling constitutes a form of dissociation, which, according to the literature on trauma, can occur when deeply disturbing events force one to shift the field of vision and attention from the site of threat and menace to a "safer place." Ideal places, some inside discursive precincts, are always safer; the "ideal" bodies discovered there, always easier to edit, to manipulate, and control. Fantasy, too, is such a place.

My fantasy of inhabiting another body not my own comes in part from my body's memory, clearly not traumatic, of the sedimented gait and posture I was driven to perform so as to assume a specific racial role prescribed by the ideals of a specific class. But it also comes from the piercing awareness of what William Wordsworth termed "the touch of earthly years," greedily demanding their due. Mine is, in other words, a body in time, showing all the signs that flesh is indeed corruptible, insolid, and bodies pass away. Tina, on the other hand, seems to have mocked and defeated time, arm wrestled gravity to the ground. At sixty, her age-defying body sometimes make me doubt the testimony of my bedimming eyes, makes me forget, if only for the duration of a song, that gravity is the undisputed victor in my war with time. Because my daily walking regimen has only done so much, I have lately had fantasies of studying dance. I think, if I danced as much as Tina does, I, too, could reverse the clock.

But all of this amounts to the sheerest folly, the baldest frivolity. Moreover, it loses sight of the fact that Tina Turner is a stage name, a persona far removed from the Anna Mae Bullock formerly of Nutbush, Tennessee. By her own account, the costumes, the wild blond wigs, the shakes and gyrations are the opposite of the sober, contemplative life she leads offstage. And focusing on that stage persona and how Tina's body performs misses the fact that the broader appeal of Tina Turner lies well beyond her visible body or any of its parts, well beyond the realm of sight. It is sound, combined with spectacle, that makes for Tina's greatest appeal, the voice that emanates from the body's inside, unseen parts.

We need not relinquish entirely the fantasy of "owning" a body just like Tina Turner's nor the "self" that body seems to represent in order to shoulder the demands that this moment imposes. As rates of various diseases escalate exponentially, along with escalating rates of mortality, as the prospects of universally accessible health care are steadily receding, the threats to black women's health, and thus their recovery, seem everywhere apparent. To summon once again one of this volume's privileged terms, the times call for resisting the lure of the ideal body, while mobilizing to keep the real ones alive, lest we be left with ever-dwindling bodies to represent, bodies to recover. These times call for resistance that stretches beyond discursive realms, resistance though it often seems much easier to dissociate, to withdraw inside the ample and yet weightless "flesh" of dreams.

NOTES

Thanks to Michael Bennett, Kendra Hamilton, Farzaneh Milani, and David Morrison for their helpful comments on earlier drafts.

1. "Writ about [our] privates" refers to Sherley Anne Williams's novel *Dessa Rose* (New York: William Morrow, 1986).
2. As Nell Painter notes, "the symbol of Sojourner Truth that is most popular today turns on two speeches of the 1850s: one in Akron, Ohio, in 1851, the other in Siler Lake, a small town in northern Indiana, in 1858," although the two are often conflated to form, mistakenly, a single episode.
3. Interestingly, on the 5 October 1998 issue of *Time*, by contrast, Oprah did appear *en role*. On that cover, she is a decidedly deglamorized Oprah, shorn of makeup and without processed hair. Her features seem noticeably blunted. Placed side by side with the *Vogue* cover, they hardly seem to be the same woman.

WORKS CITED

Abraham, Nicolas, and Maria Torok. *The Shell and the Kernel*. Ed., trans., and with an intro. by Nicholas Rand. Chicago: U of Chicago P, 1994.

Bly, Nellie. *Oprah: Up Close and Down Home*. New York: Kensington, 1993.

Eagleton, Terry. *The Illusions of Post-Modernism*. Oxford: Blackwell, 1996.

Gage, Francis. "Ar'n't I a Woman." In *The Norton Anthology of African American Literature*, edited by Henry Louis Gates, Jr., and Nellie McKay. New York: Norton, 1997.

Herndl, Diane Price. "The Invisible (Invalid) Woman: African-American Women, Illness, and Nineteenth-Century Narrative." *Women's Studies* 24 (1995): 553–72.

Jones, Amelia. *Body Art: Performing the Subject*. Minneapolis: U of Minnesota P, 1998.

Kapsalis, Terri. *Public Privates: Performing Gynecology from Both Ends of the Speculum*. Durham, NC: Duke UP, 1997.

Kleinman, Arthur, and Joan Kleinman. "How Bodies Remember: Social Memory and Bodily Experience of Criticism, Resistance, and Delegitimation Following China's Cultural Revolution." *New Literary History* 25 (1994): 707–23.

Lorde, Audre. *A Burst of Light: Living with Cancer*. Ithaca, NY: Firebrand Books, 1988.

———. *The Cancer Journals* . New York: Spinster's Ink, 1980.

Morrison, Toni. *Beloved*. New York: Penguin, 1987.

Noden, Merrell. *People Profiles Oprah Winfrey*. New York: Time, Inc., 1999.

O'Grady, Lorraine. "Olympia's Maid: Reclaiming Black Female Subjectivity." *New Feminist Criticism: Art/Identity/Action*. Ed. Joanna Frueh, Cassandra Langer, and Arlene Raven. New York: HarperCollins, 1994.

Painter, Nell Irvin. "Sojourner Truth." *Black Women in America: An Historical Encyclopedia*. Ed. Darlene Clark Hine, Elsa Barkley Brown, and Rosalyn Terborg-Penn. Bloomington: Indiana UP, l994. 1172–76.

Peterson, Carla. *"Doers of the Word": African American Speakers and Writers in the North, 1830–1880*. New Brunswick, NJ: Rutgers UP, 1998.

Roberts, Dorothy. *Killing the Black Body: Race, Reproduction, and the Meaning of Liberty*. New York: Pantheon, 1997.

Sontag, Susan. *Illness as Metaphor.* New York: Farrar, Straus and Giroux, 1977.

Van Metter, Jonathan. "Oprah's Moment." *Vogue* (October 1998): 322–30, 392–93.

Washington, Joseph R. Jr. *Marriage in Black and White.* Boston: Beacon, 1970.

Witt, Doris Smith. *Black Hunger: Food and the Politics of U.S. Identity.* New York: Oxford UP, 1999.

Woods, Patricia Mason. "You Can Heal Your Fibroids." *Essence* (April 2000): 52, 55.

Notes on Contributors

MARGARET K. BASS is assistant professor of English at the University of Iowa. Her areas of specialization are Caribbean literature, autobiography studies, and African American literature. She is committed to redefining "academic scholarship" and writing in ways that are relevant and accessible to members of the citizenry outside the academy. Her passion for teaching, commitment to undergraduate education, and conviction that every campus must have an African American professorial presence led her to St. Lawrence University in Canton, New York. She continues to struggle with her weight.

DORRI RABUNG BEAM is completing her Ph.D. in English at the University of Virginia. Her dissertation recovers and analyzes "highly wrought" novels, as reviewers called them, written by women in the mid to late nineteenth century. She currently teaches at Randolph-Macon College in Ashland, Virginia.

MICHAEL BENNETT is associate professor of English at Long Island University, Brooklyn. He is the coeditor, with David Teague, of *The Nature of Cities: Ecocriticism and Urban Environments* (University of Arizona Press, 1999) and has published essays on African American families and public policy, computers and composition, ecocriticism, and African American literary theory. He is currently at work on a manuscript entitled "The Imprisonment of American Culture."

JACQUELINE E. BRADY teaches English at Pace University. Trained in comparative literature and cinema studies, she is writing a cultural history of bodybuilding, focusing on constructions of gender. She is also a bodybuilder and personal trainer.

DAPHNE A. BROOKS is an assistant professor in the Department of Literature at the University of California, San Diego. Her interests include performance studies, popular culture, and nineteenth-century African American literature and culture. She is currently completing her first book, *Bodies in Dissent: Performing Race, Gender, and Nation in the Trans-Atlantic Imaginary*, forthcoming from Duke University Press.

VANESSA D. DICKERSON, associate professor of English at DePauw University, is the author of *Victorian Ghosts in the Noontide: Women Writers and the Supernatural* (University of Missouri Press, 1996) and the editor of a collection of essays entitled *Keeping the Victorian House* (Garland, 1995). She has also published essays on Victorian women and on contemporary black women writers and is currently researching a book on black Victorians.

BILL GASKINS has been a visiting artist at the University of Minnesota, Syracuse University, the American Photography Institute at New York University, and a visiting professor in photography at The School of the Art Institute of Chicago. Presently, he is a lecturer in photography in the Division of Fine Art at Howard University. As an artist, Gaskins has concentrated on the diversity, complexity, rituals, and gestures of African American life through the medium of photography. His work has earned critical attention through solo and group exhibitions, exhibition catalogs, and other publications. *Good and Bad Hair: Photographs by Bill Gaskins*, a monograph celebrating the role and significance of hairstyling in African American identity, was published by Rutgers University Press in 1997.

MEREDITH GOLDSMITH is a visiting assistant professor in the Department of English, Linguistics, and Speech at Mary Washington College. Her interests include African American and ethnic women's writing and nineteenth- and twentieth-century American literature, particularly the novel of manners. She is working on a book manuscript entitled "Convincing Personations: Theatricality, Ethnicity, and Race in the Turn-of-the-Century American Novel."

YVETTE LOUIS is a doctoral candidate in the Department of Comparative Literature at Princeton University. She is currently at work on a thesis entitled "Body Language: The Slave Body and the Word in the Literature of the African Americas."

DEBORAH E. MCDOWELL is professor of English at the University of Virginia. The author of numerous articles and essays on black American literature and culture, she is also the founding editor of the Beacon Black Women Writer Series, coeditor (with Arnold Rampersad) of *Slavery and the Literary Imagination* (Johns Hopkins University Press, 1989), and author of *"The Changing Same": Black Women's Literature, Criticism, and Theory* (Indiana University Press, 1995) and *Leaving Pipe Shop: Memories of Kin* (Scribner's, 1997).

AJUAN MARIA MANCE is a visual artist and assistant professor of English at Mills College in Oakland, California. An African American literature specialist, she also spent several years on the faculty of the University of Oregon. Her current research is on the development of black female identity in African American women's poetry since Reconstruction.

CARLA L. PETERSON is professor of English and comparative literature at the University of Maryland (College Park), where she chairs the Committee on Africa and the Americas. She has published numerous essays on African American writers, including Jarena Lee, Frederick Douglass, Frances Ellen Watkins Harper, and Pauline Hopkins. She is the author of *The Determined Reader: Gender and Culture in the Novel from Napoleon to Victoria* (Rutgers University Press, 1986). *"Doers of the Word": African-American Women Speakers and Writers in the North (1830–1860)* was published in 1995 as part of Oxford University Press's series on Race and American Culture; it was republished in paperback by Rutgers University Press in 1998.

NOLIWE ROOKS is a visiting assistant professor in history and African American studies at Princeton University. She is the author of *Hair Raising: Beauty, Culture and African American Women* (Rutgers University Press, 1996), as well as articles that have appeared in such journals as *The Black Scholar, Iowa Journal of Cultural Studies,* and *Camera Obscura.* She is currently working on a book-length manuscript on the history of African American women's magazines, 1891–1975.

MARK WINOKUR is an associate professor in the Department of English at the University of Colorado, Boulder. He writes about race, ethnicity, and gender in film and has published in such journals as *Film History*, *Cinema Journal*, *The Velvet Light Trap*, and *Sight and Sound*. He is the author of *American Laughter* (St, Martin's, 1995), a study of ethnicity and American film comedy.

DORIS WITT teaches twentieth-century United States literature and culture at the University of Iowa. She is the author of *Black Hunger: Food and the Politics of U.S. Identity* (Oxford University Press, 1999).

Index

abolitionist movement, x, 32
acting, and sexuality, 60
"Address" (Gage), 45
adolescence. *See The Bluest Eye*
adornment, 98. *See also* hairstyle
affirmative action, xv–xvi
African American Feminist Health
    Campaign, 271–72
Afro-Americanists, male, 47
Agnew, Jean-Christophe, 100
AIDS, 38n13, 309
American Renaissance, 6, 19
Ammons, Elizabeth, 25
Angel in the House, 196
antimiscegenation laws, 91
anti-oedipal paradigm, lesbian, 232
"Ar'n't I a Woman?" (Truth), 299–300,
    300, 309
Arthurs, Jane, 3
Arzner, Dorothy, 234
Asian women, 184–85
atomization of the black body, 113–14
Aunt Jemima, 5

Baartman, Saartjie, 263. *See also*
    Hottentot Venus
Bakhtin, Mikhail, 185, 254
Balsamo, Anne, 254, 256
Barclay, G. Lippard, 41, 44
Baum, L. Frank, 117n7
"Be Active" (Watkins), 24–25
beauty, xv, 137, 181. *See also* hair,

nappy; *Passing*
Beavers, Louise, 178
Belenky, Mary, 273
Bell, John, 58
The Bell Curve (Herrnstein and
    Murray), 174
Beloved (Morrison), xvi, 23, 196, 197,
    208, 237, 308–9; bodily represen-
    tation in, 197; community in, 212–
    13; recovery of the body in, 197,
    211–13; role of hunger in, 210–11;
    role of talk in, 210; self-hatred in,
    211; transgenerational haunting in,
    314
Bennett, Paula, 77, 82
Berlant, Lauren, 22, 71
Berson, Misha, 61
biggerexia, 258
biological determinism, 173–75
birthmark, in *Sula*, 206–7
Black Arts movement, 124
black body: as animal-like, 21, 196;
    atomization of, 113–14; as body in
    pain, xii; decorporealizing, xi–xiii,
    xv, 21, 299; dominant culture's
    morbid fascination with, xv; as
    machine, x; media portrayal of, xv;
    normalizing, xiii, xiv–xv; as object
    of gaze, 4, 44, 59–61, 177, 197;
    subjectivity of, ix, 4, 46; visibility/
    invisibility of, xi, 22. *See also*
    black female body

323

CPSIA information can be obtained
at www.ICGtesting.com
Printed in the USA
BVHW011636080420
576728BV00035B/18